BLACK CLOVER
VOLUME 23
SHONEN JUMP Manga Edition

Story and Art by YŪKI TABATA

Translation ● TAYLOR ENGEL,
HC LANGUAGE SOLUTIONS, INC.

Touch-Up Art & Lettering ● ANNALIESE CHRISTMAN

Design ● KAM LI

Editor ● ALEXIS KIRSCH

Printed in the U.S.A.

Published by VIZ Media, LLC
P.O. Box 77010
San Francisco, CA 94107

10 9 8 7 6 5 4 3 2 1
First printing, November 2020

ratings.viz.com RATED T TEEN

PARENTAL ADVISORY
BLACK CLOVER is rated T for Teen and is recommended for ages 13 and up. This volume contains realistic and fantasy violence.

VIZ MEDIA
viz.com

SHONEN JUMP

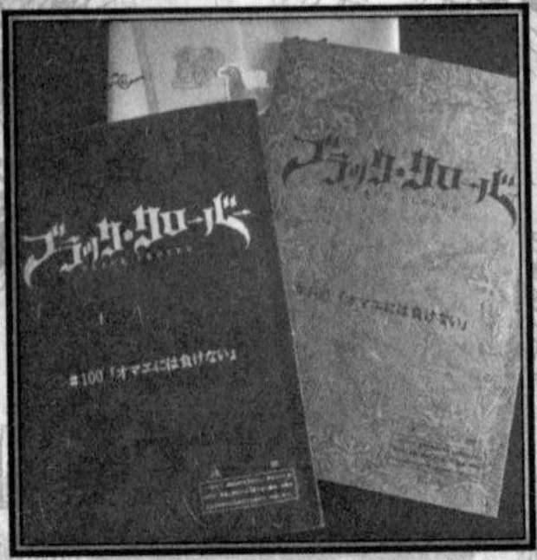
ブラッククローバー
ブラッククローバー

Studio Pierrot gave me a special script to commemorate the 100th episode of the *Black Clover* anime!! It's soooo cooool!! Get this! It's jam-packed with the voice actors' signatures!! Coooooool!! I'm deeply moved!! Thank you so much for all your work on the anime!! I'll work really hard on the manga too!!

—Yūki Tabata, 2020

YŪKI TABATA
was born in Fukuoka Prefecture and got his big break in the 2011 Shonen Jump Golden Future Cup with his winning entry, *Hungry Joker*. He started the magical fantasy series *Black Clover* in 2015.

Secre

Black✿Clover

YŪKI TABATA · 23 · AS PITCH-BLACK AS IT GETS

Asta

Member of: The Black Bulls
Magic: None (Anti-Magic)

He has no magic, but he's working to become the Wizard King through sheer guts and his well-trained body. He fights with anti-magic swords.

Yuno

Member of: The Golden Dawn
Magic: Wind

Asta's best friend, and a good rival who's also been working to become the Wizard King. He controls Sylph, the spirit of wind.

Yami Sukehiro

Member of: The Black Bulls
Magic: Dark

A captain who looks fierce, but is very popular with his brigade, which has a deep-rooted confidence in him. Heavy smoker.

Finral Roulacase

Member of: The Black Bulls
Magic: Spatial

A playboy who immediately chats up any woman he sees. He can't attack, but he has high-level abilities.

Noelle Silva

Member of: The Black Bulls
Magic: Water

A royal. She feels inferior to her brilliant siblings. Her latent abilities are an unknown quantity.

Gordon Agrippa

Member of: The Black Bulls
Magic: Poison

He looks scary, so it's easy to get the wrong idea, but he's actually incredibly bad at communicating. He

Noznel Silva

Member of:
The Silver Eagles
Magic: Mercury

Noelle's older brother. A captain who values his pride as a royal. Considers Fuegoleon a friendly rival.

Mimosa Vermillion

Member of:
The Golden Dawn
Magic: Plant

Noelle's cousin. She's ladylike and a bit of an airhead, but she can be rude. She just might like Asta...

Dorothy Unsworth

Member of:
The Coral Peacocks
Magic: Dream

A brigade captain. She's usually fast asleep. She's able to use Dream Magic to make a world that's exactly how she wants it to be.

Charlotte Roselei

Member of:
The Blue Rose Knights
Magic: Briar

Has a cool personality. As a rule, she doesn't like men, but she seems to make an exception for Yami...

Secre Swallowtail (Nero)

Magic: Sealing

She paid for using forbidden magic by becoming a bird 500 years ago. She watched over Licht's grimoire.

Damnatio Kira

Magic: Scale

The head of the Magic Parliament, which makes and enforces the kingdom's laws. He respects the royal family above all else.

STORY

In a world where magic is everything, Asta and Yuno are both found abandoned on the same day at a church in the remote village of Hage. Both dream of becoming the Wizard King, the highest of all mages, and they spend their days working toward that dream.

The year they turn 15, both receive grimoires, magic books that amplify their bearer's magic. They take the entrance exam for the Magic Knights, nine groups of mages under the direct control of the Wizard King. Yuno, whose magic is strong, joins the Golden Dawn, an elite group, while Asta, who has no magic at all, joins the Black Bulls, a group of misfits. With this, the two finally take their first step toward becoming the Wizard King...

With the help of Lumiere and Licht, Asta and Yuno are finally able to defeat the devil and make peace with the elves. The Wizard King, Julius, turns out to have survived, although he has physically reverted to childhood. But just when it looks as though life will be peaceful again, Asta and Nero are summoned before the Magic Parliament and accused of having caused the war!!

CONTENTS

BLACK ❖ CLOVER

23

Page 218: The Worst of the Worst

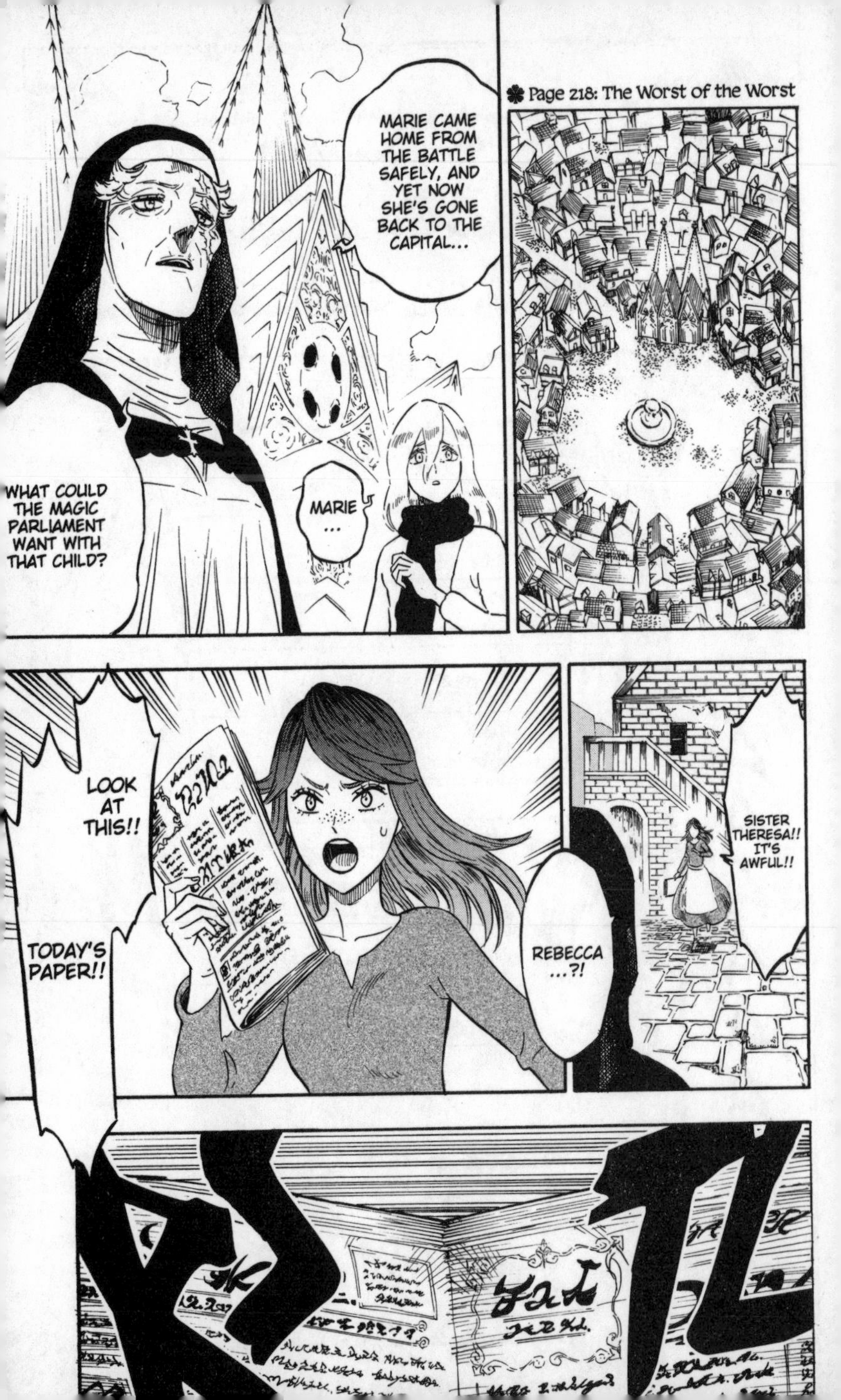
MARIE CAME HOME FROM THE BATTLE SAFELY, AND YET NOW SHE'S GONE BACK TO THE CAPITAL...
MARIE ...
WHAT COULD THE MAGIC PARLIAMENT WANT WITH THAT CHILD?
SISTER THERESA!! IT'S AWFUL!!
REBECCA ...?!
LOOK AT THIS!!
TODAY'S PAPER!!

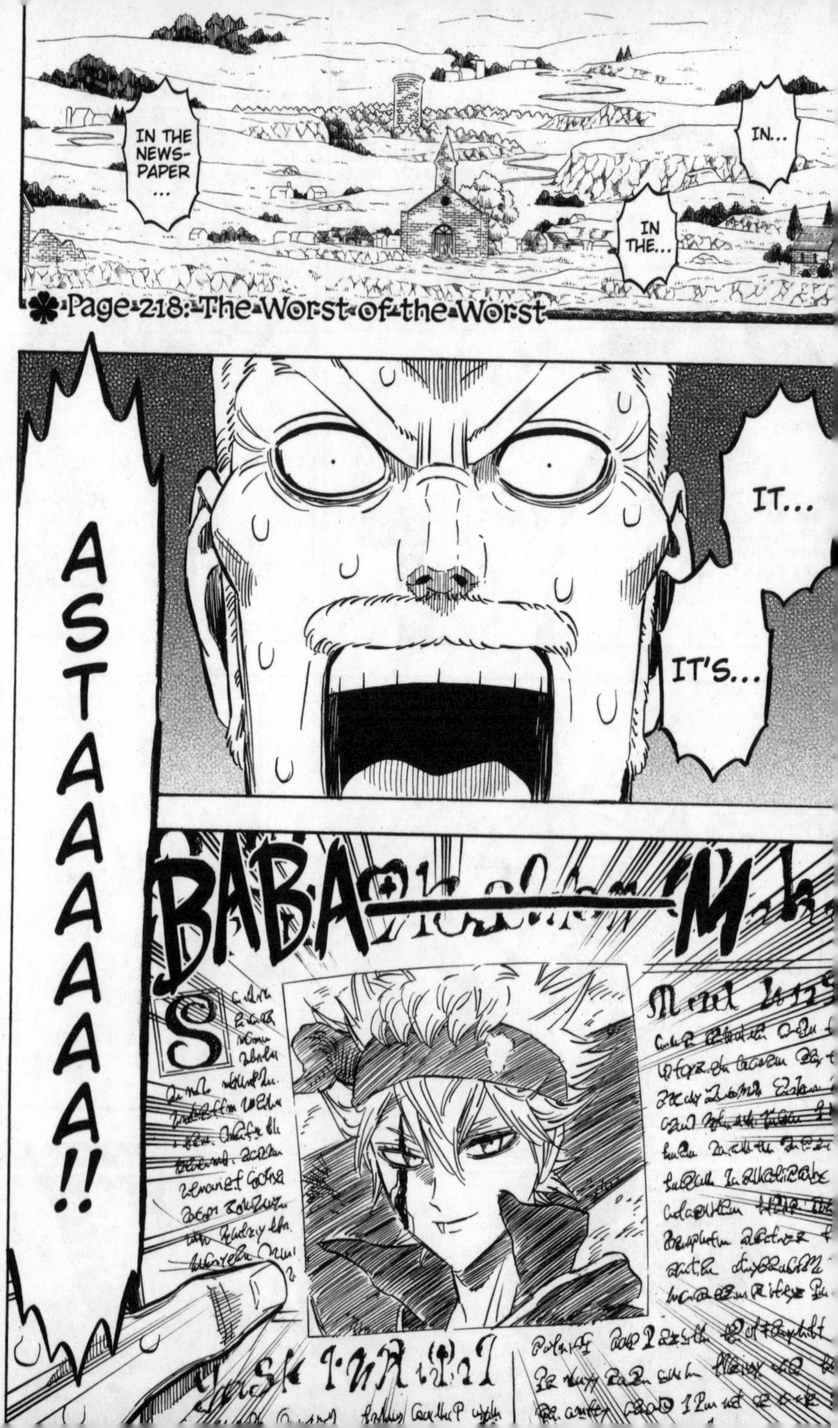

IN...
IN THE...
IN THE NEWS-PAPER...
Page 218: The Worst of the Worst
IT...
IT'S...
ASTAAAAAAA!!
BABA

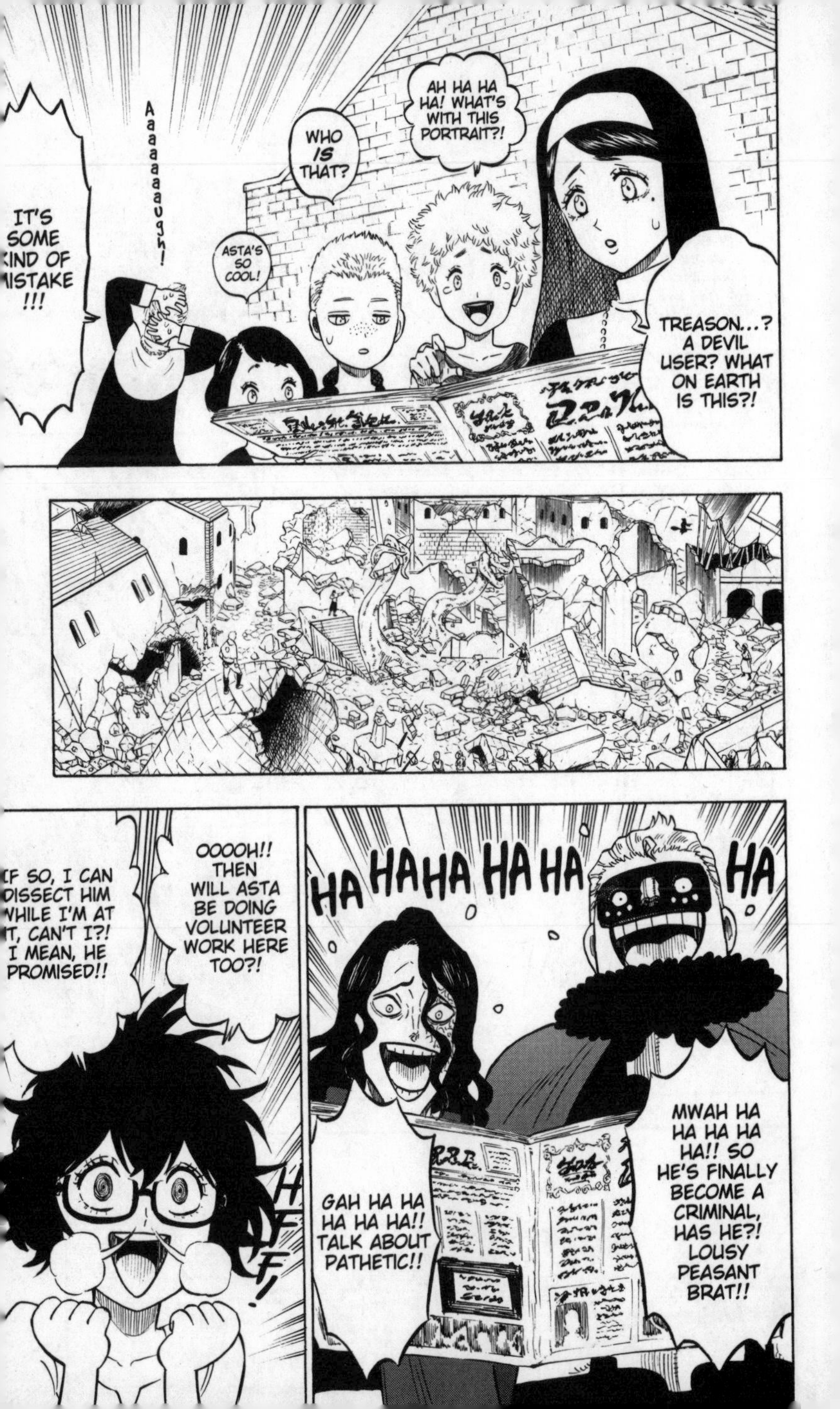

AH HA HA HA! WHAT'S WITH THIS PORTRAIT?!
WHO IS THAT?
TREASON...? A DEVIL USER? WHAT ON EARTH IS THIS?!
Aaaaaaaaaugh!
ASTA'S SO COOL!
IT'S SOME KIND OF MISTAKE!!!
HA HAHA HA HA HA
MWAH HA HA HA HA HA!! SO HE'S FINALLY BECOME A CRIMINAL, HAS HE?! LOUSY PEASANT BRAT!!
GAH HA HA HA HA!! TALK ABOUT PATHETIC!!
OOOOH!! THEN WILL ASTA BE DOING VOLUNTEER WORK HERE TOO?!
IF SO, I CAN DISSECT HIM WHILE I'M AT IT, CAN'T I?! I MEAN, HE PROMISED!!
HFF!

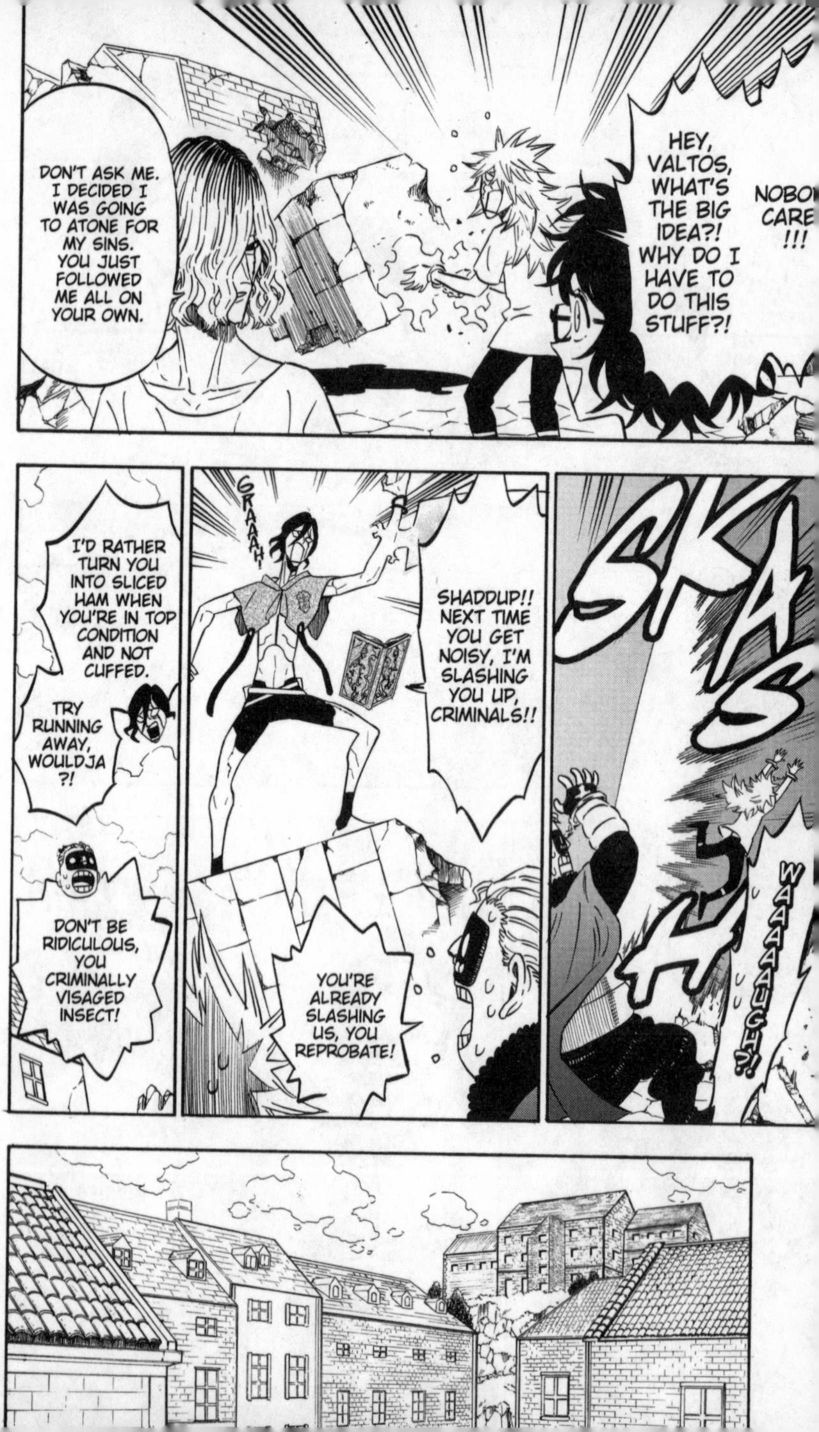
NOBO
CARE
!!!
HEY, VALTOS, WHAT'S THE BIG IDEA?! WHY DO I HAVE TO DO THIS STUFF?!
DON'T ASK ME. I DECIDED I WAS GOING TO ATONE FOR MY SINS. YOU JUST FOLLOWED ME ALL ON YOUR OWN.
WAAAAAUGH?!
GRAAAAH!
SHADDUP!! NEXT TIME YOU GET NOISY, I'M SLASHING YOU UP, CRIMINALS!!
YOU'RE ALREADY SLASHING US, YOU REPROBATE!
I'D RATHER TURN YOU INTO SLICED HAM WHEN YOU'RE IN TOP CONDITION AND NOT CUFFED.
TRY RUNNING AWAY, WOULDJA?!
DON'T BE RIDICULOUS, YOU CRIMINALLY VISAGED INSECT!

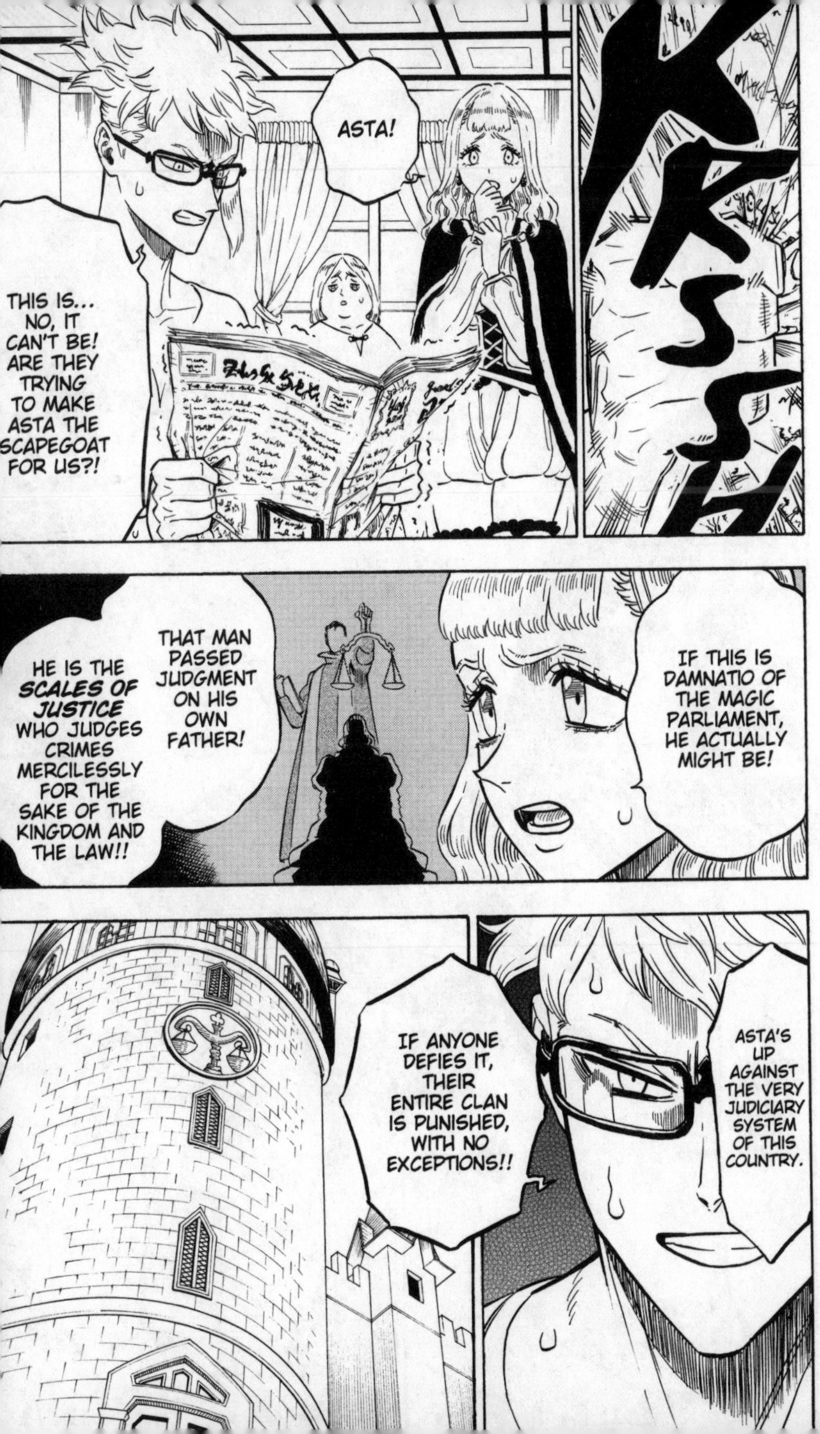
KSSH
ASTA!
THIS IS... NO, IT CAN'T BE! ARE THEY TRYING TO MAKE ASTA THE SCAPEGOAT FOR US?!
IF THIS IS DAMNATIO OF THE MAGIC PARLIAMENT, HE ACTUALLY MIGHT BE!
THAT MAN PASSED JUDGMENT ON HIS OWN FATHER!
HE IS THE *SCALES OF JUSTICE* WHO JUDGES CRIMES MERCILESSLY FOR THE SAKE OF THE KINGDOM AND THE LAW!!
ASTA'S UP AGAINST THE VERY JUDICIARY SYSTEM OF THIS COUNTRY.
IF ANYONE DEFIES IT, THEIR ENTIRE CLAN IS PUNISHED, WITH NO EXCEPTIONS!!

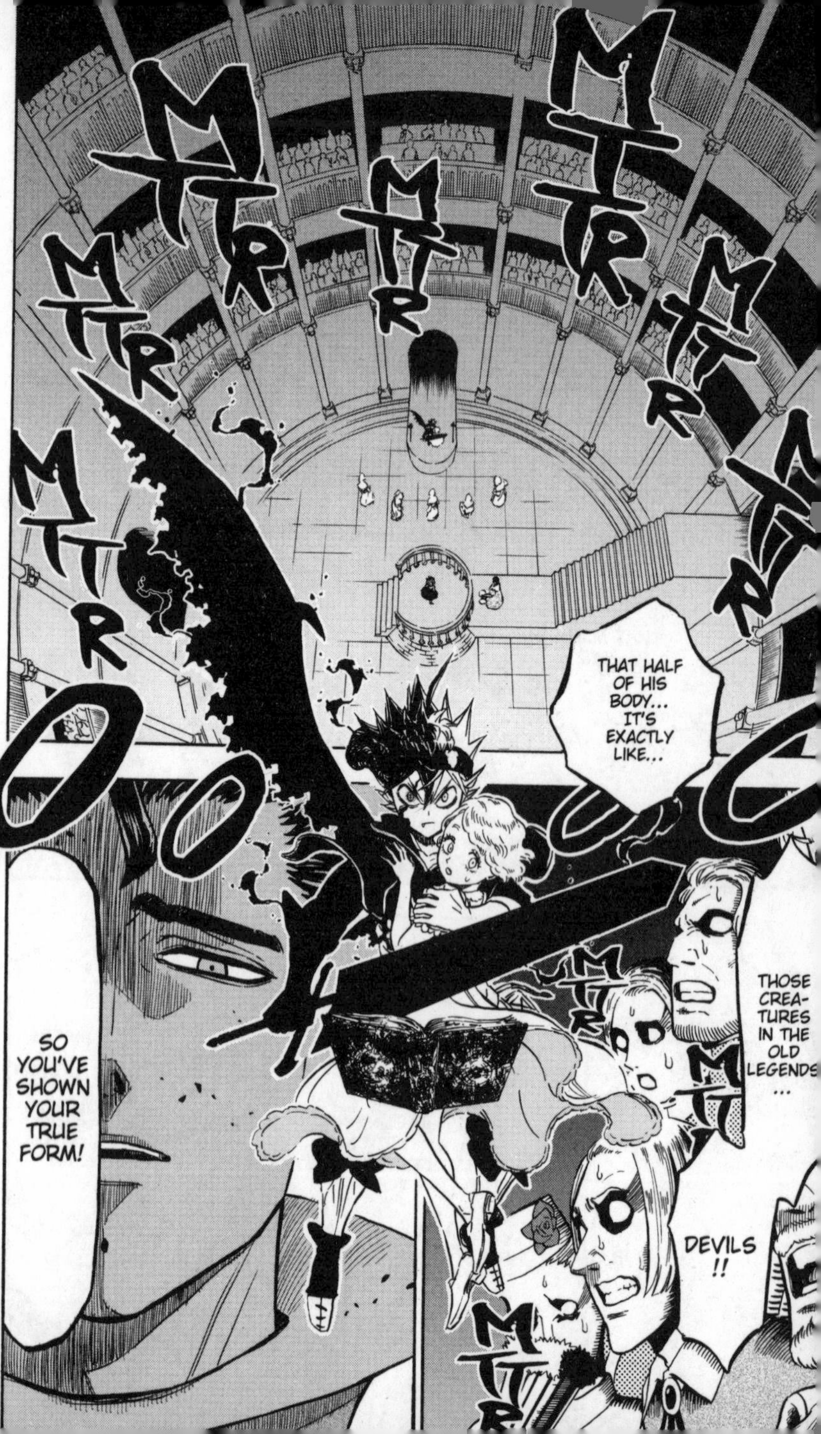
MTTR
MTTR
THAT HALF OF HIS BODY... IT'S EXACTLY LIKE...
THOSE CREATURES IN THE OLD LEGENDS...
DEVILS!!
SO YOU'VE SHOWN YOUR TRUE FORM!

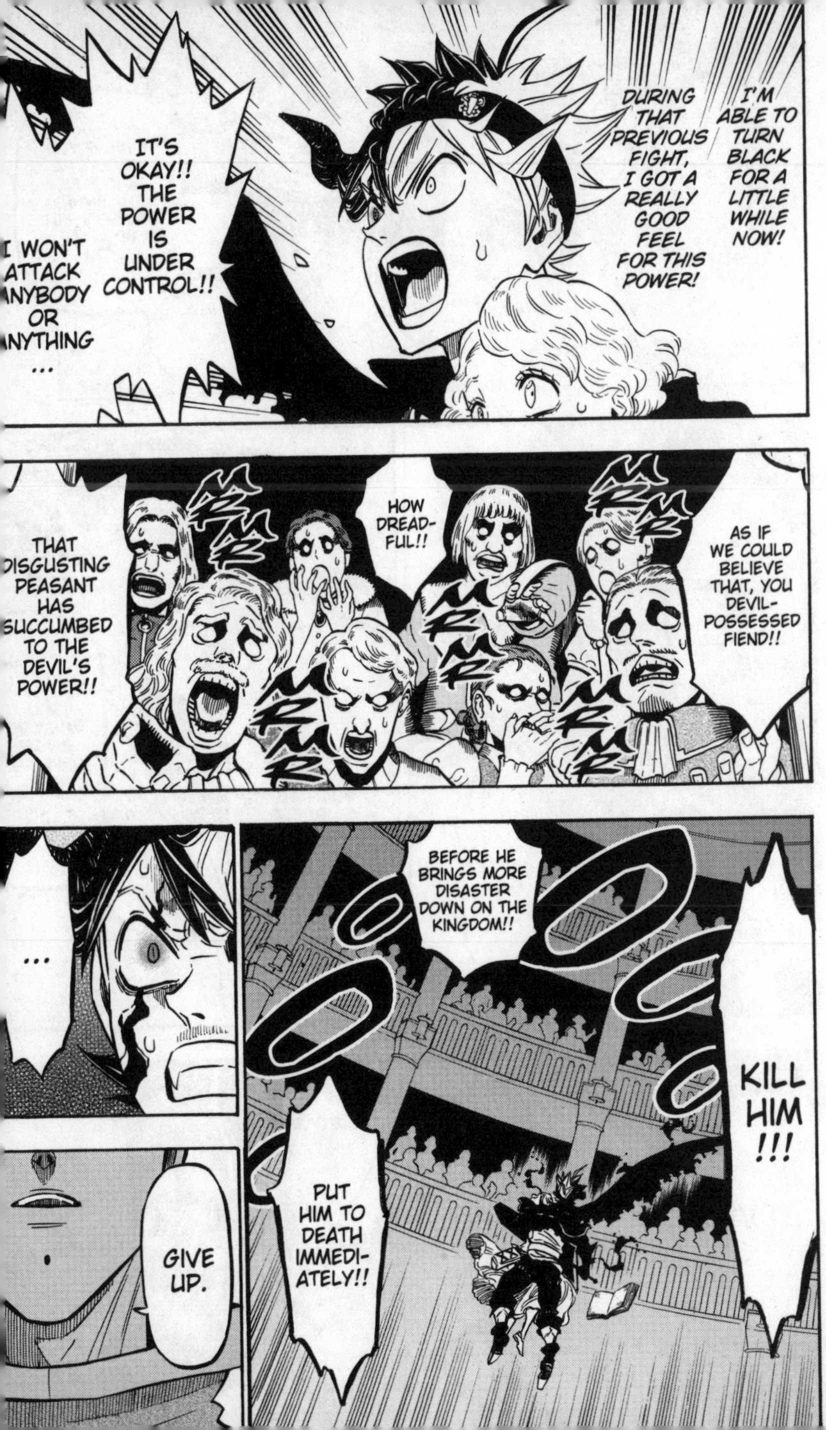
I'M ABLE TO TURN BLACK FOR A LITTLE WHILE NOW!
DURING THAT PREVIOUS FIGHT, I GOT A REALLY GOOD FEEL FOR THIS POWER!
IT'S OKAY!! THE POWER IS UNDER CONTROL!!
I WON'T ATTACK ANYBODY OR ANYTHING ...
AS IF WE COULD BELIEVE THAT, YOU DEVIL-POSSESSED FIEND!!
HOW DREAD-FUL!!
THAT DISGUSTING PEASANT HAS SUCCUMBED TO THE DEVIL'S POWER!!
KILL HIM!!!
BEFORE HE BRINGS MORE DISASTER DOWN ON THE KINGDOM!!
PUT HIM TO DEATH IMMEDI-ATELY!!
...
GIVE UP.

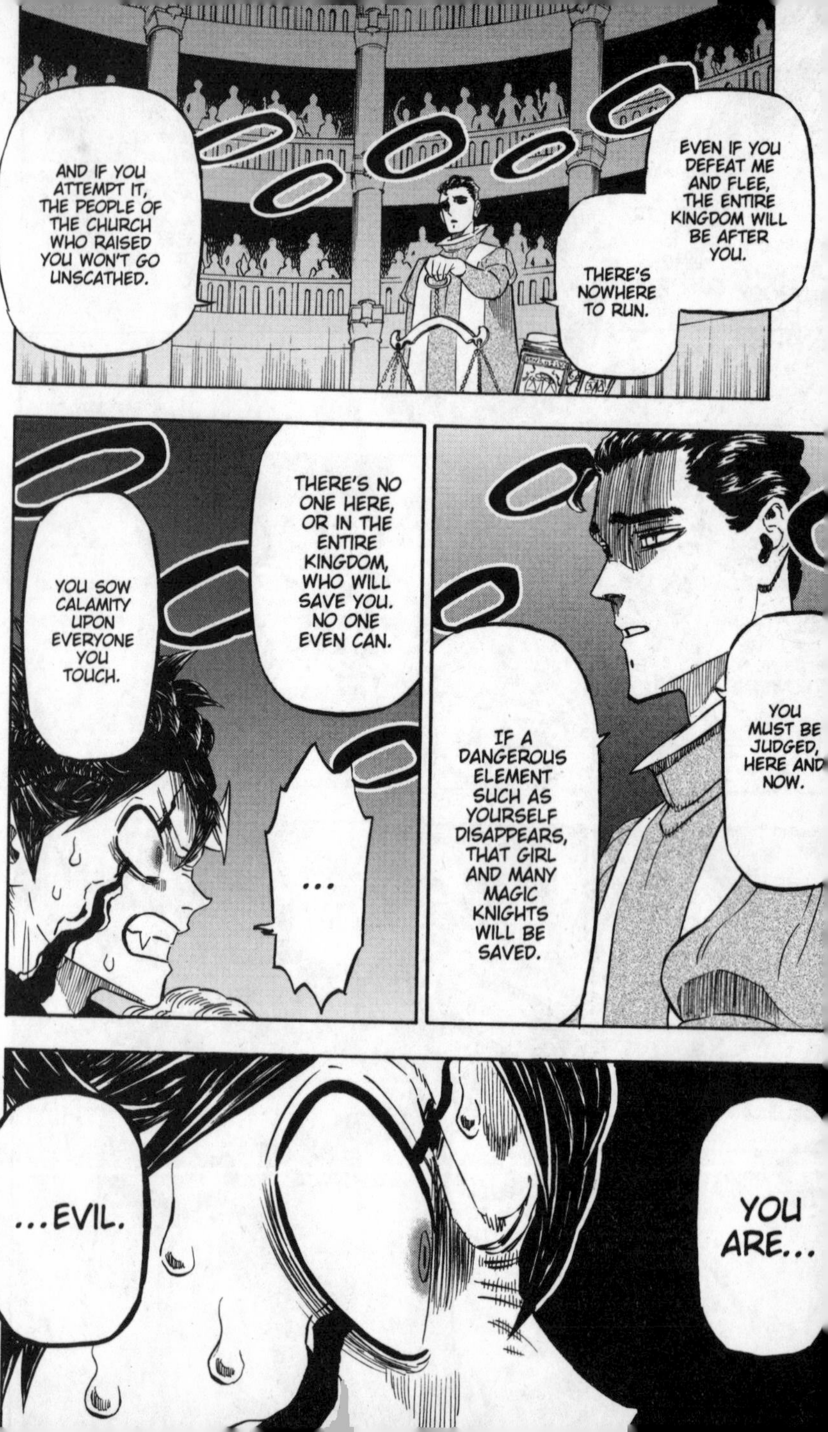
EVEN IF YOU DEFEAT ME AND FLEE, THE ENTIRE KINGDOM WILL BE AFTER YOU.
THERE'S NOWHERE TO RUN.
AND IF YOU ATTEMPT IT, THE PEOPLE OF THE CHURCH WHO RAISED YOU WON'T GO UNSCATHED.
YOU MUST BE JUDGED, HERE AND NOW.
IF A DANGEROUS ELEMENT SUCH AS YOURSELF DISAPPEARS, THAT GIRL AND MANY MAGIC KNIGHTS WILL BE SAVED.
THERE'S NO ONE HERE, OR IN THE ENTIRE KINGDOM, WHO WILL SAVE YOU. NO ONE EVEN CAN.
YOU SOW CALAMITY UPON EVERYONE YOU TOUCH.
...
YOU ARE...
...EVIL.

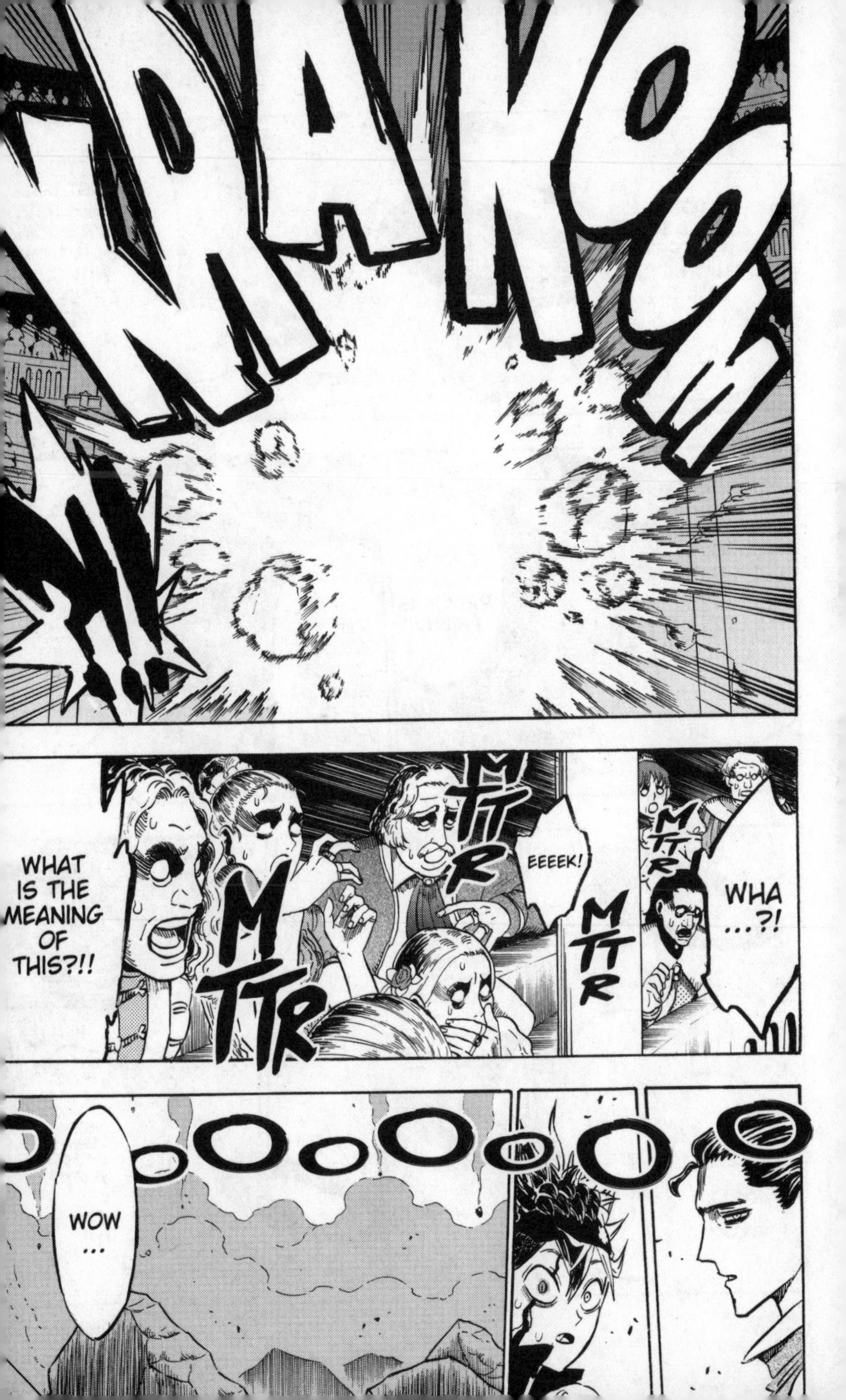
WHA ...?!
MTTR
MTTR
EEEEK!
MTTR
WHAT IS THE MEANING OF THIS?!!
MTTR
WOW ...

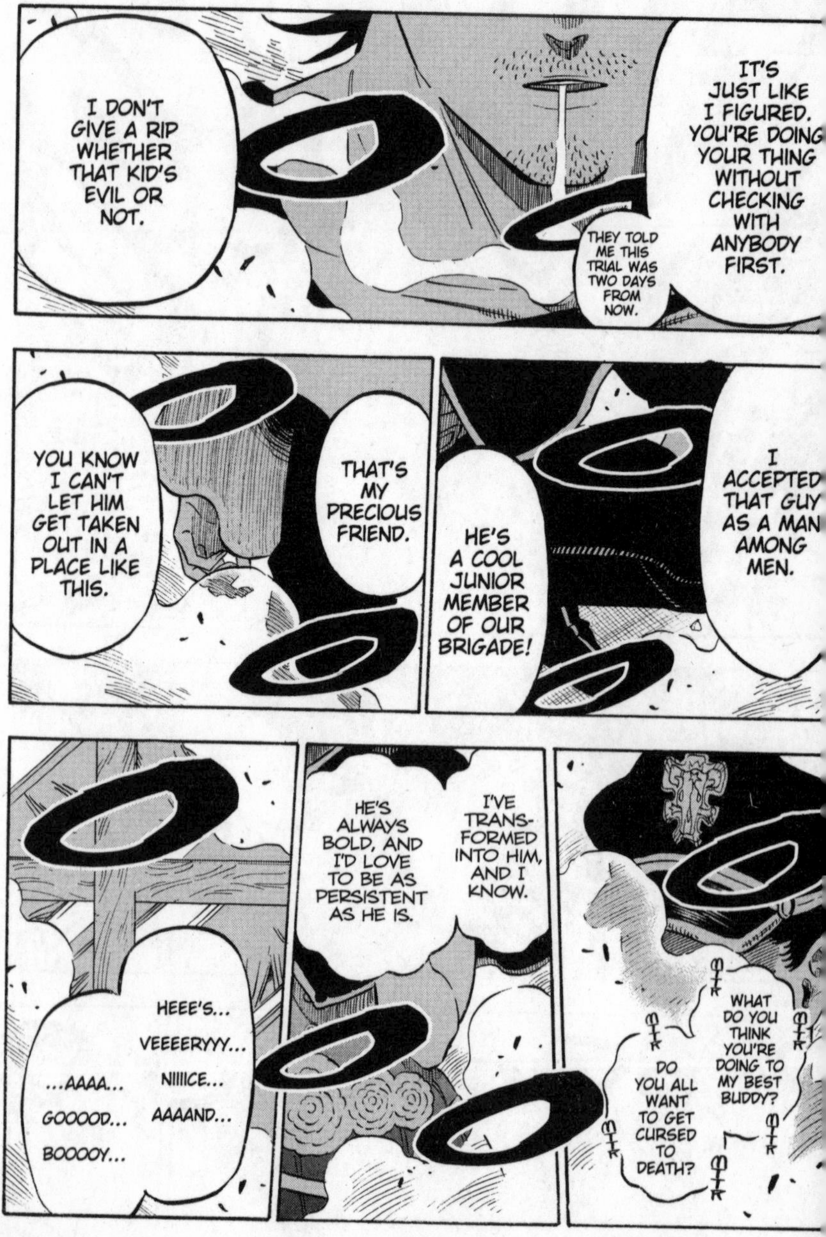
IT'S JUST LIKE I FIGURED. YOU'RE DOING YOUR THING WITHOUT CHECKING WITH ANYBODY FIRST.
THEY TOLD ME THIS TRIAL WAS TWO DAYS FROM NOW.
I DON'T GIVE A RIP WHETHER THAT KID'S EVIL OR NOT.
I ACCEPTED THAT GUY AS A MAN AMONG MEN.
HE'S A COOL JUNIOR MEMBER OF OUR BRIGADE!
THAT'S MY PRECIOUS FRIEND.
YOU KNOW I CAN'T LET HIM GET TAKEN OUT IN A PLACE LIKE THIS.
WHAT DO YOU THINK YOU'RE DOING TO MY BEST BUDDY?
DO YOU ALL WANT TO GET CURSED TO DEATH?
I'VE TRANS-FORMED INTO HIM, AND I KNOW.
HE'S ALWAYS BOLD, AND I'D LOVE TO BE AS PERSISTENT AS HE IS.
HEEE'S... VEEEERYYY... NIIIICE... AAAAND...
...AAAA... GOOOOD... BOOOOY...

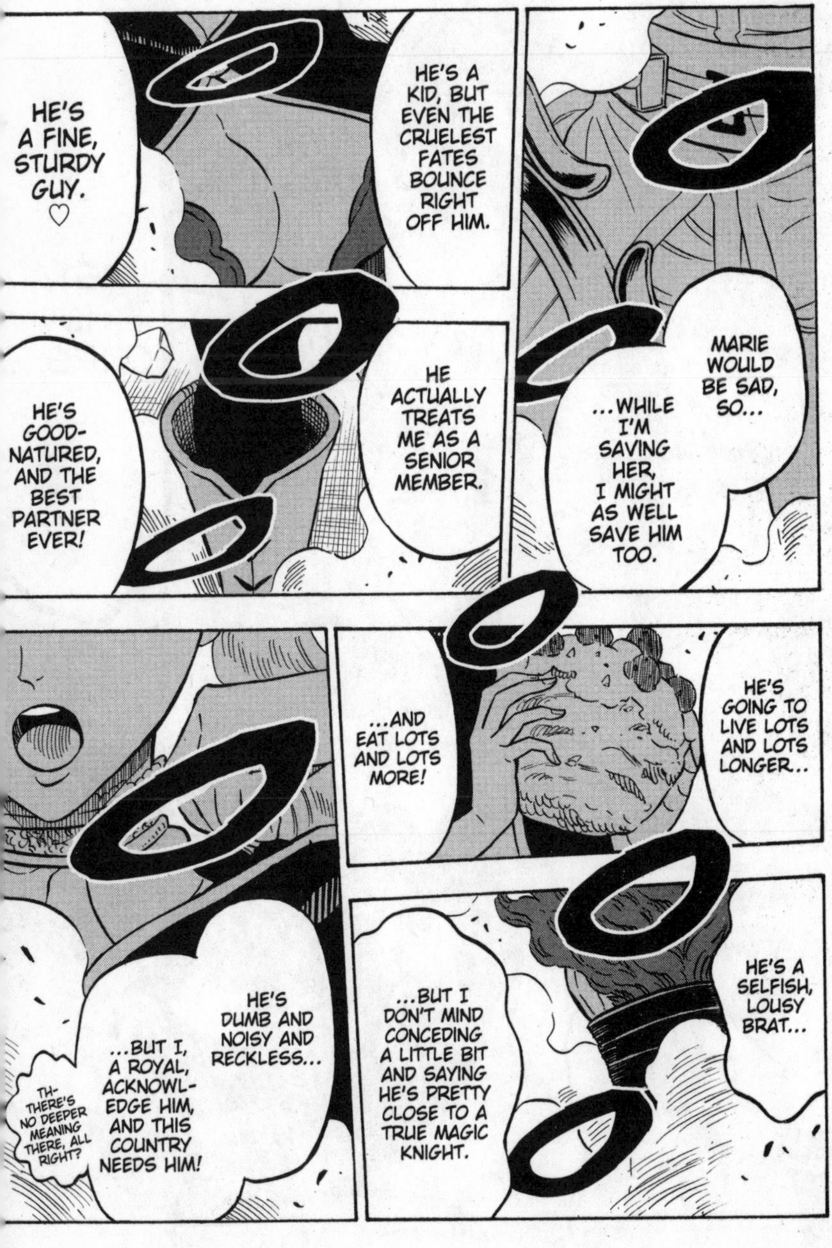
MARIE WOULD BE SAD, SO...
...WHILE I'M SAVING HER, I MIGHT AS WELL SAVE HIM TOO.
HE'S A KID, BUT EVEN THE CRUELEST FATES BOUNCE RIGHT OFF HIM.
HE'S A FINE, STURDY GUY. ♡
HE ACTUALLY TREATS ME AS A SENIOR MEMBER.
HE'S GOOD-NATURED, AND THE BEST PARTNER EVER!
HE'S GOING TO LIVE LOTS AND LOTS LONGER...
...AND EAT LOTS AND LOTS MORE!
HE'S A SELFISH, LOUSY BRAT...
...BUT I DON'T MIND CONCEDING A LITTLE BIT AND SAYING HE'S PRETTY CLOSE TO A TRUE MAGIC KNIGHT.
HE'S DUMB AND NOISY AND RECKLESS...
...BUT I, A ROYAL, ACKNOWLEDGE HIM, AND THIS COUNTRY NEEDS HIM!
TH-THERE'S NO DEEPER MEANING THERE, ALL RIGHT?

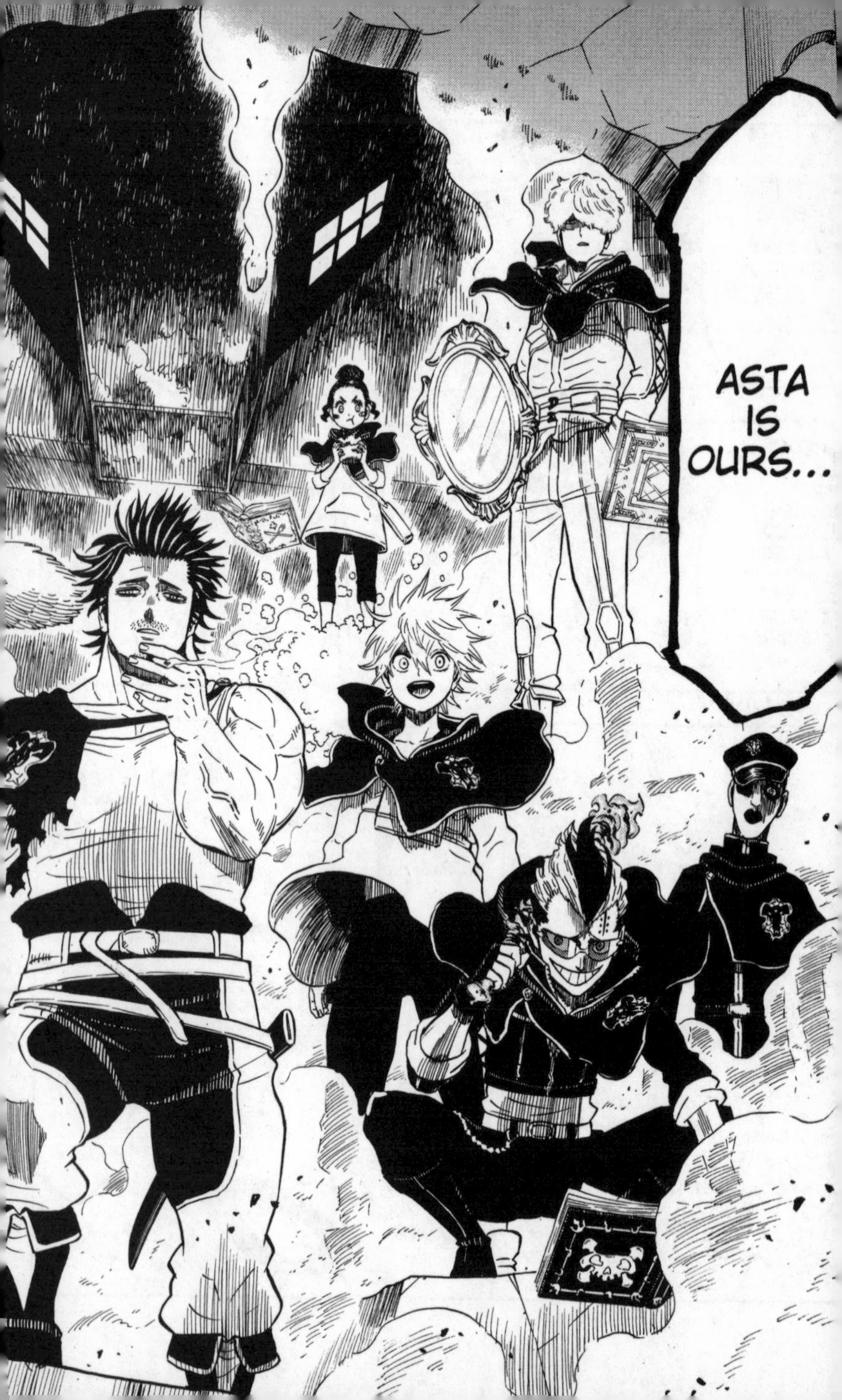
ASTA IS OURS...

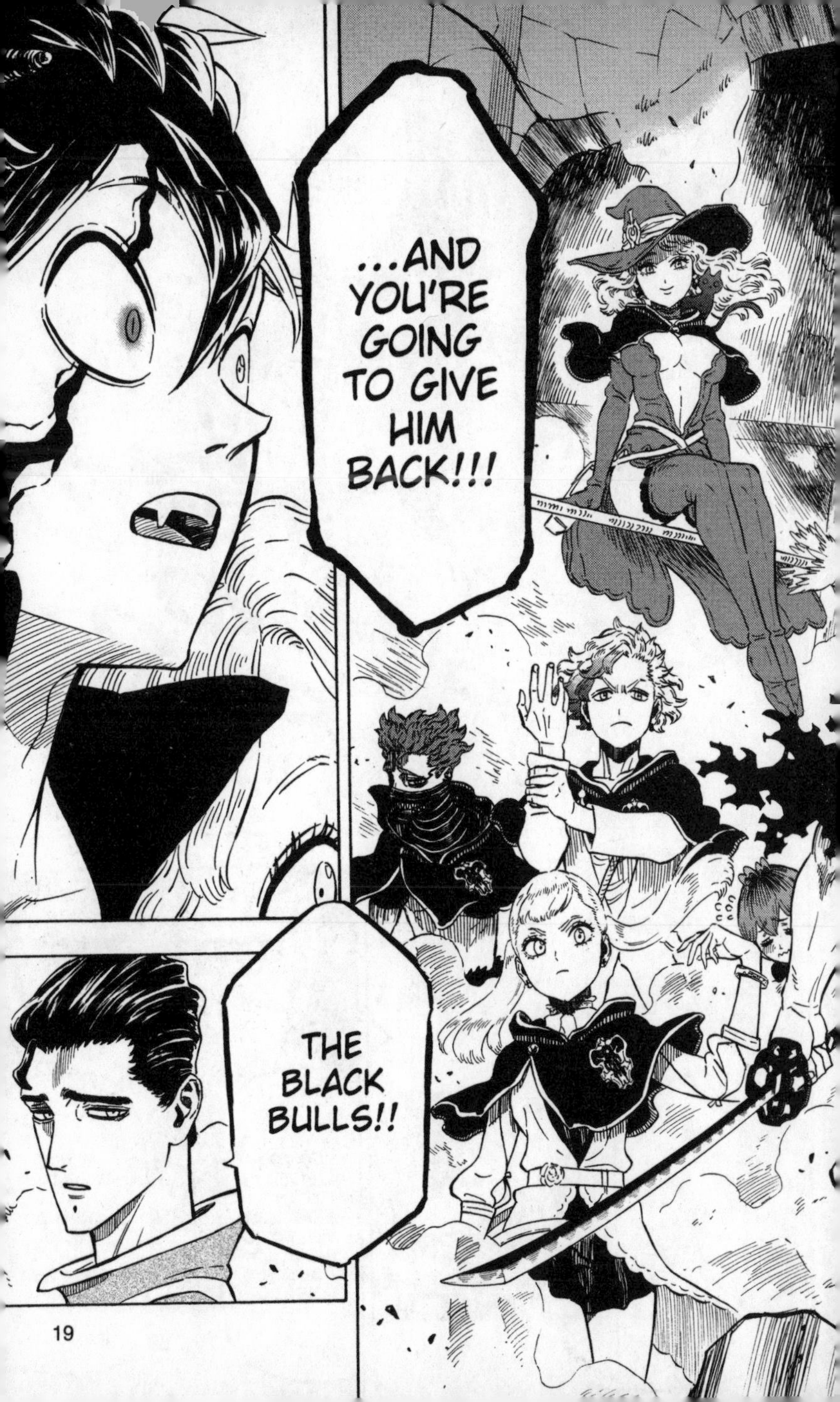

...AND YOU'RE GOING TO GIVE HIM BACK!!!
THE BLACK BULLS!!

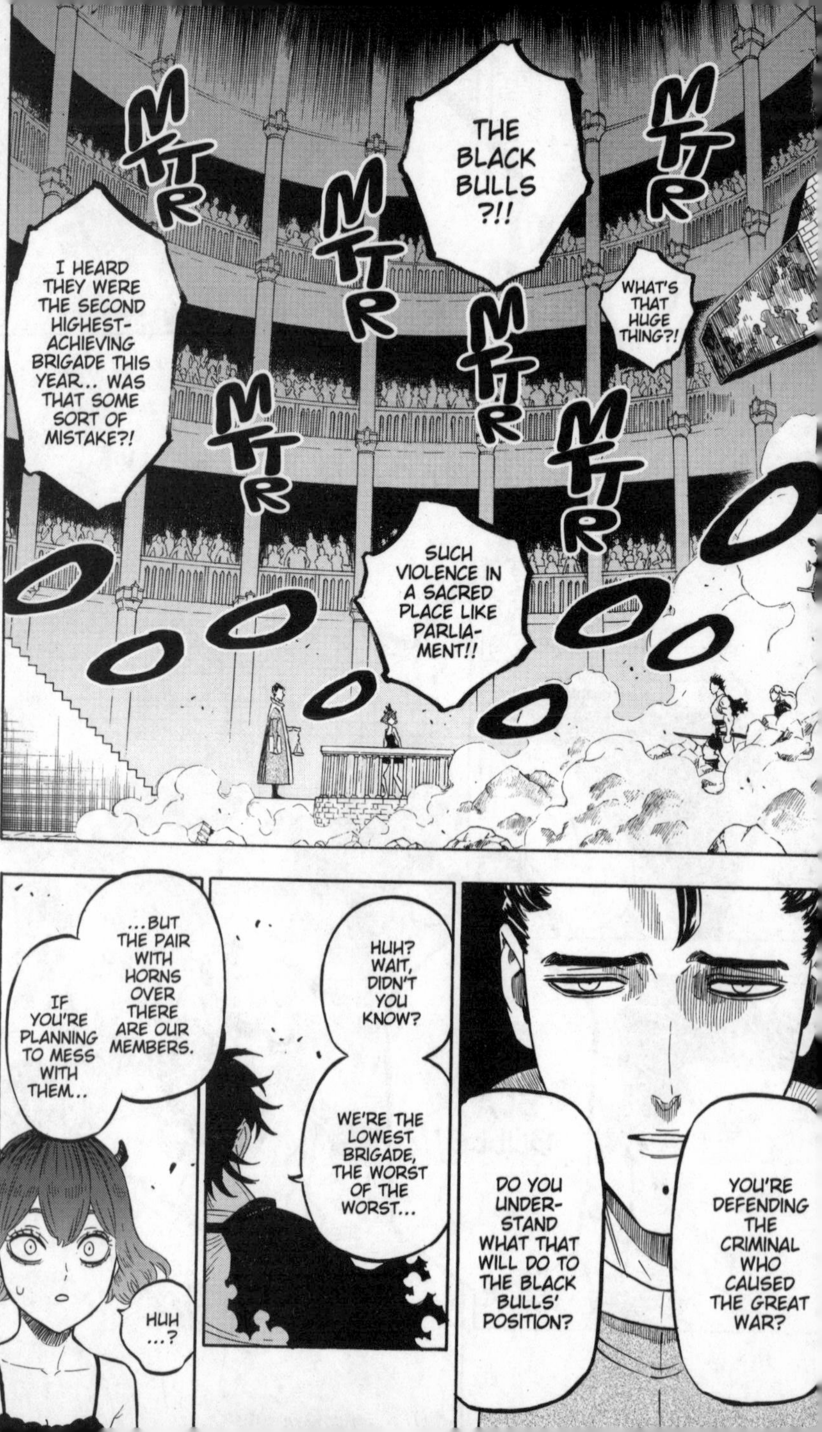
MTTR
THE BLACK BULLS?!!
MTTR
WHAT'S THAT HUGE THING?!
MTTR
MTTR
I HEARD THEY WERE THE SECOND HIGHEST-ACHIEVING BRIGADE THIS YEAR... WAS THAT SOME SORT OF MISTAKE?!
MTTR
MTTR
OOOO
SUCH VIOLENCE IN A SACRED PLACE LIKE PARLIA-MENT!!
OOOO
YOU'RE DEFENDING THE CRIMINAL WHO CAUSED THE GREAT WAR?
DO YOU UNDER-STAND WHAT THAT WILL DO TO THE BLACK BULLS' POSITION?
HUH? WAIT, DIDN'T YOU KNOW?
WE'RE THE LOWEST BRIGADE, THE WORST OF THE WORST...
...BUT THE PAIR WITH HORNS OVER THERE ARE OUR MEMBERS.
IF YOU'RE PLANNING TO MESS WITH THEM...
HUH ...?

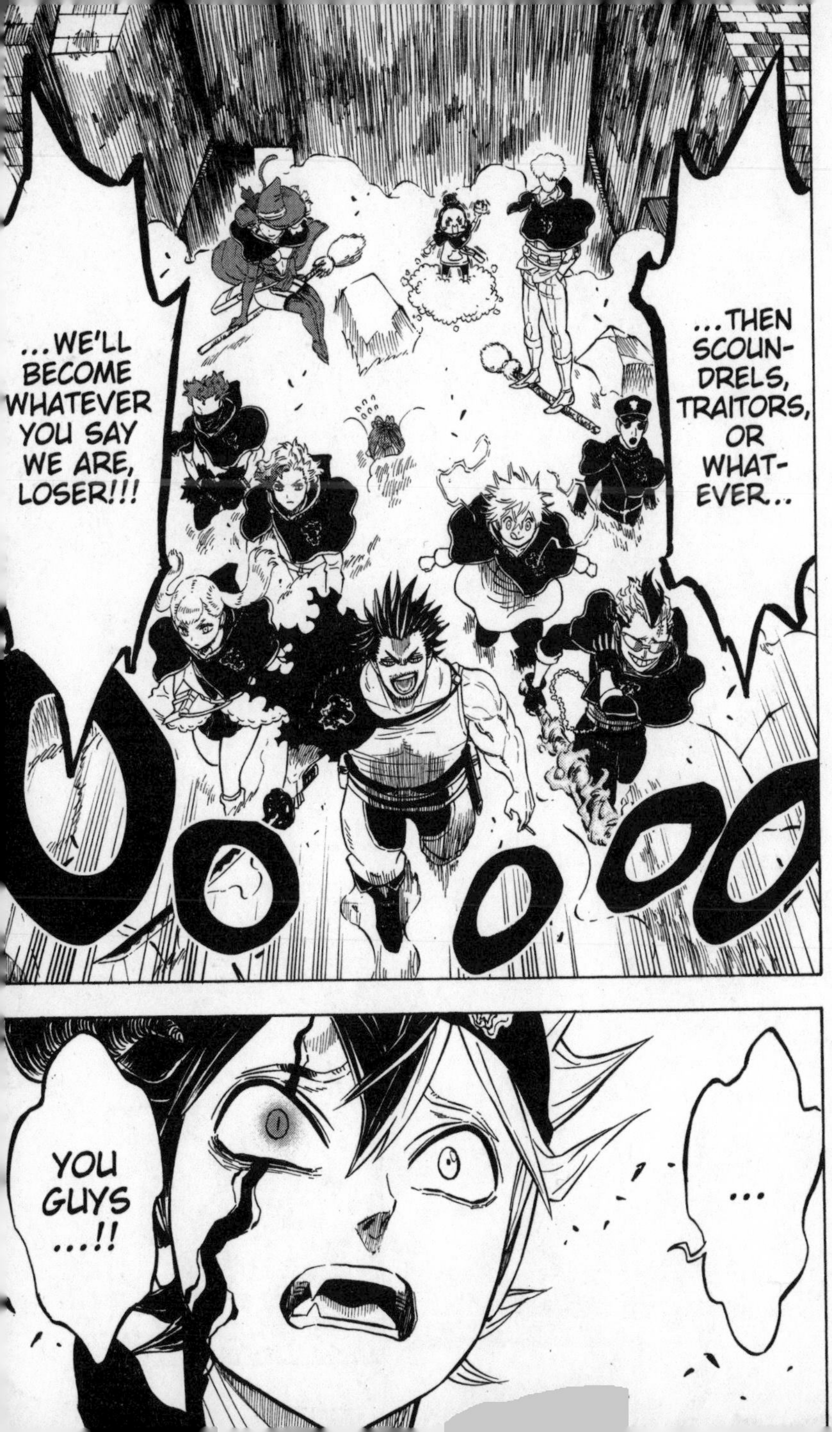
...THEN SCOUNDRELS, TRAITORS, OR WHATEVER...
...WE'LL BECOME WHATEVER YOU SAY WE ARE, LOSER!!!
OOOOO
...
YOU GUYS ...!!

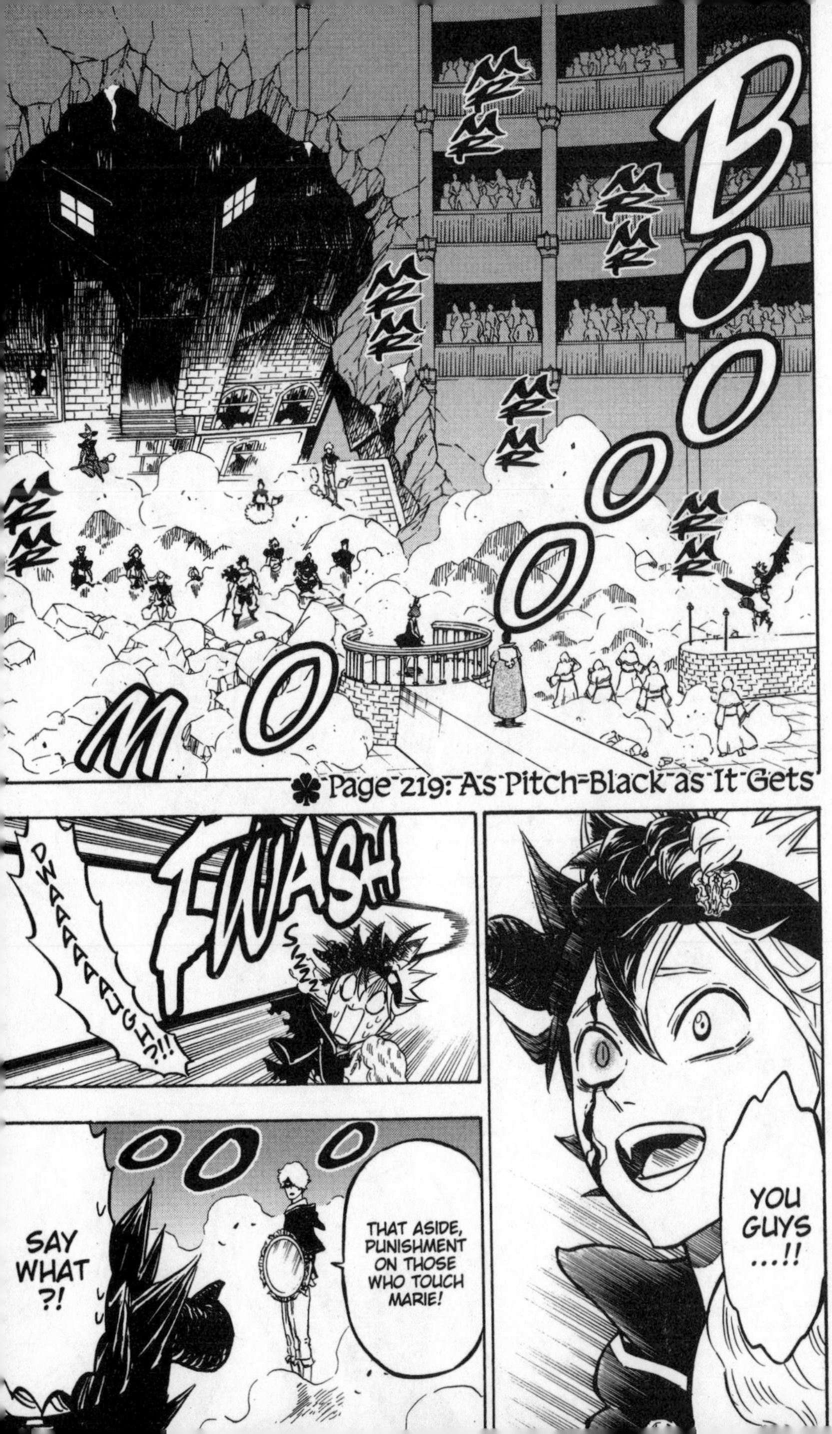
BOOOOOOOM
MRMR
MRMR
MRMR
MRMR
MRMR
MRMR
Page 219: As Pitch-Black as It Gets
YOU GUYS ...!!
FWASH
DWAAAAAAAUGH?!!
SWZZ
OOO
SAY WHAT ?!
THAT ASIDE, PUNISHMENT ON THOSE WHO TOUCH MARIE!

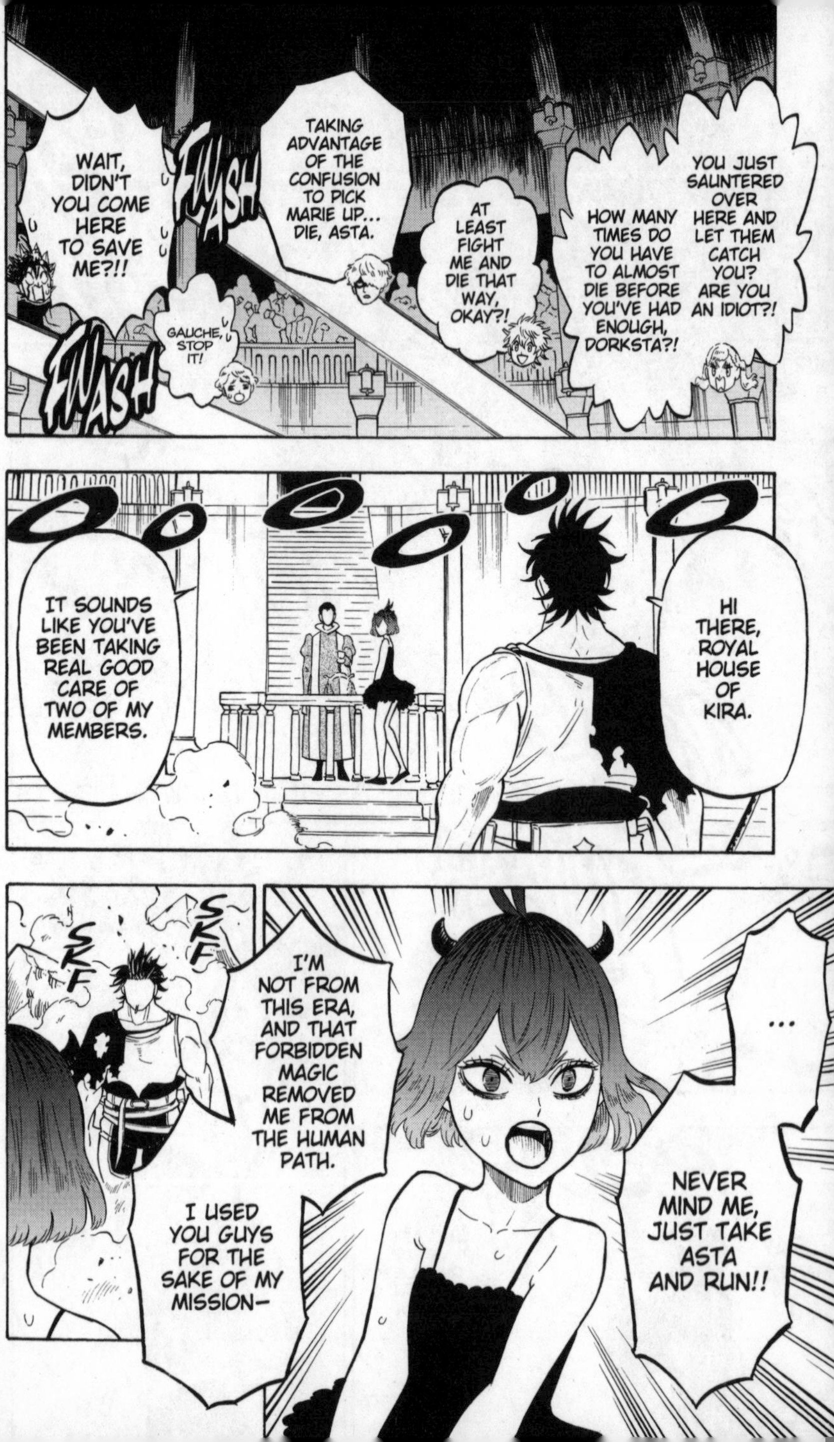
YOU JUST SAUNTERED OVER HERE AND LET THEM CATCH YOU? ARE YOU AN IDIOT?!
HOW MANY TIMES DO YOU HAVE TO ALMOST DIE BEFORE YOU'VE HAD ENOUGH, DORKSTA?!
AT LEAST FIGHT ME AND DIE THAT WAY, OKAY?!
TAKING ADVANTAGE OF THE CONFUSION TO PICK MARIE UP... DIE, ASTA.
FWASH
GAUCHE, STOP IT!
WAIT, DIDN'T YOU COME HERE TO SAVE ME?!!
FWASH
HI THERE, ROYAL HOUSE OF KIRA.
IT SOUNDS LIKE YOU'VE BEEN TAKING REAL GOOD CARE OF TWO OF MY MEMBERS.
...
NEVER MIND ME, JUST TAKE ASTA AND RUN!!
I'M NOT FROM THIS ERA, AND THAT FORBIDDEN MAGIC REMOVED ME FROM THE HUMAN PATH.
I USED YOU GUYS FOR THE SAKE OF MY MISSION—
SKF
SKF

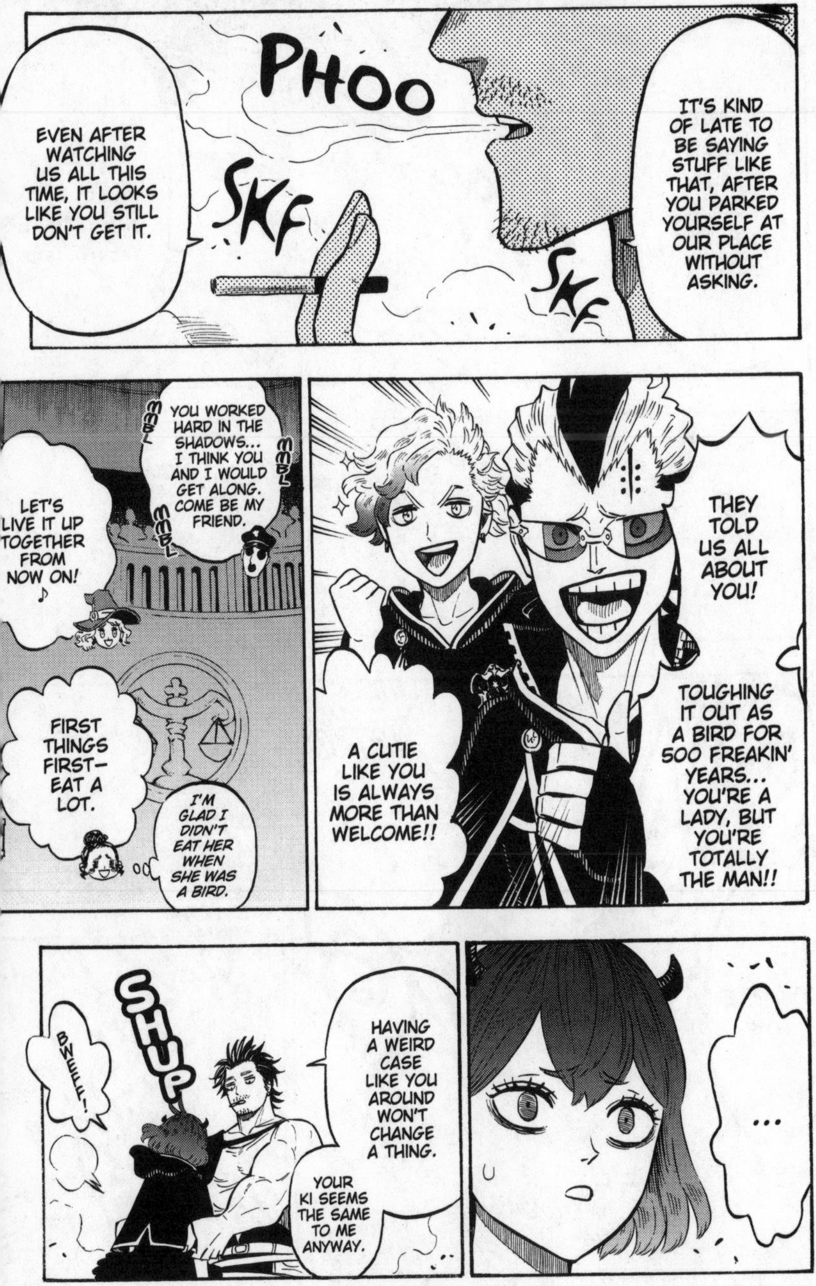
PHOO
IT'S KIND OF LATE TO BE SAYING STUFF LIKE THAT, AFTER YOU PARKED YOURSELF AT OUR PLACE WITHOUT ASKING.
SKF
SKF
EVEN AFTER WATCHING US ALL THIS TIME, IT LOOKS LIKE YOU STILL DON'T GET IT.
THEY TOLD US ALL ABOUT YOU!
TOUGHING IT OUT AS A BIRD FOR 500 FREAKIN' YEARS... YOU'RE A LADY, BUT YOU'RE TOTALLY THE MAN!!
A CUTIE LIKE YOU IS ALWAYS MORE THAN WELCOME!!
YOU WORKED HARD IN THE SHADOWS... I THINK YOU AND I WOULD GET ALONG. COME BE MY FRIEND.
MMBL
MMBL
MMBL
LET'S LIVE IT UP TOGETHER FROM NOW ON! ♪
FIRST THINGS FIRST—EAT A LOT.
I'M GLAD I DIDN'T EAT HER WHEN SHE WAS A BIRD.
...
SHUP
HAVING A WEIRD CASE LIKE YOU AROUND WON'T CHANGE A THING.
YOUR KI SEEMS THE SAME TO ME ANYWAY.
BWEFF!

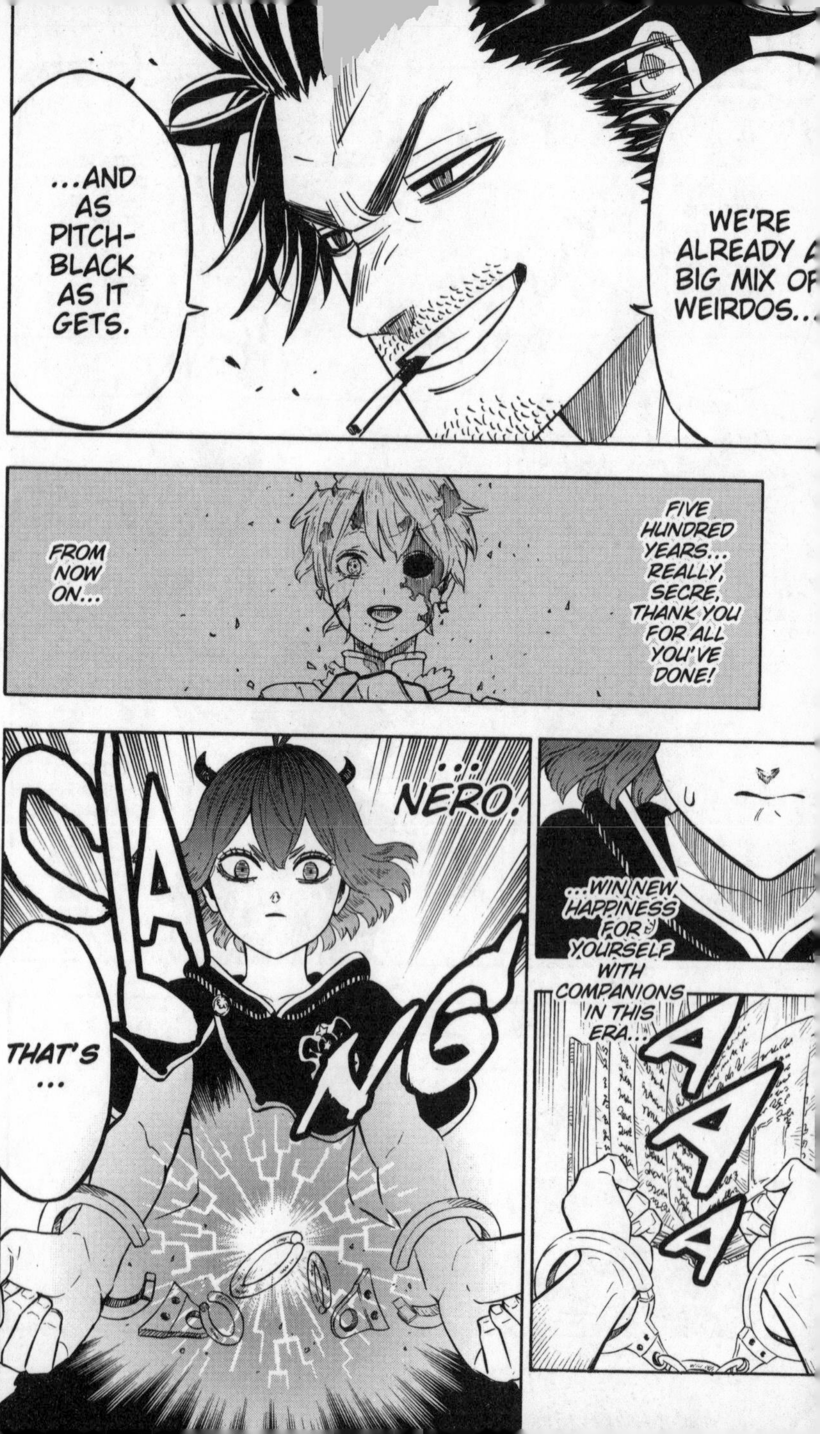

WE'RE ALREADY A BIG MIX OF WEIRDOS...
...AND AS PITCH-BLACK AS IT GETS.
FIVE HUNDRED YEARS... REALLY, SECRE, THANK YOU FOR ALL YOU'VE DONE!
FROM NOW ON...
...WIN NEW HAPPINESS FOR YOURSELF WITH COMPANIONS IN THIS ERA...
AAAA
...NERO.
CLANG
THAT'S ...

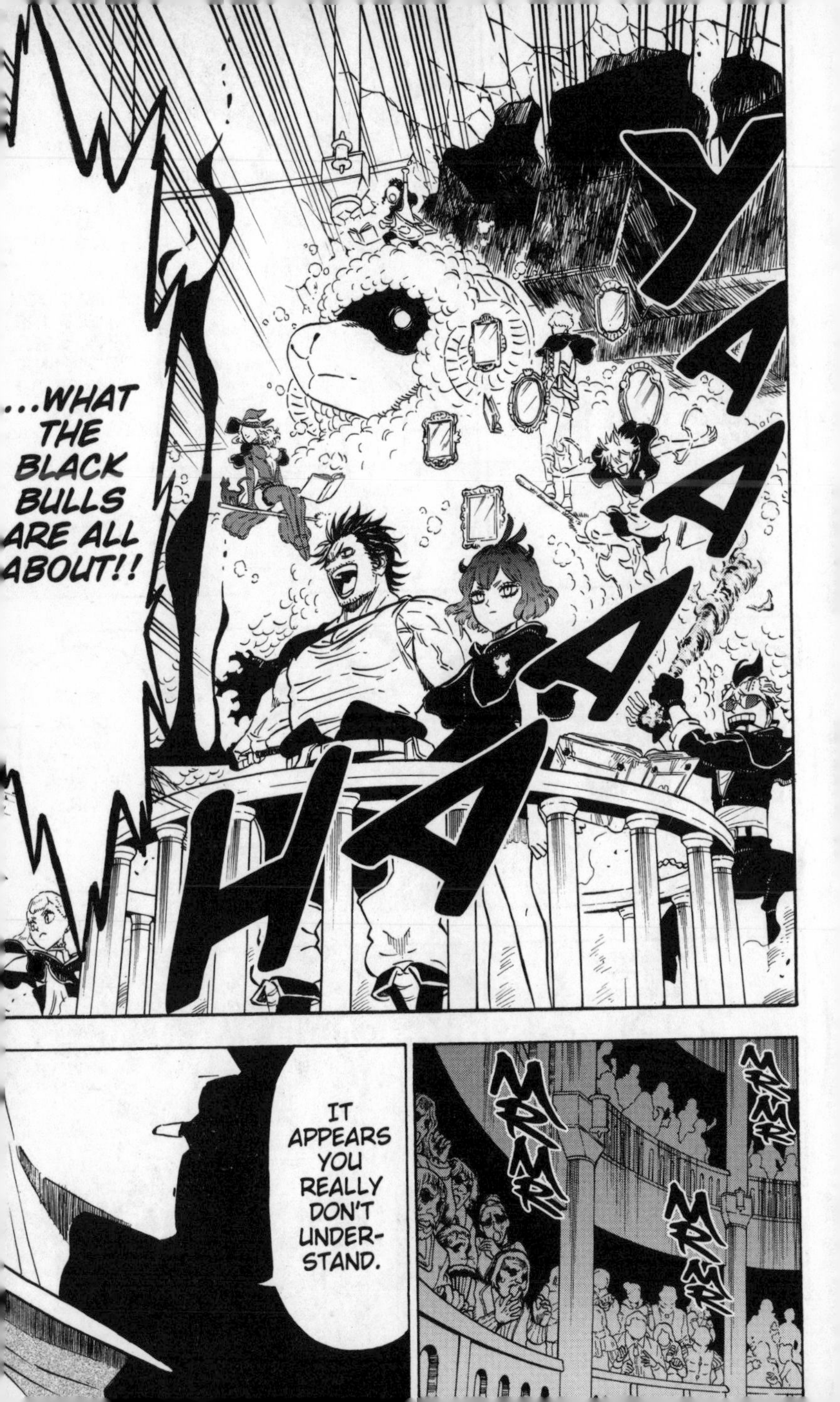
...WHAT THE BLACK BULLS ARE ALL ABOUT!!
HAAAAAY
MRMR
MRMR
MRMR
IT APPEARS YOU REALLY DON'T UNDER-STAND.

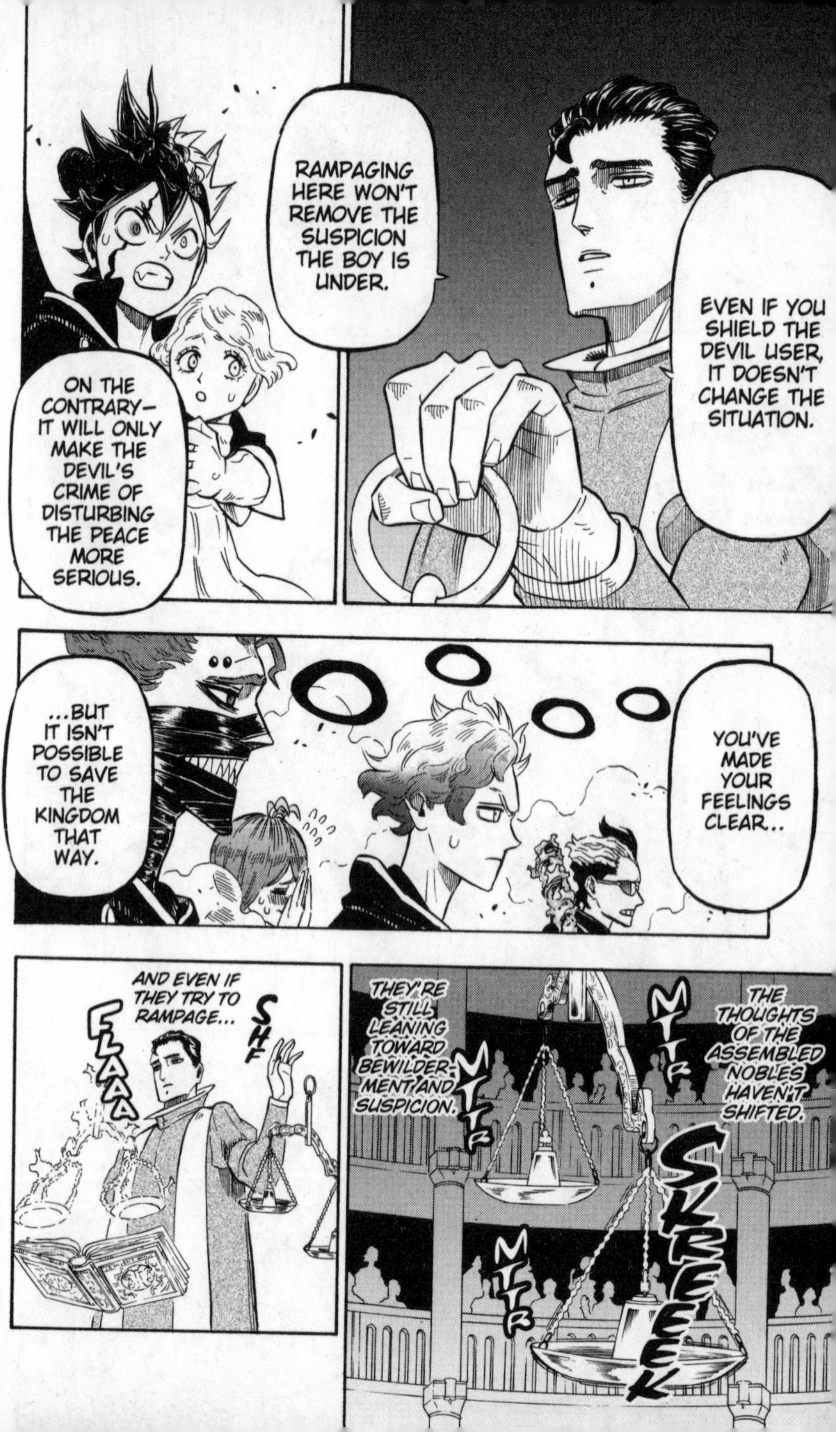
EVEN IF YOU SHIELD THE DEVIL USER, IT DOESN'T CHANGE THE SITUATION.
RAMPAGING HERE WON'T REMOVE THE SUSPICION THE BOY IS UNDER.
ON THE CONTRARY—IT WILL ONLY MAKE THE DEVIL'S CRIME OF DISTURBING THE PEACE MORE SERIOUS.
YOU'VE MADE YOUR FEELINGS CLEAR...
...BUT IT ISN'T POSSIBLE TO SAVE THE KINGDOM THAT WAY.
THE THOUGHTS OF THE ASSEMBLED NOBLES HAVEN'T SHIFTED.
MTR
THEY'RE STILL LEANING TOWARD BEWILDERMENT AND SUSPICION.
MTR
SKREEEEK
MTR
AND EVEN IF THEY TRY TO RAMPAGE...
SHF
FLAAA

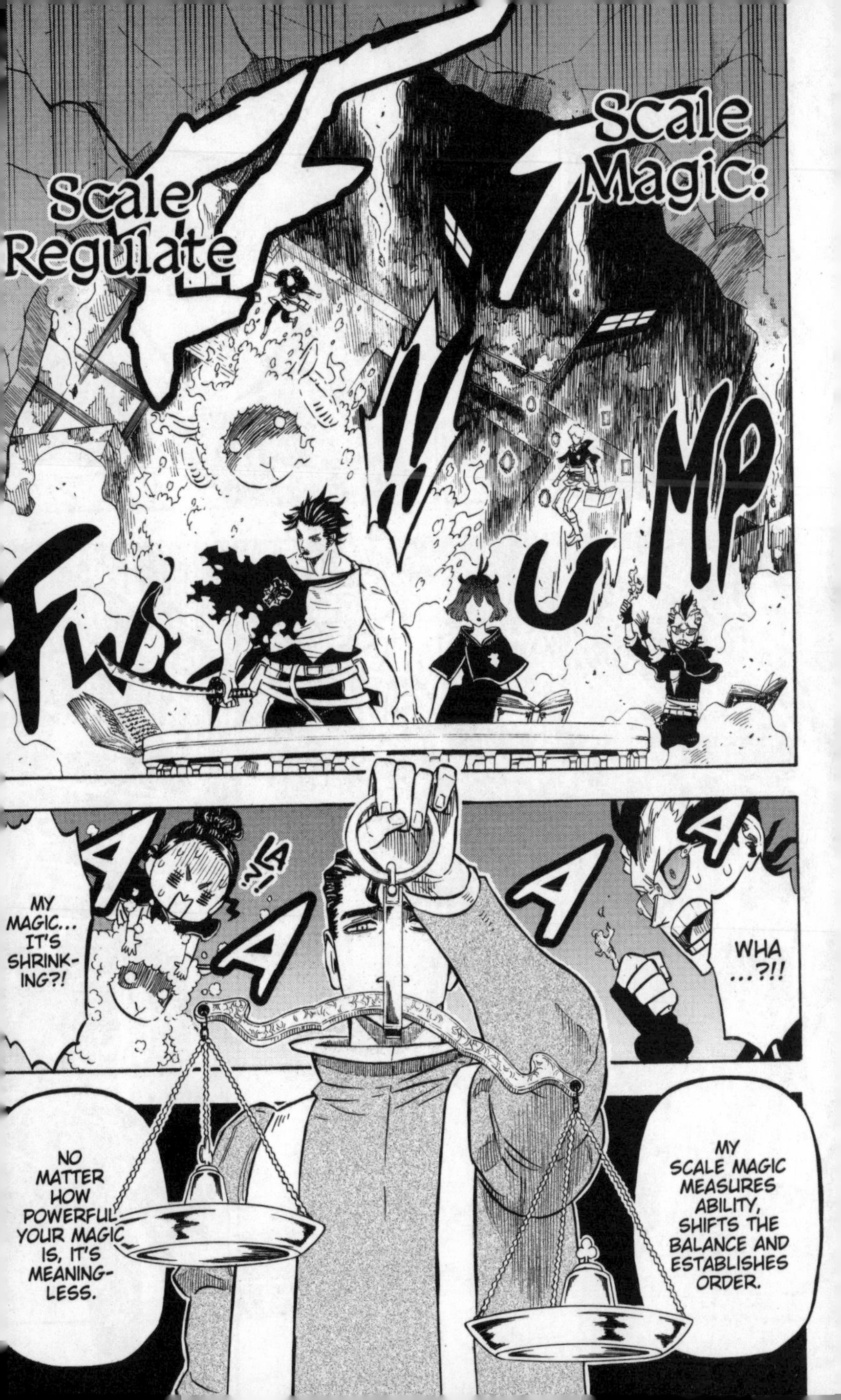
Scale Magic:
Scale Regulate
WHA ...?!!
MY MAGIC... IT'S SHRINKING?!
MY SCALE MAGIC MEASURES ABILITY, SHIFTS THE BALANCE AND ESTABLISHES ORDER.
NO MATTER HOW POWERFUL YOUR MAGIC IS, IT'S MEANINGLESS.

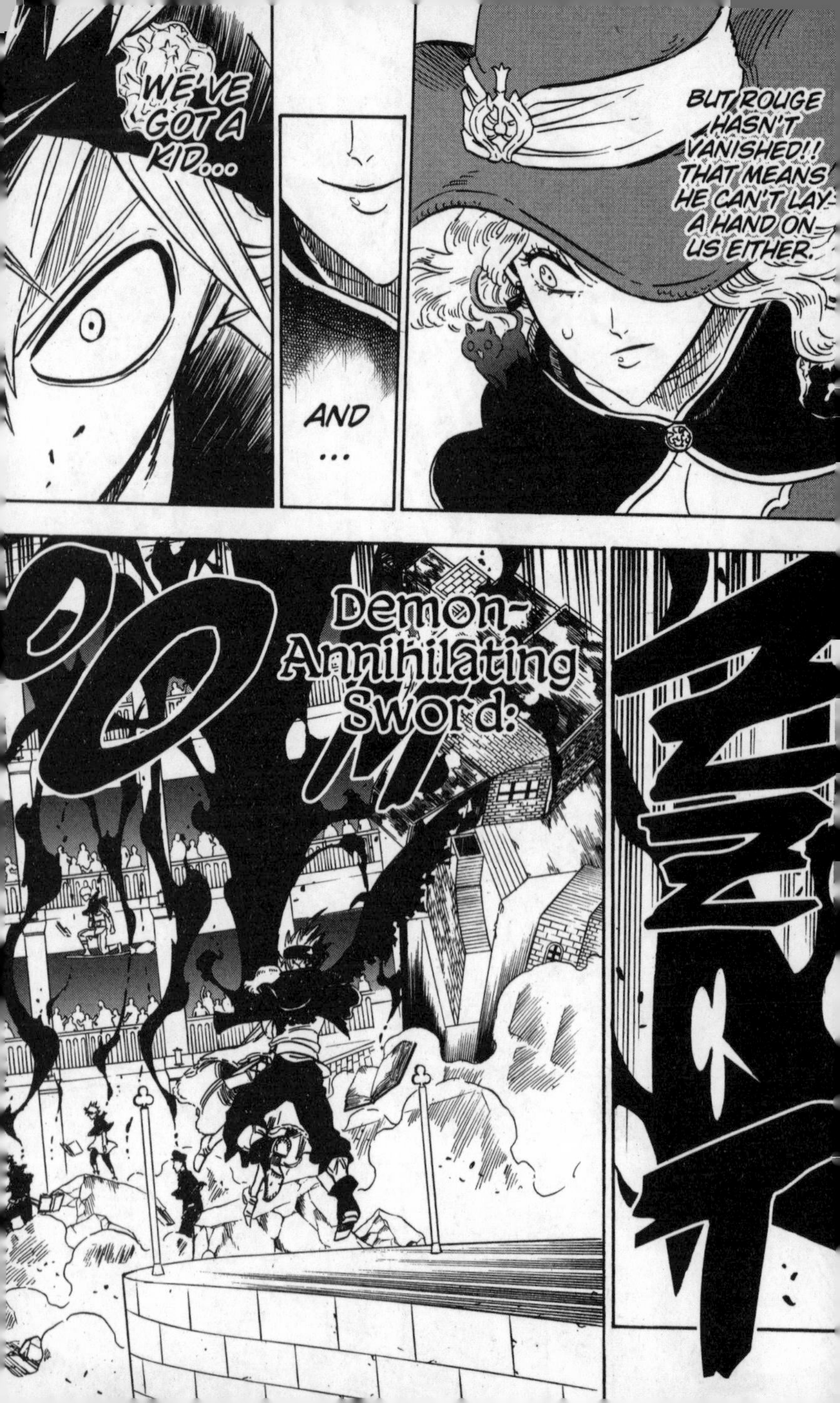
BUT ROUGE HASN'T VANISHED!! THAT MEANS HE CAN'T LAY A HAND ON US EITHER.
AND ...
WE'VE GOT A KID...
Demon-Annihilating Sword:

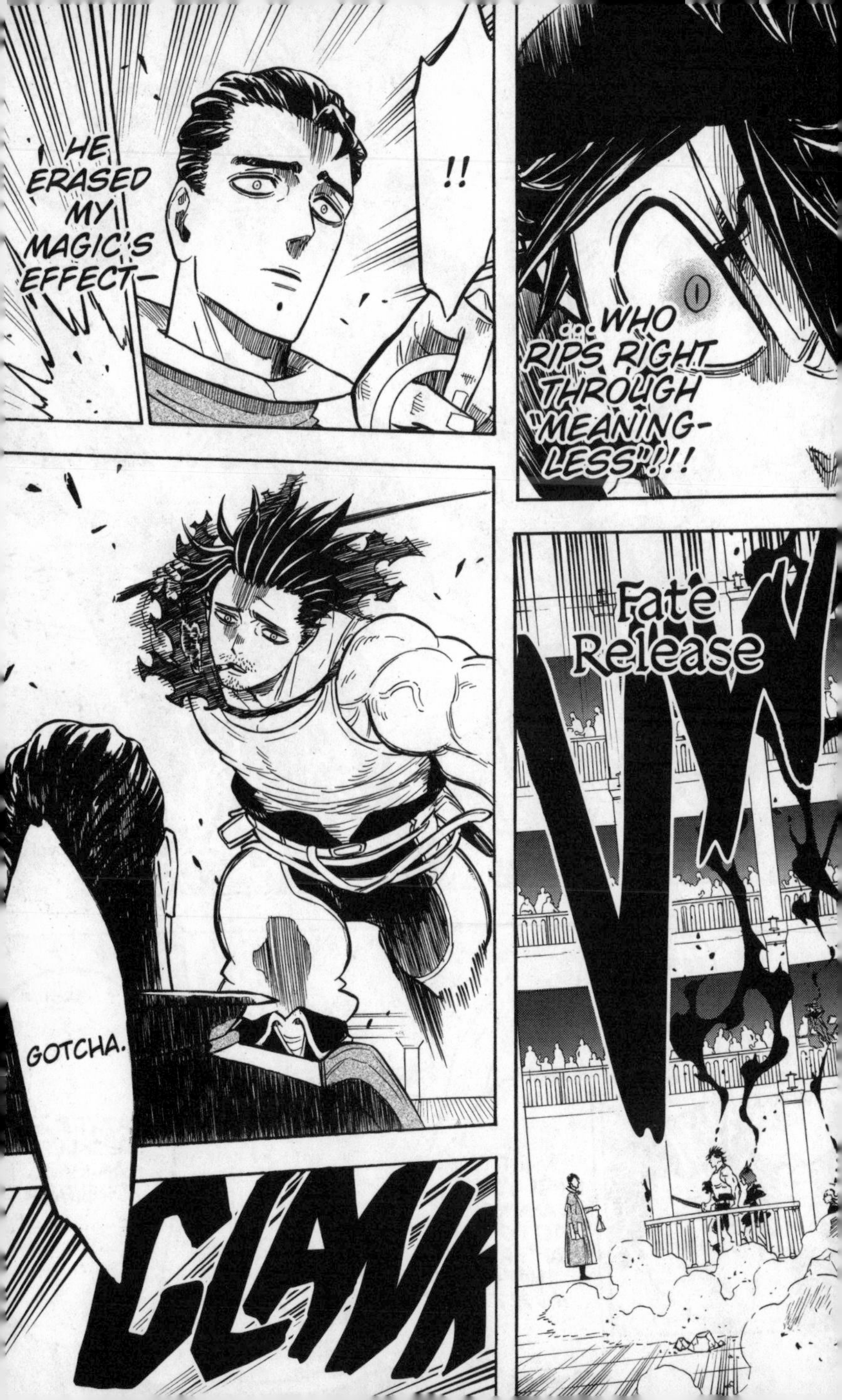
...WHO RIPS RIGHT THROUGH "MEANING-LESS"!!!
HE ERASED MY MAGIC'S EFFECT—
!!
Fate Release
GOTCHA.
CLAN

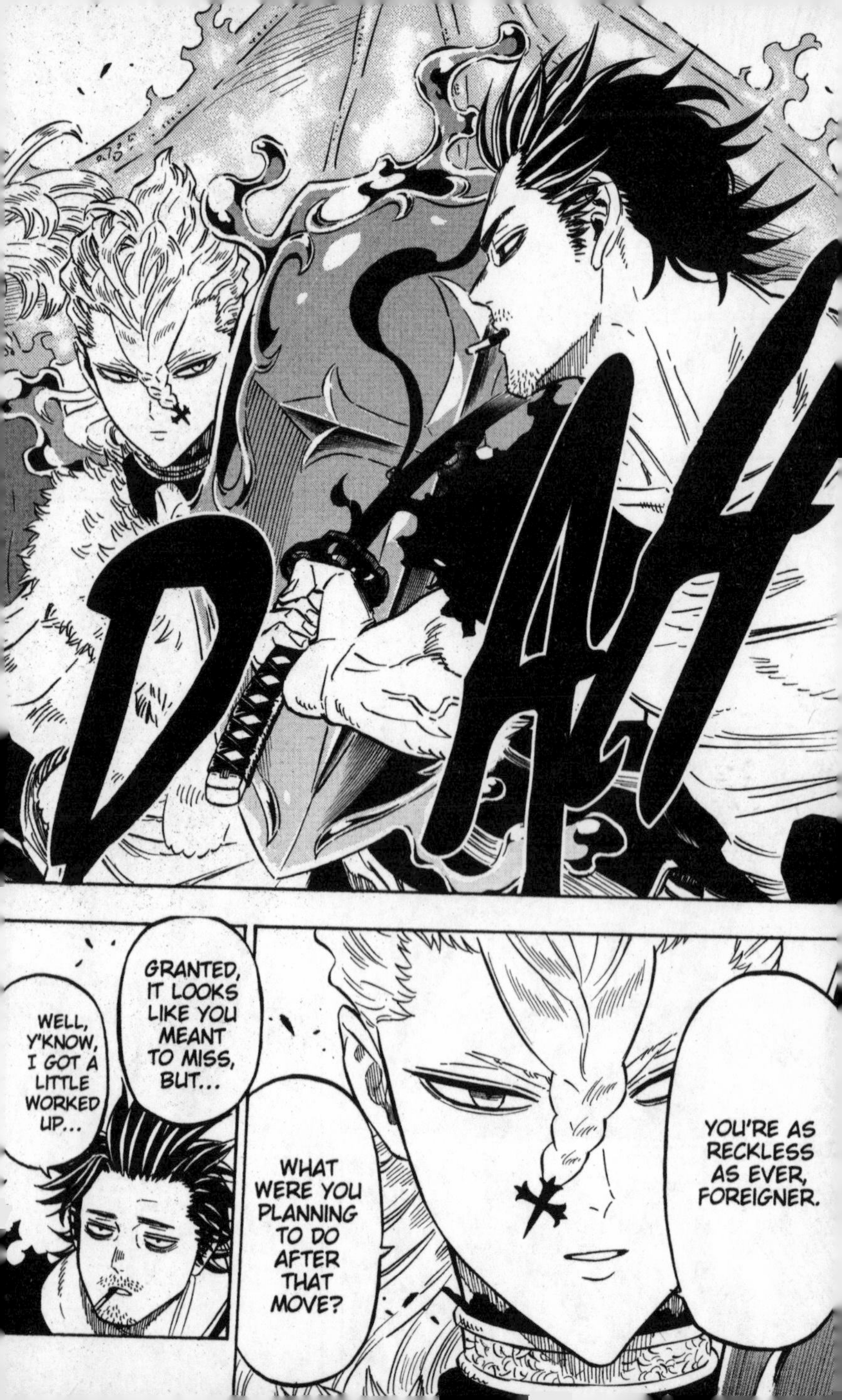
DAH
YOU'RE AS RECKLESS AS EVER, FOREIGNER.
WHAT WERE YOU PLANNING TO DO AFTER THAT MOVE?
GRANTED, IT LOOKS LIKE YOU MEANT TO MISS, BUT...
WELL, Y'KNOW, I GOT A LITTLE WORKED UP...

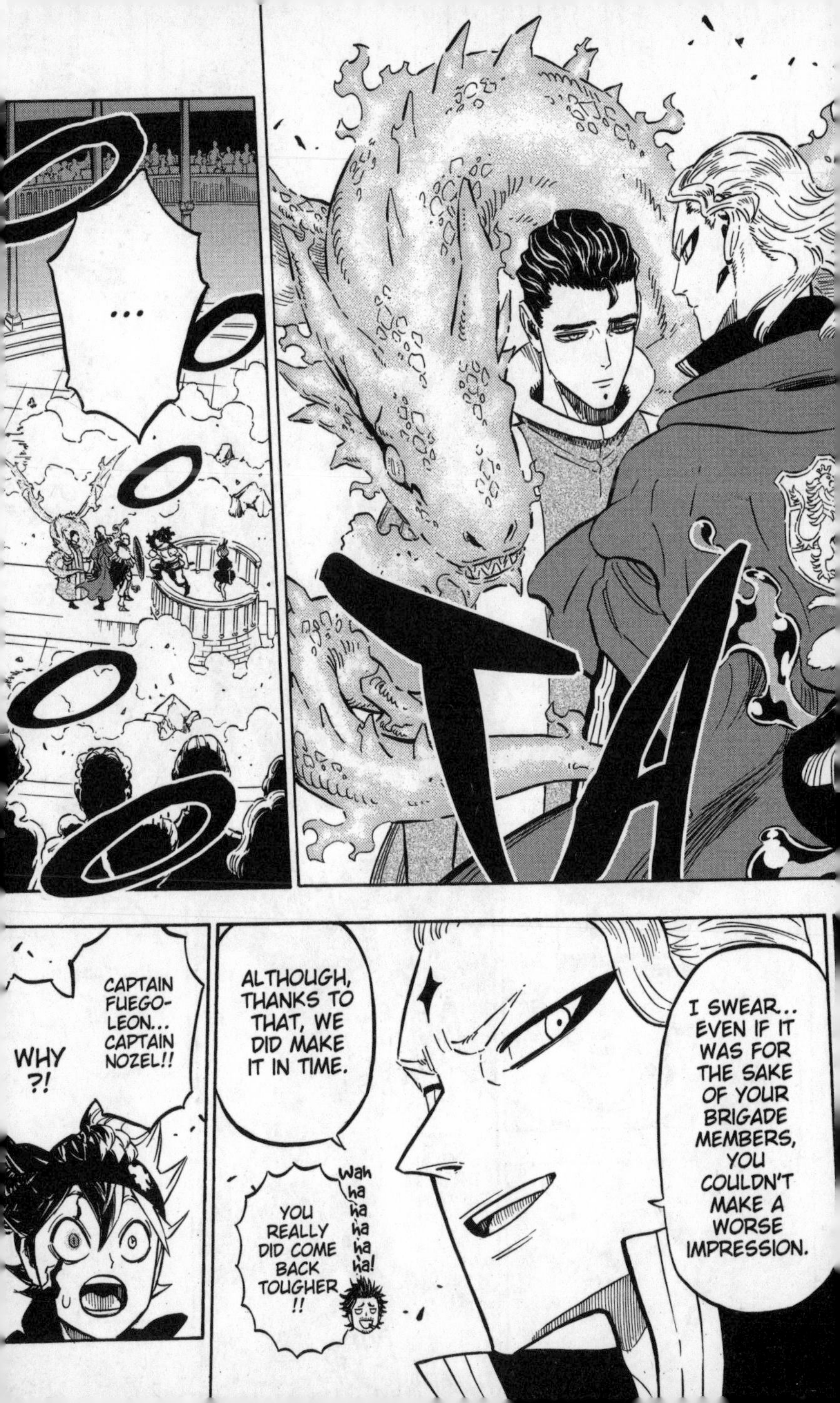
TA
...
I SWEAR... EVEN IF IT WAS FOR THE SAKE OF YOUR BRIGADE MEMBERS, YOU COULDN'T MAKE A WORSE IMPRESSION.
ALTHOUGH, THANKS TO THAT, WE DID MAKE IT IN TIME.
Wah ha ha ha ha ha!
YOU REALLY DID COME BACK TOUGHER!!
CAPTAIN FUEGO-LEON... CAPTAIN NOZEL!!
WHY?!

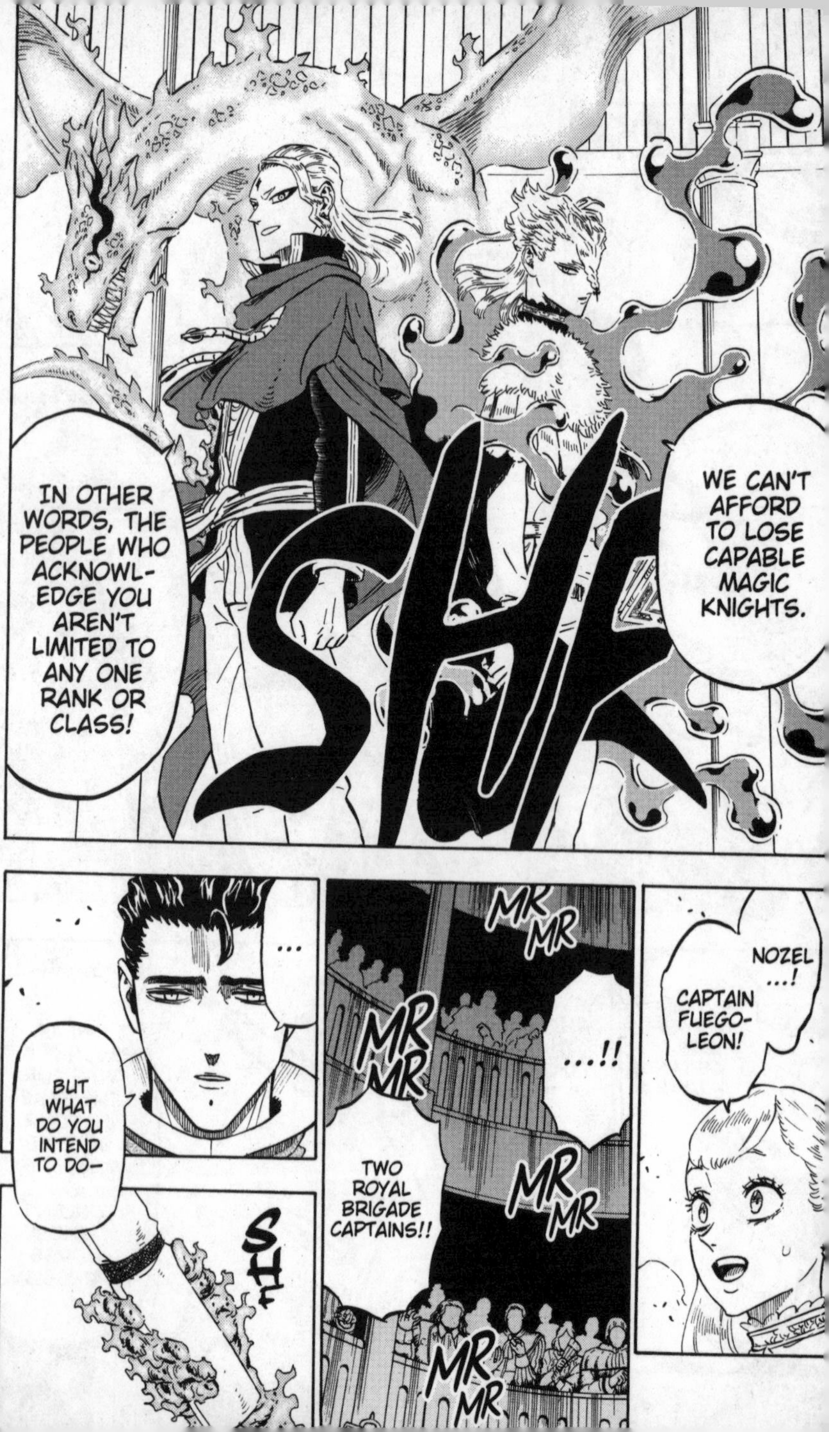
WE CAN'T AFFORD TO LOSE CAPABLE MAGIC KNIGHTS.
IN OTHER WORDS, THE PEOPLE WHO ACKNOWL-EDGE YOU AREN'T LIMITED TO ANY ONE RANK OR CLASS!
SHK
NOZEL...!
CAPTAIN FUEGO-LEON!
MK MR
...!!
MR MR
MR MR
TWO ROYAL BRIGADE CAPTAINS!!
MR MR
...
BUT WHAT DO YOU INTEND TO DO—
SHF

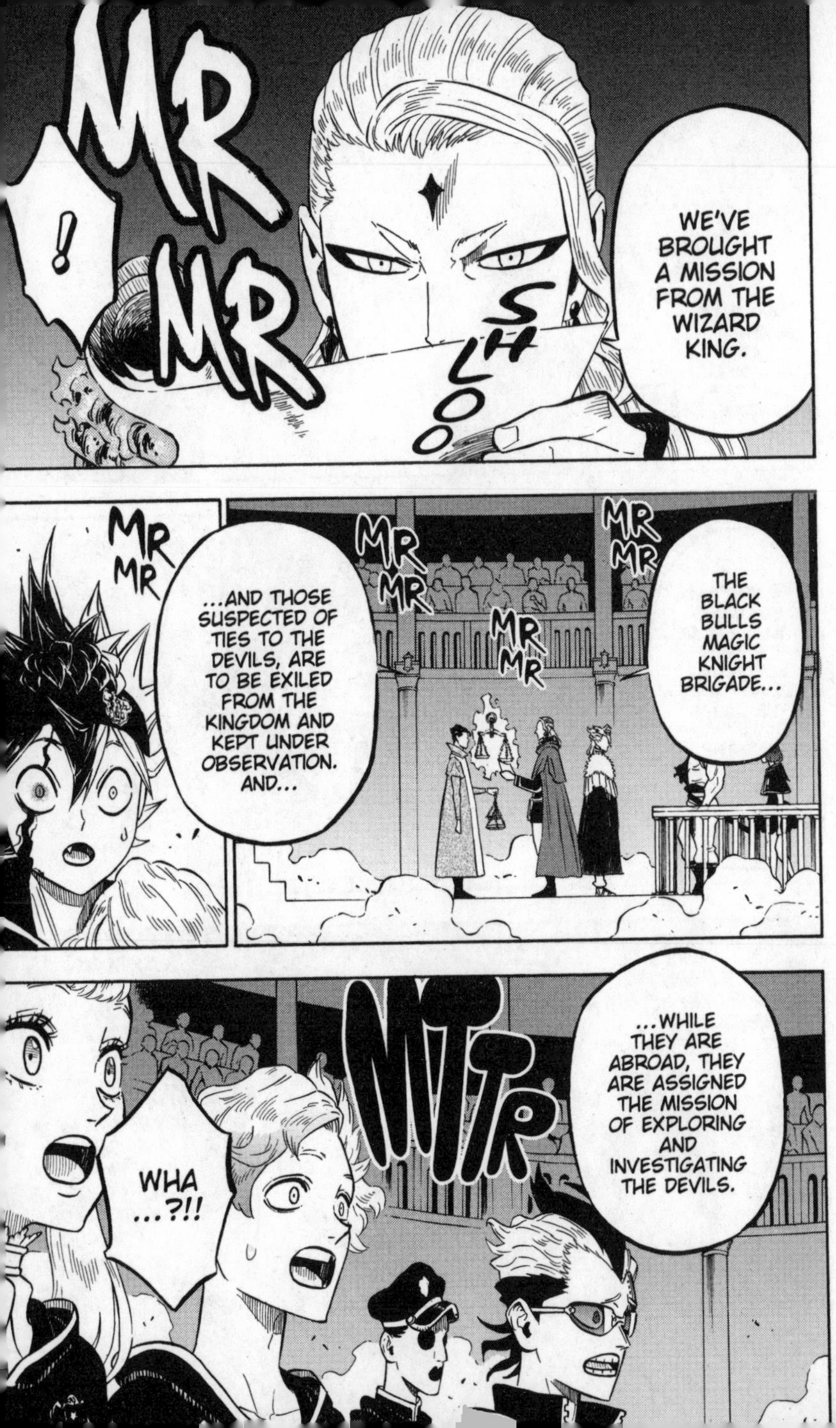
WE'VE BROUGHT A MISSION FROM THE WIZARD KING.
SHLOOO
MR MR
!
THE BLACK BULLS MAGIC KNIGHT BRIGADE...
MR MR
MR MR
MR MR
...AND THOSE SUSPECTED OF TIES TO THE DEVILS, ARE TO BE EXILED FROM THE KINGDOM AND KEPT UNDER OBSERVATION. AND...
MR MR
...WHILE THEY ARE ABROAD, THEY ARE ASSIGNED THE MISSION OF EXPLORING AND INVESTIGATING THE DEVILS.
WHA...?!!

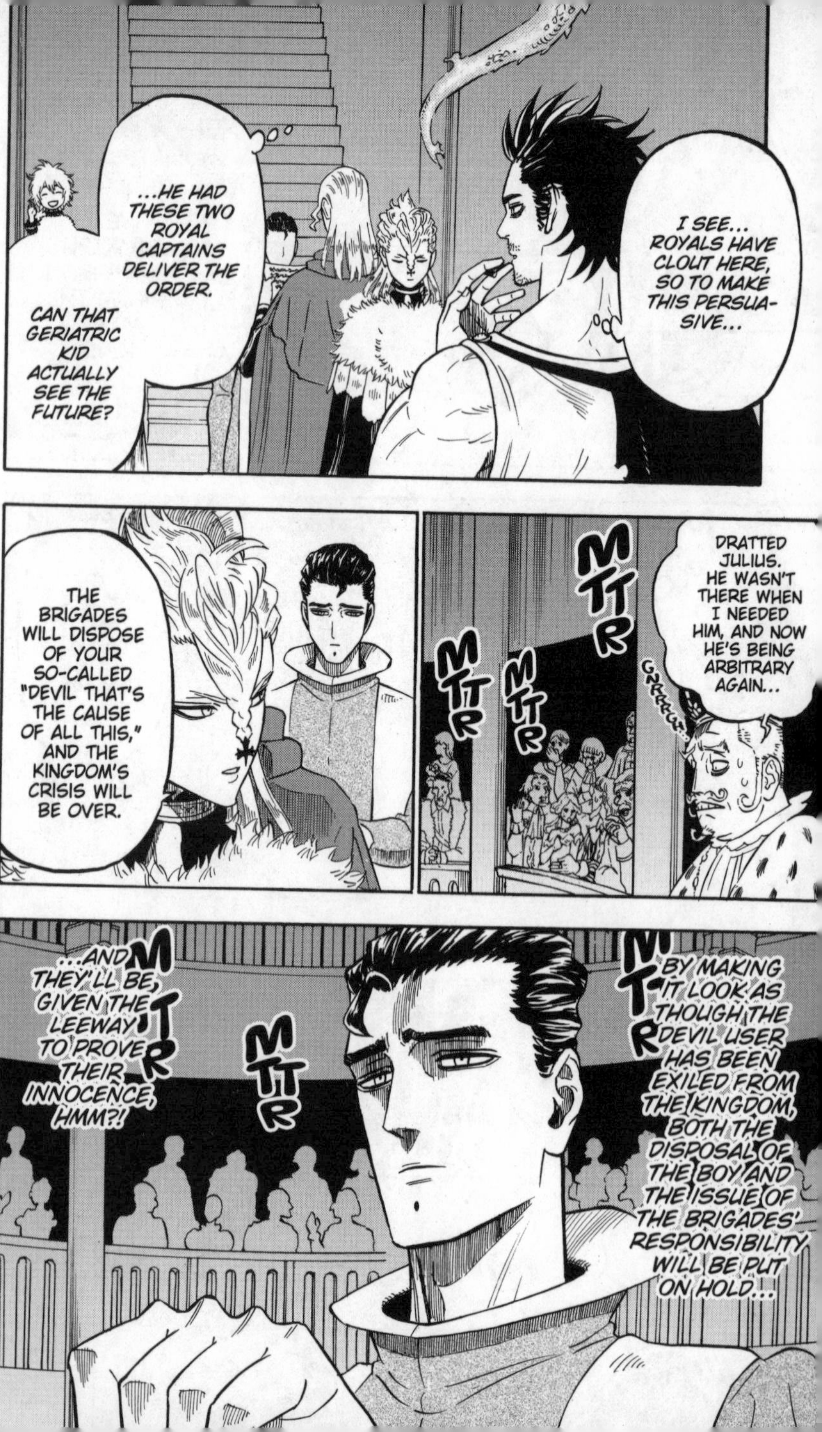
I SEE... ROYALS HAVE CLOUT HERE, SO TO MAKE THIS PERSUA-SIVE...
...HE HAD THESE TWO ROYAL CAPTAINS DELIVER THE ORDER.
CAN THAT GERIATRIC KID ACTUALLY SEE THE FUTURE?
DRATTED JULIUS. HE WASN'T THERE WHEN I NEEDED HIM, AND NOW HE'S BEING ARBITRARY AGAIN...
GNRRRGH
MTTR
MTTR
MTTR
THE BRIGADES WILL DISPOSE OF YOUR SO-CALLED "DEVIL THAT'S THE CAUSE OF ALL THIS," AND THE KINGDOM'S CRISIS WILL BE OVER.
MTTR
BY MAKING IT LOOK AS THOUGH THE DEVIL USER HAS BEEN EXILED FROM THE KINGDOM, BOTH THE DISPOSAL OF THE BOY AND THE ISSUE OF THE BRIGADES' RESPONSIBILITY WILL BE PUT ON HOLD...
MTTR
MTTR
...AND THEY'LL BE GIVEN THE LEEWAY TO PROVE THEIR INNOCENCE, HMM?!

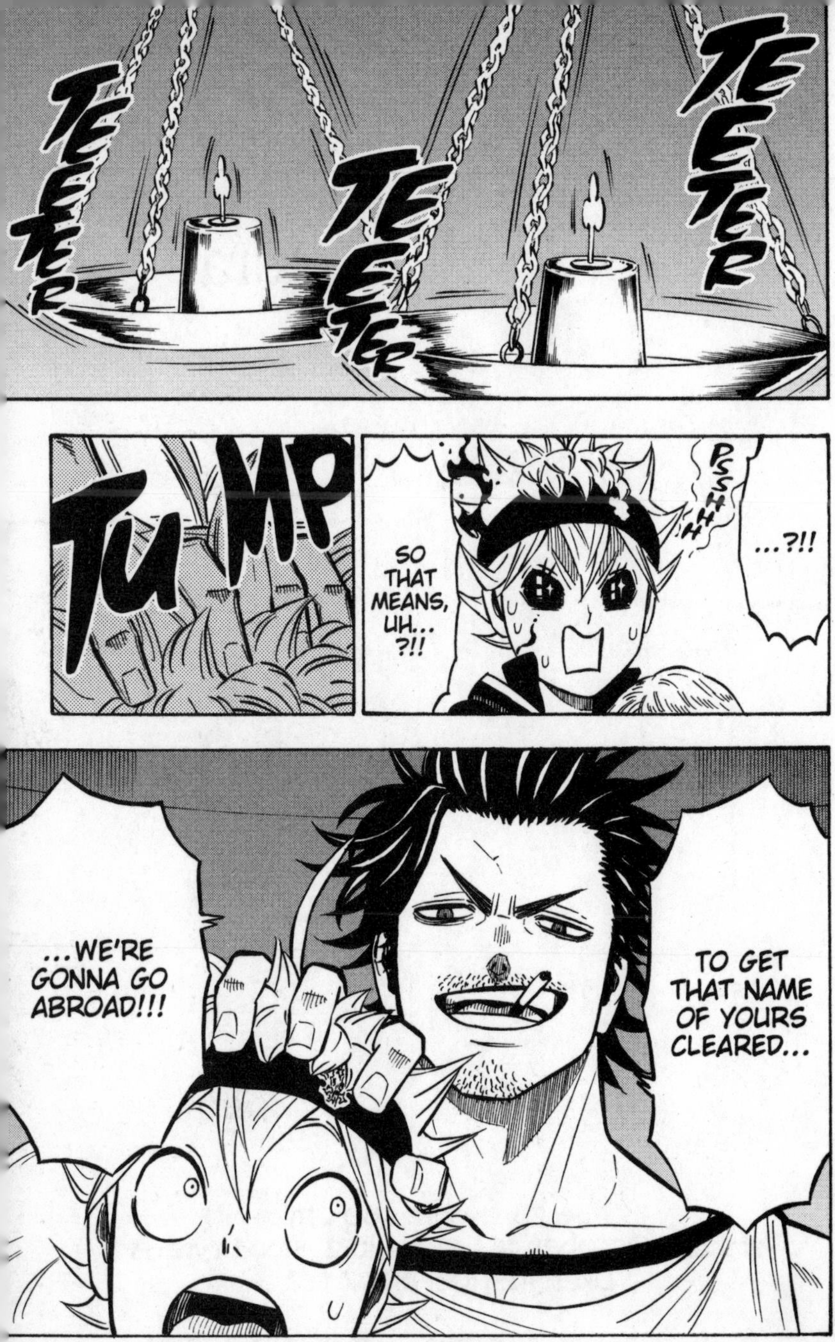
TEETER
TEETER
TEETER
...?!!
PSSHHH
SO THAT MEANS, UH... ?!!
TUMP
TO GET THAT NAME OF YOURS CLEARED...
...WE'RE GONNA GO ABROAD!!!

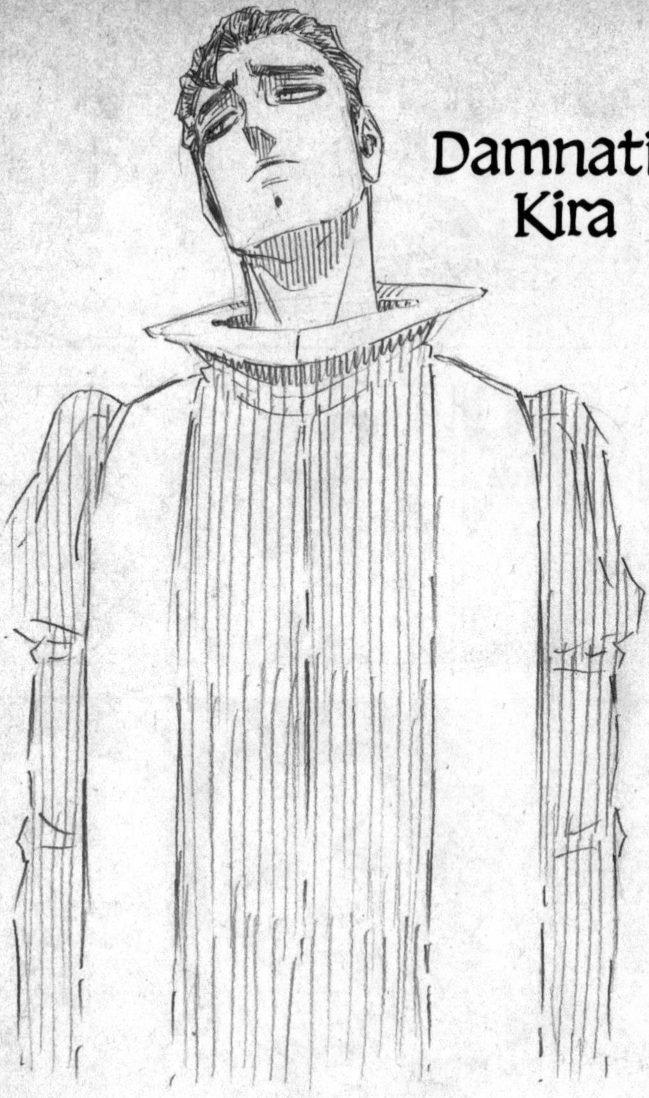

Damnatio Kira

Age: 28 Height: 180 cm
Birthday: October 16 Sign: Libra Blood Type: A
Likes: Justice, black tea

Character Profile

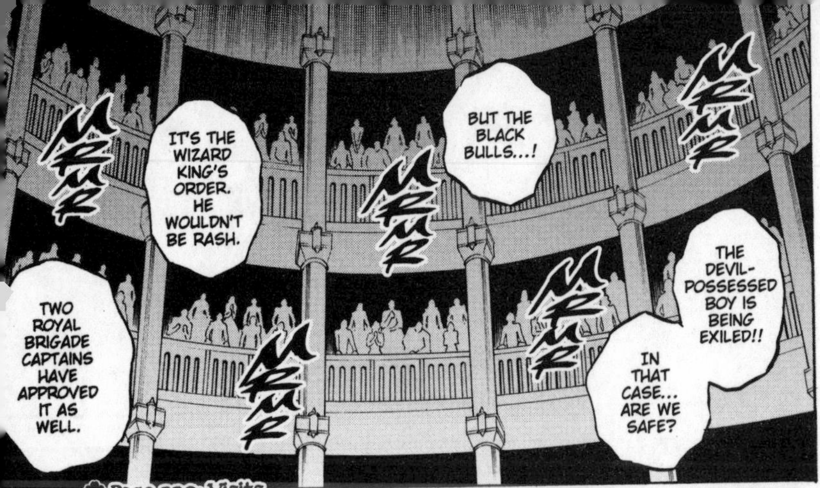
MRMR
BUT THE BLACK BULLS...!
THE DEVIL-POSSESSED BOY IS BEING EXILED!!
IN THAT CASE... ARE WE SAFE?
MRMR
MRMR
MRMR
IT'S THE WIZARD KING'S ORDER. HE WOULDN'T BE RASH.
MRMR
TWO ROYAL BRIGADE CAPTAINS HAVE APPROVED IT AS WELL.

Page 220: Visits

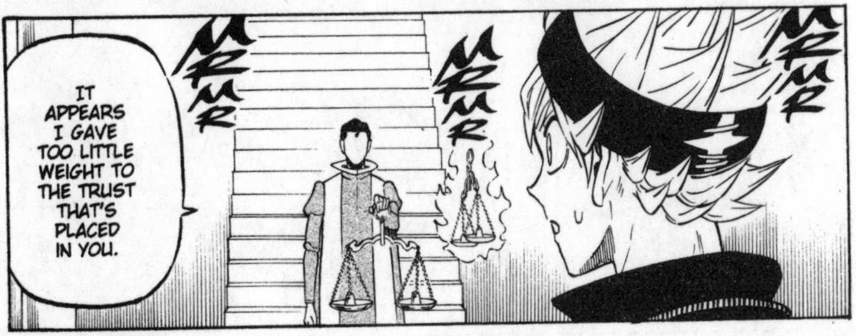
MRMR
MRMR
MRMR
IT APPEARS I GAVE TOO LITTLE WEIGHT TO THE TRUST THAT'S PLACED IN YOU.

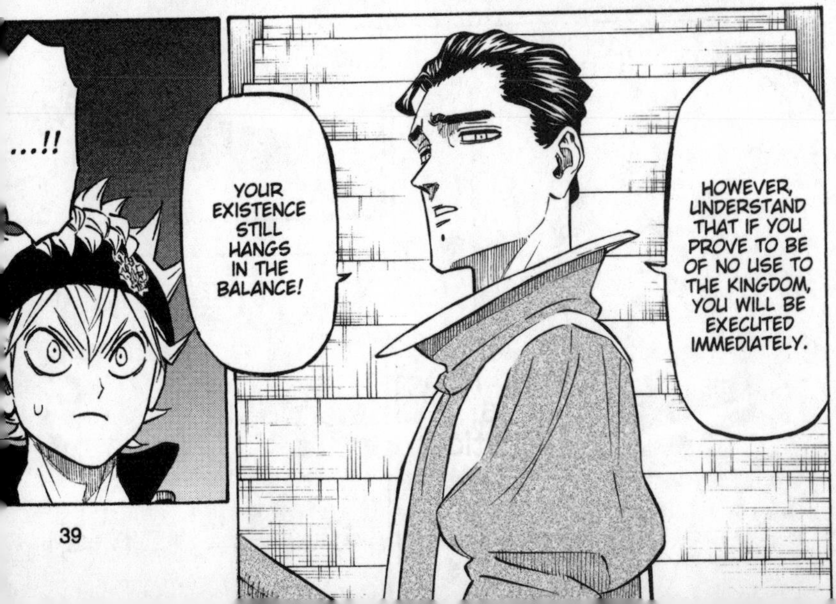
HOWEVER, UNDERSTAND THAT IF YOU PROVE TO BE OF NO USE TO THE KINGDOM, YOU WILL BE EXECUTED IMMEDIATELY.
YOUR EXISTENCE STILL HANGS IN THE BALANCE!
...!!

Page 220: Visits

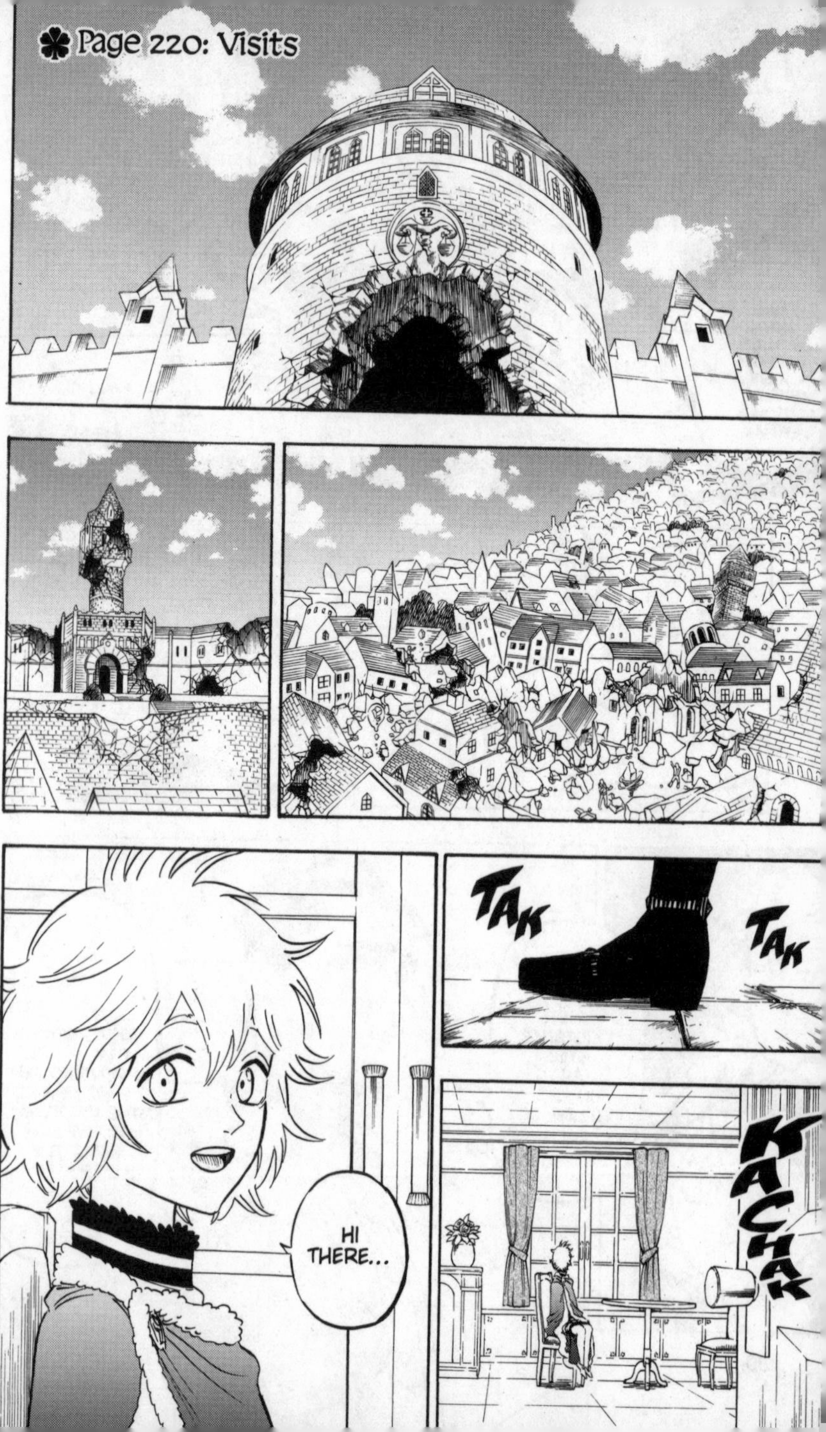
TAK
TAK
KACHAK
HI THERE...

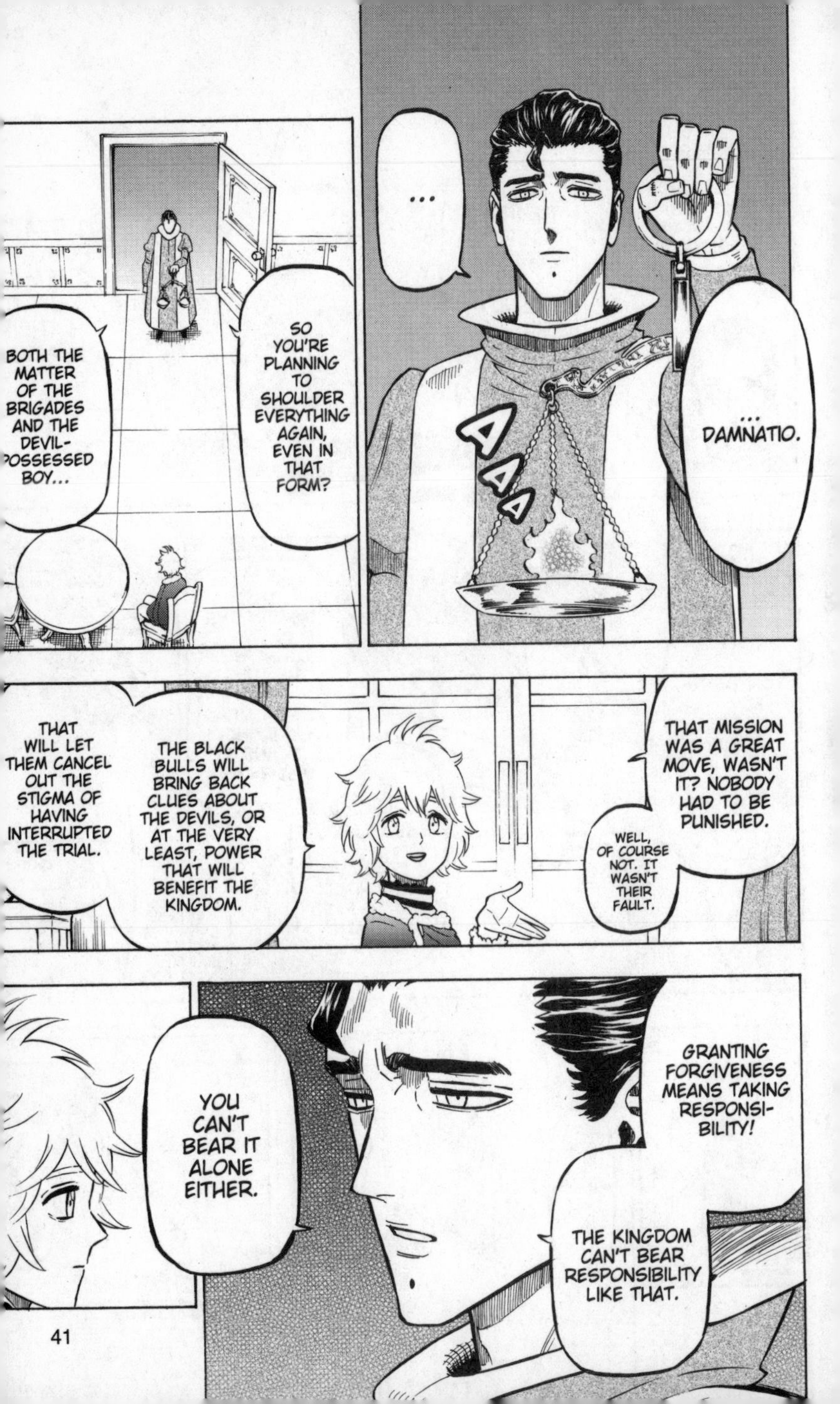
...
... DAMNATIO.
AAA
SO YOU'RE PLANNING TO SHOULDER EVERYTHING AGAIN, EVEN IN THAT FORM?
BOTH THE MATTER OF THE BRIGADES AND THE DEVIL-POSSESSED BOY...
THAT MISSION WAS A GREAT MOVE, WASN'T IT? NOBODY HAD TO BE PUNISHED.
WELL, OF COURSE NOT. IT WASN'T THEIR FAULT.
THE BLACK BULLS WILL BRING BACK CLUES ABOUT THE DEVILS, OR AT THE VERY LEAST, POWER THAT WILL BENEFIT THE KINGDOM.
THAT WILL LET THEM CANCEL OUT THE STIGMA OF HAVING INTERRUPTED THE TRIAL.
GRANTING FORGIVENESS MEANS TAKING RESPONSIBILITY!
THE KINGDOM CAN'T BEAR RESPONSIBILITY LIKE THAT.
YOU CAN'T BEAR IT ALONE EITHER.

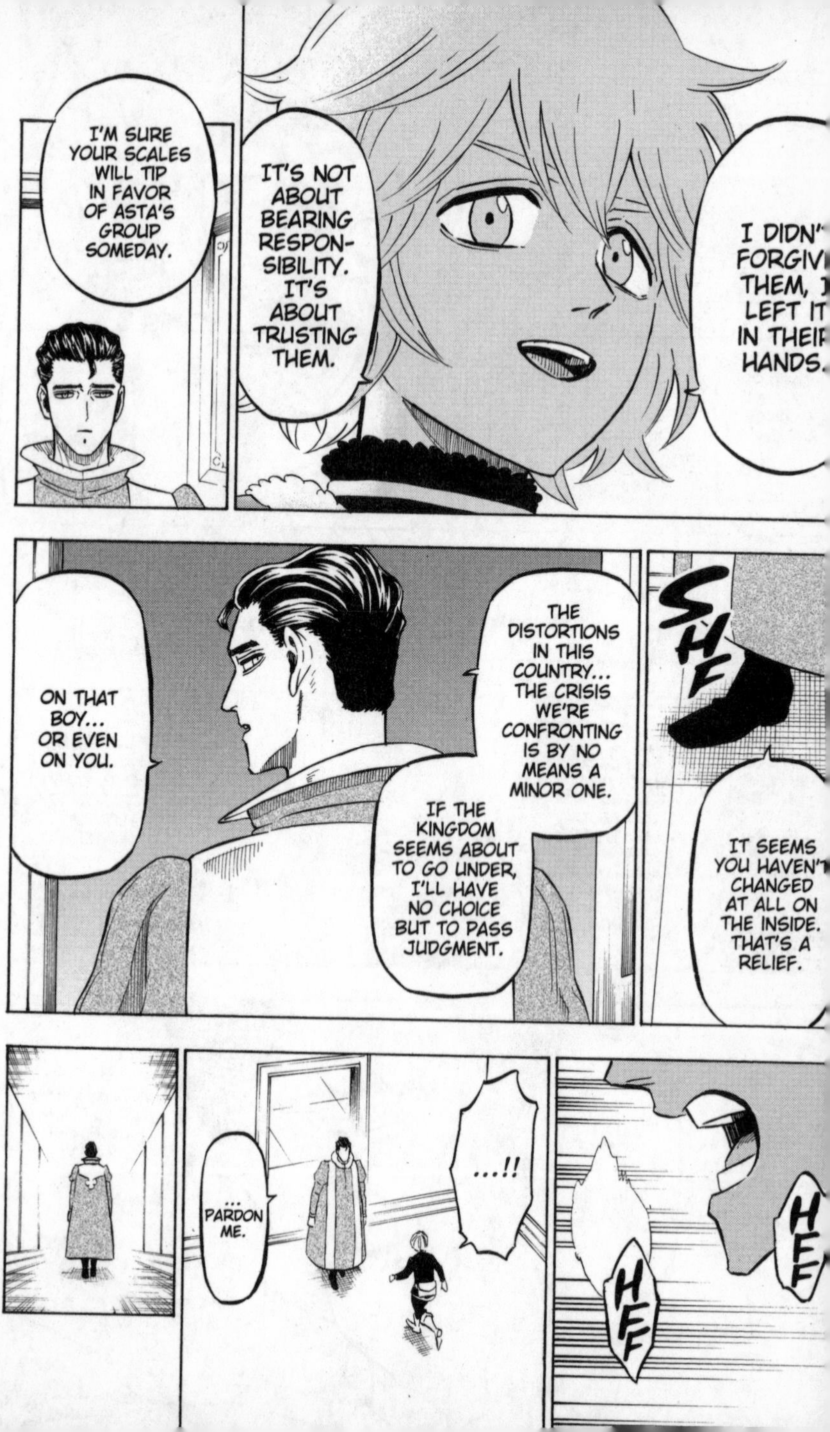
I DIDN' FORGIV THEM, I LEFT IT IN THEIF HANDS.
IT'S NOT ABOUT BEARING RESPON-SIBILITY. IT'S ABOUT TRUSTING THEM.
I'M SURE YOUR SCALES WILL TIP IN FAVOR OF ASTA'S GROUP SOMEDAY.
SHF
IT SEEMS YOU HAVEN'T CHANGED AT ALL ON THE INSIDE. THAT'S A RELIEF.
THE DISTORTIONS IN THIS COUNTRY... THE CRISIS WE'RE CONFRONTING IS BY NO MEANS A MINOR ONE.
IF THE KINGDOM SEEMS ABOUT TO GO UNDER, I'LL HAVE NO CHOICE BUT TO PASS JUDGMENT.
ON THAT BOY... OR EVEN ON YOU.
HEF
HEF
...!!
... PARDON ME.

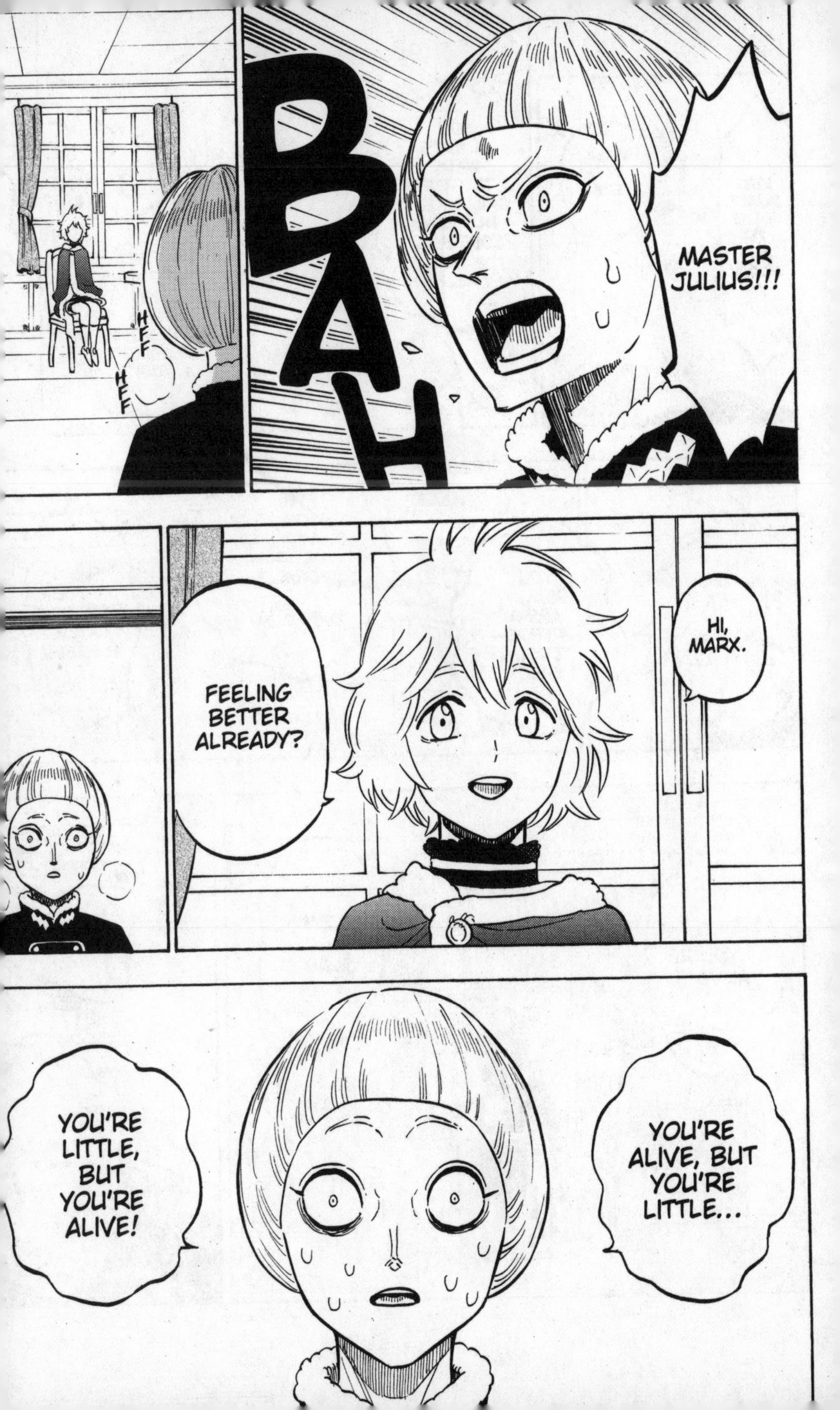
MASTER JULIUS!!!
BAH
HFF HFF
HI, MARX.
FEELING BETTER ALREADY?
YOU'RE ALIVE, BUT YOU'RE LITTLE...
YOU'RE LITTLE, BUT YOU'RE ALIVE!

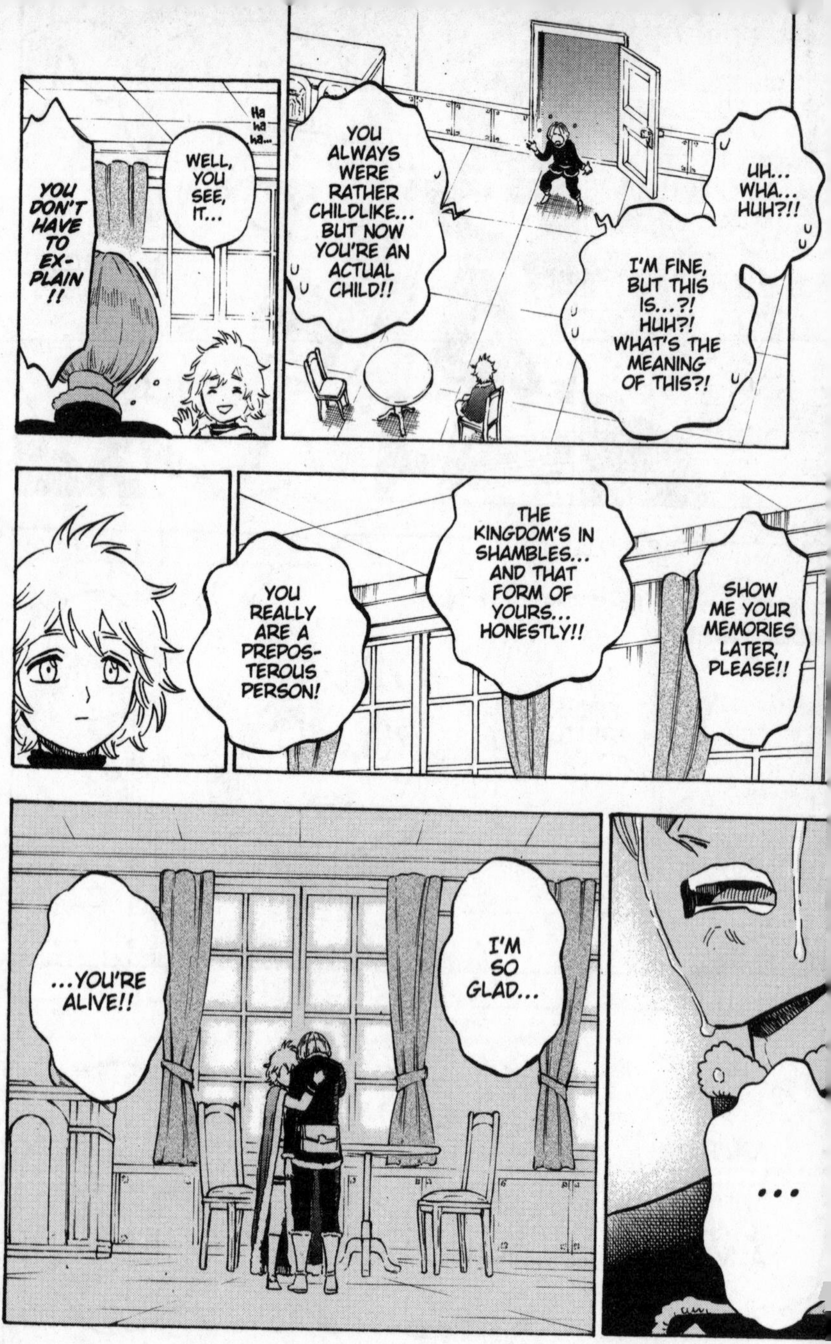
UH... WHA... HUH?!!
YOU ALWAYS WERE RATHER CHILDLIKE... BUT NOW YOU'RE AN ACTUAL CHILD!!
I'M FINE, BUT THIS IS...?! HUH?! WHAT'S THE MEANING OF THIS?!
Ha ha ha...
WELL, YOU SEE, IT...
YOU DON'T HAVE TO EX-PLAIN!!
SHOW ME YOUR MEMORIES LATER, PLEASE!!
THE KINGDOM'S IN SHAMBLES... AND THAT FORM OF YOURS... HONESTLY!!
YOU REALLY ARE A PREPOS-TEROUS PERSON!
...
I'M SO GLAD...
...YOU'RE ALIVE!!

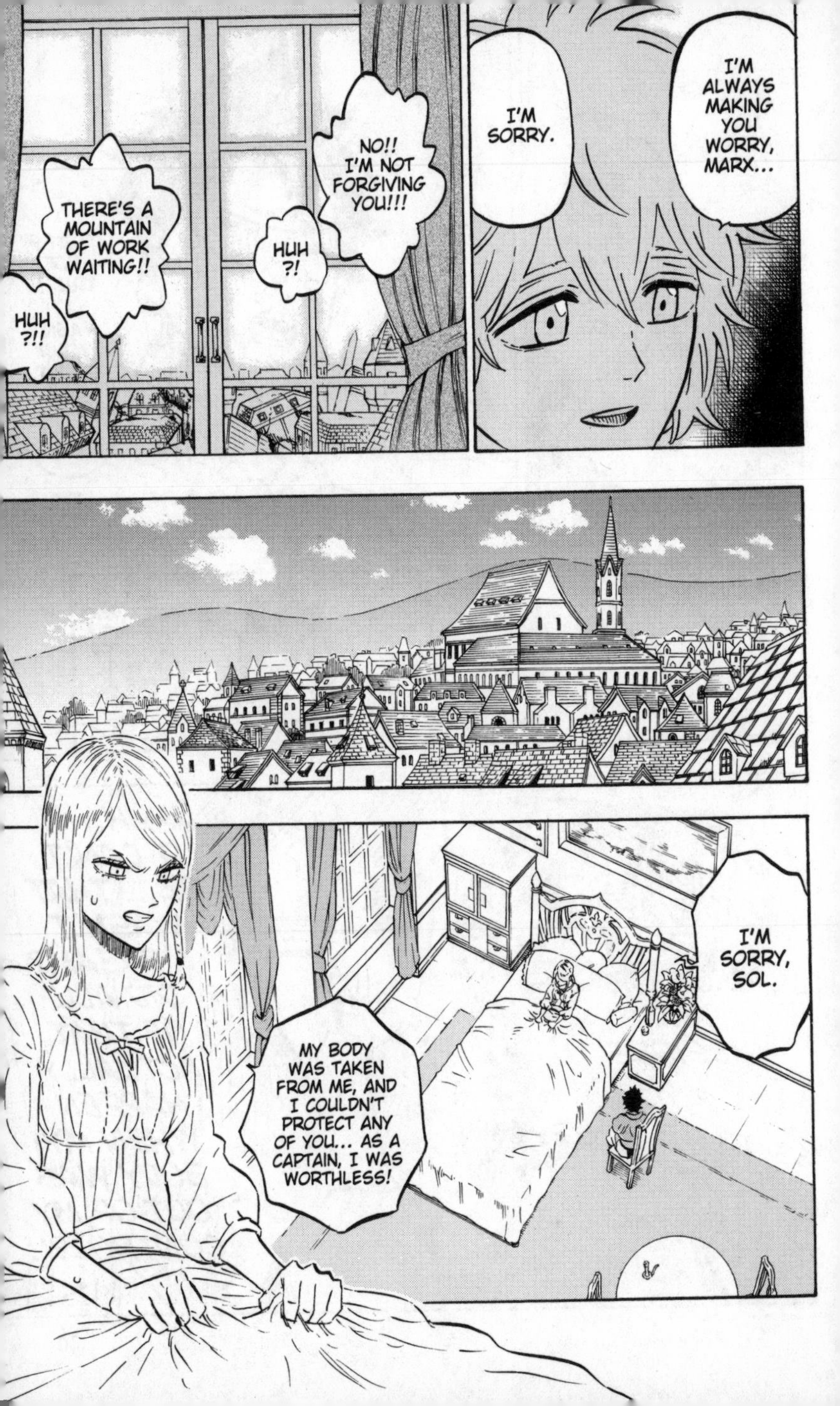
I'M ALWAYS MAKING YOU WORRY, MARX...
I'M SORRY.
NO!! I'M NOT FORGIVING YOU!!!
HUH ?!
THERE'S A MOUNTAIN OF WORK WAITING!!
HUH ?!!
I'M SORRY, SOL.
MY BODY WAS TAKEN FROM ME, AND I COULDN'T PROTECT ANY OF YOU... AS A CAPTAIN, I WAS WORTHLESS!

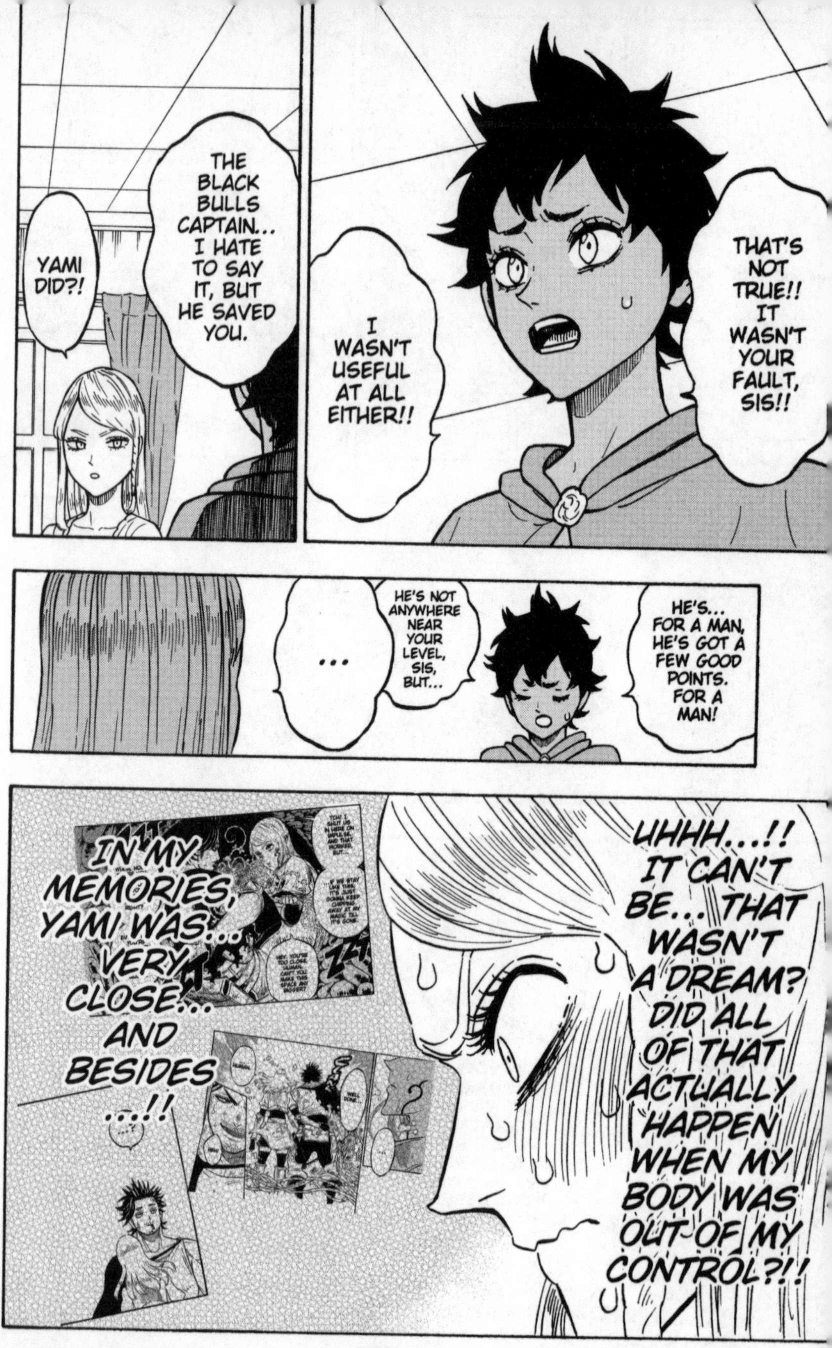

THAT'S NOT TRUE!! IT WASN'T YOUR FAULT, SIS!!
I WASN'T USEFUL AT ALL EITHER!!
THE BLACK BULLS CAPTAIN... I HATE TO SAY IT, BUT HE SAVED YOU.
YAMI DID?!
HE'S... FOR A MAN, HE'S GOT A FEW GOOD POINTS. FOR A MAN!
HE'S NOT ANYWHERE NEAR YOUR LEVEL, SIS, BUT...
...
UHHH...!! IT CAN'T BE... THAT WASN'T A DREAM? DID ALL OF THAT ACTUALLY HAPPEN WHEN MY BODY WAS OUT OF MY CONTROL?!!
IN MY MEMORIES, YAMI WAS... VERY CLOSE... AND BESIDES...!!

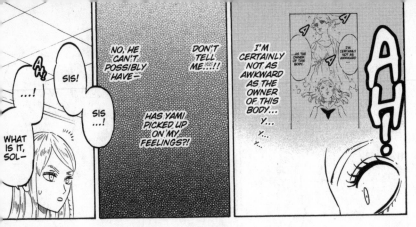

SIS!

...!

SIS...!

WHAT IS IT, SOL—

NO, HE CAN'T POSSIBLY HAVE—

DON'T TELL ME...!!

HAS YAMI PICKED UP ON MY FEELINGS?!

I'M CERTAINLY NOT AS AWKWARD AS THE OWNER OF THIS BODY... Y... Y... Y...

...AS THE OWNER OF THIS BODY...

I'M CERTAINLY NOT AS AWKWARD...

AH!

YO.

THE BLACK BULLS CAPTAIN IS HERE.

YAMI-IIIII?!!!

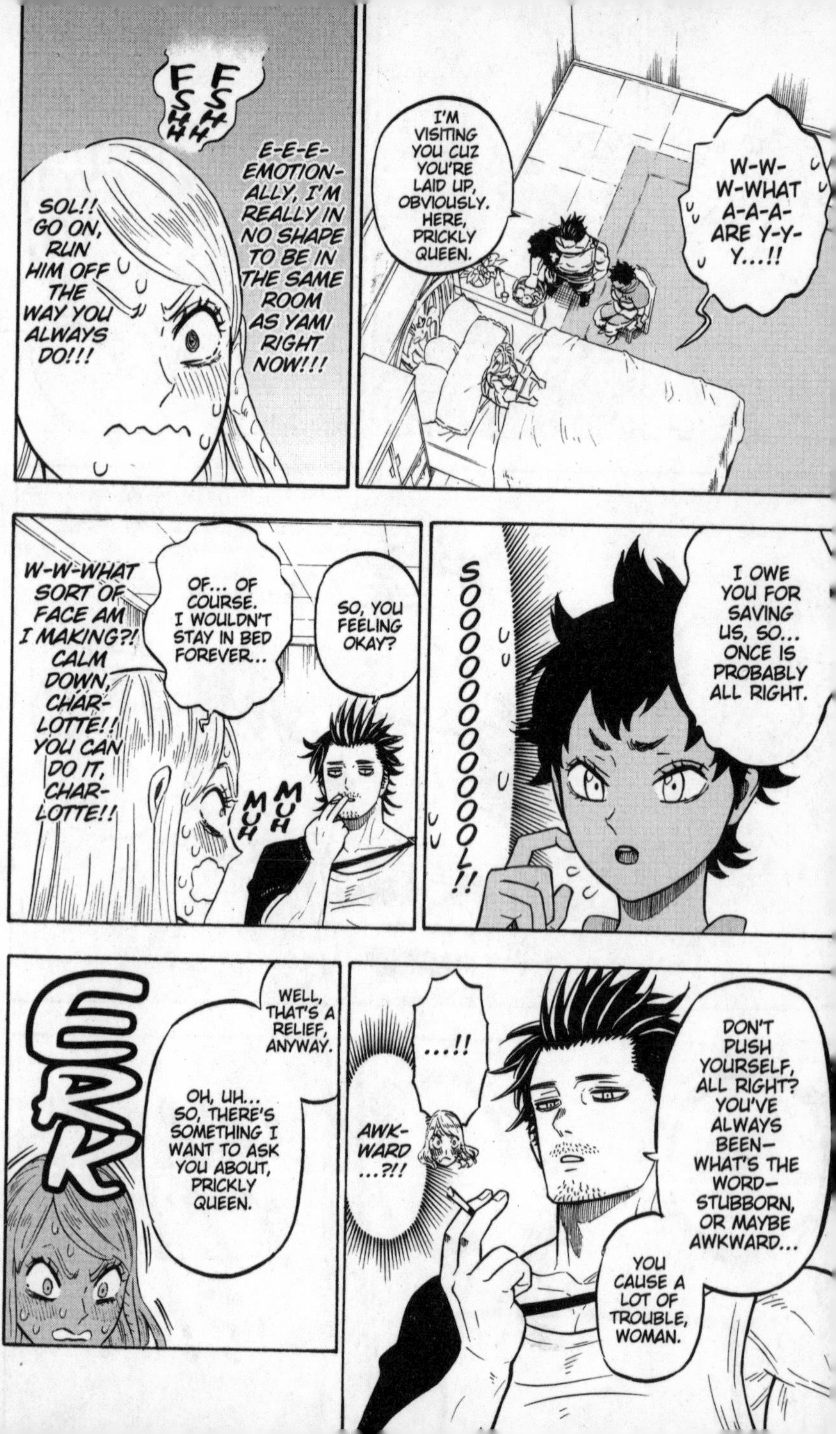
W-W-W-WHAT A-A-A-ARE Y-Y-Y...!!
I'M VISITING YOU CUZ YOU'RE LAID UP, OBVIOUSLY. HERE, PRICKLY QUEEN.
FSHHH FSHHH
E-E-E-EMOTIONALLY, I'M REALLY IN NO SHAPE TO BE IN THE SAME ROOM AS YAMI RIGHT NOW!!!
SOL!! GO ON, RUN HIM OFF THE WAY YOU ALWAYS DO!!!
I OWE YOU FOR SAVING US, SO... ONCE IS PROBABLY ALL RIGHT.
SOOOOOOOOOOOOL!!
SO, YOU FEELING OKAY?
OF... OF COURSE. I WOULDN'T STAY IN BED FOREVER...
W-W-WHAT SORT OF FACE AM I MAKING?! CALM DOWN, CHARLOTTE!! YOU CAN DO IT, CHARLOTTE!!
MUH MUH
DON'T PUSH YOURSELF, ALL RIGHT? YOU'VE ALWAYS BEEN—WHAT'S THE WORD—STUBBORN, OR MAYBE AWKWARD...
...!!
YOU CAUSE A LOT OF TROUBLE, WOMAN.
AWKWARD...?!!
WELL, THAT'S A RELIEF, ANYWAY.
OH, UH... SO, THERE'S SOMETHING I WANT TO ASK YOU ABOUT, PRICKLY QUEEN.
ERK

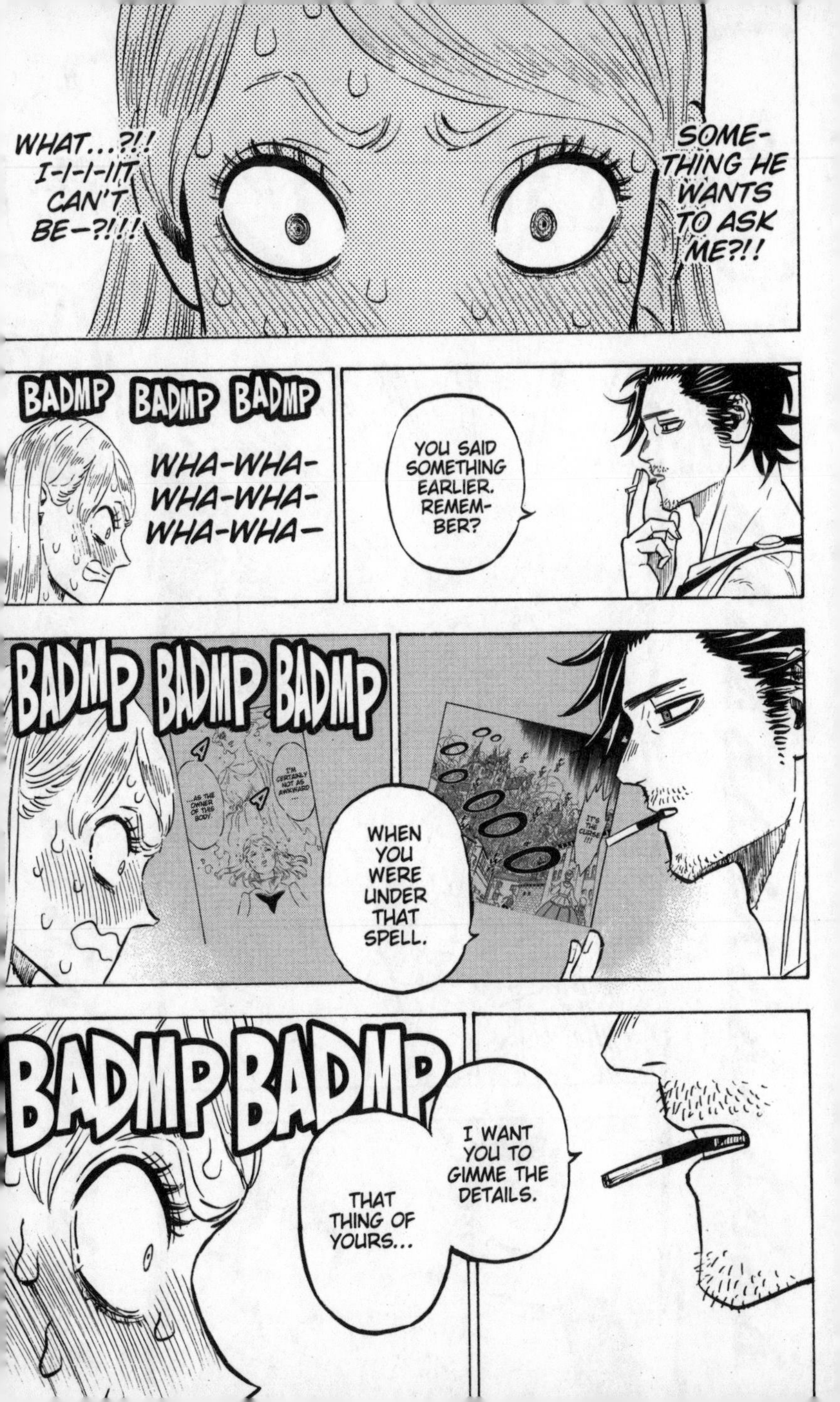

SOME-THING HE WANTS TO ASK ME?!!
WHAT...?!! I-I-I-IIT CAN'T BE—?!!!
YOU SAID SOMETHING EARLIER. REMEMBER?
BADMP BADMP BADMP
WHA-WHA-WHA-WHA-WHA-WHA-
WHEN YOU WERE UNDER THAT SPELL.
IT'S THE CURSE!!!
I'M CERTAINLY NOT AS AWKWARD...
...AS THE OWNER OF THIS BODY.
BADMP BADMP BADMP
I WANT YOU TO GIMME THE DETAILS.
THAT THING OF YOURS...
BADMP BADMP

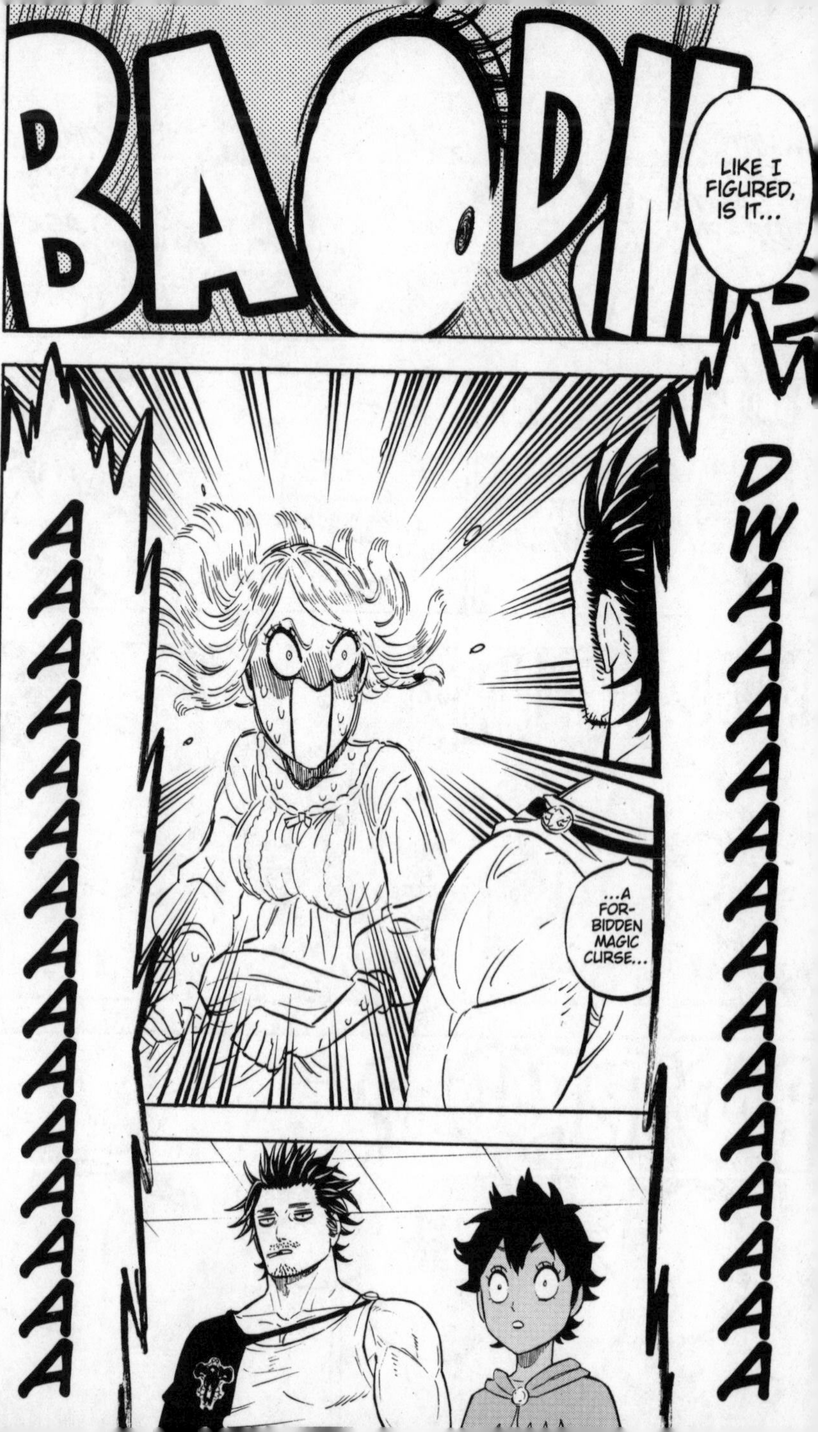
LIKE I FIGURED, IS IT...
BA-DMP
...A FORBIDDEN MAGIC CURSE...
DWAAAAAAAAAAAAAAA
AAAAAAAAAAAAAAAA

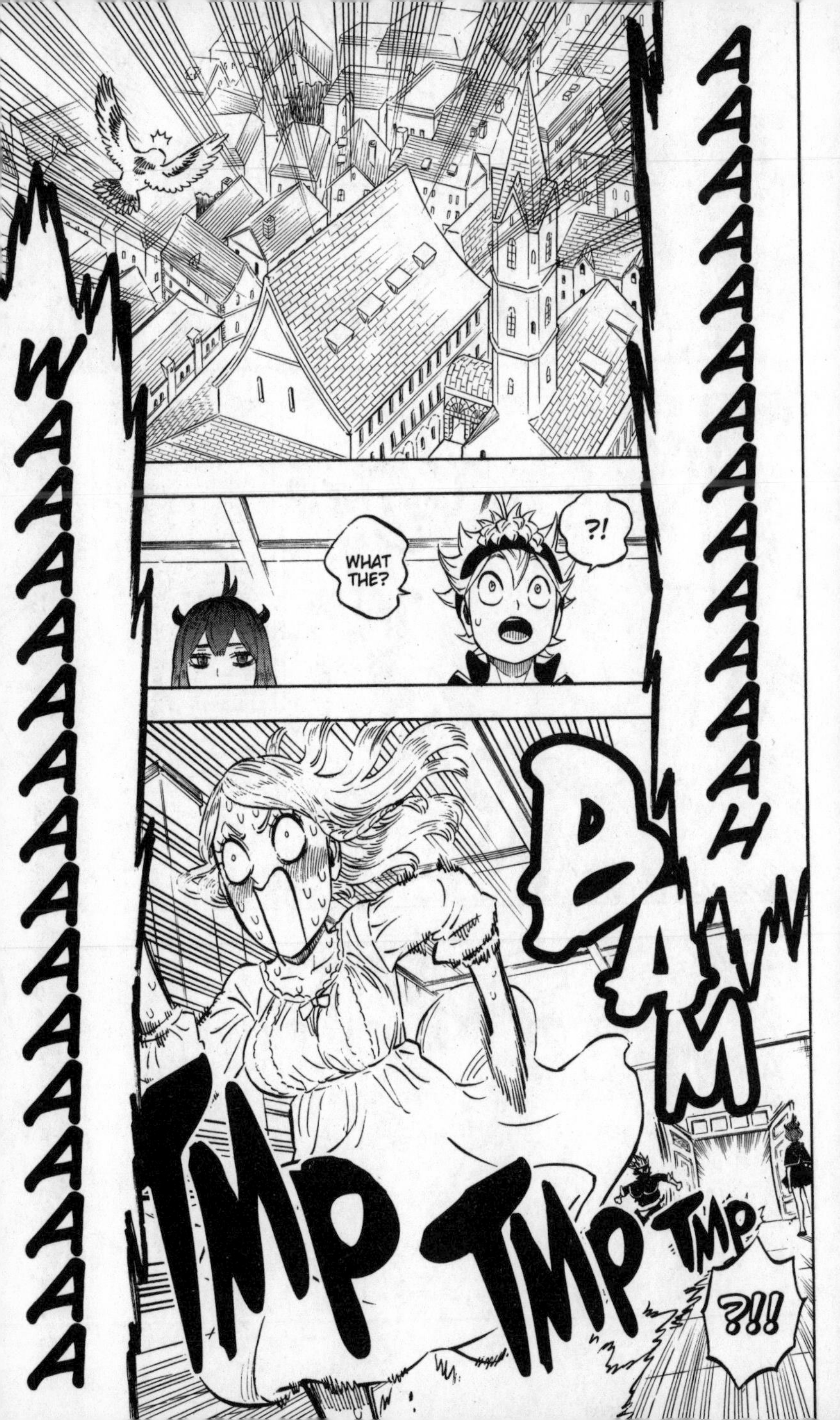
WAAAAAAAAAAAAAAAAAAAA
AAAAAAAAAAAAAAAH
?!
WHAT THE?
BAM
TMP TMP TMP
?!!

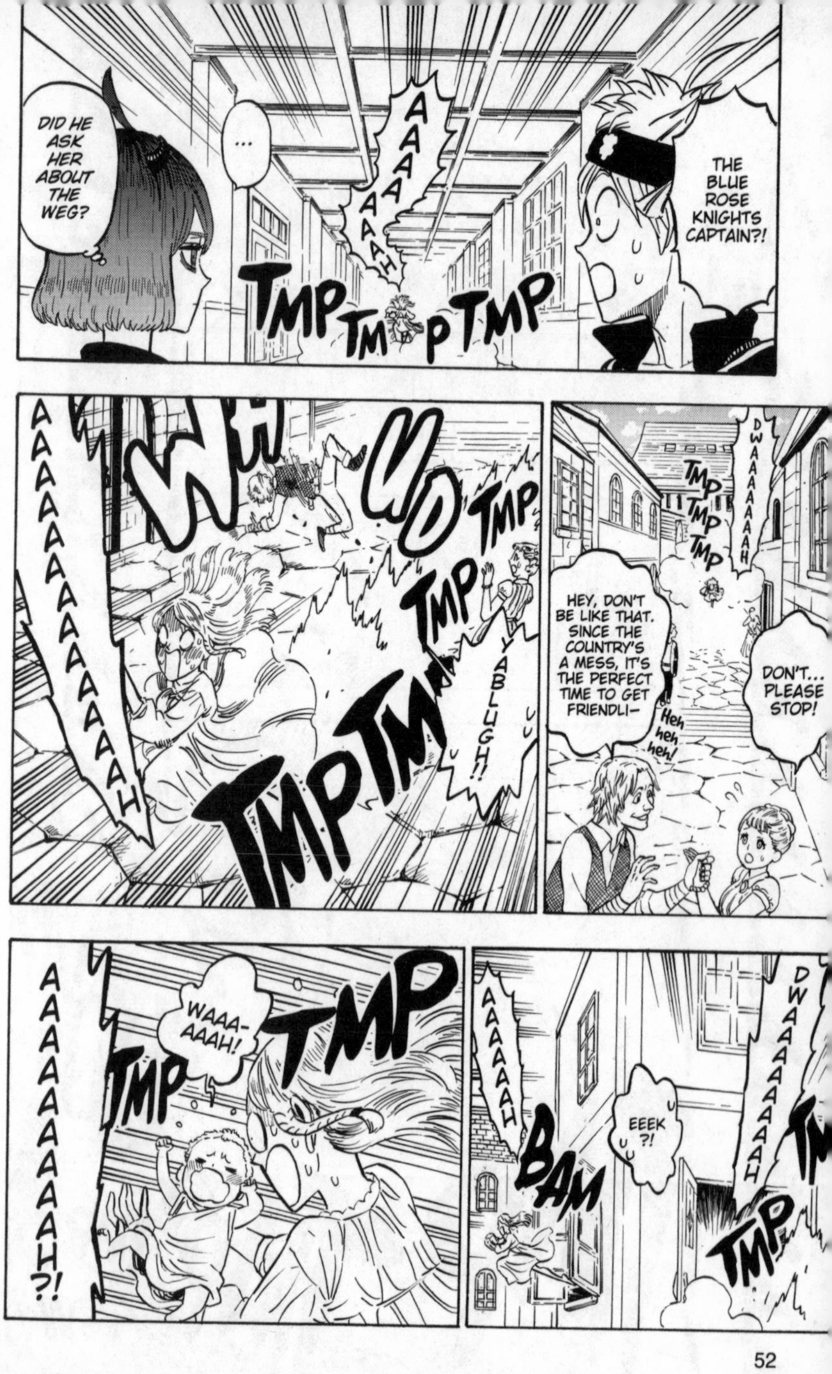
THE BLUE ROSE KNIGHTS CAPTAIN?!
AAAAAAAH
TMP TMP TMP TMP
...
DID HE ASK HER ABOUT THE WEG?
DWAAAAAAAAH
TMP TMP TMP
DON'T... PLEASE STOP!
HEY, DON'T BE LIKE THAT. SINCE THE COUNTRY'S A MESS, IT'S THE PERFECT TIME TO GET FRIENDLI-
Heh heh heh!
TMP TMP
WHUD
YABLUGH!!
TMPTM
AAAAAAAAAAAAAAAAH
DWAAAAAAAAAH
TMP
EEEK?!
BAM
AAAAAAH
TMP
WAAA-AAAH!
TMP
AAAAAAAAAAAAAAH?!

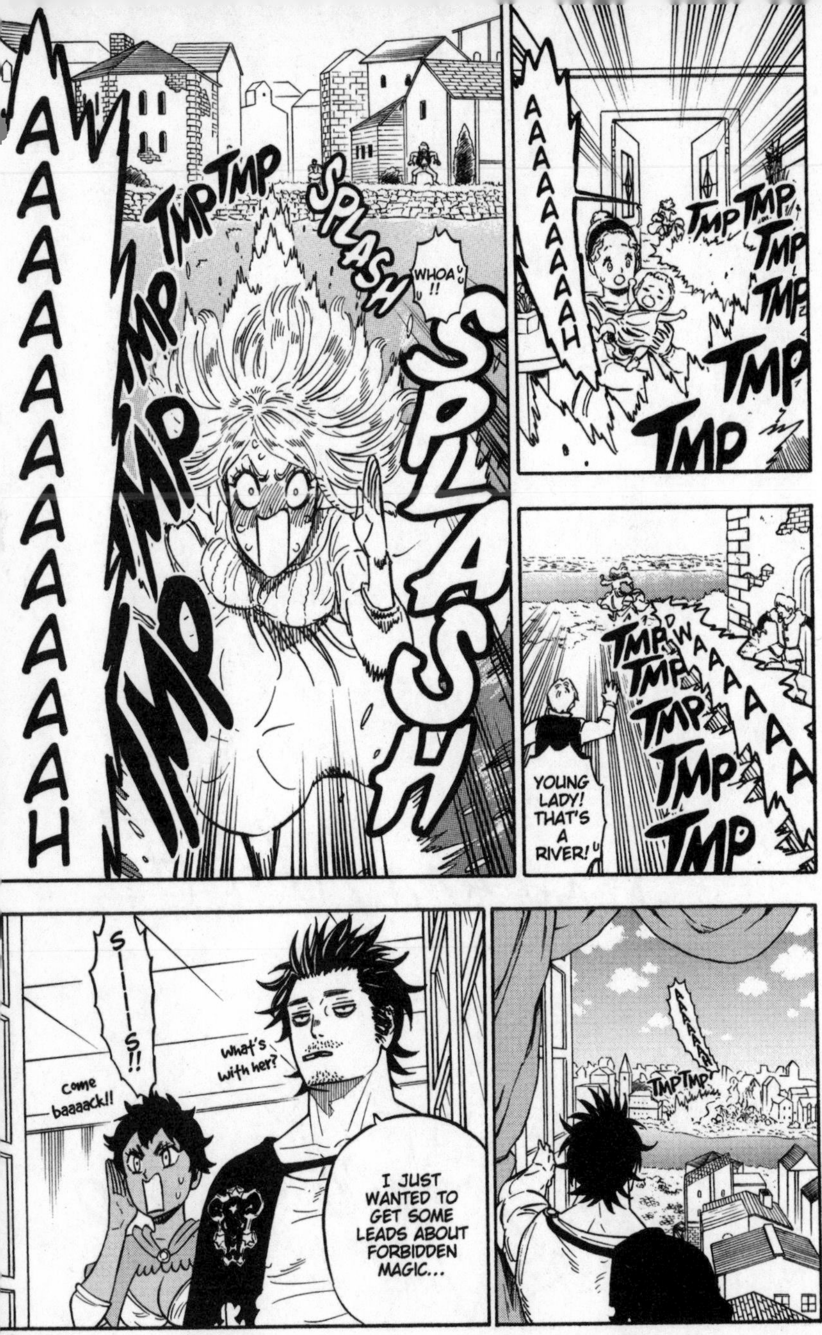
AAAAAAAAAAH
TMP TMP
TMP
TMP
TMP
TMP
TMP
TMP
TMP
TMP
TMP
WAAAAAA
YOUNG LADY! THAT'S A RIVER!
AAAAAAAAAAAAAH
TMP TMP
TMP
TMP
TMP
SPLASH
WHOA!!
SPLASH
AAAAAAAH
TMP TMP
S----S!!
come baaaack!!
what's with her?
I JUST WANTED TO GET SOME LEADS ABOUT FORBIDDEN MAGIC...

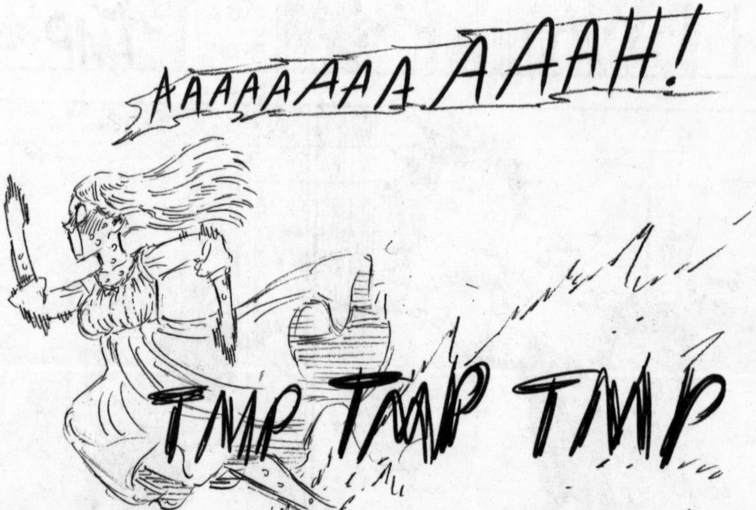
AAAAAAAAAAAH!
TMP TMP TMP

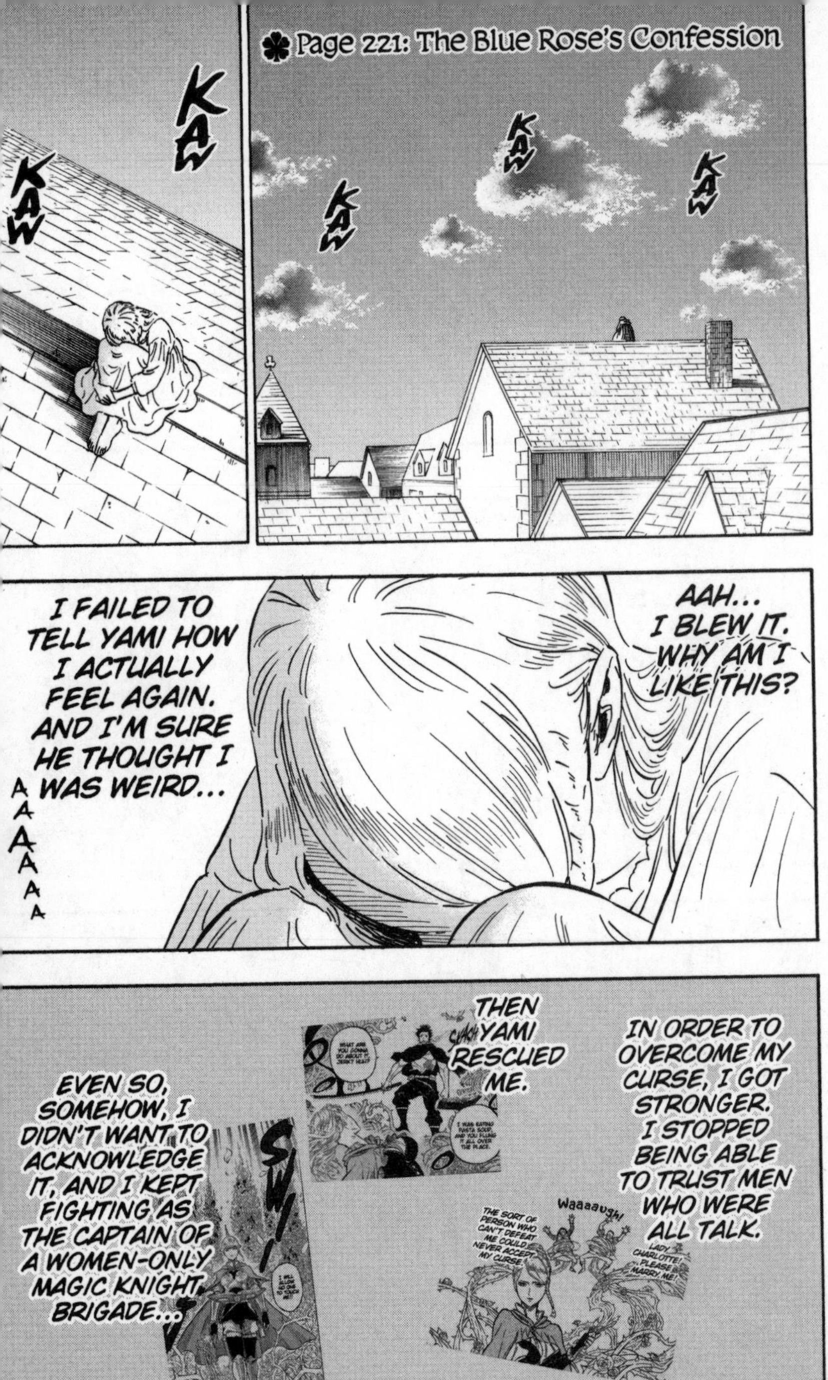
Page 221: The Blue Rose's Confession
KAW
KAW
KAW
KAW
KAW
AAH... I BLEW IT. WHY AM I LIKE THIS?
I FAILED TO TELL YAMI HOW I ACTUALLY FEEL AGAIN. AND I'M SURE HE THOUGHT I WAS WEIRD...
AAAAAAA
IN ORDER TO OVERCOME MY CURSE, I GOT STRONGER. I STOPPED BEING ABLE TO TRUST MEN WHO WERE ALL TALK.
Waaaaugh!
LADY CHARLOTTE! PLEASE MARRY ME!
THE SORT OF PERSON WHO CAN'T DEFEAT ME COULD NEVER ACCEPT MY CURSE.
THEN YAMI RESCUED ME.
EVEN SO, SOMEHOW, I DIDN'T WANT TO ACKNOWLEDGE IT, AND I KEPT FIGHTING AS THE CAPTAIN OF A WOMEN-ONLY MAGIC KNIGHT BRIGADE...
SW!

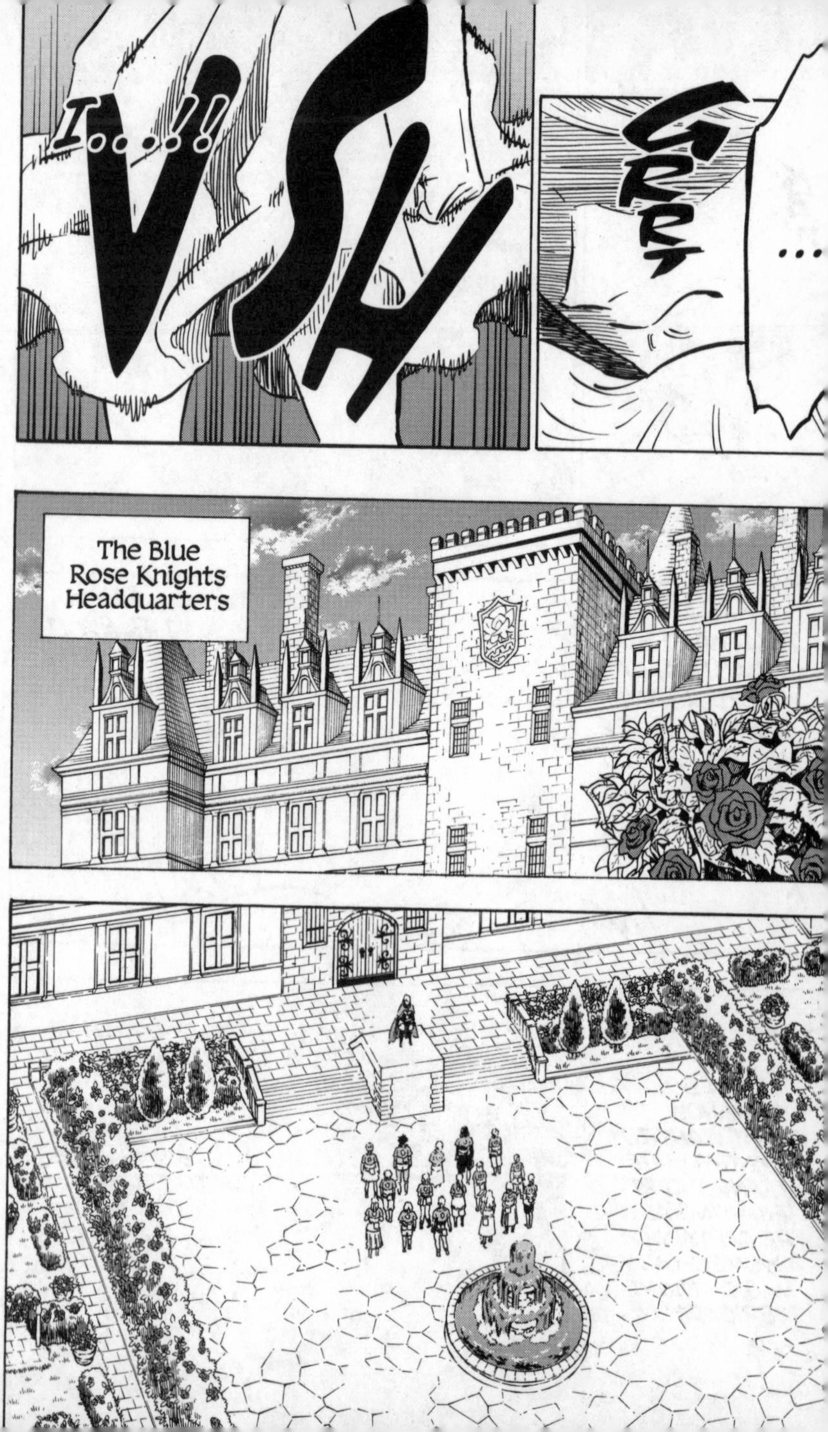

GRRT
...
VSH
I...!!
The Blue Rose Knights Headquarters

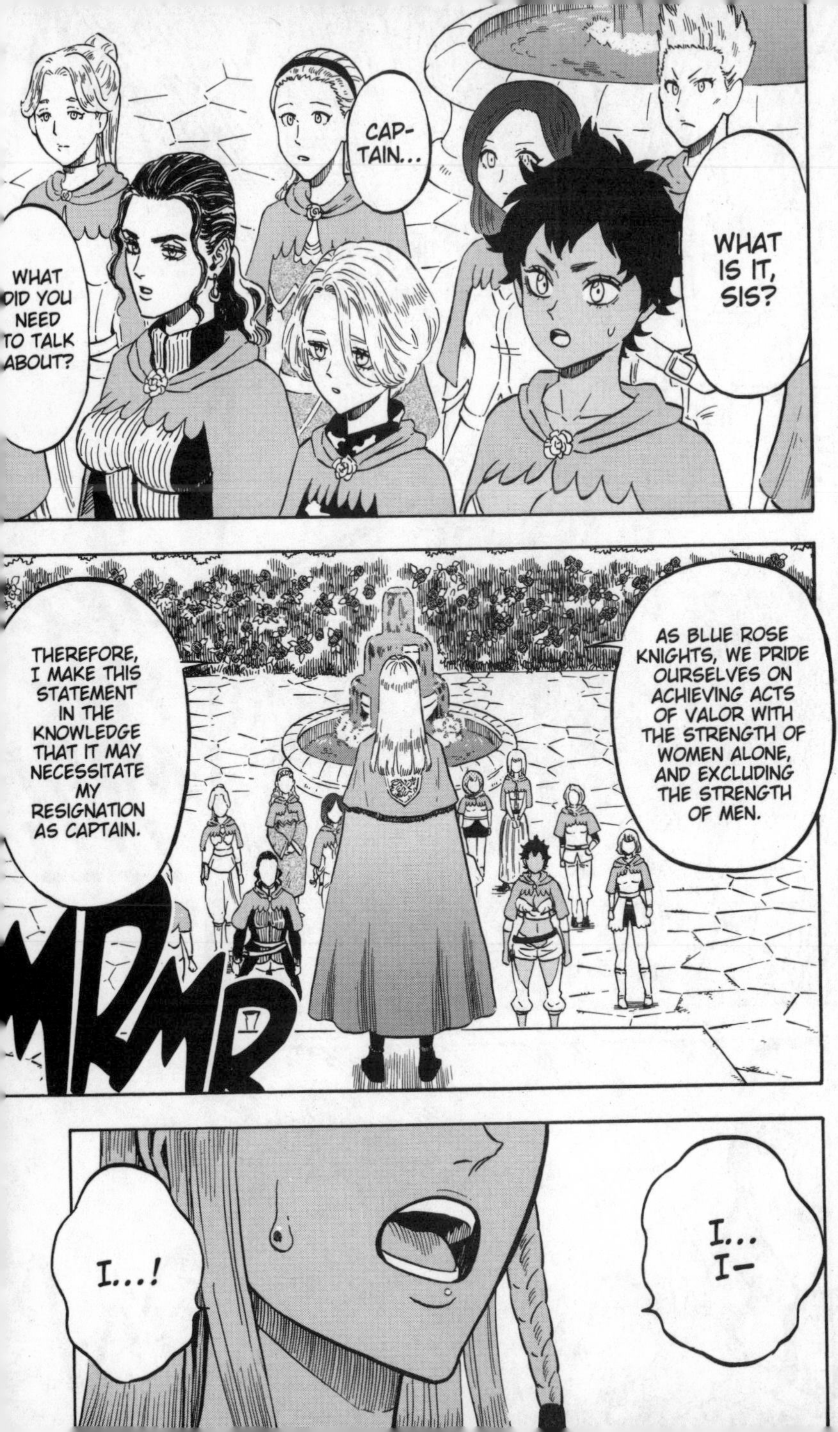
WHAT IS IT, SIS?
CAP-TAIN...
WHAT DID YOU NEED TO TALK ABOUT?
AS BLUE ROSE KNIGHTS, WE PRIDE OURSELVES ON ACHIEVING ACTS OF VALOR WITH THE STRENGTH OF WOMEN ALONE, AND EXCLUDING THE STRENGTH OF MEN.
THEREFORE, I MAKE THIS STATEMENT IN THE KNOWLEDGE THAT IT MAY NECESSITATE MY RESIGNATION AS CAPTAIN.
MRMR
I... I—
I...!

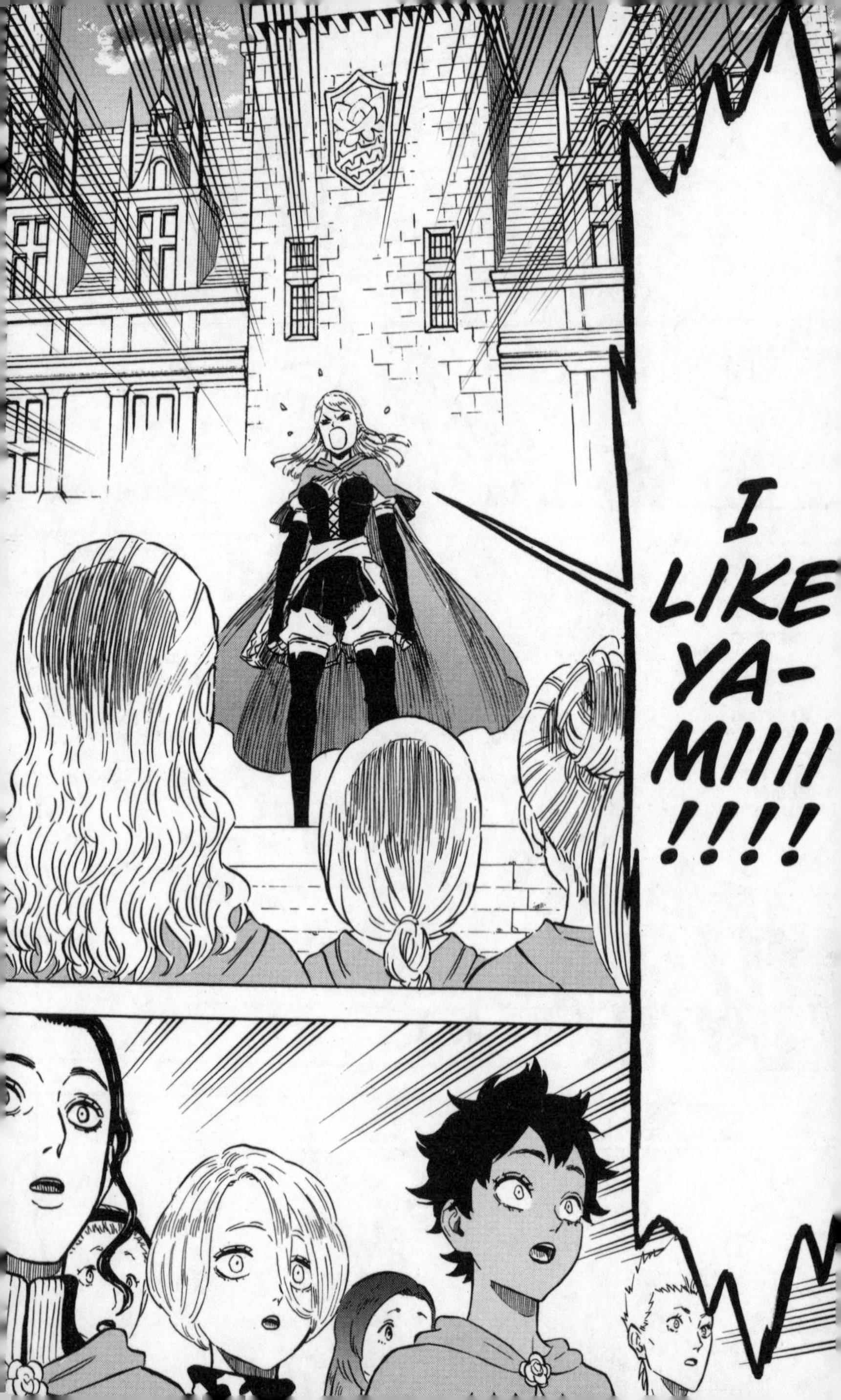
I LIKE YA-MIIII !!!!

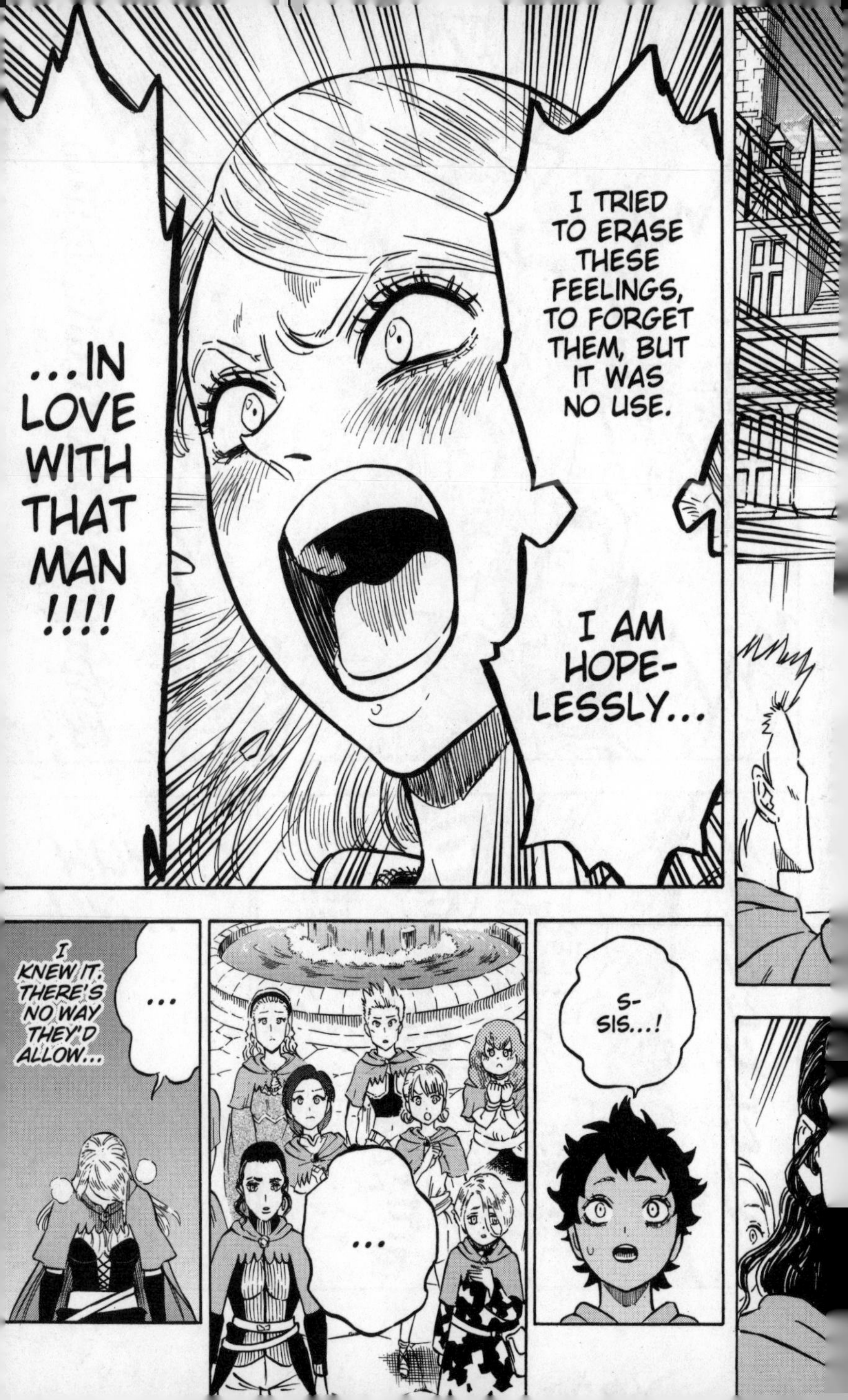
I TRIED TO ERASE THESE FEELINGS, TO FORGET THEM, BUT IT WAS NO USE.
I AM HOPELESSLY...
...IN LOVE WITH THAT MAN!!!!
S- SIS...!
...
...
I KNEW IT. THERE'S NO WAY THEY'D ALLOW...

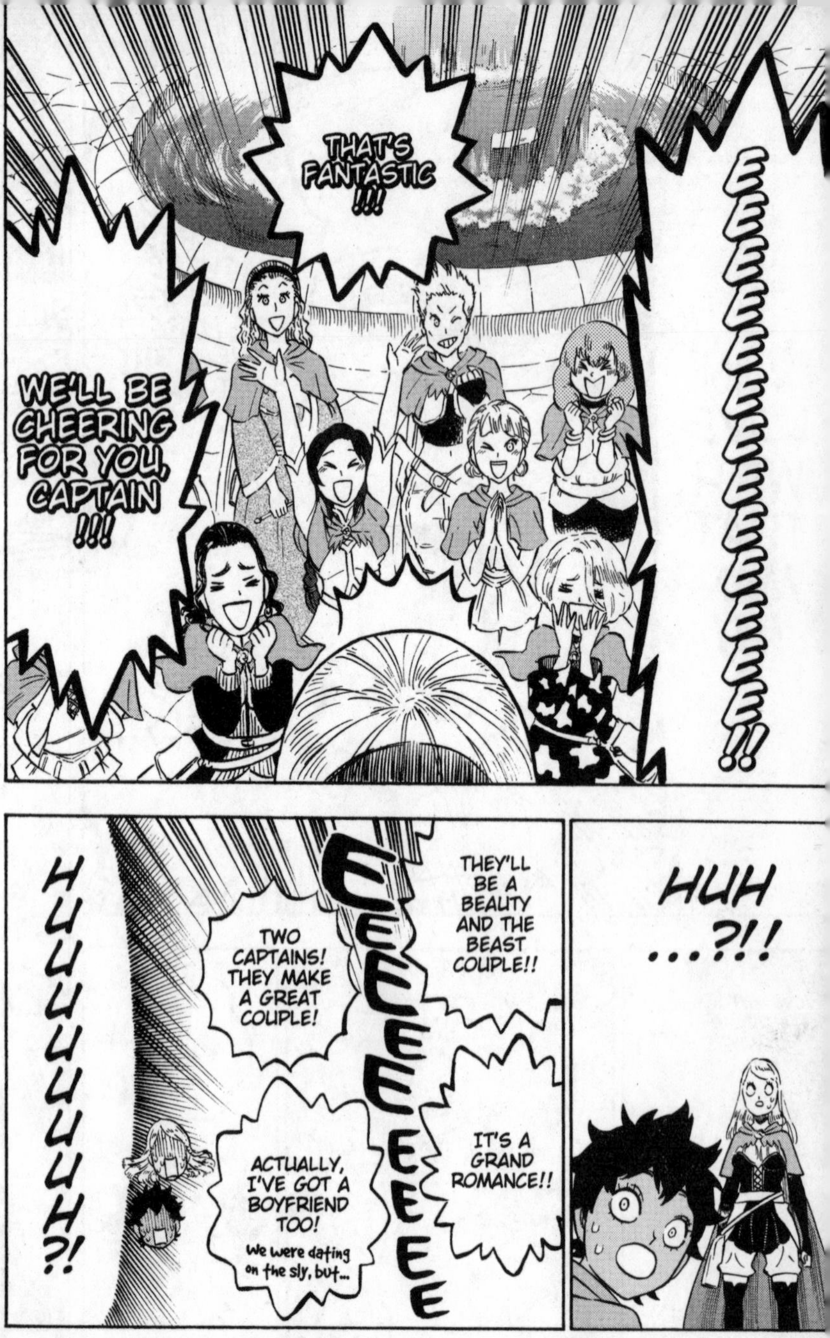
EEEEEEEEEEEEEEEEE!!
THAT'S FANTASTIC!!!
WE'LL BE CHEERING FOR YOU, CAPTAIN!!!
HUH...?!!
THEY'LL BE A BEAUTY AND THE BEAST COUPLE!!
TWO CAPTAINS! THEY MAKE A GREAT COUPLE!
EEEEEEEEEEEE
IT'S A GRAND ROMANCE!!
ACTUALLY, I'VE GOT A BOYFRIEND TOO!
We were dating on the sly, but...
HUUUUUUUUH?!

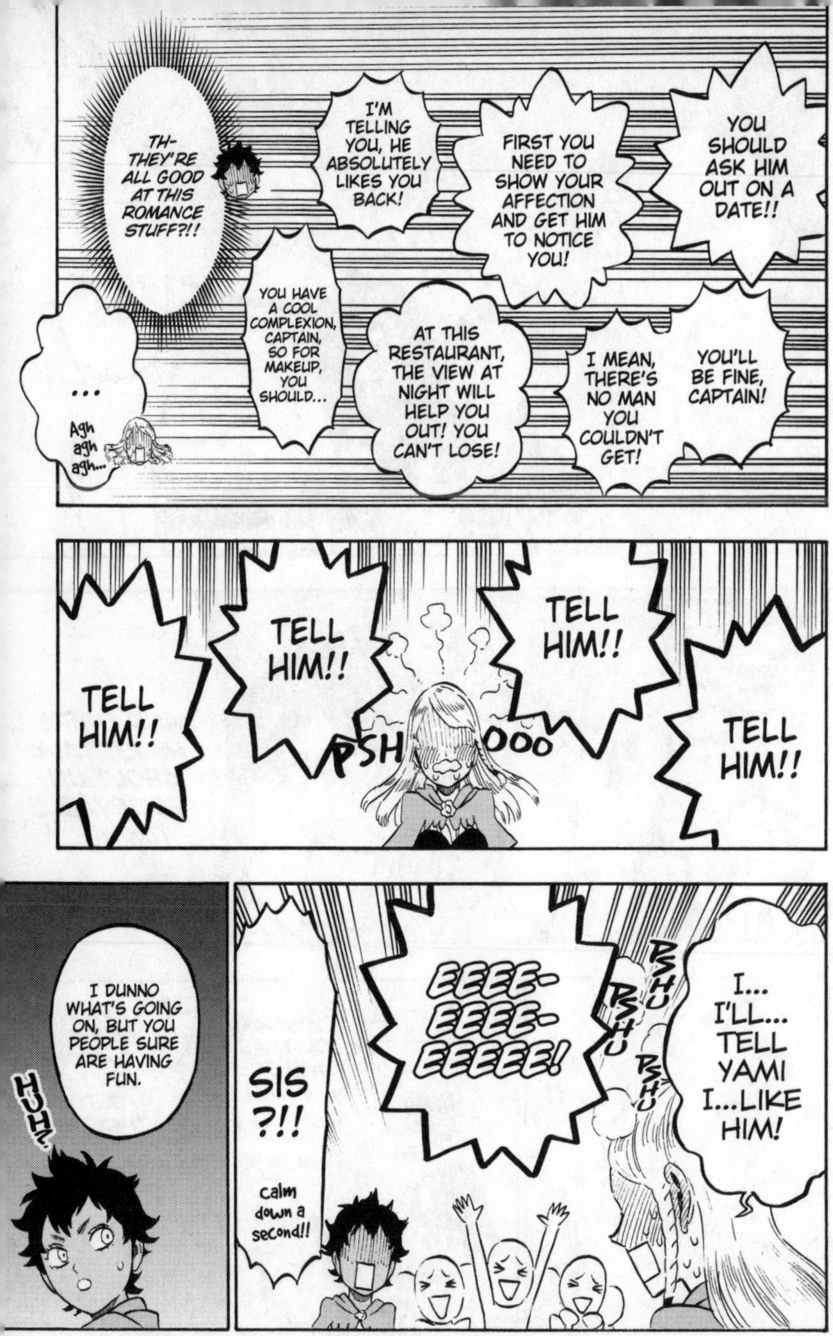
YOU SHOULD ASK HIM OUT ON A DATE!!
FIRST YOU NEED TO SHOW YOUR AFFECTION AND GET HIM TO NOTICE YOU!
I'M TELLING YOU, HE ABSOLUTELY LIKES YOU BACK!
TH- THEY'RE ALL GOOD AT THIS ROMANCE STUFF?!!
YOU'LL BE FINE, CAPTAIN!
I MEAN, THERE'S NO MAN YOU COULDN'T GET!
AT THIS RESTAURANT, THE VIEW AT NIGHT WILL HELP YOU OUT! YOU CAN'T LOSE!
YOU HAVE A COOL COMPLEXION, CAPTAIN, SO FOR MAKEUP, YOU SHOULD...
...
Agh agh agh...
TELL HIM!!
TELL HIM!!
PSHOOO
TELL HIM!!
TELL HIM!!
I... I'LL... TELL YAMI I...LIKE HIM!
PSHU
PSHU
PSHU
EEEE-EEEE-EEEEE!
SIS?!!
calm down a second!!
I DUNNO WHAT'S GOING ON, BUT YOU PEOPLE SURE ARE HAVING FUN.
HUH?

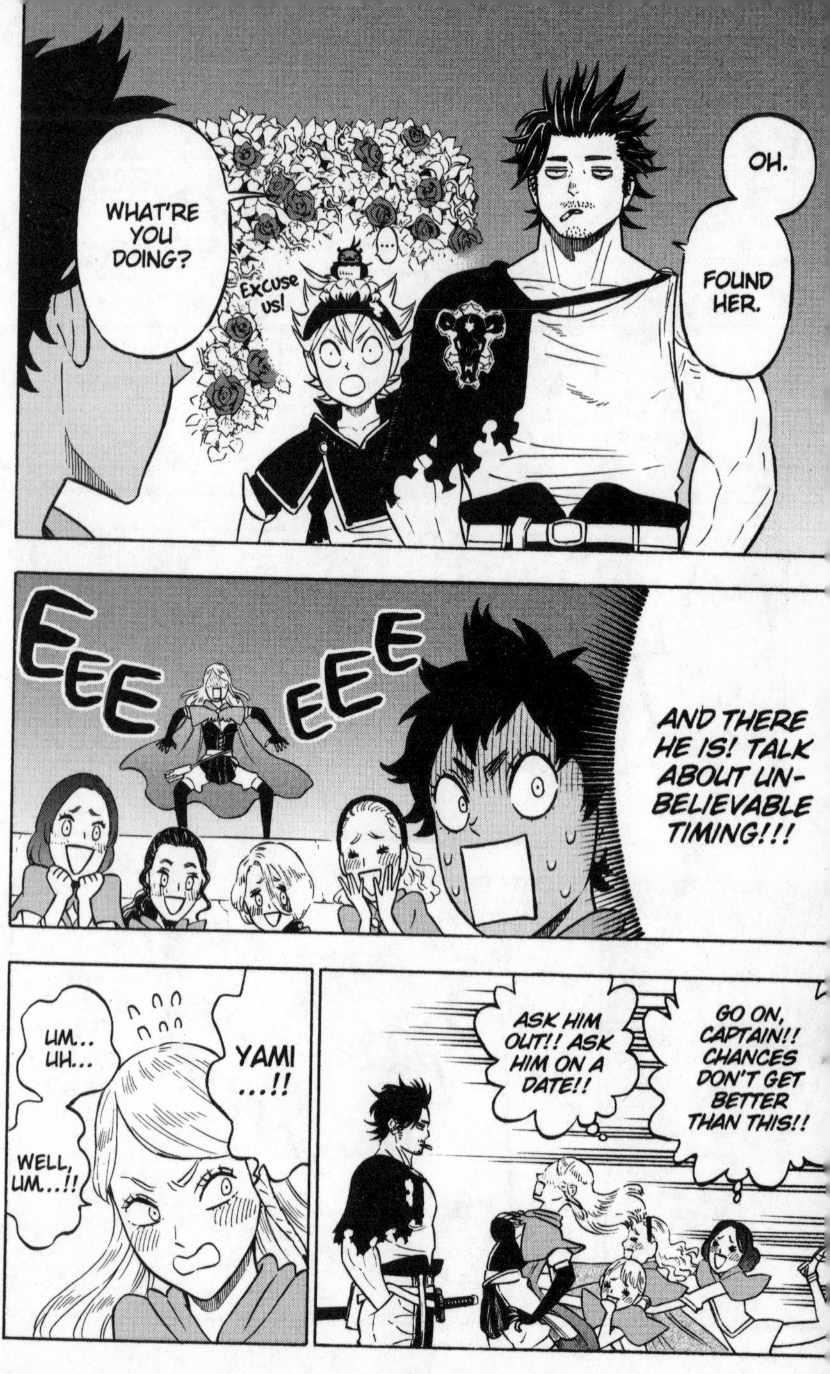
OH.
FOUND HER.
...
EXCUSE US!
WHAT'RE YOU DOING?
AND THERE HE IS! TALK ABOUT UN-BELIEVABLE TIMING!!!
EEEEEE
GO ON, CAPTAIN!! CHANCES DON'T GET BETTER THAN THIS!!
ASK HIM OUT!! ASK HIM ON A DATE!!
YAMI ...!!
UM... UH...
WELL, UM...!!

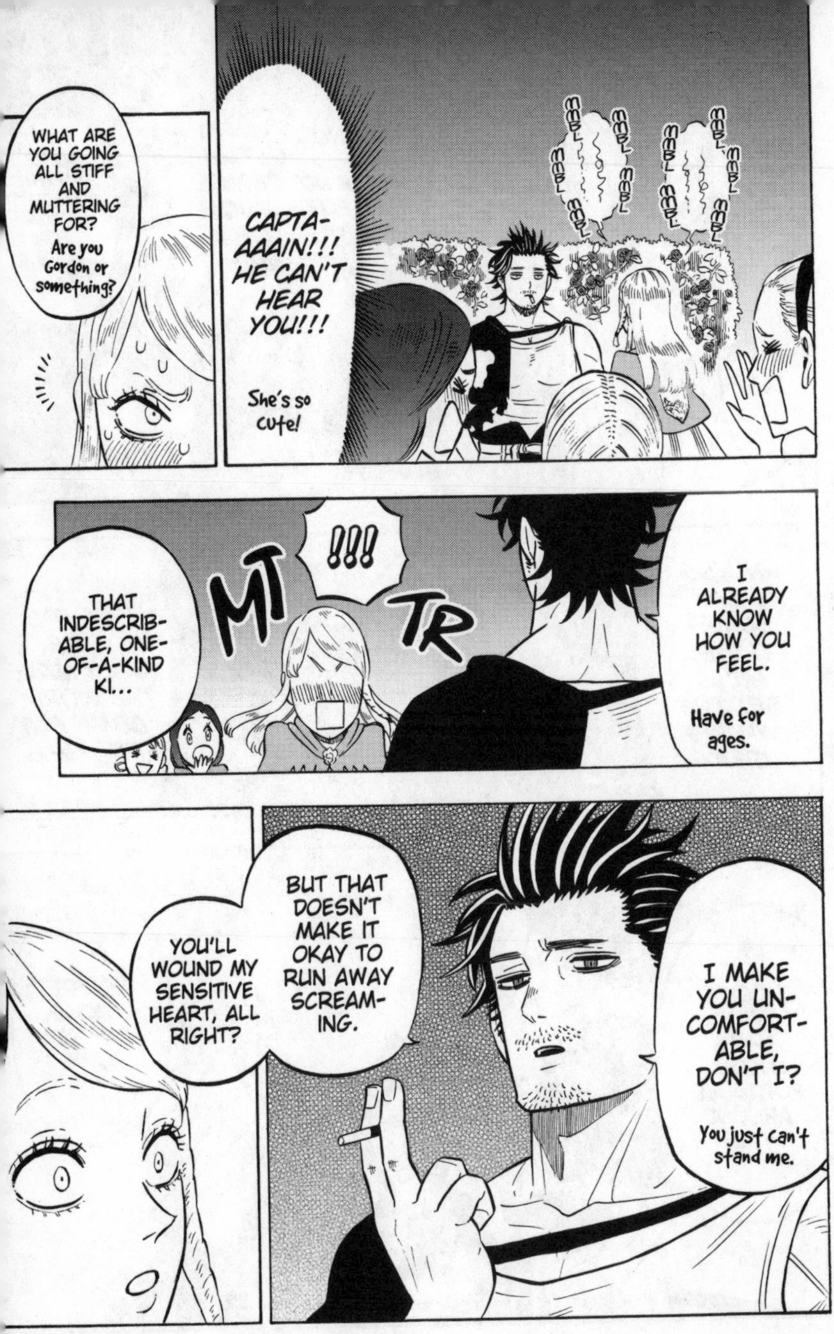
MMBL MMBL MMBL MMBL
MMBL MMBL MMBL MMBL MMBL
CAPTA-AAAIN!!! HE CAN'T HEAR YOU!!!
She's so cute!
WHAT ARE YOU GOING ALL STIFF AND MUTTERING FOR? Are you Gordon or something?
I ALREADY KNOW HOW YOU FEEL. Have for ages.
!!!
MT TR
THAT INDESCRIB-ABLE, ONE-OF-A-KIND KI...
I MAKE YOU UN-COMFORT-ABLE, DON'T I? You just can't stand me.
BUT THAT DOESN'T MAKE IT OKAY TO RUN AWAY SCREAM-ING.
YOU'LL WOUND MY SENSITIVE HEART, ALL RIGHT?

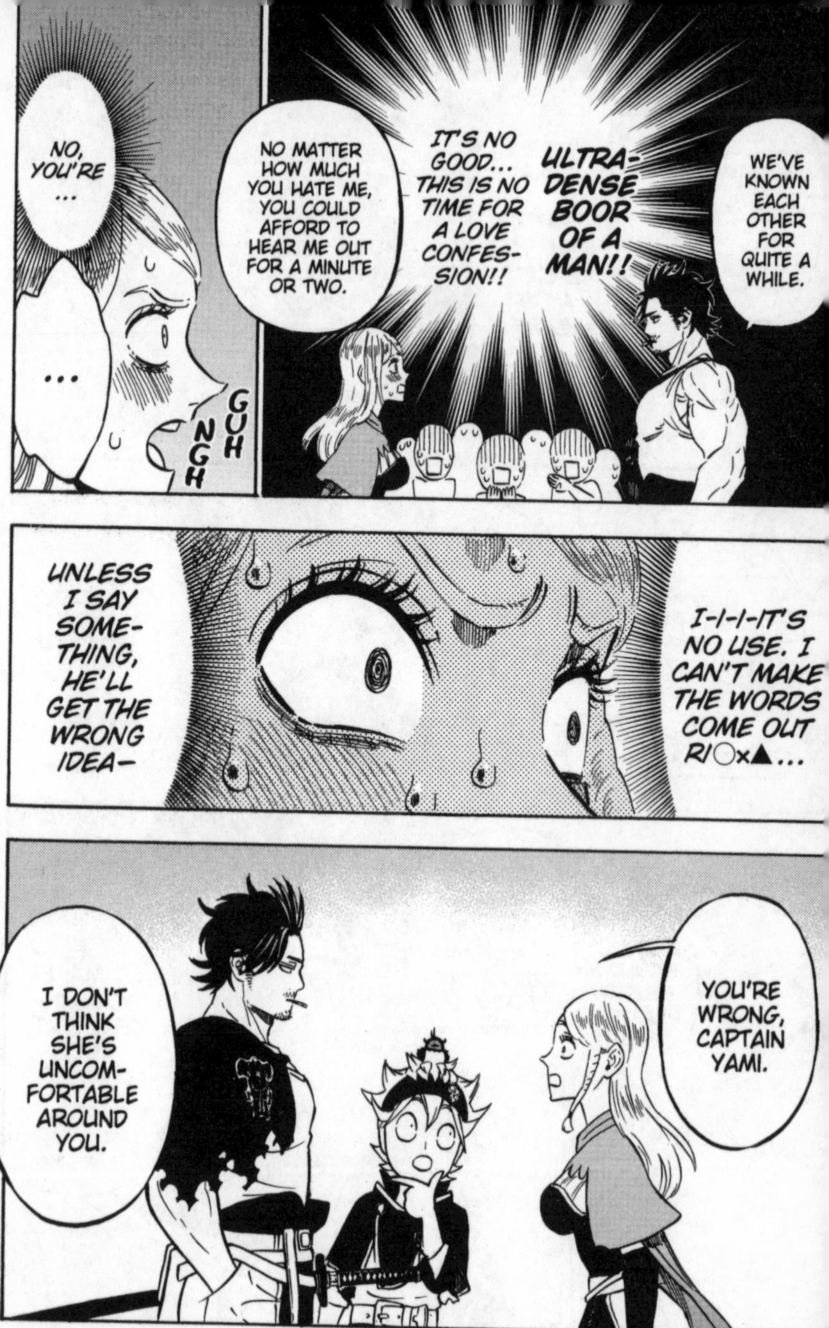
WE'VE KNOWN EACH OTHER FOR QUITE A WHILE.
ULTRA-DENSE BOOR OF A MAN!!
IT'S NO GOOD... THIS IS NO TIME FOR A LOVE CONFES-SION!!
NO MATTER HOW MUCH YOU HATE ME, YOU COULD AFFORD TO HEAR ME OUT FOR A MINUTE OR TWO.
NO, YOU'RE ...
...
GUH
NGH
I-I-I-IT'S NO USE. I CAN'T MAKE THE WORDS COME OUT RI○x▲...
UNLESS I SAY SOME-THING, HE'LL GET THE WRONG IDEA—
YOU'RE WRONG, CAPTAIN YAMI.
I DON'T THINK SHE'S UNCOM-FORTABLE AROUND YOU.

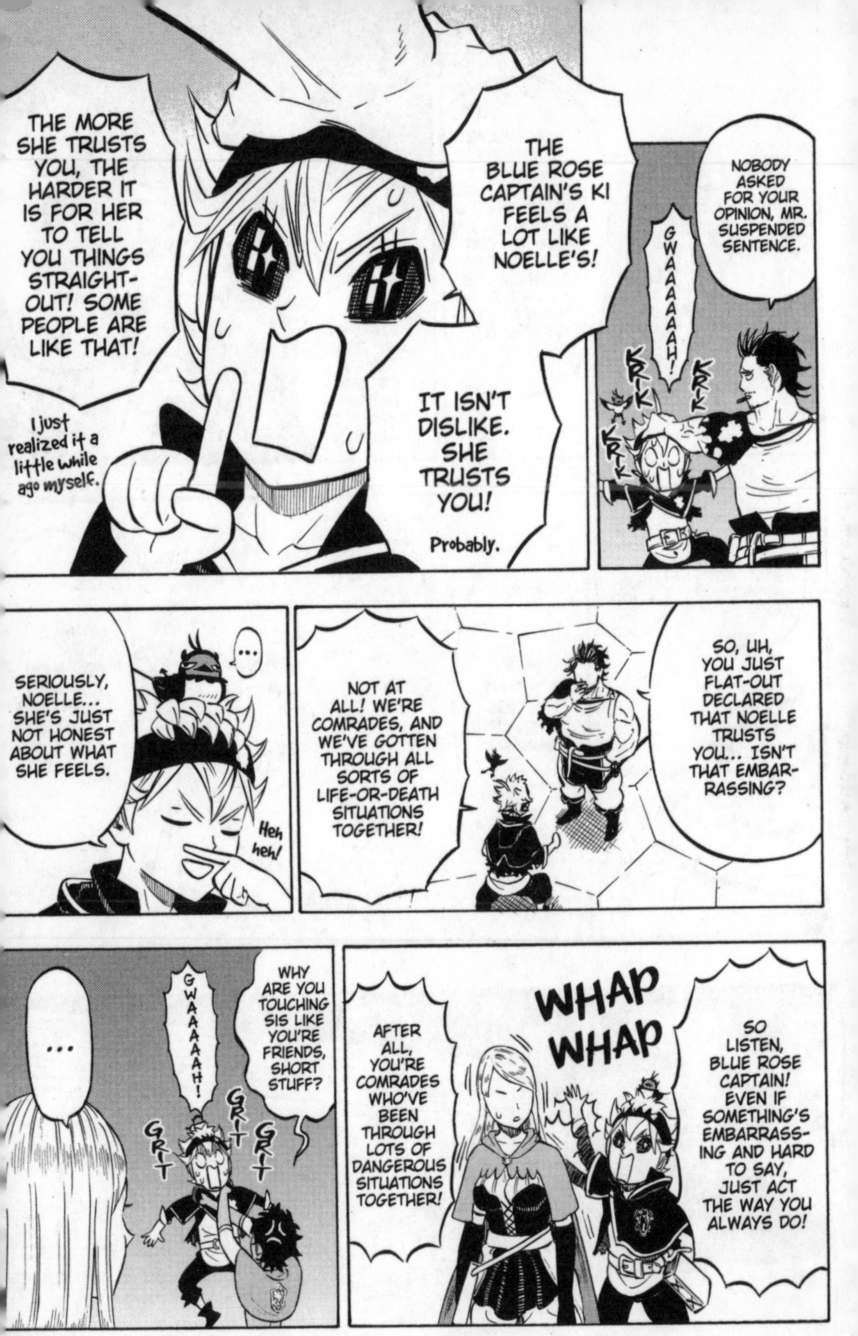
NOBODY ASKED FOR YOUR OPINION, MR. SUSPENDED SENTENCE.
GWAAAAAAAH!
KRIK KRIK KRIK
THE BLUE ROSE CAPTAIN'S KI FEELS A LOT LIKE NOELLE'S!
IT ISN'T DISLIKE. SHE TRUSTS YOU!
Probably.
THE MORE SHE TRUSTS YOU, THE HARDER IT IS FOR HER TO TELL YOU THINGS STRAIGHT-OUT! SOME PEOPLE ARE LIKE THAT!
I just realized it a little while ago myself.
SO, UH, YOU JUST FLAT-OUT DECLARED THAT NOELLE TRUSTS YOU... ISN'T THAT EMBARRASSING?
NOT AT ALL! WE'RE COMRADES, AND WE'VE GOTTEN THROUGH ALL SORTS OF LIFE-OR-DEATH SITUATIONS TOGETHER!
...
SERIOUSLY, NOELLE... SHE'S JUST NOT HONEST ABOUT WHAT SHE FEELS.
Heh heh!
SO LISTEN, BLUE ROSE CAPTAIN! EVEN IF SOMETHING'S EMBARRASSING AND HARD TO SAY, JUST ACT THE WAY YOU ALWAYS DO!
WHAP WHAP
AFTER ALL, YOU'RE COMRADES WHO'VE BEEN THROUGH LOTS OF DANGEROUS SITUATIONS TOGETHER!
WHY ARE YOU TOUCHING SIS LIKE YOU'RE FRIENDS, SHORT STUFF?
GWAAAAAAH!
GRIT GRIT GRIT
...

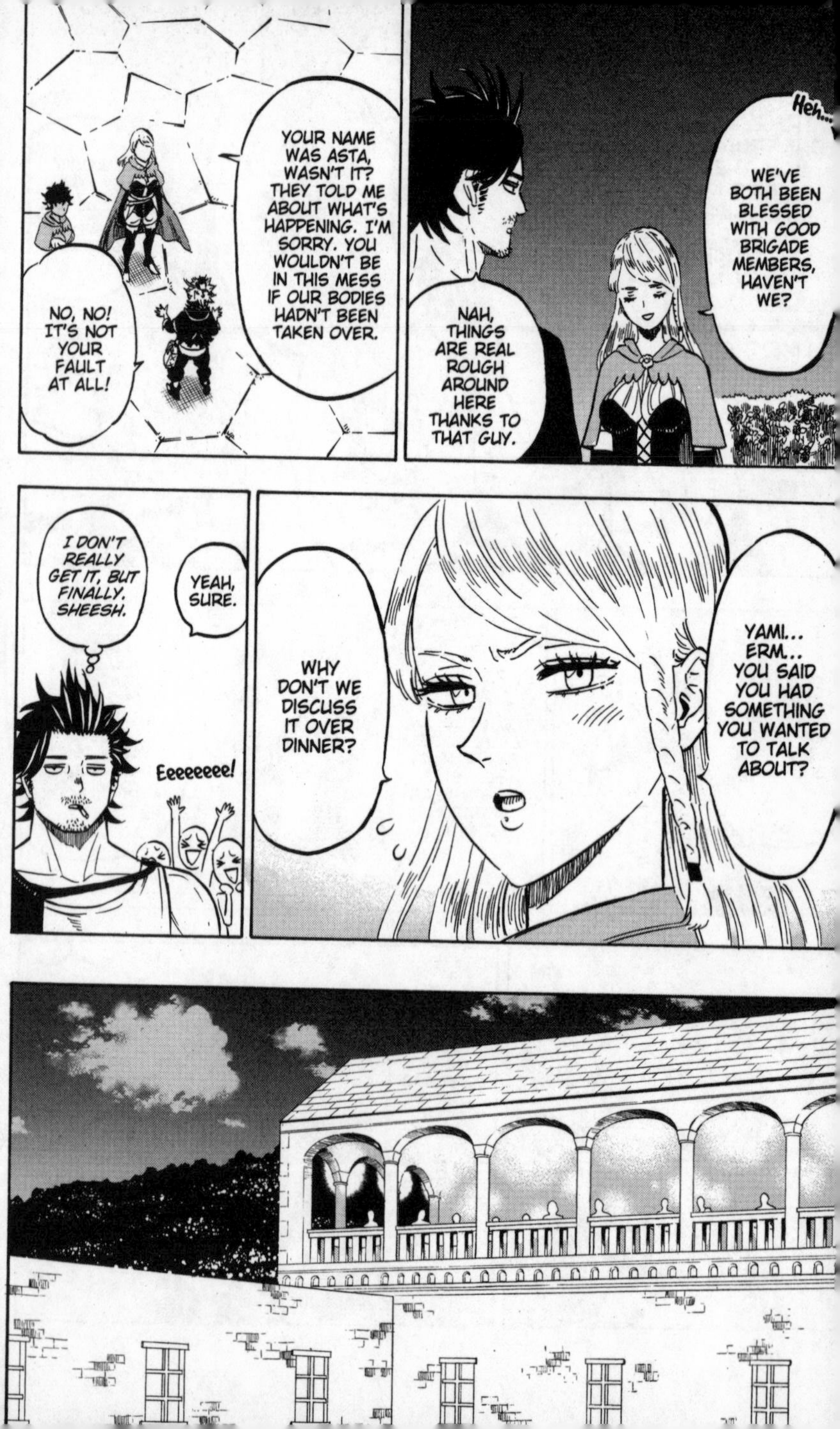
Heh...
WE'VE BOTH BEEN BLESSED WITH GOOD BRIGADE MEMBERS, HAVEN'T WE?
NAH, THINGS ARE REAL ROUGH AROUND HERE THANKS TO THAT GUY.
YOUR NAME WAS ASTA, WASN'T IT? THEY TOLD ME ABOUT WHAT'S HAPPENING. I'M SORRY. YOU WOULDN'T BE IN THIS MESS IF OUR BODIES HADN'T BEEN TAKEN OVER.
NO, NO! IT'S NOT YOUR FAULT AT ALL!
YAMI... ERM... YOU SAID YOU HAD SOMETHING YOU WANTED TO TALK ABOUT?
WHY DON'T WE DISCUSS IT OVER DINNER?
YEAH, SURE.
I DON'T REALLY GET IT, BUT FINALLY. SHEESH.
Eeeeeeee!

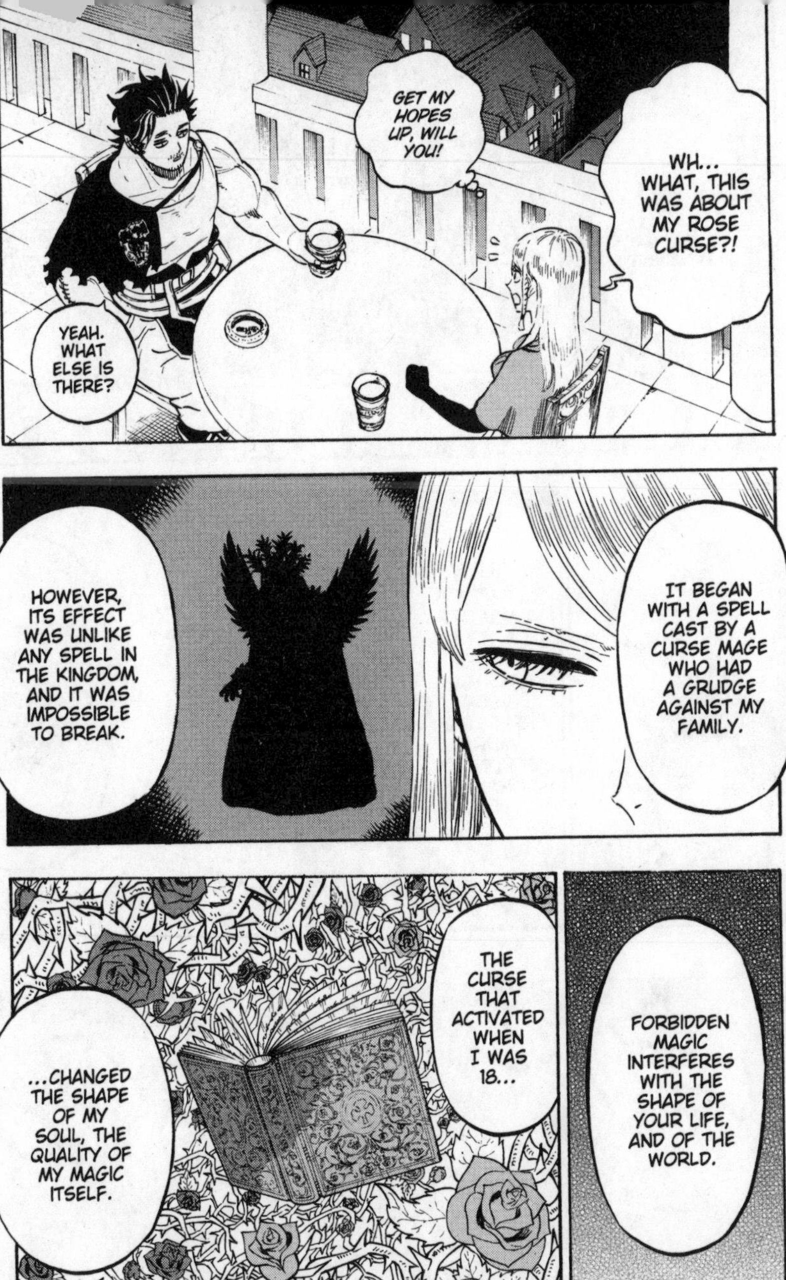
WH... WHAT, THIS WAS ABOUT MY ROSE CURSE?!
GET MY HOPES UP, WILL YOU!
YEAH. WHAT ELSE IS THERE?
IT BEGAN WITH A SPELL CAST BY A CURSE MAGE WHO HAD A GRUDGE AGAINST MY FAMILY.
HOWEVER, ITS EFFECT WAS UNLIKE ANY SPELL IN THE KINGDOM, AND IT WAS IMPOSSIBLE TO BREAK.
FORBIDDEN MAGIC INTERFERES WITH THE SHAPE OF YOUR LIFE, AND OF THE WORLD.
THE CURSE THAT ACTIVATED WHEN I WAS 18...
...CHANGED THE SHAPE OF MY SOUL, THE QUALITY OF MY MAGIC ITSELF.

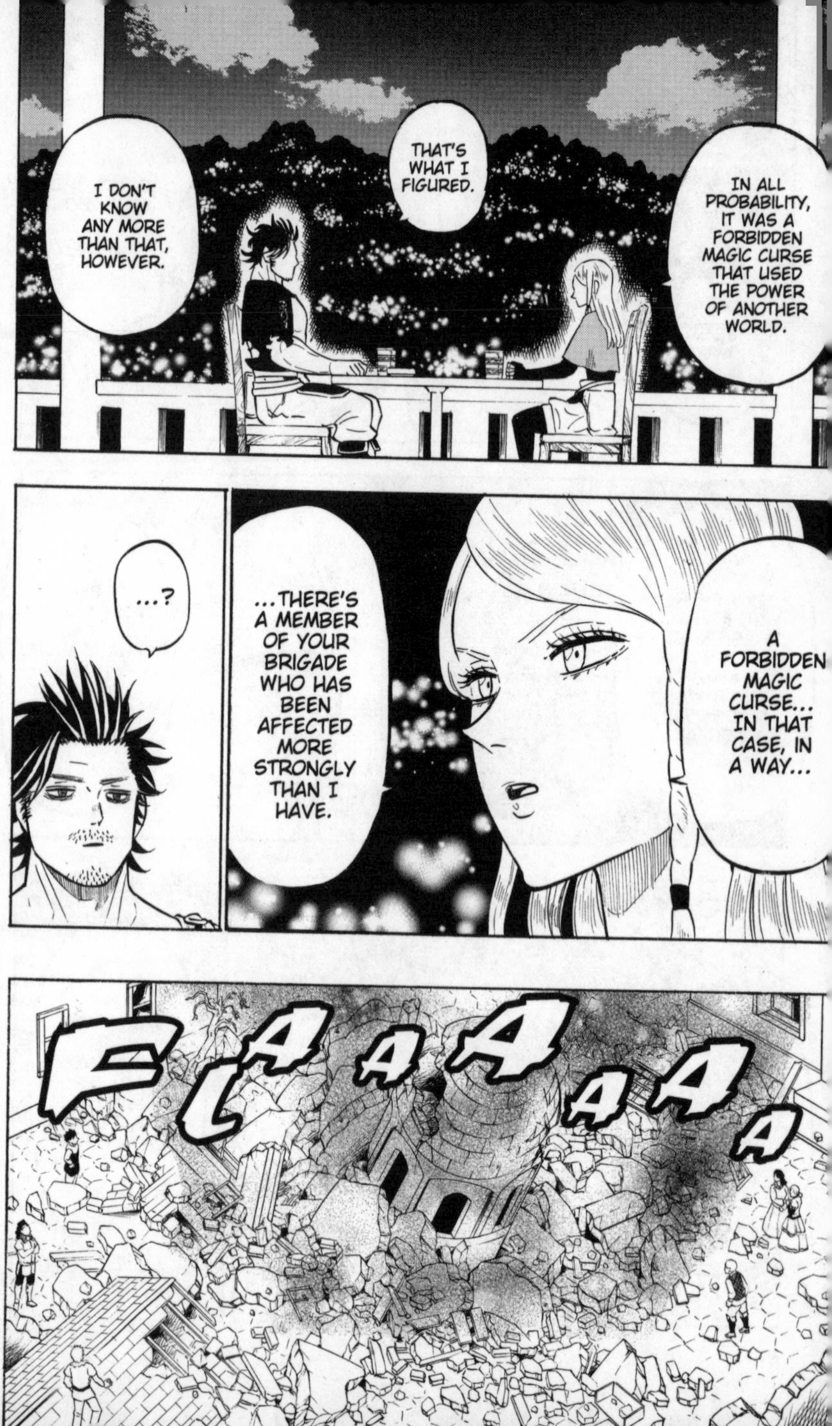
IN ALL PROBABILITY, IT WAS A FORBIDDEN MAGIC CURSE THAT USED THE POWER OF ANOTHER WORLD.
THAT'S WHAT I FIGURED.
I DON'T KNOW ANY MORE THAN THAT, HOWEVER.
A FORBIDDEN MAGIC CURSE... IN THAT CASE, IN A WAY...
...THERE'S A MEMBER OF YOUR BRIGADE WHO HAS BEEN AFFECTED MORE STRONGLY THAN I HAVE.
...?
FLAAAAAAA

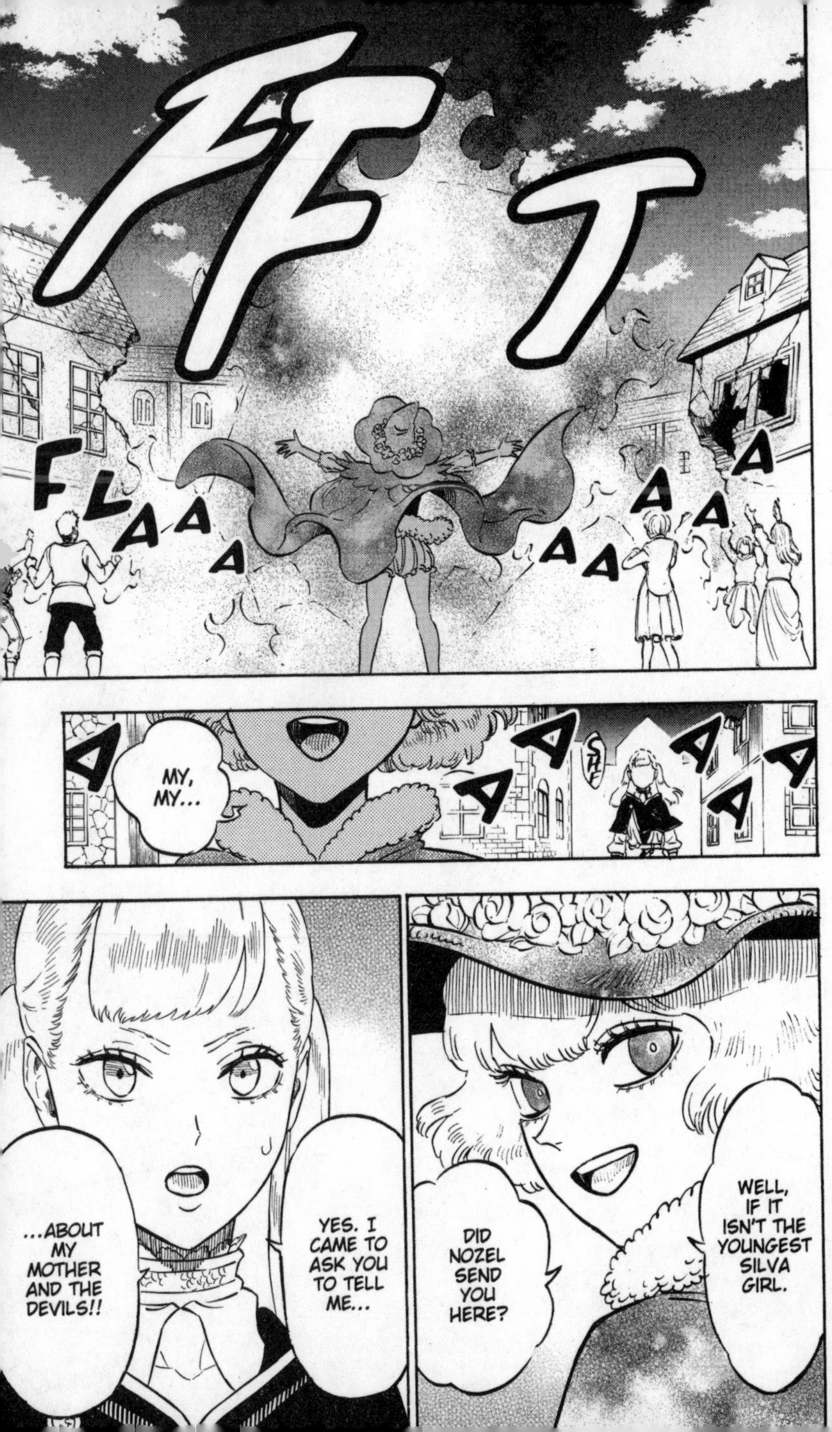
FFT
FLAAAAAAAAAA
SHF
AAAAAA
MY, MY...
WELL, IF IT ISN'T THE YOUNGEST SILVA GIRL.
DID NOZEL SEND YOU HERE?
YES. I CAME TO ASK YOU TO TELL ME...
...ABOUT MY MOTHER AND THE DEVILS!!

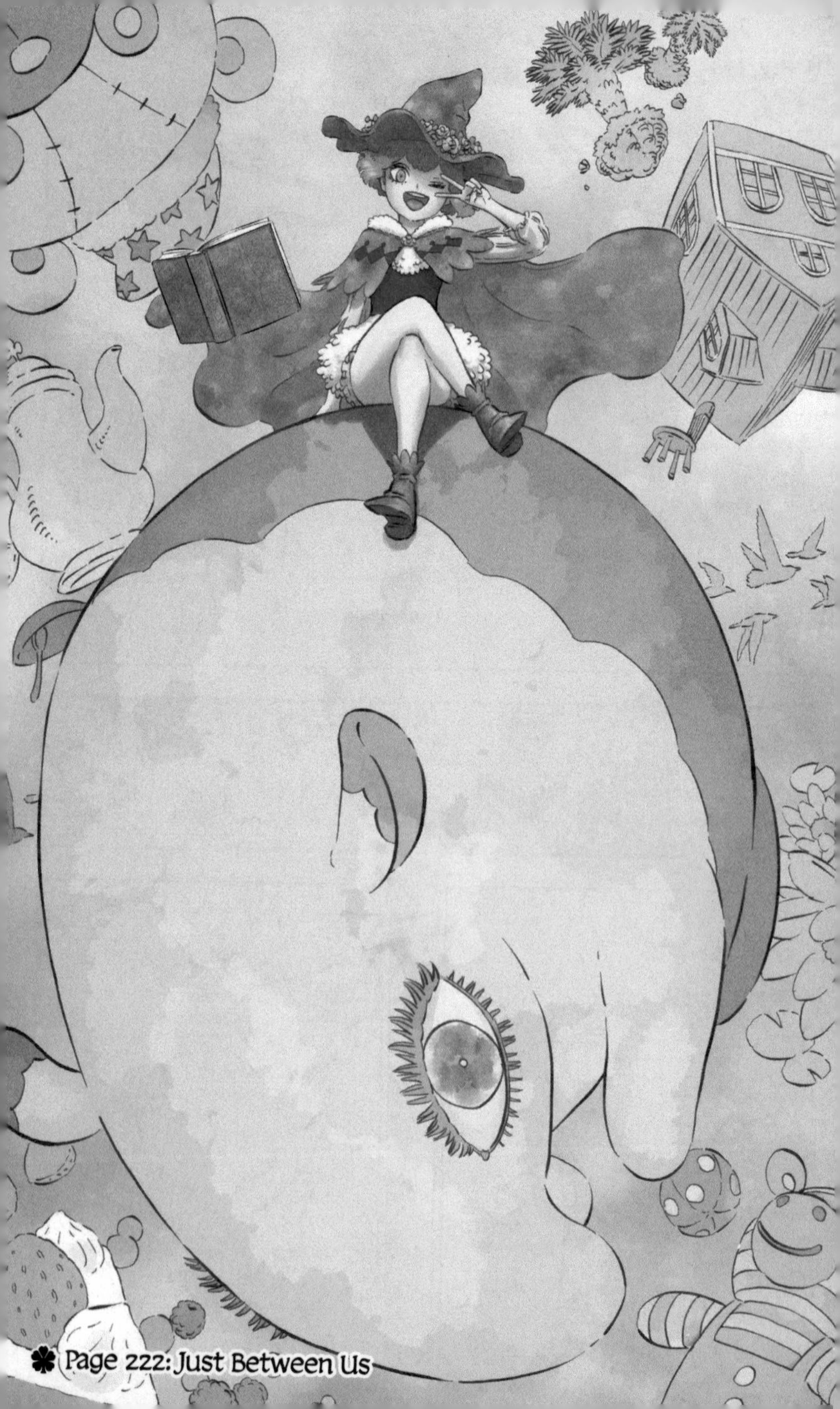

Page 222: Just Between Us

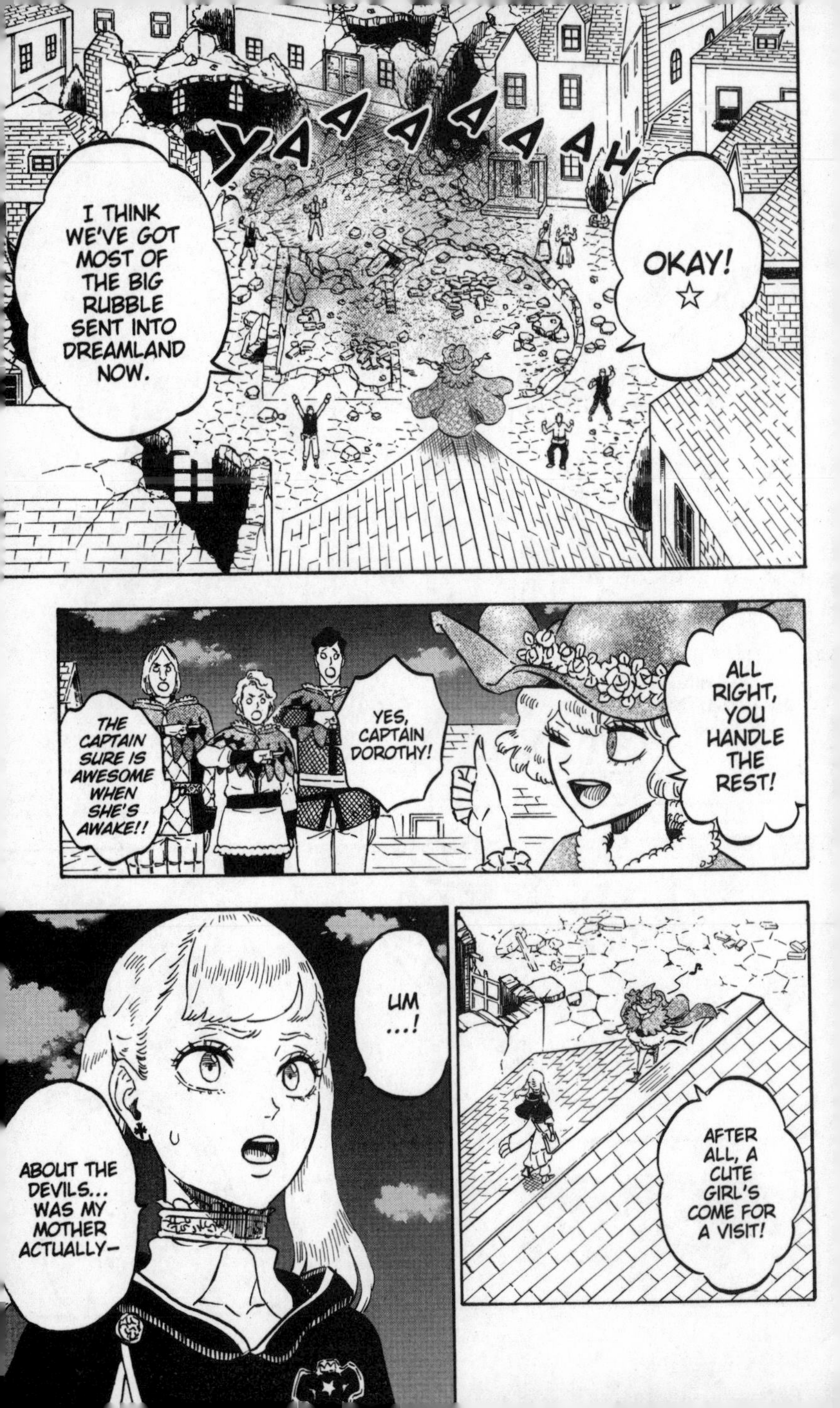
YAAAAAAH
I THINK WE'VE GOT MOST OF THE BIG RUBBLE SENT INTO DREAMLAND NOW.
OKAY! ☆
ALL RIGHT, YOU HANDLE THE REST!
YES, CAPTAIN DOROTHY!
THE CAPTAIN SURE IS AWESOME WHEN SHE'S AWAKE!!
AFTER ALL, A CUTE GIRL'S COME FOR A VISIT!
UM ...!
ABOUT THE DEVILS... WAS MY MOTHER ACTUALLY—

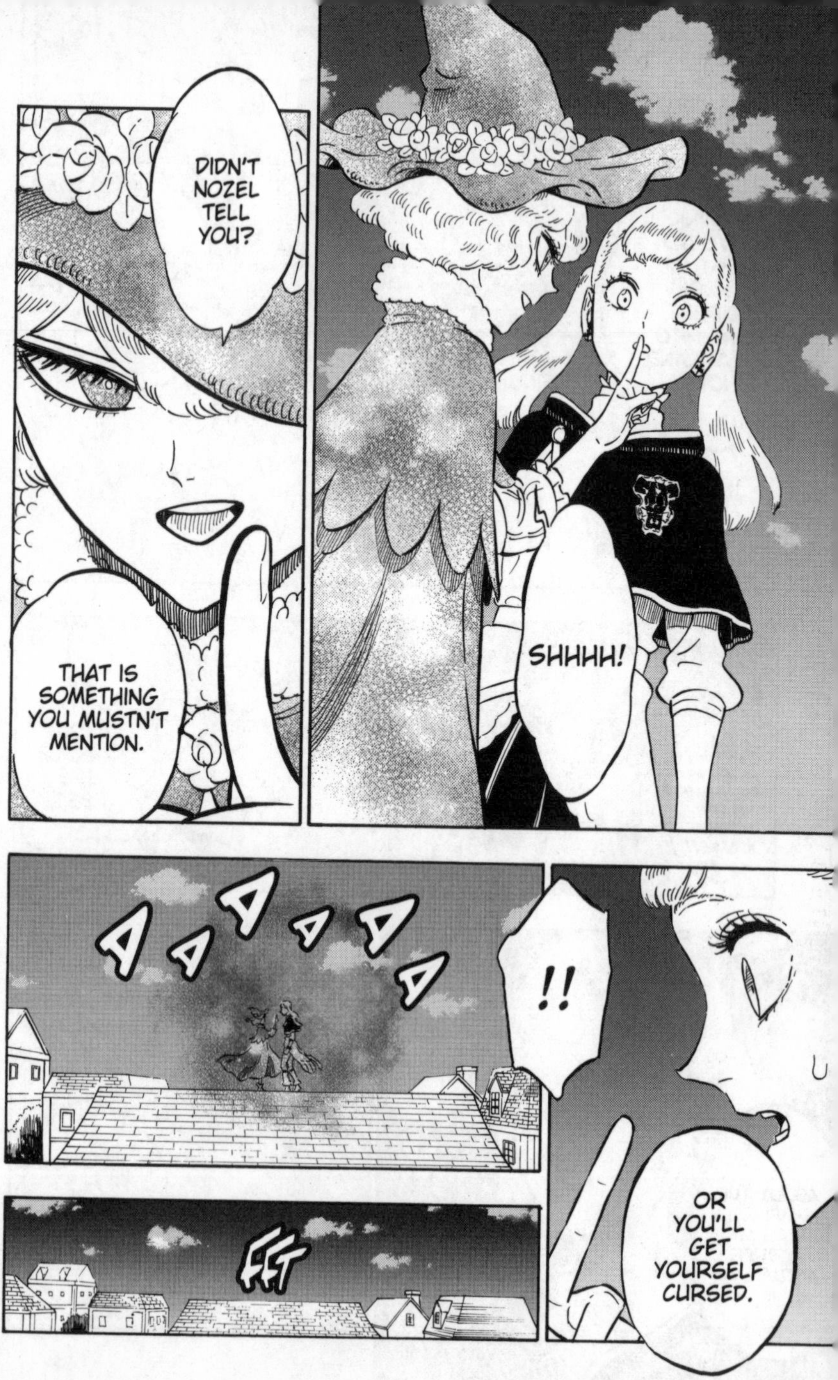
SHHHH!
DIDN'T NOZEL TELL YOU?
THAT IS SOMETHING YOU MUSTN'T MENTION.
!!
OR YOU'LL GET YOURSELF CURSED.
AAAAAA
FFT

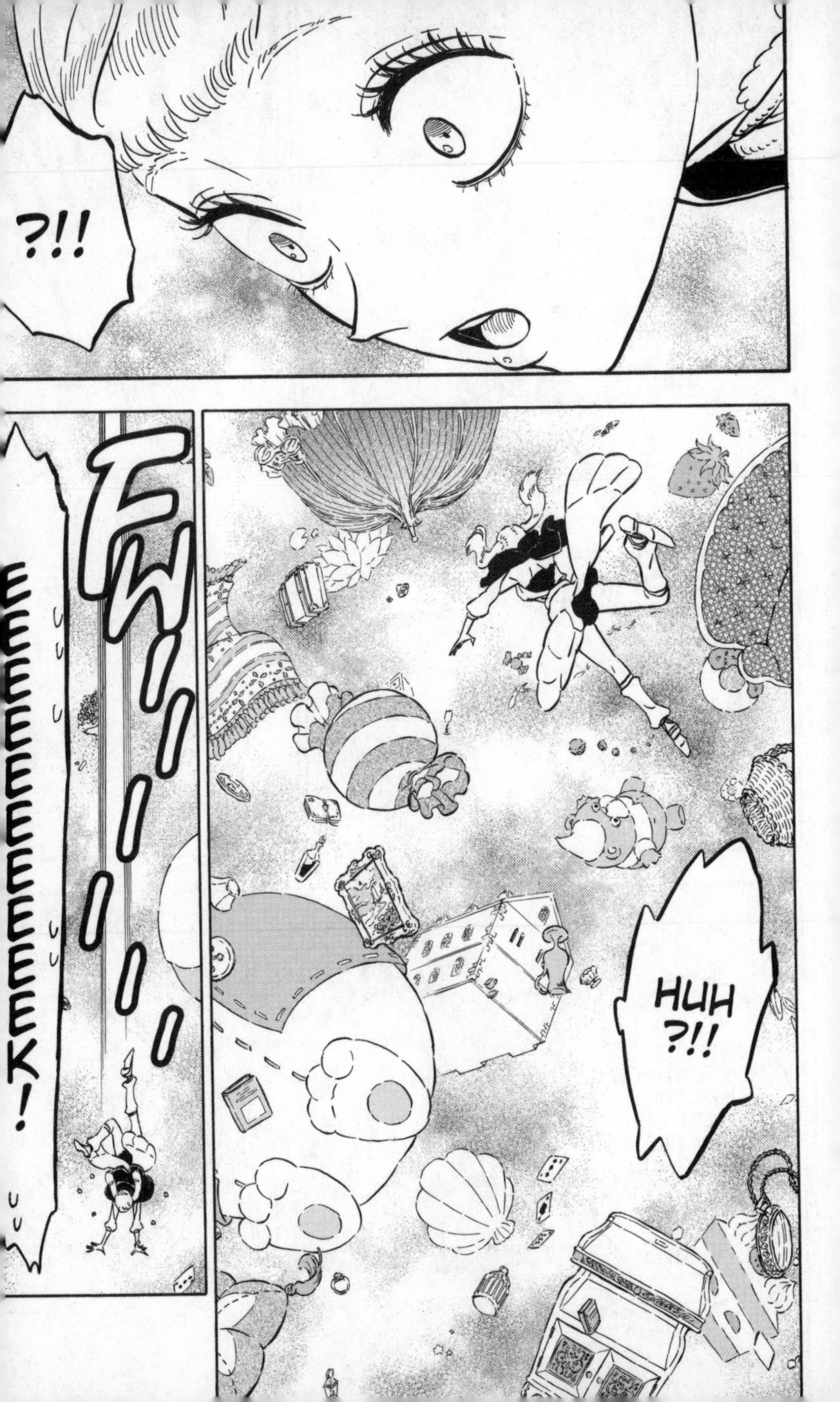

?!!
HUH ?!!
FWIIIIIIII
EEEEEEEEEEEEEEEK!

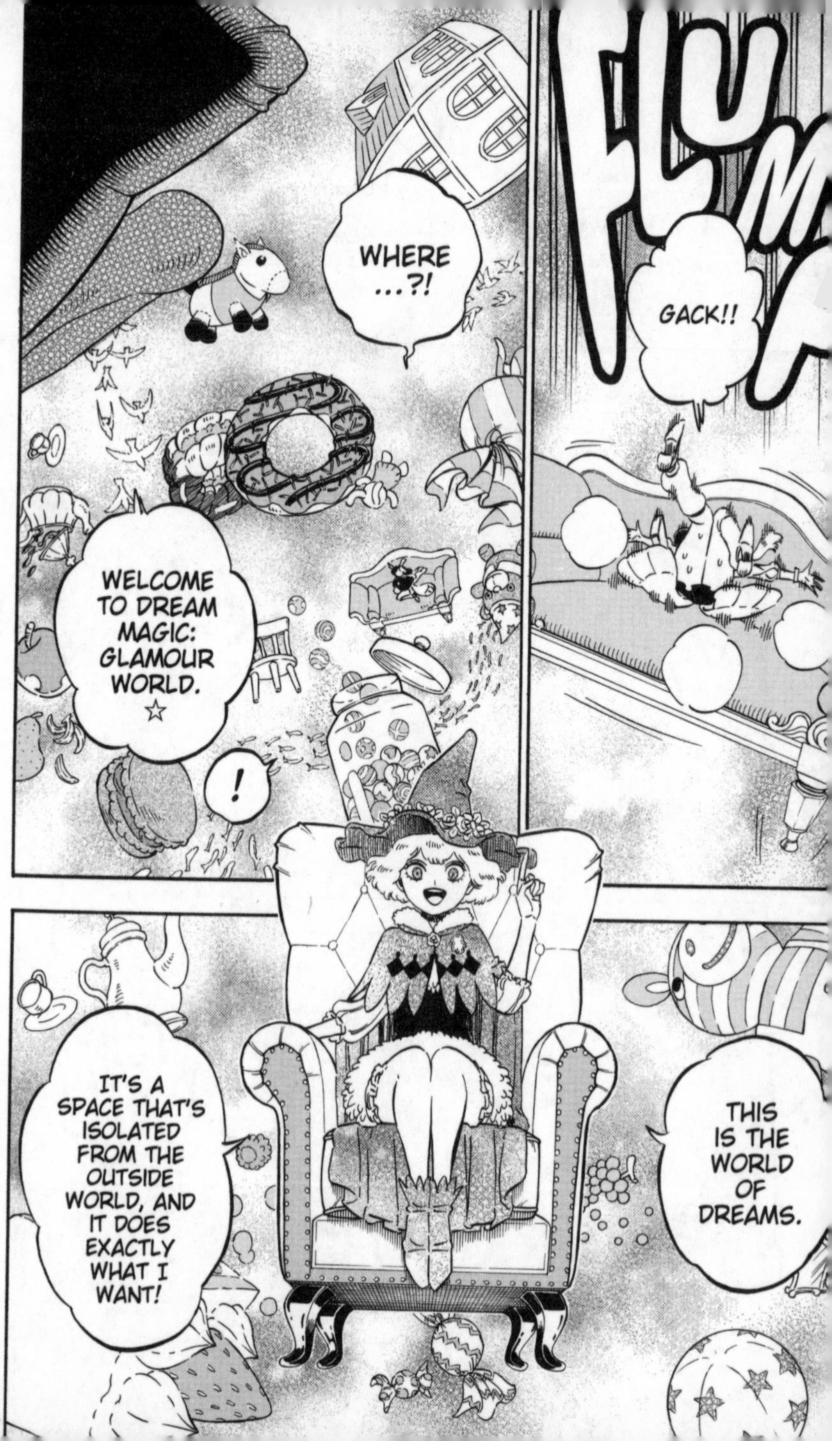
GACK!!
WHERE ...?!
WELCOME TO DREAM MAGIC: GLAMOUR WORLD. ☆
!
THIS IS THE WORLD OF DREAMS.
IT'S A SPACE THAT'S ISOLATED FROM THE OUTSIDE WORLD, AND IT DOES EXACTLY WHAT I WANT!

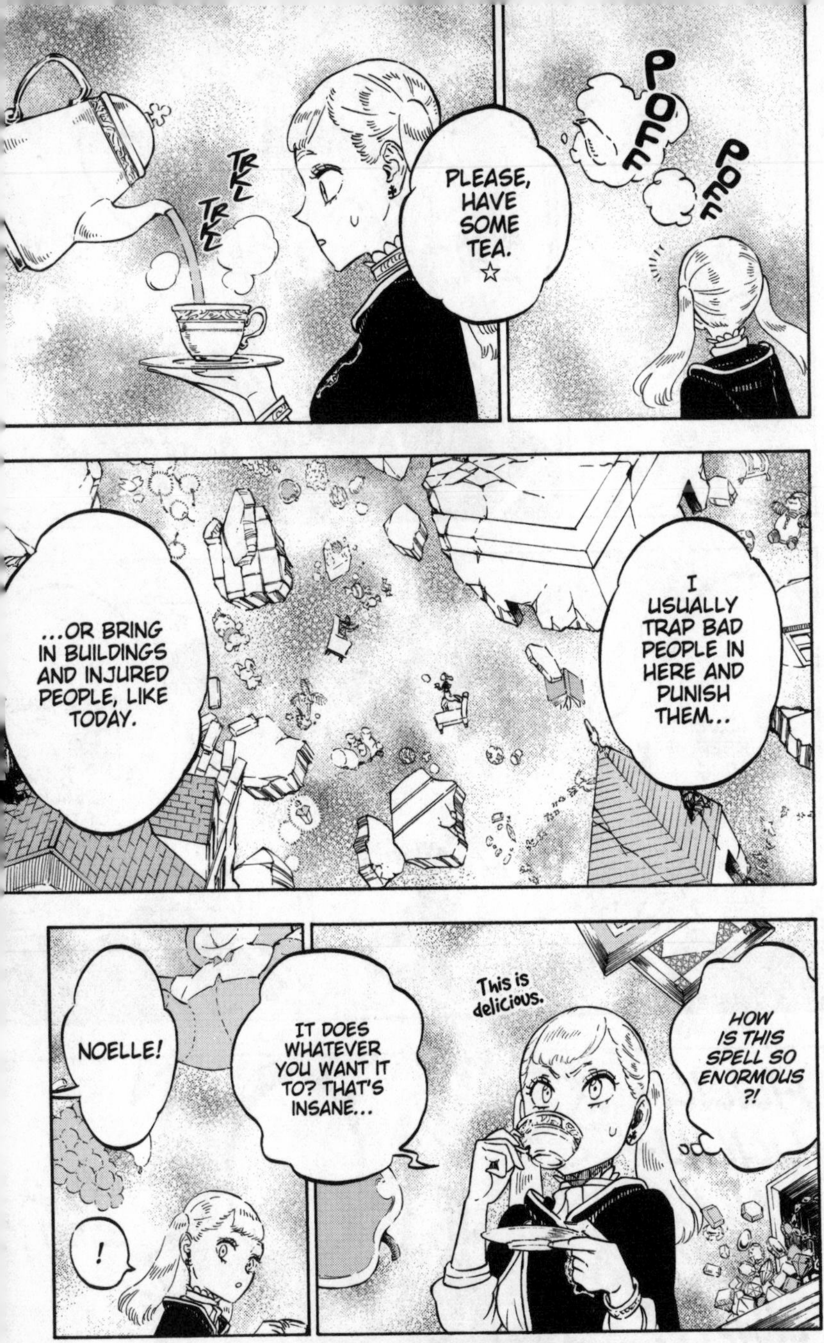
POFF
POFF
PLEASE, HAVE SOME TEA. ☆
TRKL
TRKL
I USUALLY TRAP BAD PEOPLE IN HERE AND PUNISH THEM...
...OR BRING IN BUILDINGS AND INJURED PEOPLE, LIKE TODAY.
HOW IS THIS SPELL SO ENORMOUS?!
This is delicious.
IT DOES WHATEVER YOU WANT IT TO? THAT'S INSANE...
NOELLE!
!

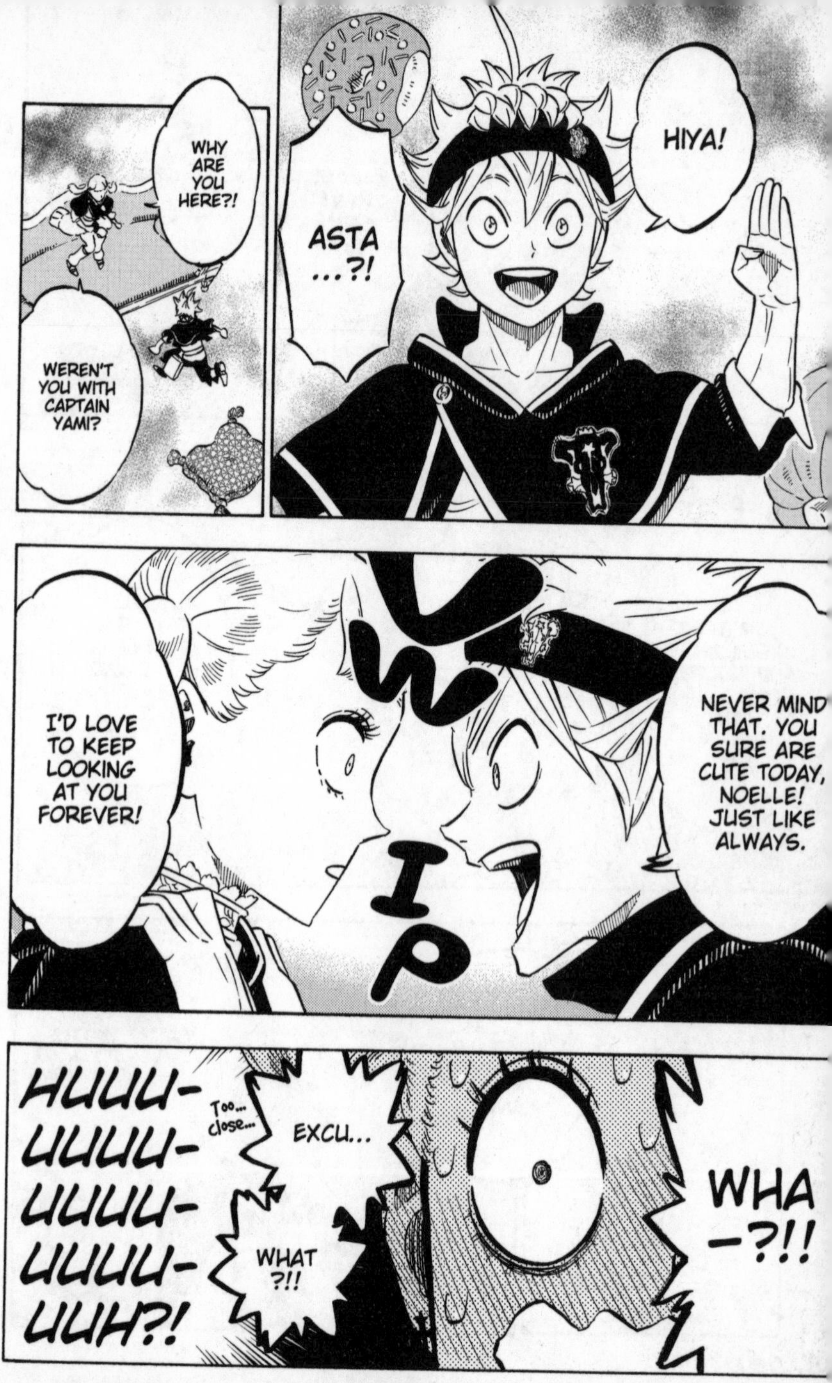
HIYA!
ASTA ...?!
WHY ARE YOU HERE?!
WEREN'T YOU WITH CAPTAIN YAMI?
NEVER MIND THAT. YOU SURE ARE CUTE TODAY, NOELLE! JUST LIKE ALWAYS.
WIP
I'D LOVE TO KEEP LOOKING AT YOU FOREVER!
WHA-?!!
EXCU...
WHAT?!!
Too... close...
HUUU-UUUUU-UUUUU-UUUUU-UUH?!

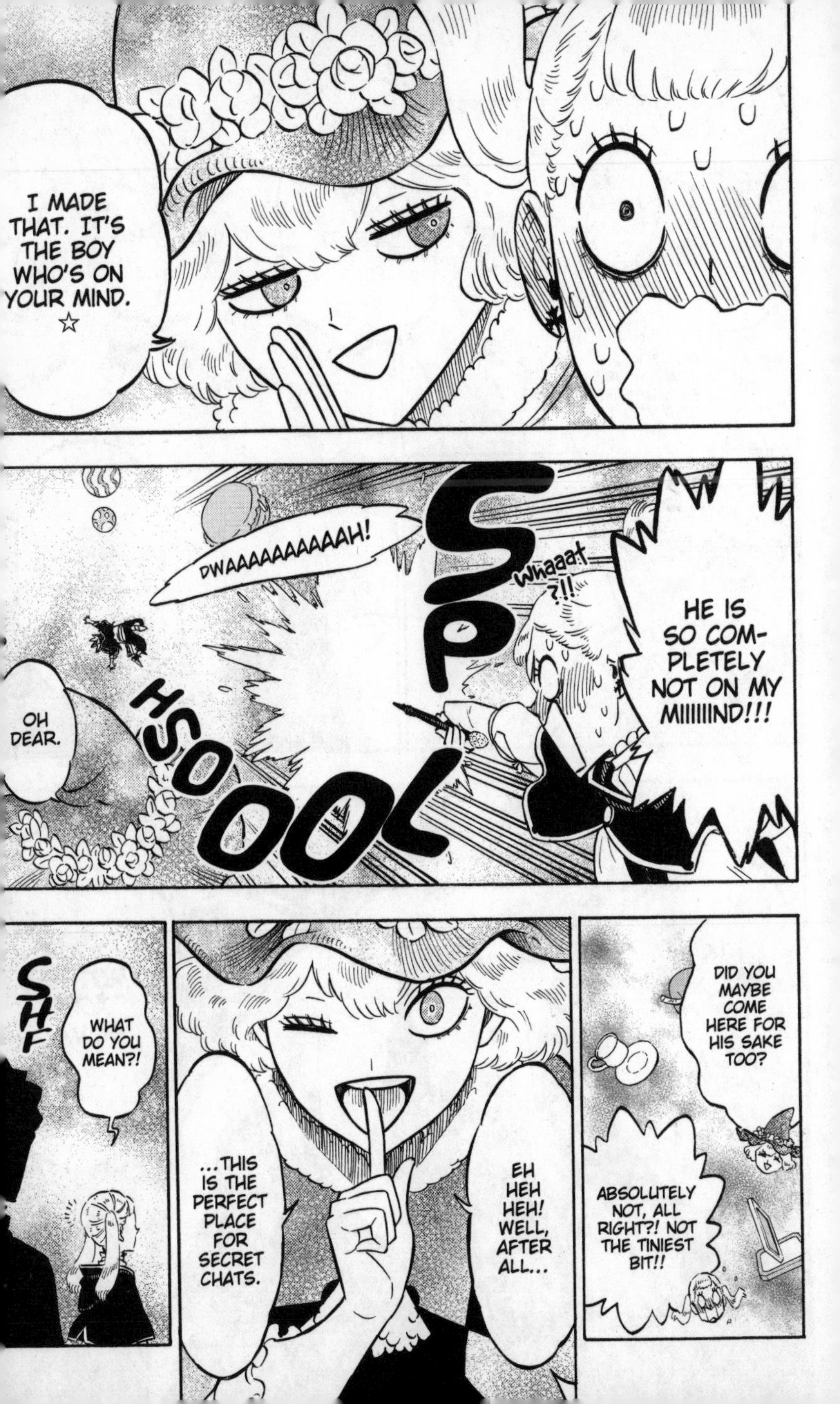
I MADE THAT. IT'S THE BOY WHO'S ON YOUR MIND. ☆
HE IS SO COMPLETELY NOT ON MY MIIIIIIND!!!
Whaaat?!!
SPLOOOSH
DWAAAAAAAAAAAH!
OH DEAR.
DID YOU MAYBE COME HERE FOR HIS SAKE TOO?
ABSOLUTELY NOT, ALL RIGHT?! NOT THE TINIEST BIT!!
EH HEH HEH! WELL, AFTER ALL...
...THIS IS THE PERFECT PLACE FOR SECRET CHATS.
SHF
WHAT DO YOU MEAN?!

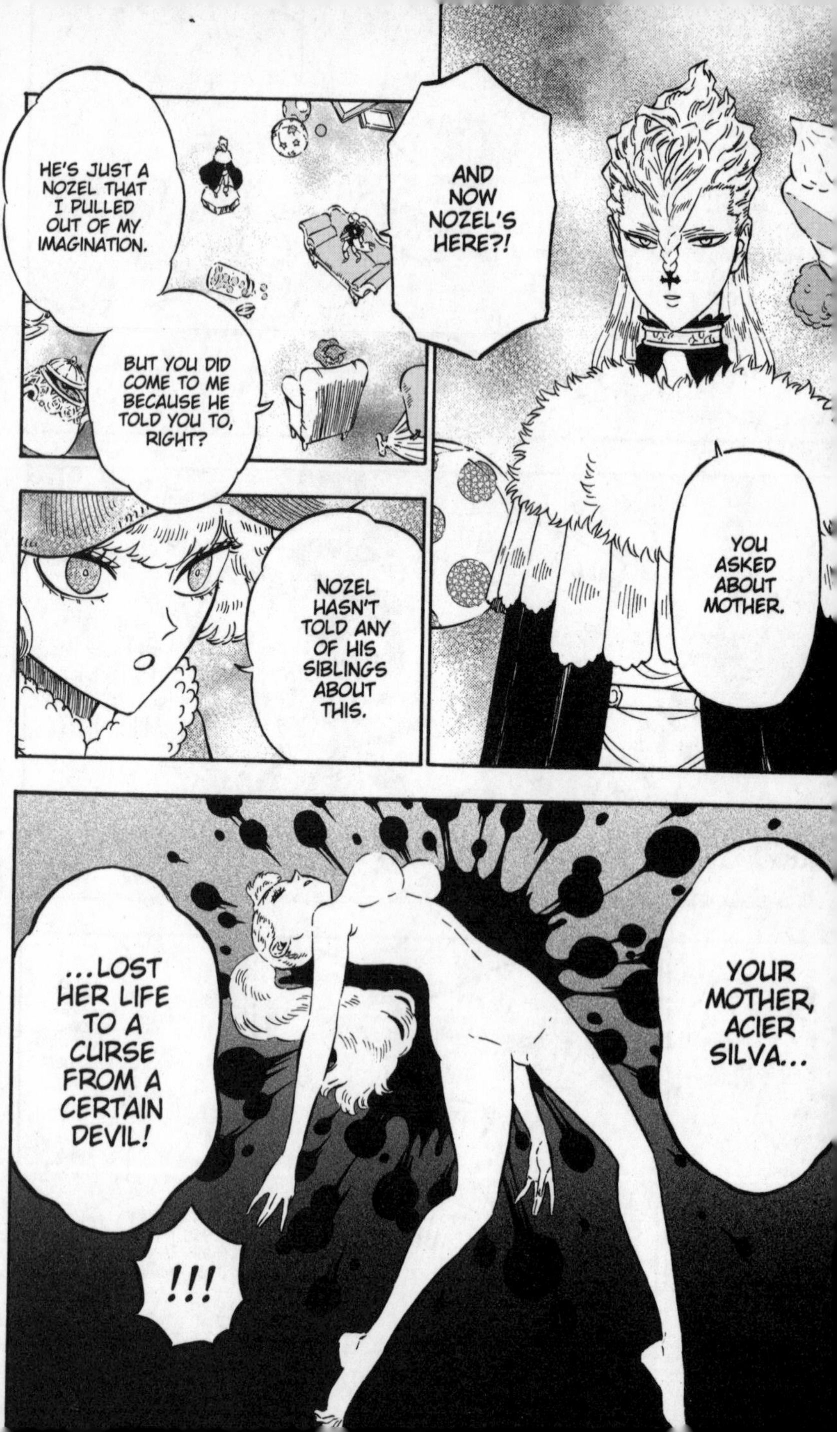
AND NOW NOZEL'S HERE?!
YOU ASKED ABOUT MOTHER.
HE'S JUST A NOZEL THAT I PULLED OUT OF MY IMAGINATION.
BUT YOU DID COME TO ME BECAUSE HE TOLD YOU TO, RIGHT?
NOZEL HASN'T TOLD ANY OF HIS SIBLINGS ABOUT THIS.
YOUR MOTHER, ACIER SILVA...
...LOST HER LIFE TO A CURSE FROM A CERTAIN DEVIL!
!!!

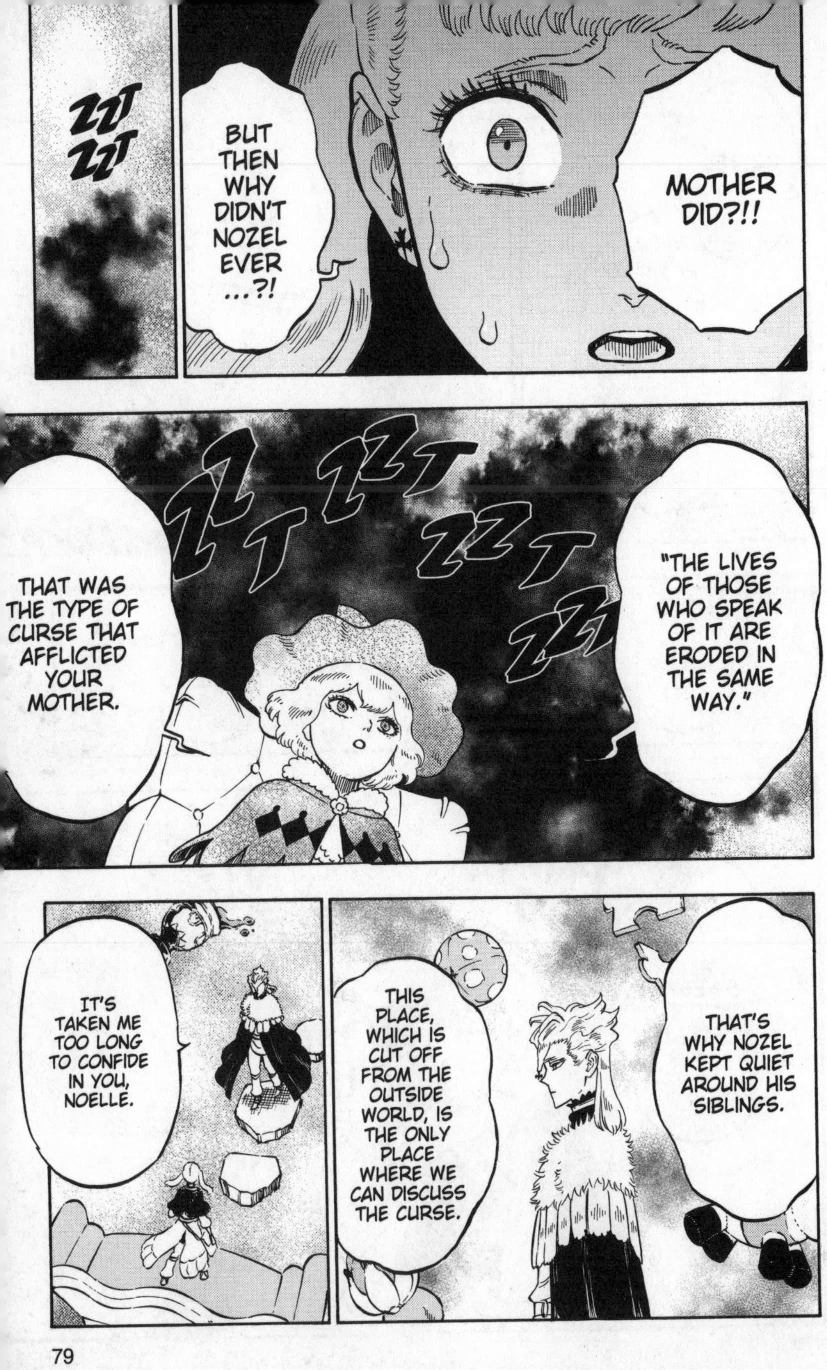
MOTHER DID?!!
BUT THEN WHY DIDN'T NOZEL EVER ...?!
ZZT ZZT
"THE LIVES OF THOSE WHO SPEAK OF IT ARE ERODED IN THE SAME WAY."
ZZT ZZT ZZT ZZT
THAT WAS THE TYPE OF CURSE THAT AFFLICTED YOUR MOTHER.
THAT'S WHY NOZEL KEPT QUIET AROUND HIS SIBLINGS.
THIS PLACE, WHICH IS CUT OFF FROM THE OUTSIDE WORLD, IS THE ONLY PLACE WHERE WE CAN DISCUSS THE CURSE.
IT'S TAKEN ME TOO LONG TO CONFIDE IN YOU, NOELLE.

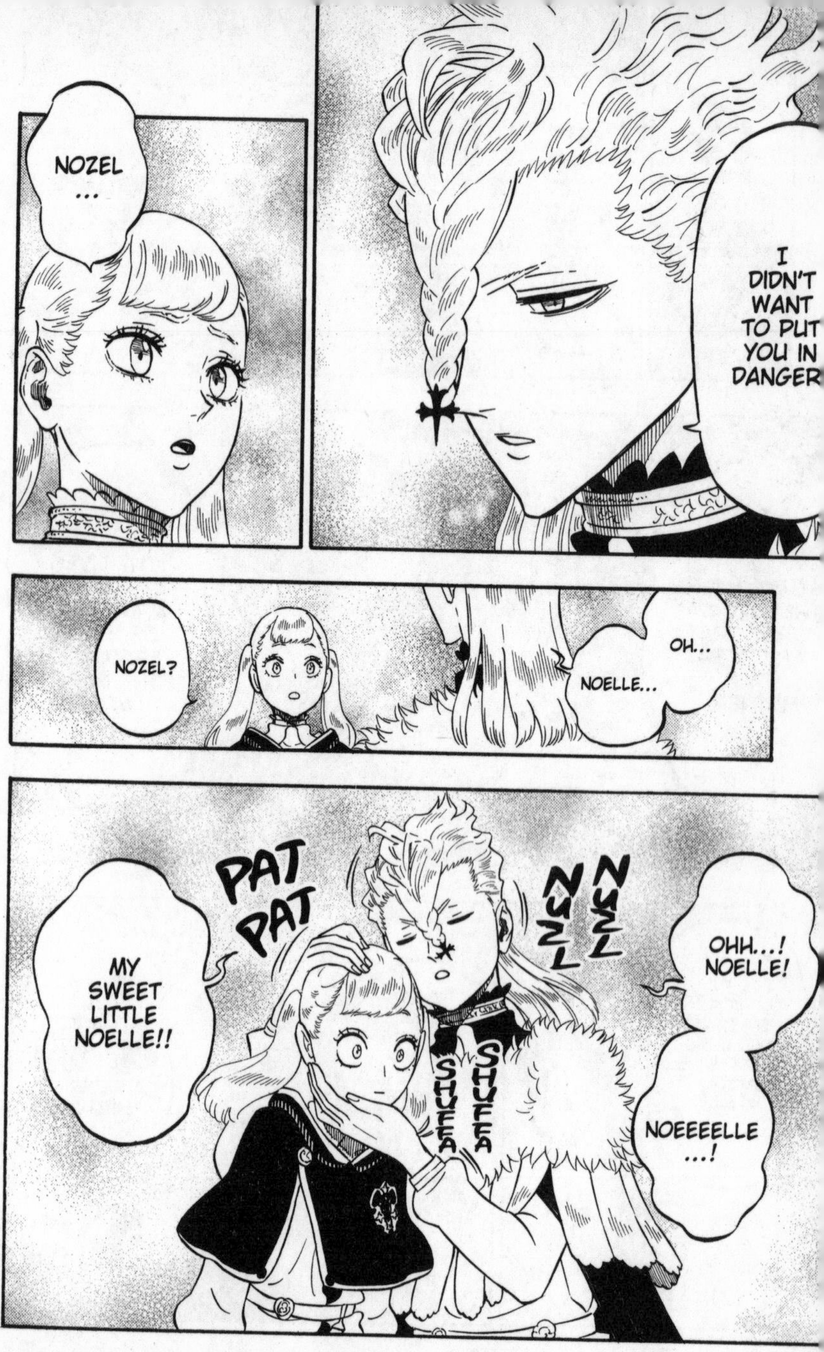
I DIDN'T WANT TO PUT YOU IN DANGER
NOZEL ...
OH... NOELLE...
NOZEL?
OHH...! NOELLE!
NOEEEELLE ...!
NUZL NUZL
SHUFFA SHUFFA
PAT PAT
MY SWEET LITTLE NOELLE!!

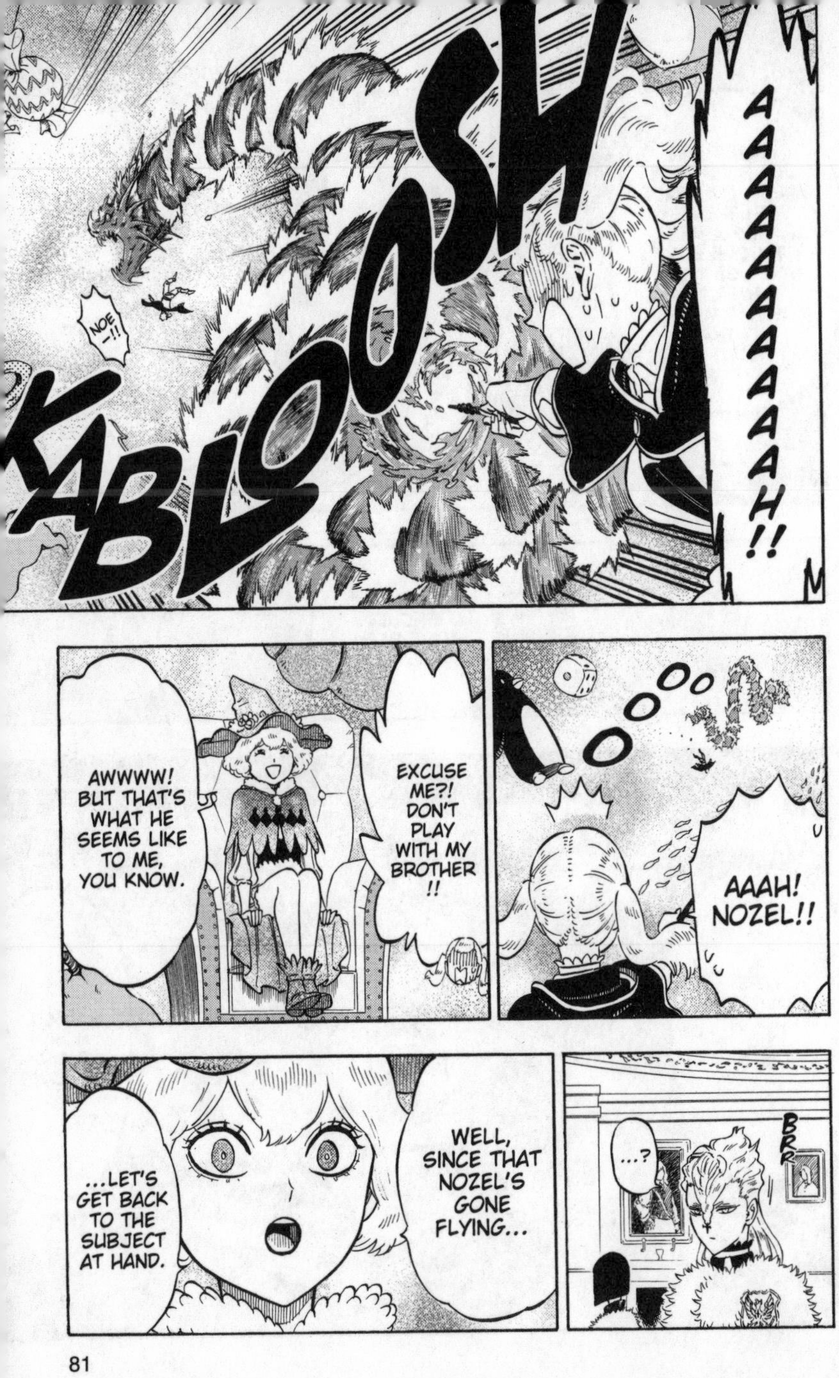
AAAAAAAAAAAH!!
KABLOOOSH
NOE—!!
OOOOO
AAAH! NOZEL!!
EXCUSE ME?! DON'T PLAY WITH MY BROTHER!!
AWWWW! BUT THAT'S WHAT HE SEEMS LIKE TO ME, YOU KNOW.
BRR
...?
WELL, SINCE THAT NOZEL'S GONE FLYING...
...LET'S GET BACK TO THE SUBJECT AT HAND.

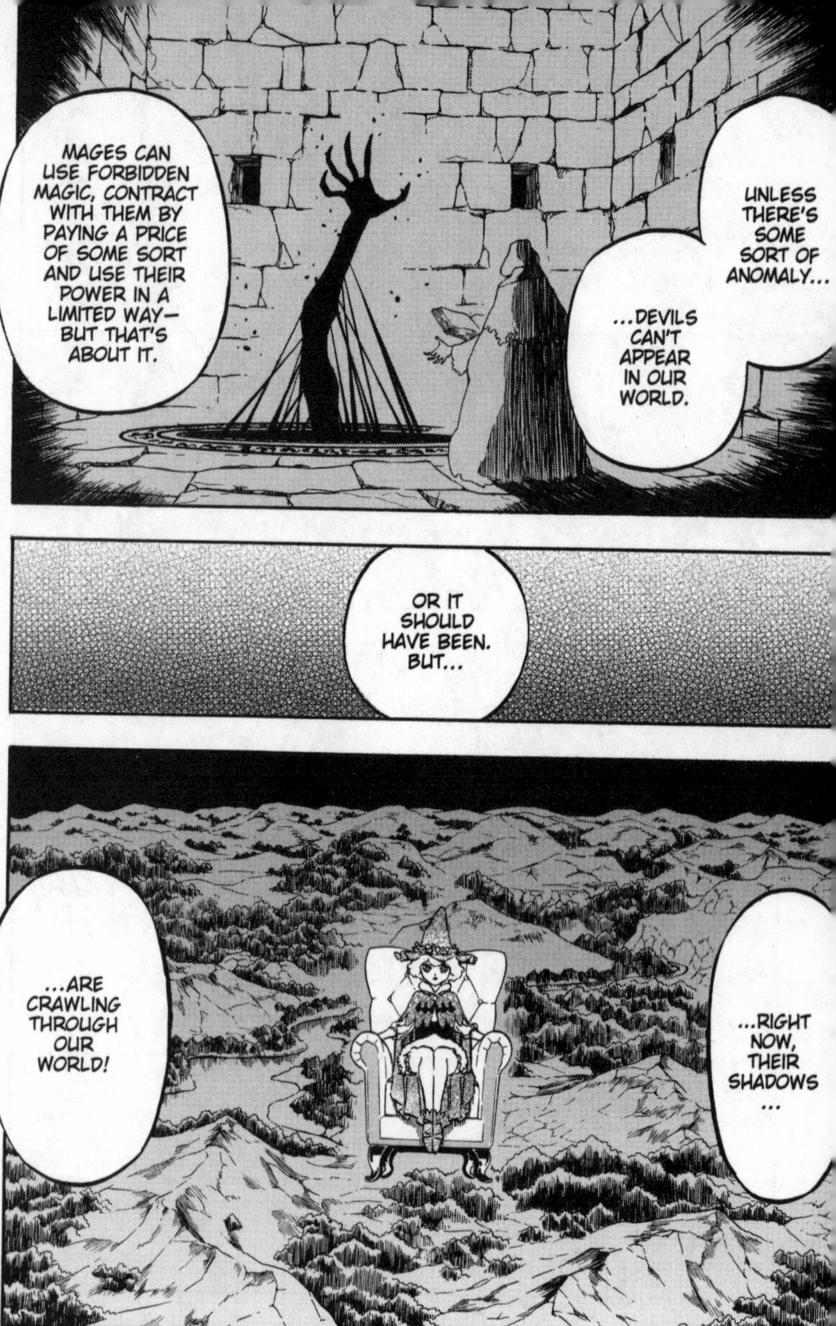
UNLESS THERE'S SOME SORT OF ANOMALY...
...DEVILS CAN'T APPEAR IN OUR WORLD.
MAGES CAN USE FORBIDDEN MAGIC, CONTRACT WITH THEM BY PAYING A PRICE OF SOME SORT AND USE THEIR POWER IN A LIMITED WAY—BUT THAT'S ABOUT IT.
OR IT SHOULD HAVE BEEN. BUT...
...RIGHT NOW, THEIR SHADOWS ...
...ARE CRAWLING THROUGH OUR WORLD!

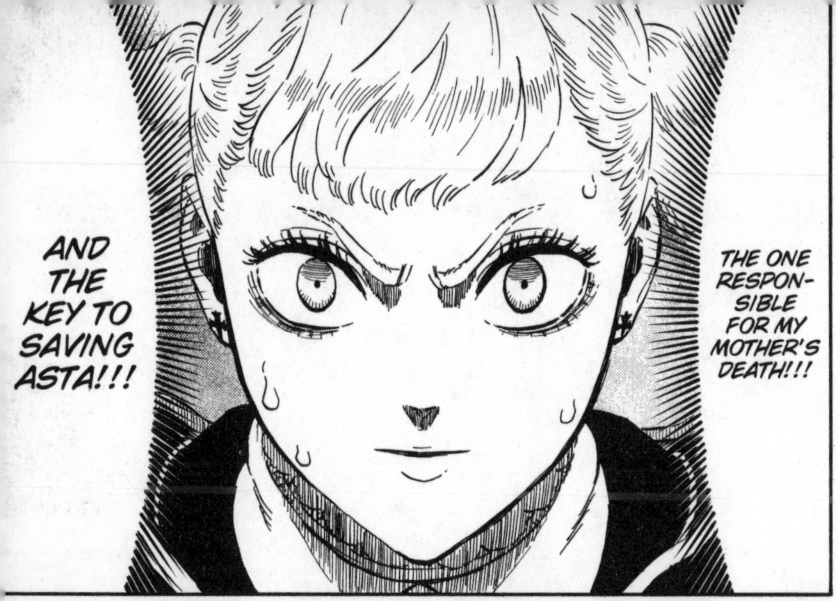
THE ONE RESPON-SIBLE FOR MY MOTHER'S DEATH!!!
AND THE KEY TO SAVING ASTA!!!

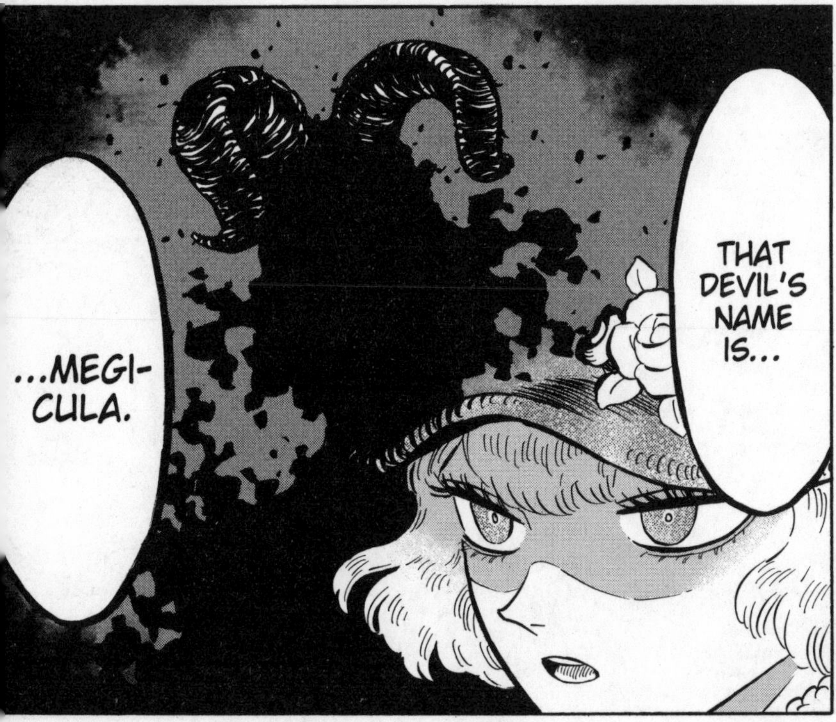
THAT DEVIL'S NAME IS...
...MEGI-CULA.

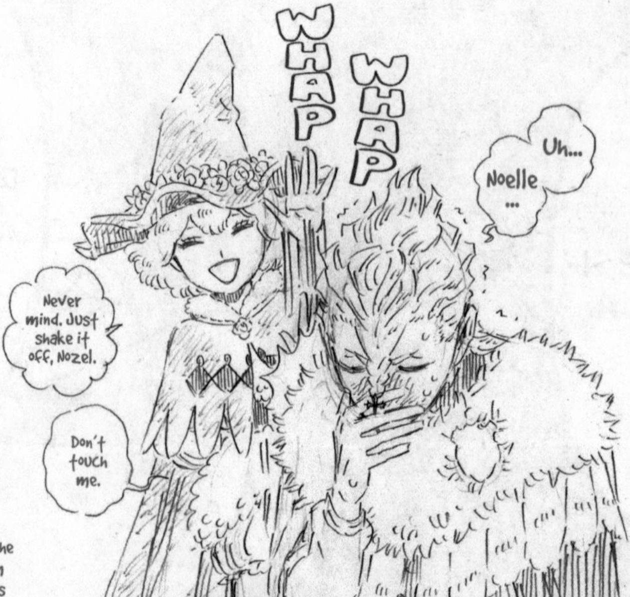
WHAP
WHAP
Uh... Noelle...
Never mind. Just shake it off, Nozel.
Don't touch me.

*This Nozel is the one from Dorothy's imagination.

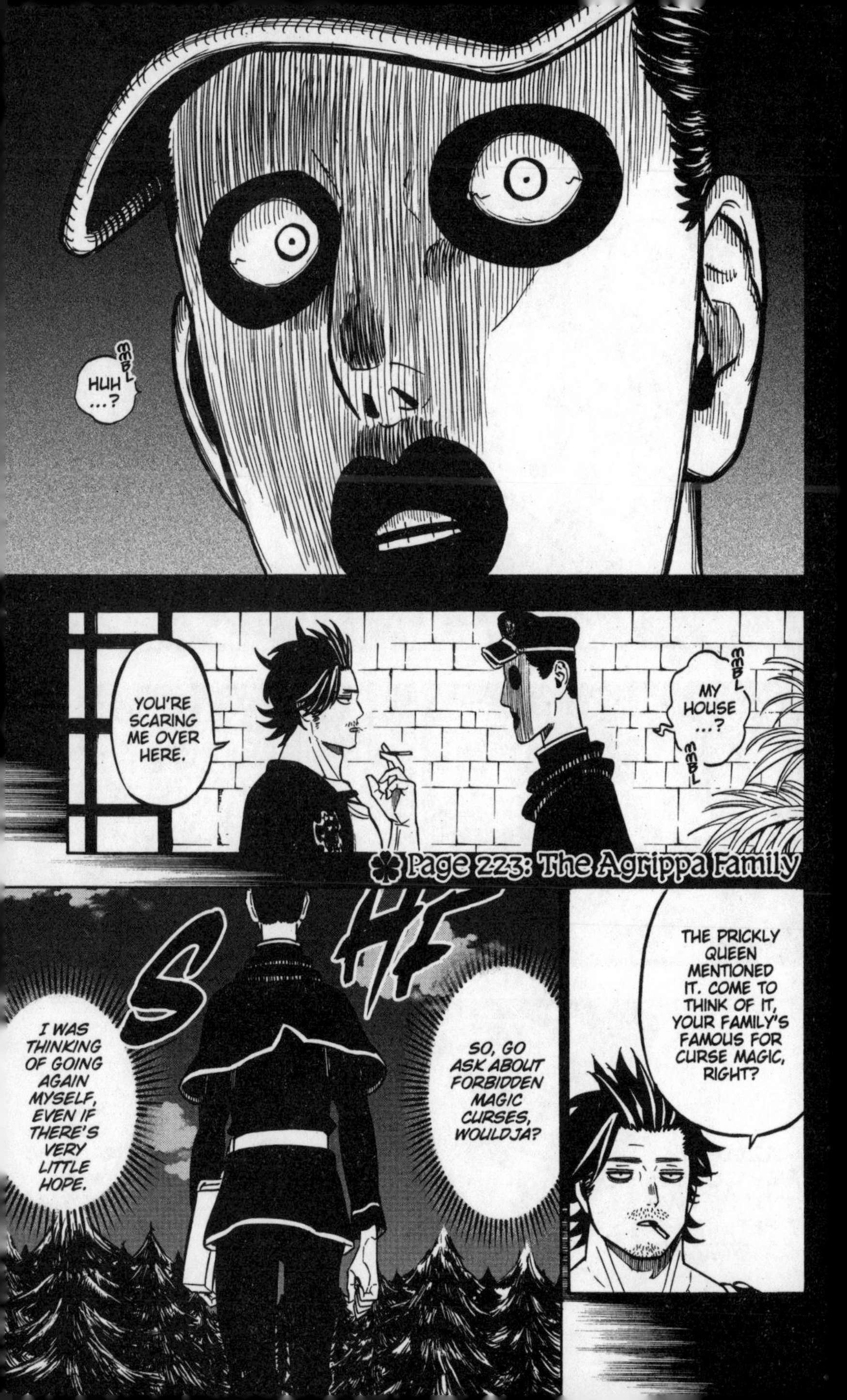
MMBL
HUH ...?
MMBL
MY HOUSE ...?
MMBL
YOU'RE SCARING ME OVER HERE.
Page 223: The Agrippa Family
THE PRICKLY QUEEN MENTIONED IT. COME TO THINK OF IT, YOUR FAMILY'S FAMOUS FOR CURSE MAGIC, RIGHT?
SHF
SO, GO ASK ABOUT FORBIDDEN MAGIC CURSES, WOULDJA?
I WAS THINKING OF GOING AGAIN MYSELF, EVEN IF THERE'S VERY LITTLE HOPE.

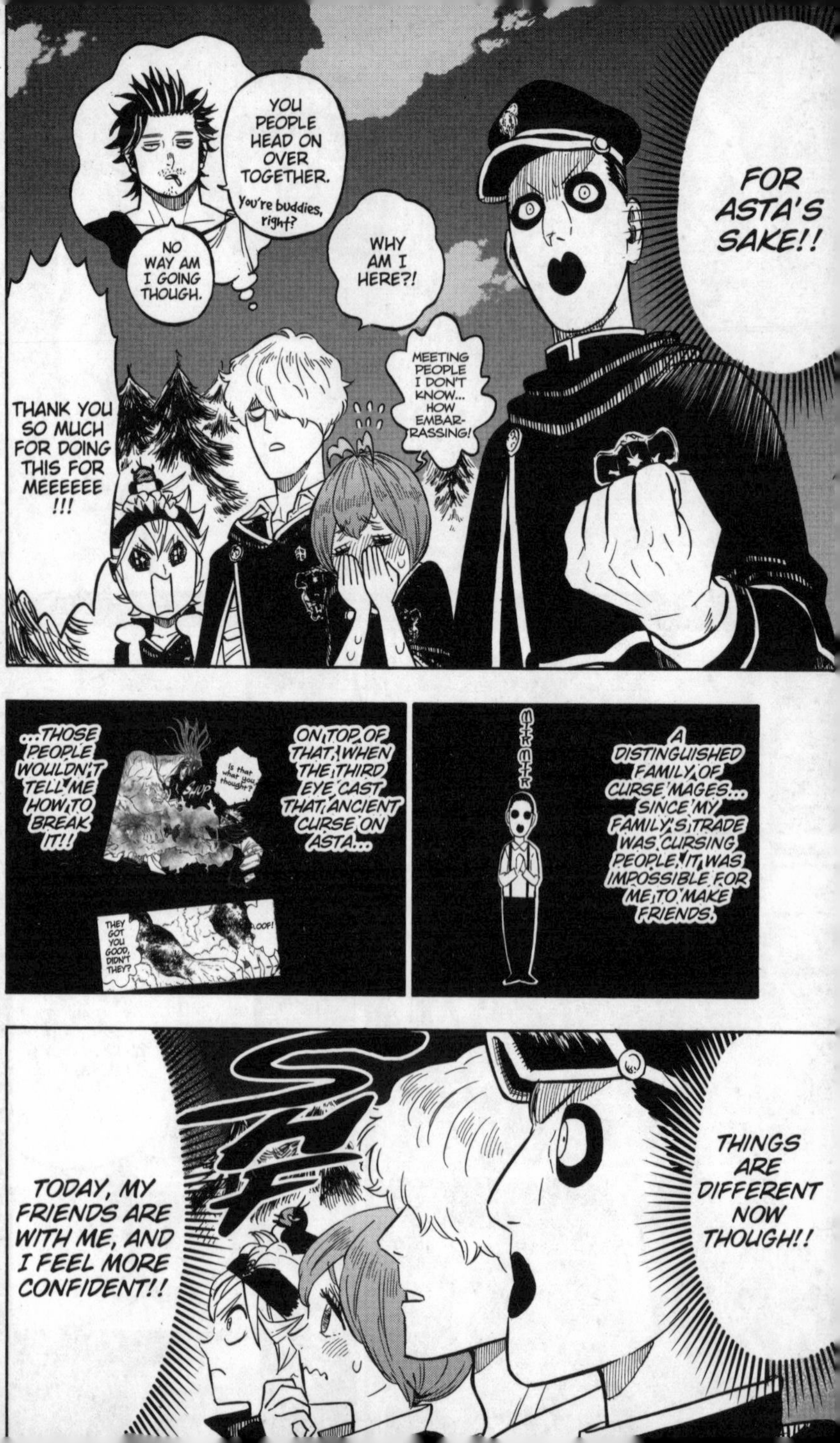
FOR ASTA'S SAKE!!
WHY AM I HERE?!
YOU PEOPLE HEAD ON OVER TOGETHER.
you're buddies, right?
NO WAY AM I GOING THOUGH.
MEETING PEOPLE I DON'T KNOW... HOW EMBARRASSING!
THANK YOU SO MUCH FOR DOING THIS FOR MEEEEEE!!!
A DISTINGUISHED FAMILY OF CURSE MAGES... SINCE MY FAMILY'S TRADE WAS CURSING PEOPLE, IT WAS IMPOSSIBLE FOR ME TO MAKE FRIENDS.
ON TOP OF THAT, WHEN THE THIRD EYE CAST THAT ANCIENT CURSE ON ASTA...
...THOSE PEOPLE WOULDN'T TELL ME HOW TO BREAK IT!!
Is that what you thought?
OOF!
THEY GOT YOU GOOD, DIDN'T THEY?
THINGS ARE DIFFERENT NOW THOUGH!!
TODAY, MY FRIENDS ARE WITH ME, AND I FEEL MORE CONFIDENT!!

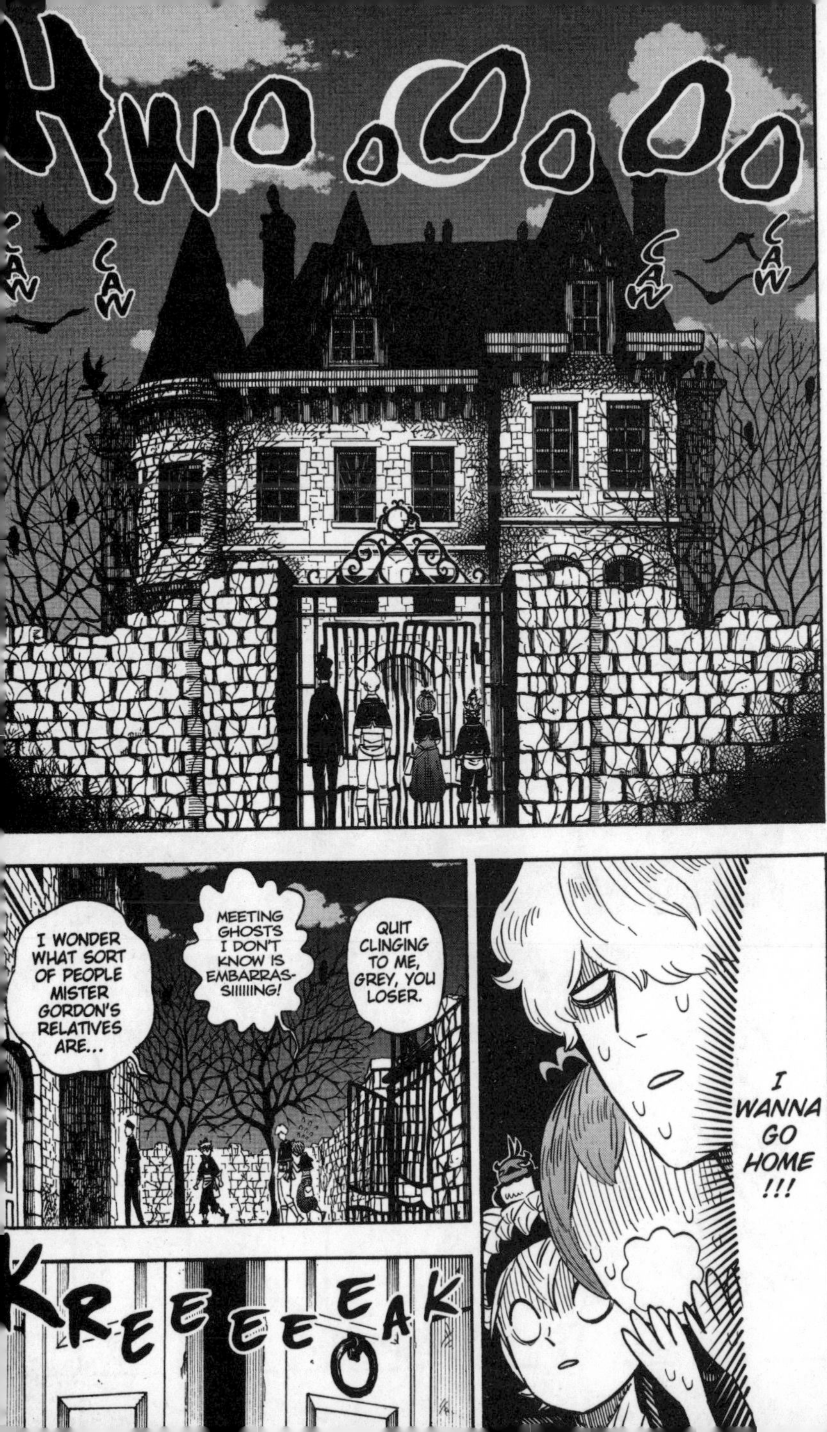
HWOOOOOOO
CAW CAW
CAW CAW
I WANNA GO HOME!!!
QUIT CLINGING TO ME, GREY, YOU LOSER.
MEETING GHOSTS I DON'T KNOW IS EMBARRAS-SIIIIIING!
I WONDER WHAT SORT OF PEOPLE MISTER GORDON'S RELATIVES ARE...
KREEEEEAK

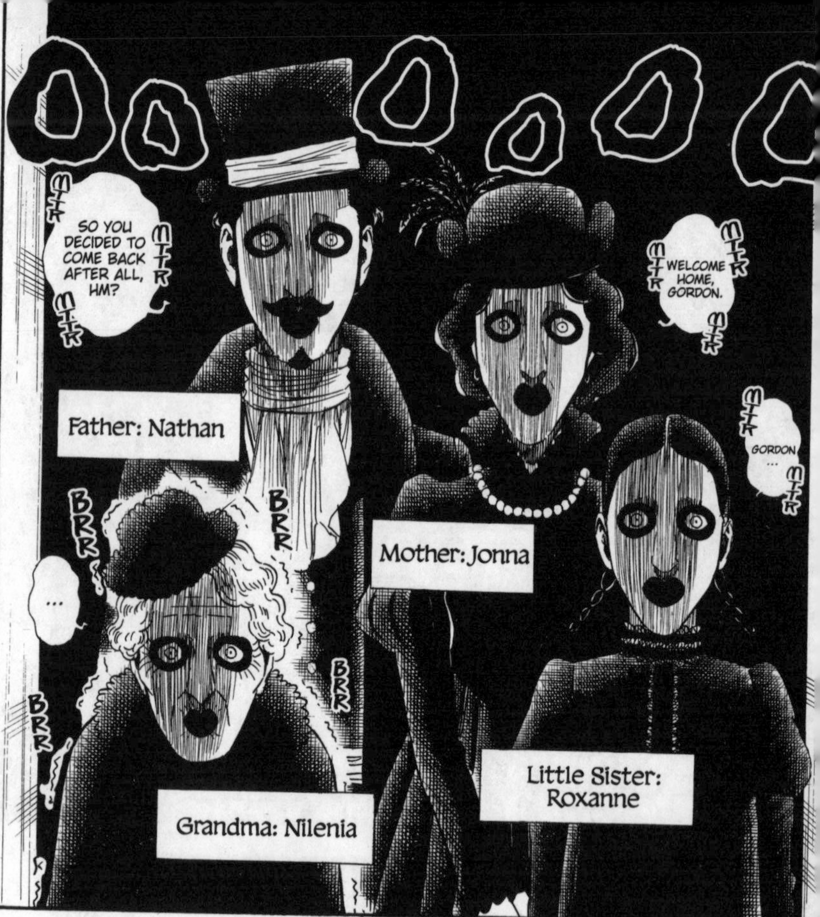
MTR MTR
WELCOME HOME, GORDON.
MTR MTR
MTR MTR
SO YOU DECIDED TO COME BACK AFTER ALL, HM?
MTR MTR
MTR
GORDON ...
MTR
Father: Nathan
Mother: Jonna
Little Sister: Roxanne
BRR
BRR
...
BRR
BRR
Grandma: Nilenia

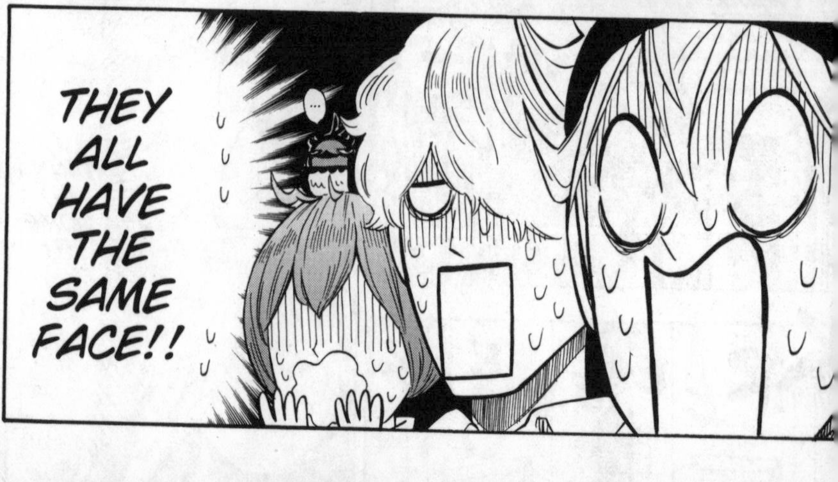
...
THEY ALL HAVE THE SAME FACE!!

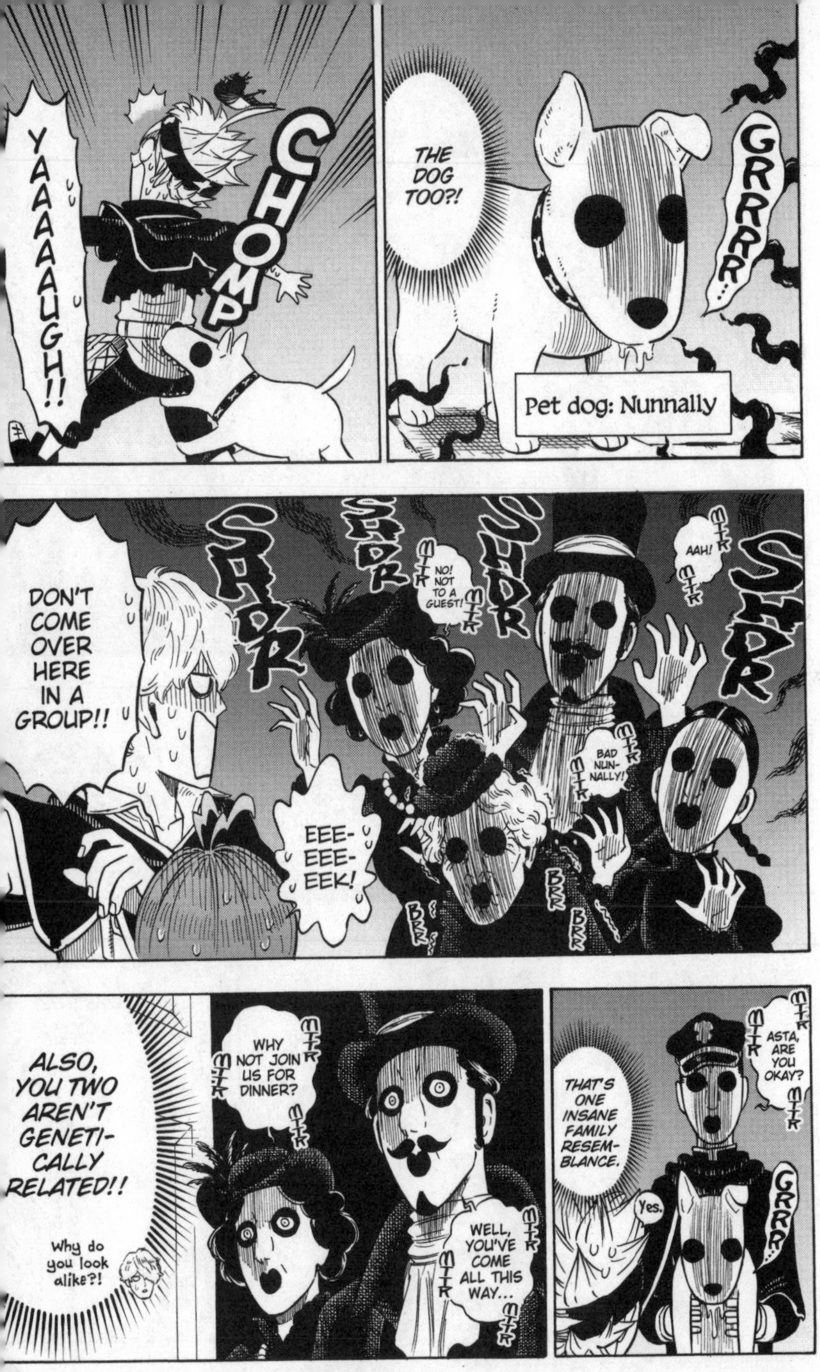
GRRRR...
THE DOG TOO?!
Pet dog: Nunnally
CHOMP
YAAAAAUGH!!
SHDR
MTTR
AAH!
MTTR
BAD NUN-NALLY!
MTTR
SHDR
NO! NOT TO A GUEST!
MTTR
SHDR
SHDR
EEE-EEE-EEK!
DON'T COME OVER HERE IN A GROUP!!
BRR
BRR
BRR
MTTR
ASTA, ARE YOU OKAY?
MTTR
THAT'S ONE INSANE FAMILY RESEMBLANCE.
GRRR...
Yes.
MTTR
WHY NOT JOIN US FOR DINNER?
MTTR
WELL, YOU'VE COME ALL THIS WAY...
MTTR
ALSO, YOU TWO AREN'T GENETICALLY RELATED!!
Why do you look alike?!

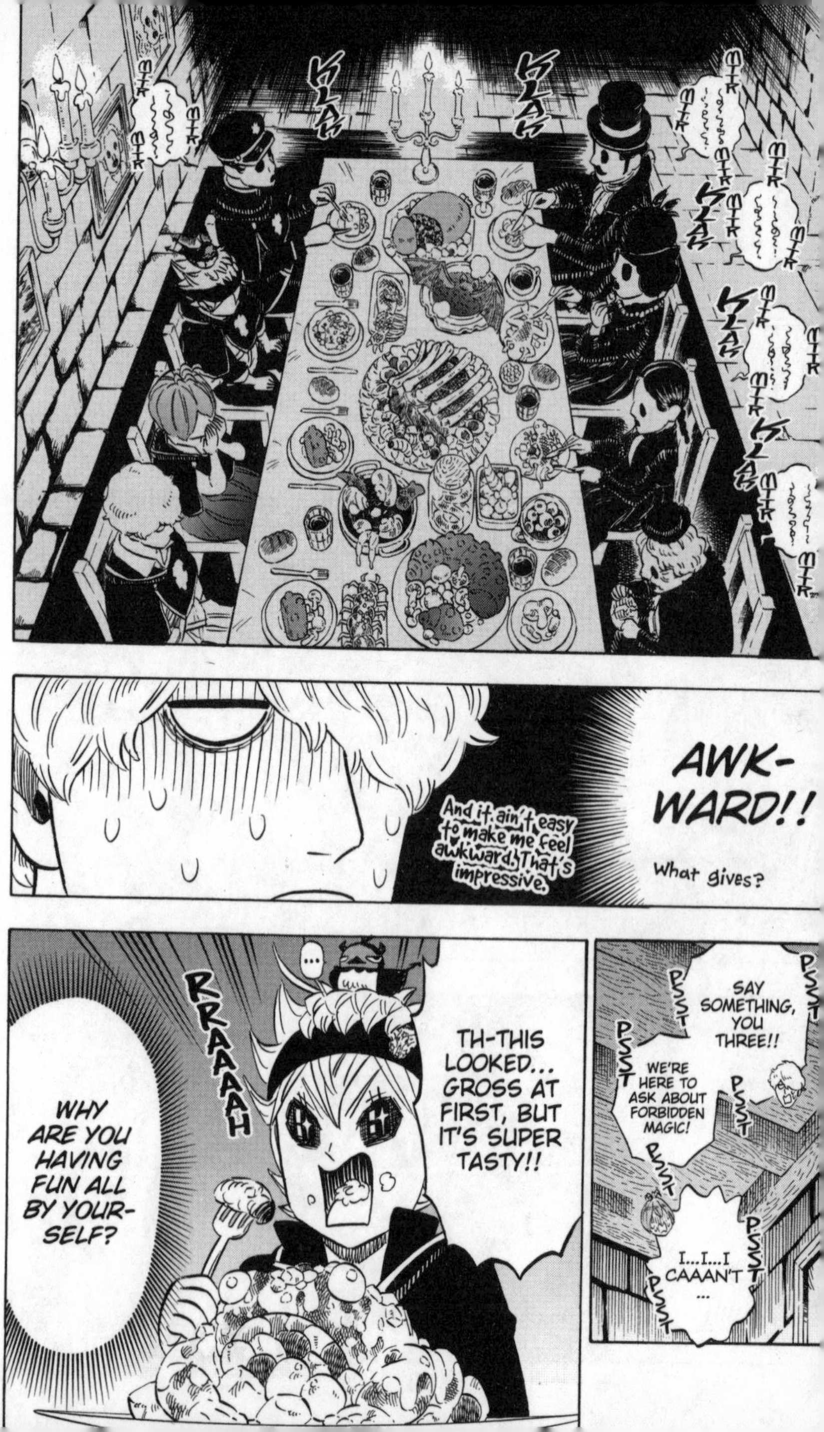
MTR MTR
KLAK
MTR MTR MTR
KLAK
MTR MTR
KLAK
MTR MTR
KLAK
MTR MTR
KLAK
MTR MTR
AWK-WARD!!
What gives?
And it ain't easy to make me feel awkward. That's impressive.
PSST PSST
SAY SOMETHING, YOU THREE!!
PSST PSST
WE'RE HERE TO ASK ABOUT FORBIDDEN MAGIC!
PSST PSST
I...I...I CAAAN'T ...
PSST
...
RRAAAAH
TH-THIS LOOKED... GROSS AT FIRST, BUT IT'S SUPER TASTY!!
WHY ARE YOU HAVING FUN ALL BY YOURSELF?

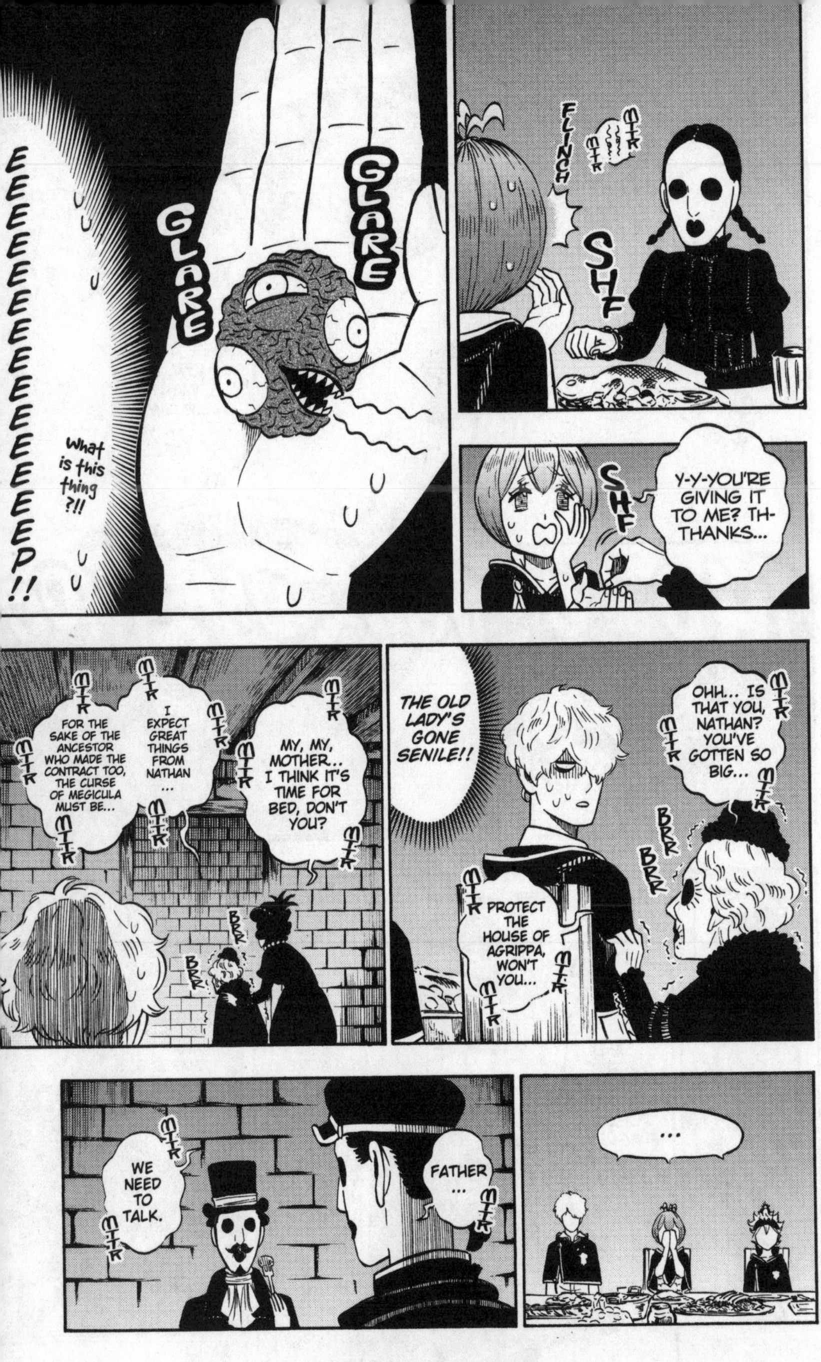

FLINCH
MTTR
MTTR
SHF
SHF
Y-Y-YOU'RE GIVING IT TO ME? TH-THANKS...
GLARE
GLARE
EEEEEEEEEEEEEEEP!!
what is this thing?!!
OHH... IS THAT YOU, NATHAN? YOU'VE GOTTEN SO BIG...
MTTR
BRR
BRR
THE OLD LADY'S GONE SENILE!!
PROTECT THE HOUSE OF AGRIPPA, WON'T YOU...
MTTR
MY, MY, MOTHER... I THINK IT'S TIME FOR BED, DON'T YOU?
MTTR
I EXPECT GREAT THINGS FROM NATHAN...
MTTR
FOR THE SAKE OF THE ANCESTOR WHO MADE THE CONTRACT TOO, THE CURSE OF MEGICULA MUST BE...
MTTR
BRR
BRR
...
FATHER...
MTTR
WE NEED TO TALK.
MTTR

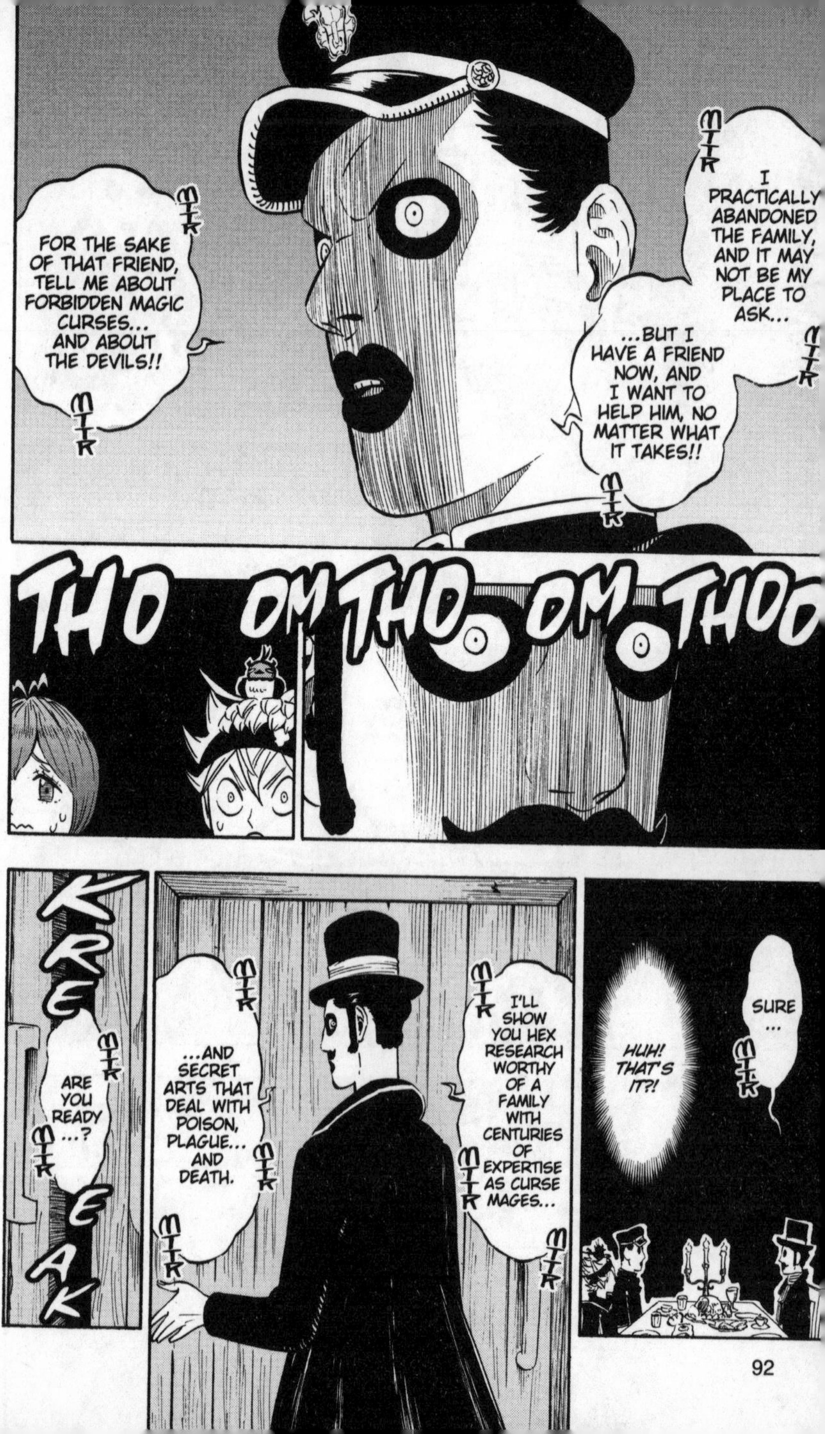
I PRACTICALLY ABANDONED THE FAMILY, AND IT MAY NOT BE MY PLACE TO ASK...
...BUT I HAVE A FRIEND NOW, AND I WANT TO HELP HIM, NO MATTER WHAT IT TAKES!!
FOR THE SAKE OF THAT FRIEND, TELL ME ABOUT FORBIDDEN MAGIC CURSES... AND ABOUT THE DEVILS!!
THOOM THOOM THOOM
SURE...
HUH! THAT'S IT?!
I'LL SHOW YOU HEX RESEARCH WORTHY OF A FAMILY WITH CENTURIES OF EXPERTISE AS CURSE MAGES...
...AND SECRET ARTS THAT DEAL WITH POISON, PLAGUE... AND DEATH.
KREEAK
ARE YOU READY...?

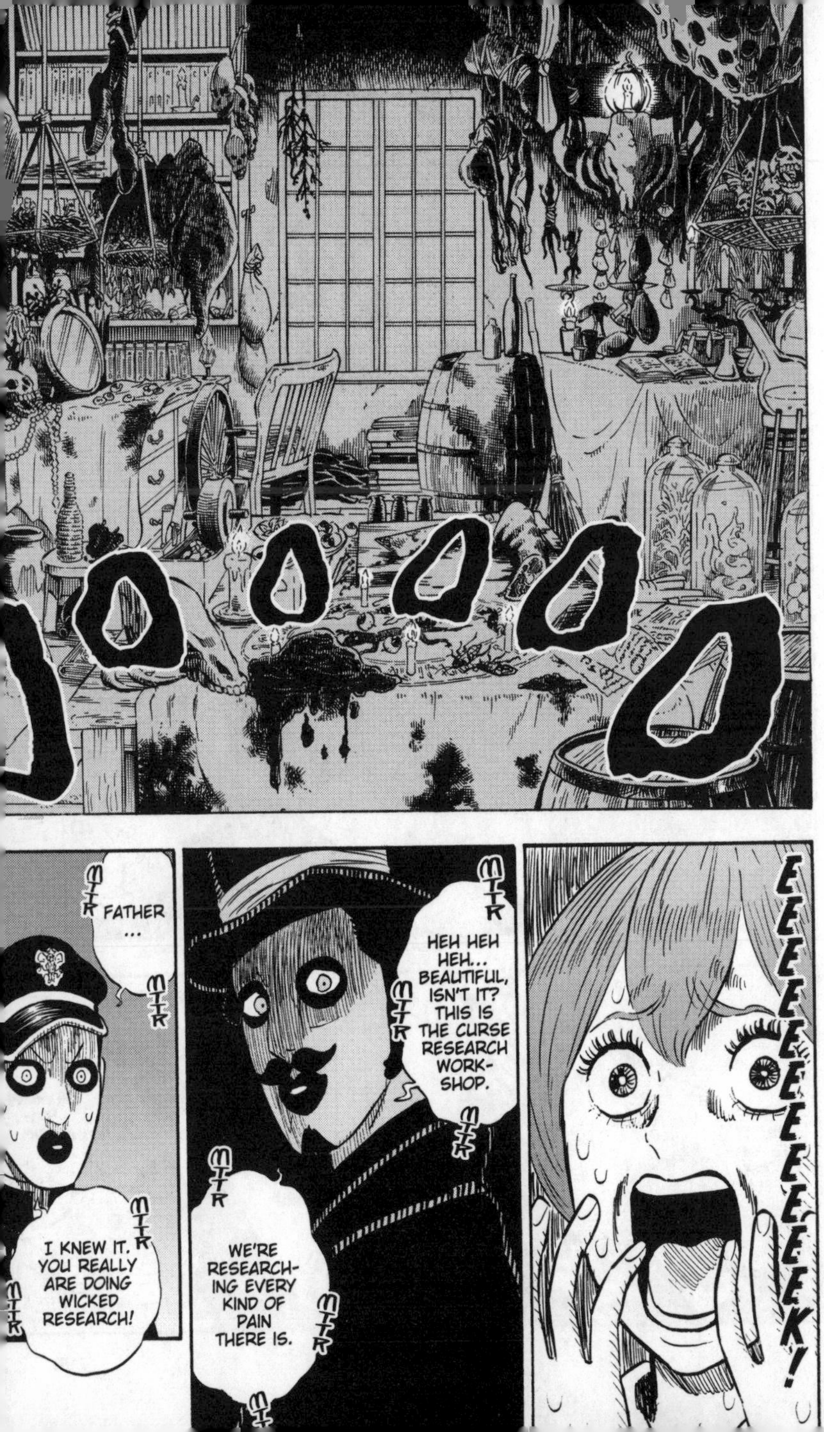
EEEEEEEEEEEEEK!
MTTR
HEH HEH HEH... BEAUTIFUL, ISN'T IT? THIS IS THE CURSE RESEARCH WORKSHOP.
MTTR
WE'RE RESEARCHING EVERY KIND OF PAIN THERE IS.
MTTR
FATHER...
MTTR
I KNEW IT. YOU REALLY ARE DOING WICKED RESEARCH!

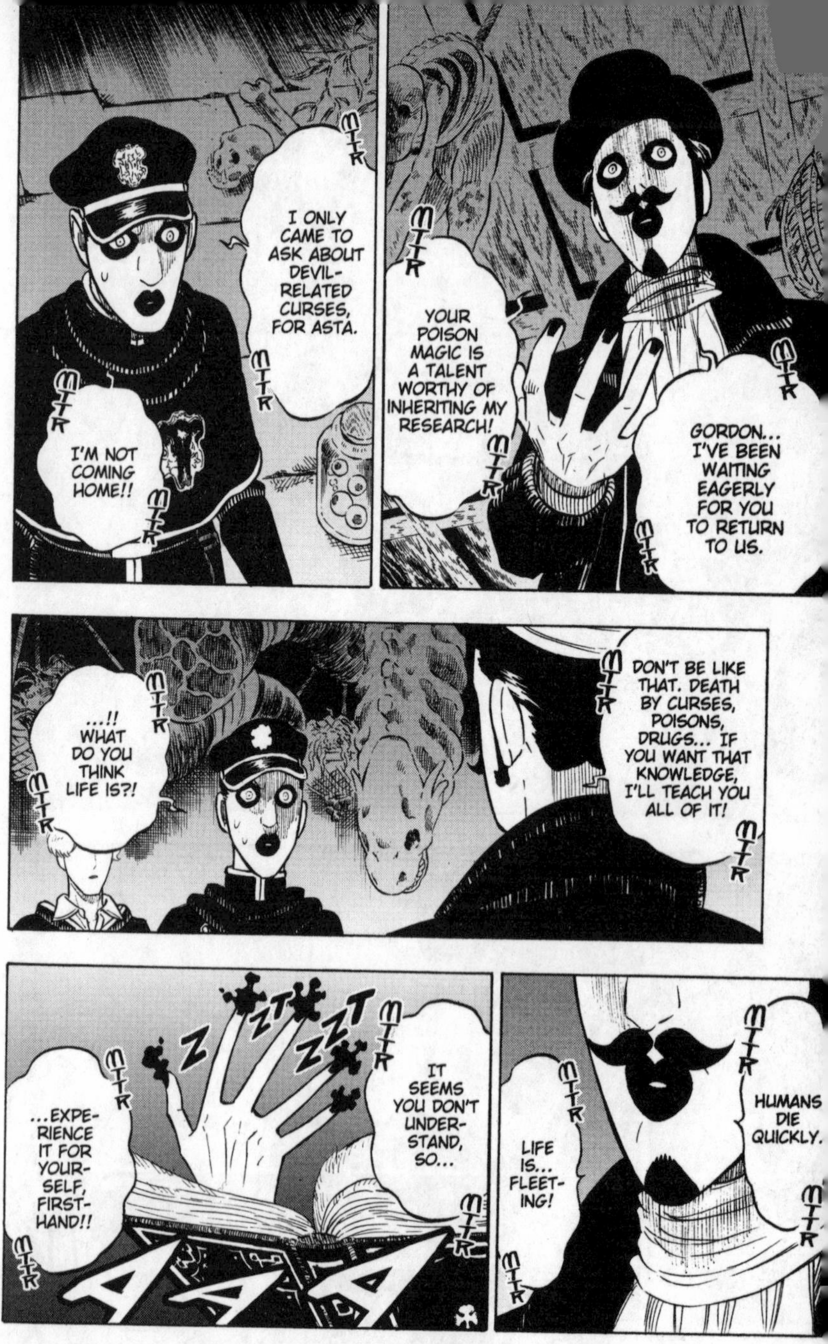

MTTR
GORDON... I'VE BEEN WAITING EAGERLY FOR YOU TO RETURN TO US.
YOUR POISON MAGIC IS A TALENT WORTHY OF INHERITING MY RESEARCH!
MTTR
I ONLY CAME TO ASK ABOUT DEVIL-RELATED CURSES, FOR ASTA.
I'M NOT COMING HOME!!
MTTR
DON'T BE LIKE THAT. DEATH BY CURSES, POISONS, DRUGS... IF YOU WANT THAT KNOWLEDGE, I'LL TEACH YOU ALL OF IT!
...!! WHAT DO YOU THINK LIFE IS?!
MTTR
HUMANS DIE QUICKLY.
LIFE IS... FLEETING!
MTTR
IT SEEMS YOU DON'T UNDERSTAND, SO...
Z ZZT ZZZT
...EXPERIENCE IT FOR YOURSELF, FIRST-HAND!!

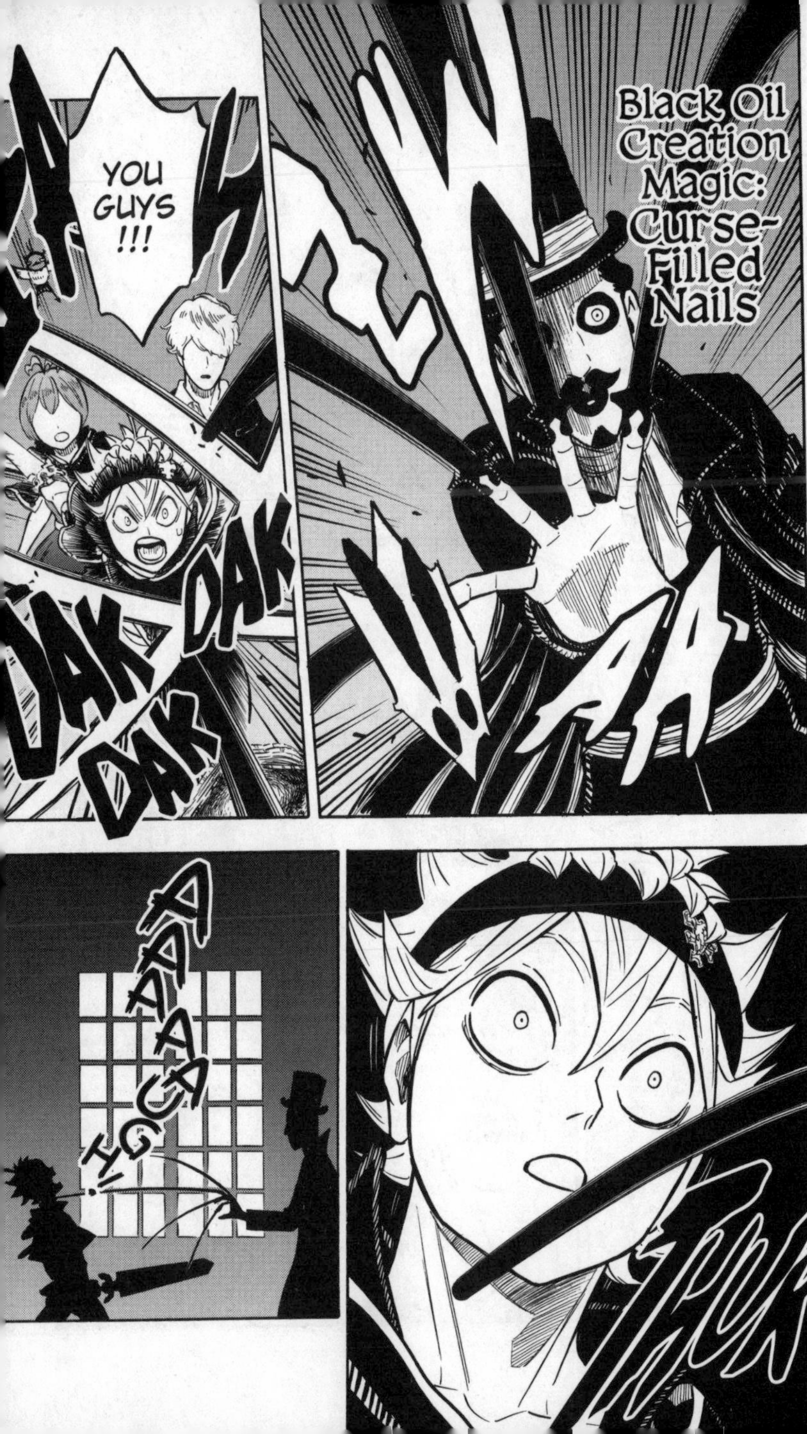
Black Oil Creation Magic: Curse-Filled Nails
YOU GUYS !!!
DAK DAK DAK
AAAAAAUGH!!

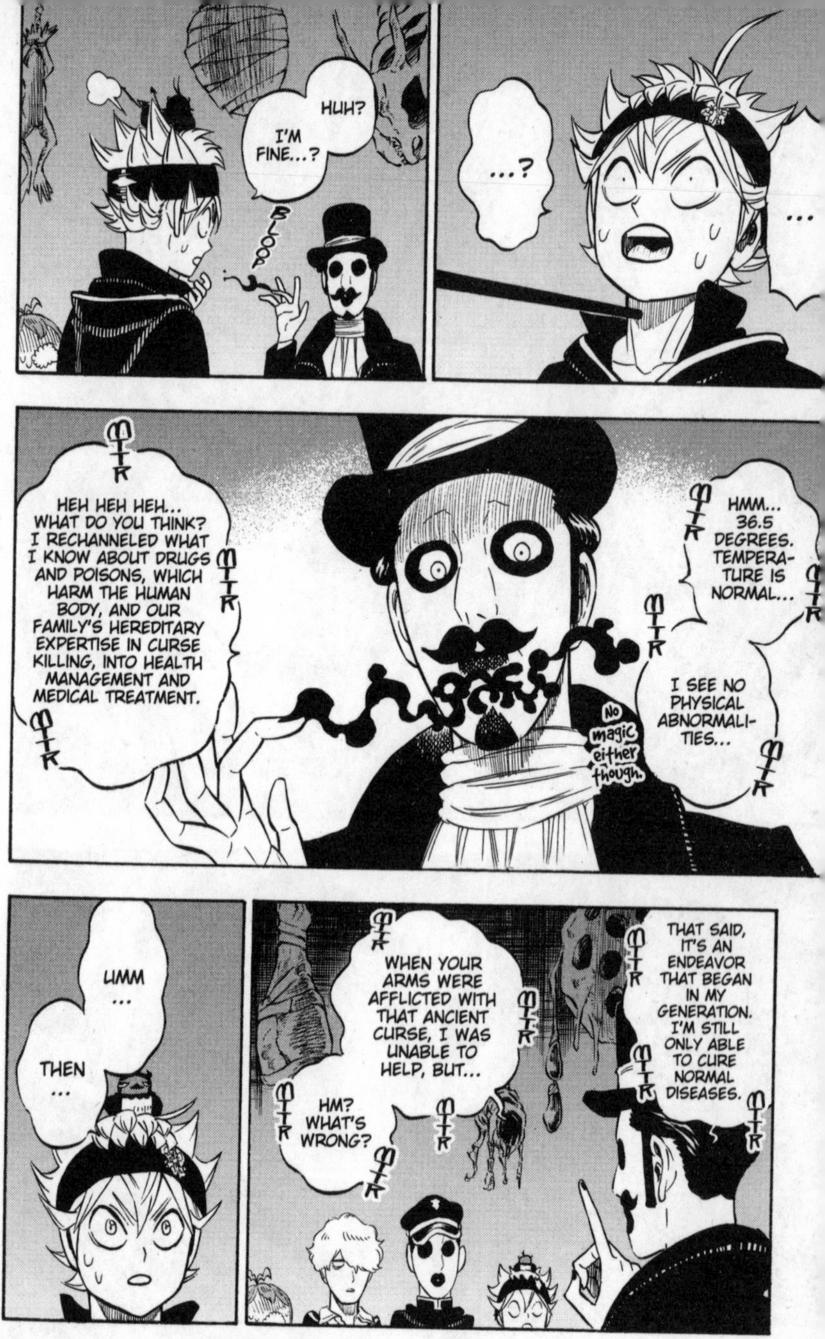
...
...?
HUH?
I'M FINE...?
BLOOP
HMM... 36.5 DEGREES. TEMPERATURE IS NORMAL...
I SEE NO PHYSICAL ABNORMALITIES...
No magic either though.
HEH HEH HEH... WHAT DO YOU THINK? I RECHANNELED WHAT I KNOW ABOUT DRUGS AND POISONS, WHICH HARM THE HUMAN BODY, AND OUR FAMILY'S HEREDITARY EXPERTISE IN CURSE KILLING, INTO HEALTH MANAGEMENT AND MEDICAL TREATMENT.
THAT SAID, IT'S AN ENDEAVOR THAT BEGAN IN MY GENERATION. I'M STILL ONLY ABLE TO CURE NORMAL DISEASES.
WHEN YOUR ARMS WERE AFFLICTED WITH THAT ANCIENT CURSE, I WAS UNABLE TO HELP, BUT...
HM? WHAT'S WRONG?
UMM...
THEN...

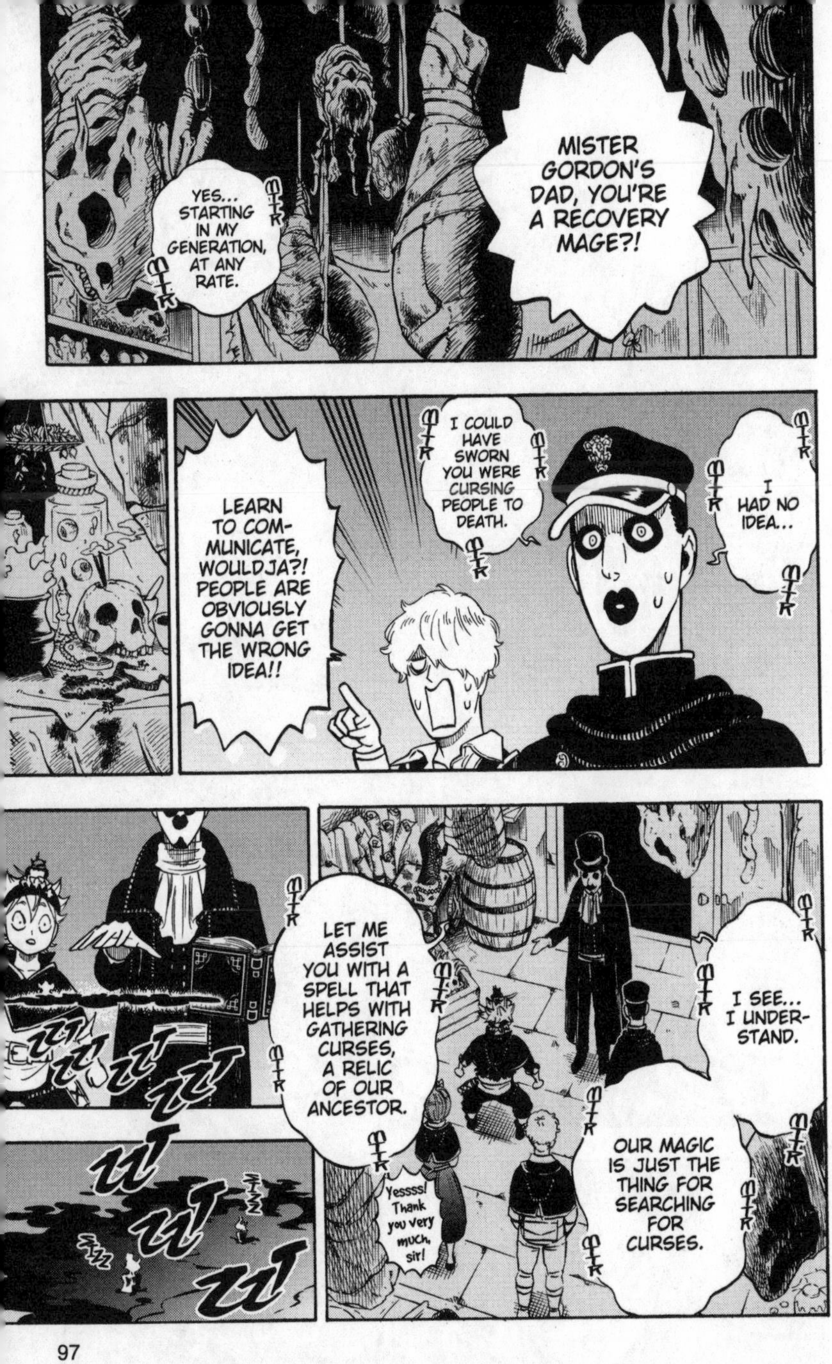
MISTER GORDON'S DAD, YOU'RE A RECOVERY MAGE?!
YES... STARTING IN MY GENERATION, AT ANY RATE.
I HAD NO IDEA...
I COULD HAVE SWORN YOU WERE CURSING PEOPLE TO DEATH.
LEARN TO COMMUNICATE, WOULDJA?! PEOPLE ARE OBVIOUSLY GONNA GET THE WRONG IDEA!!
I SEE... I UNDERSTAND.
OUR MAGIC IS JUST THE THING FOR SEARCHING FOR CURSES.
LET ME ASSIST YOU WITH A SPELL THAT HELPS WITH GATHERING CURSES, A RELIC OF OUR ANCESTOR.
Yessss! Thank you very much, sir!

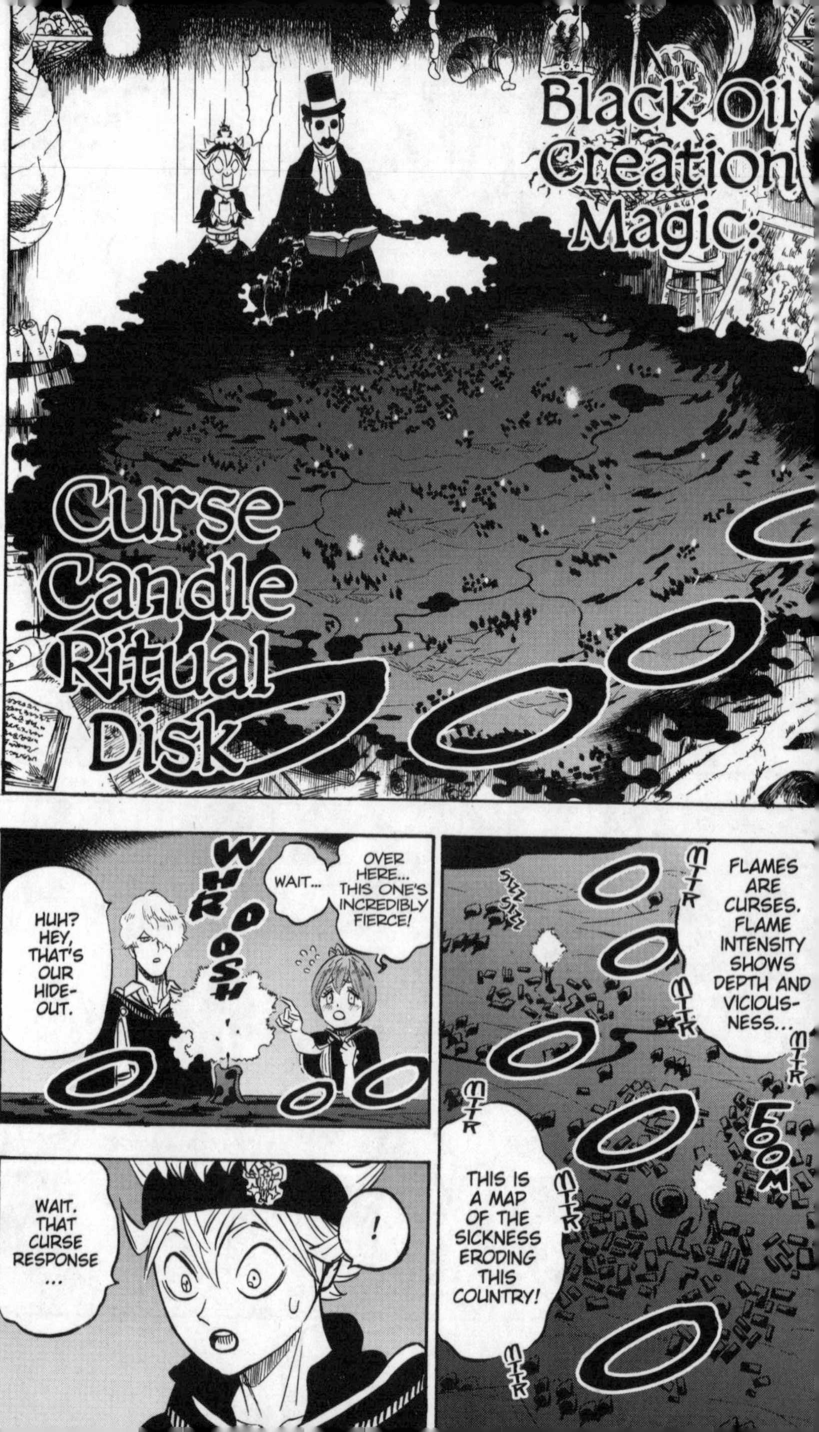

Black Oil Creation Magic:
Curse Candle Ritual Disk
FLAMES ARE CURSES. FLAME INTENSITY SHOWS DEPTH AND VICIOUSNESS...
MTTR
MTTR
SIZZ SIZZ
MTTR
FOOM
MTTR
MTTR
THIS IS A MAP OF THE SICKNESS ERODING THIS COUNTRY!
MTTR
OVER HERE... THIS ONE'S INCREDIBLY FIERCE!
WAIT...
WHROOOSH
HUH? HEY, THAT'S OUR HIDE-OUT.
!
WAIT. THAT CURSE RESPONSE ...

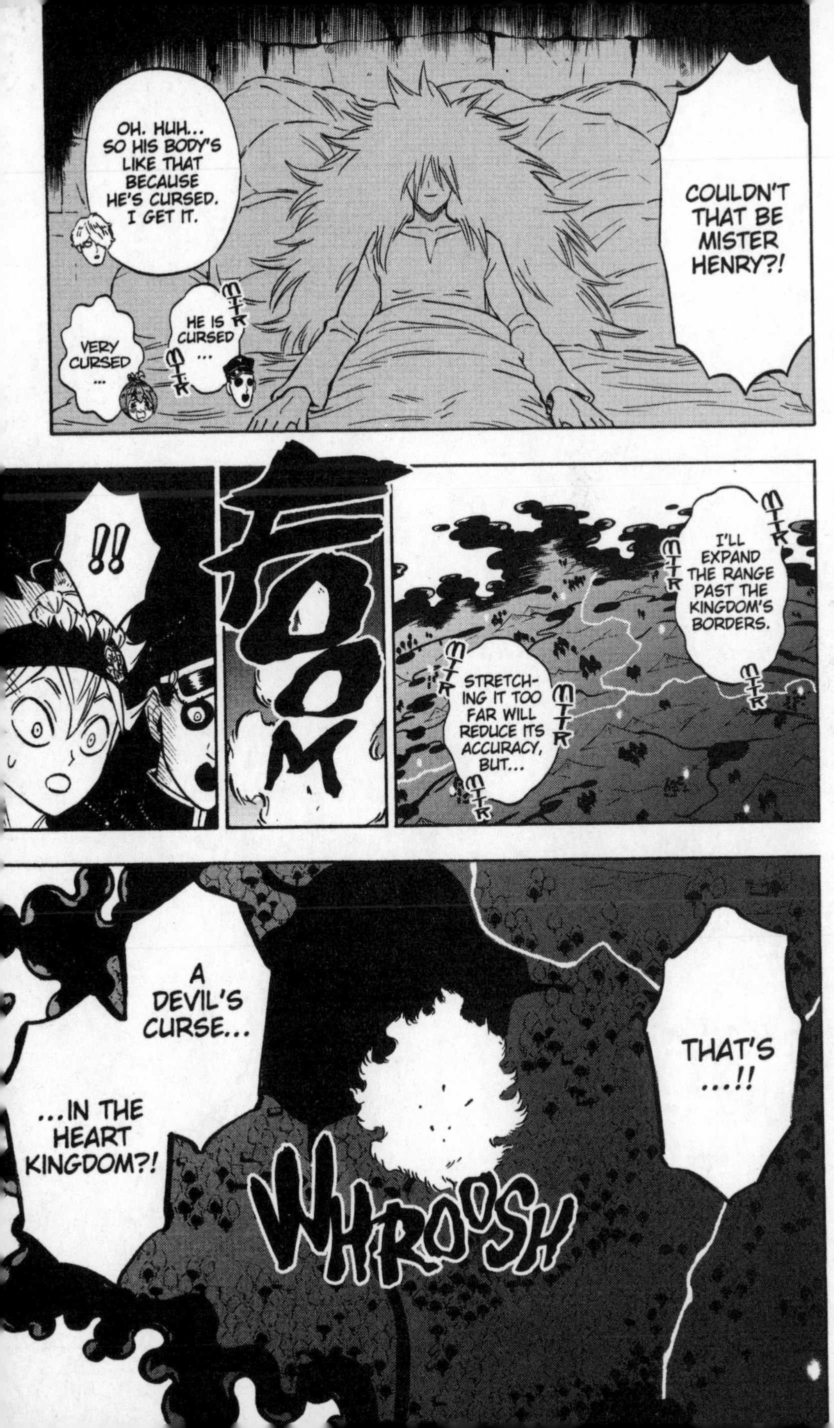
COULDN'T THAT BE MISTER HENRY?!
OH. HUH... SO HIS BODY'S LIKE THAT BECAUSE HE'S CURSED. I GET IT.
MTTR
HE IS CURSED...
MTTR
VERY CURSED...
MTTR
I'LL EXPAND THE RANGE PAST THE KINGDOM'S BORDERS.
MTTR
STRETCHING IT TOO FAR WILL REDUCE ITS ACCURACY, BUT...
!!
THAT'S ...!!
A DEVIL'S CURSE...
...IN THE HEART KINGDOM?!
WHROOSH

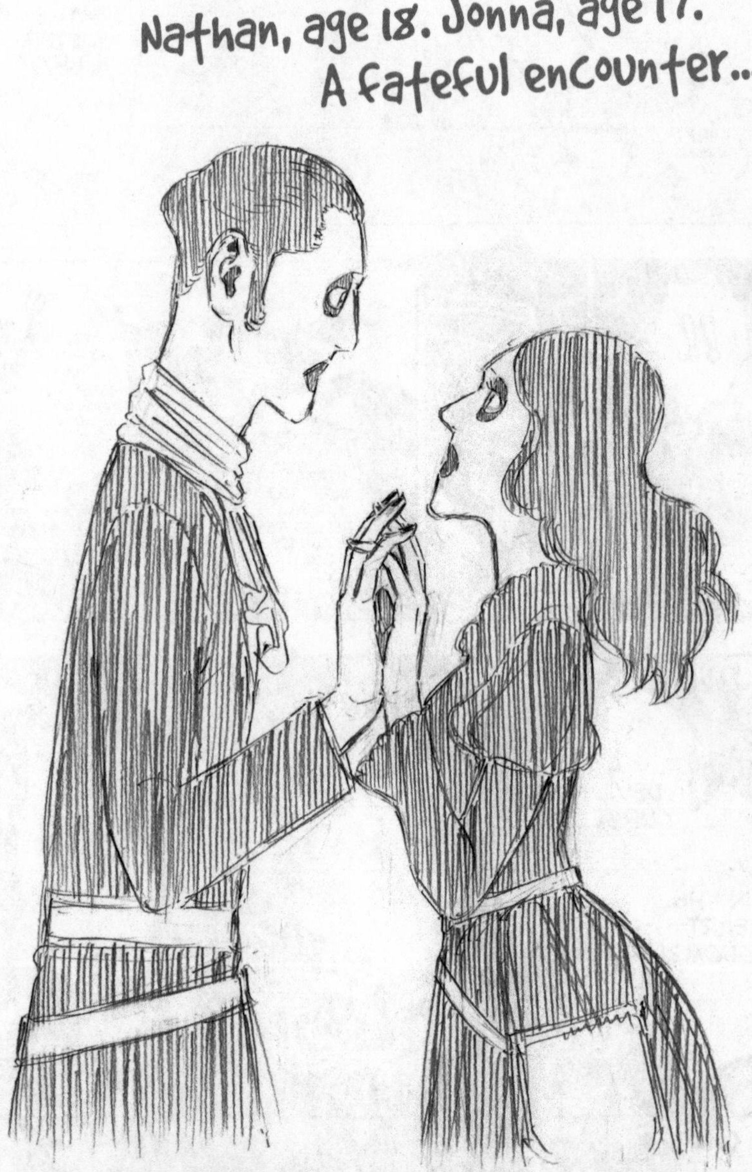
Nathan, age 18. Jonna, age 17.
A fateful encounter...

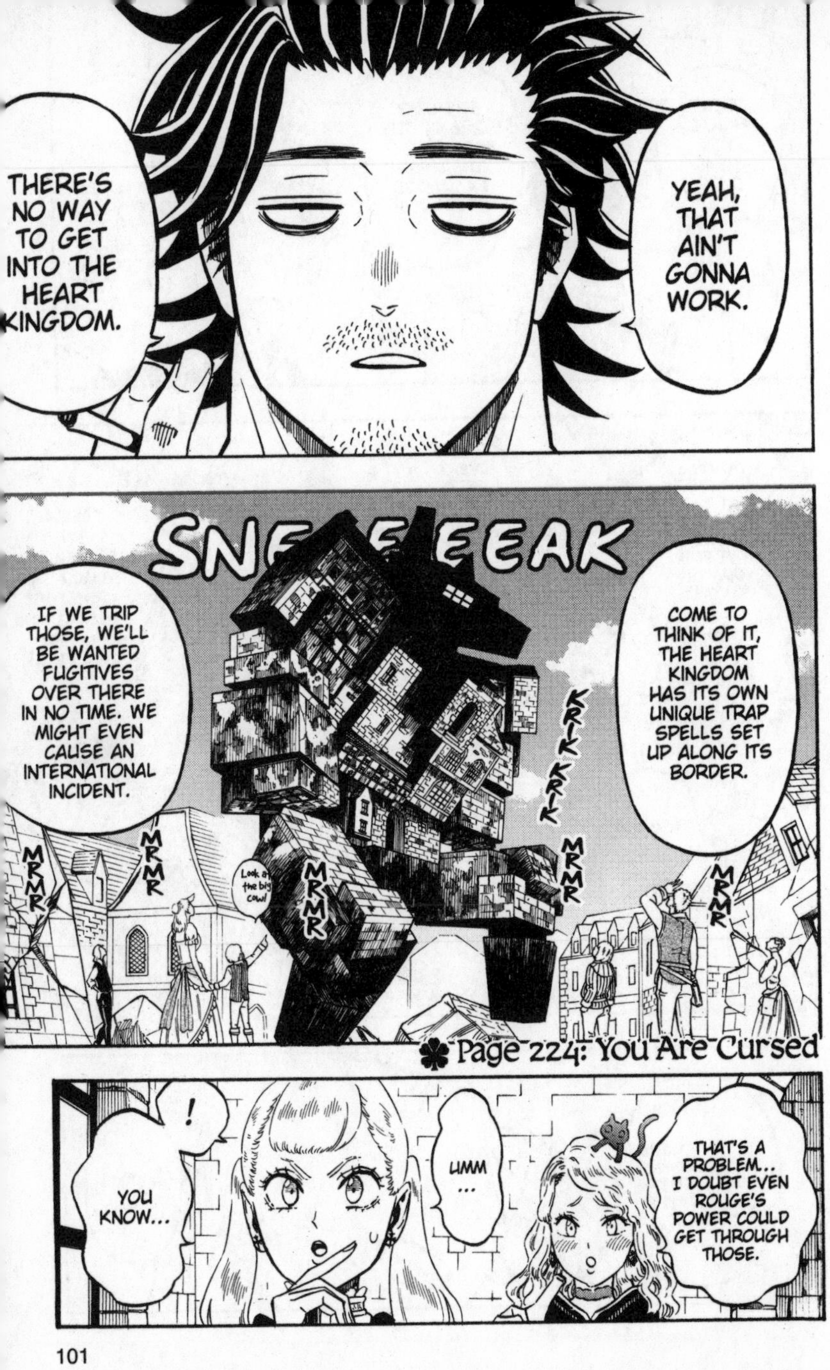
YEAH, THAT AIN'T GONNA WORK.
THERE'S NO WAY TO GET INTO THE HEART KINGDOM.
SNE EEAK
COME TO THINK OF IT, THE HEART KINGDOM HAS ITS OWN UNIQUE TRAP SPELLS SET UP ALONG ITS BORDER.
KRIK KRIK
MRMR
MRMR
MRMR
Look at the big cow!
MRMR
MRMR
IF WE TRIP THOSE, WE'LL BE WANTED FUGITIVES OVER THERE IN NO TIME. WE MIGHT EVEN CAUSE AN INTERNATIONAL INCIDENT.
Page 224: You Are Cursed
THAT'S A PROBLEM... I DOUBT EVEN ROUGE'S POWER COULD GET THROUGH THOSE.
UMM ...
!
YOU KNOW...

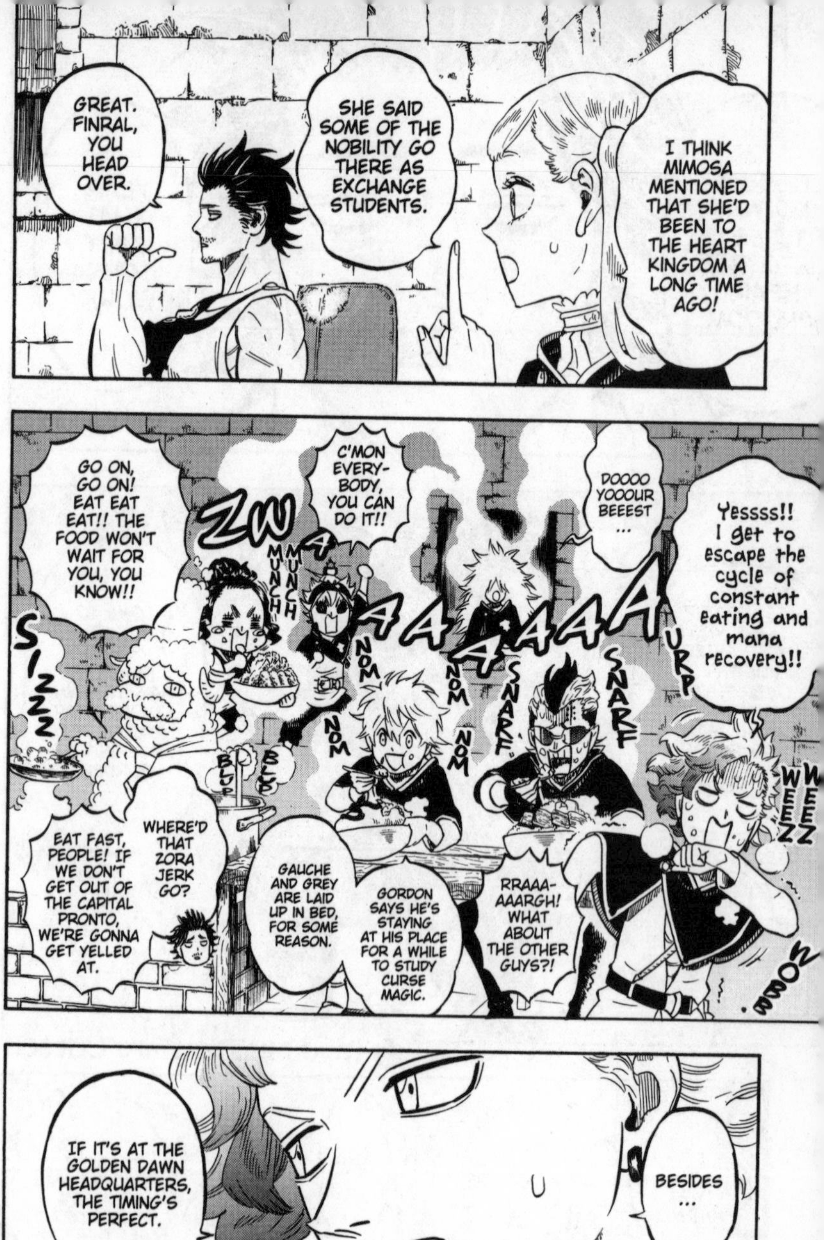
I THINK MIMOSA MENTIONED THAT SHE'D BEEN TO THE HEART KINGDOM A LONG TIME AGO!
SHE SAID SOME OF THE NOBILITY GO THERE AS EXCHANGE STUDENTS.
GREAT. FINRAL, YOU HEAD OVER.
Yessss!! I get to escape the cycle of constant eating and mana recovery!!
WEEZ WEEZ
DOOOO YOOOUR BEEEST ...
URP
C'MON EVERY-BODY, YOU CAN DO IT!!
ZWAAAAAAAA
GO ON, GO ON! EAT EAT EAT!! THE FOOD WON'T WAIT FOR YOU, YOU KNOW!!
SNARF SNARF
NOM NOM NOM NOM
MUNCH MUNCH
SIZZZ
BLUP BLUP
WOBB
RRAAA-AAARGH! WHAT ABOUT THE OTHER GUYS?!
GORDON SAYS HE'S STAYING AT HIS PLACE FOR A WHILE TO STUDY CURSE MAGIC.
GAUCHE AND GREY ARE LAID UP IN BED, FOR SOME REASON.
WHERE'D THAT ZORA JERK GO?
EAT FAST, PEOPLE! IF WE DON'T GET OUT OF THE CAPITAL PRONTO, WE'RE GONNA GET YELLED AT.
BESIDES ...
IF IT'S AT THE GOLDEN DAWN HEADQUARTERS, THE TIMING'S PERFECT.

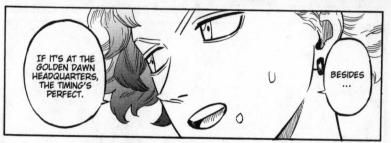

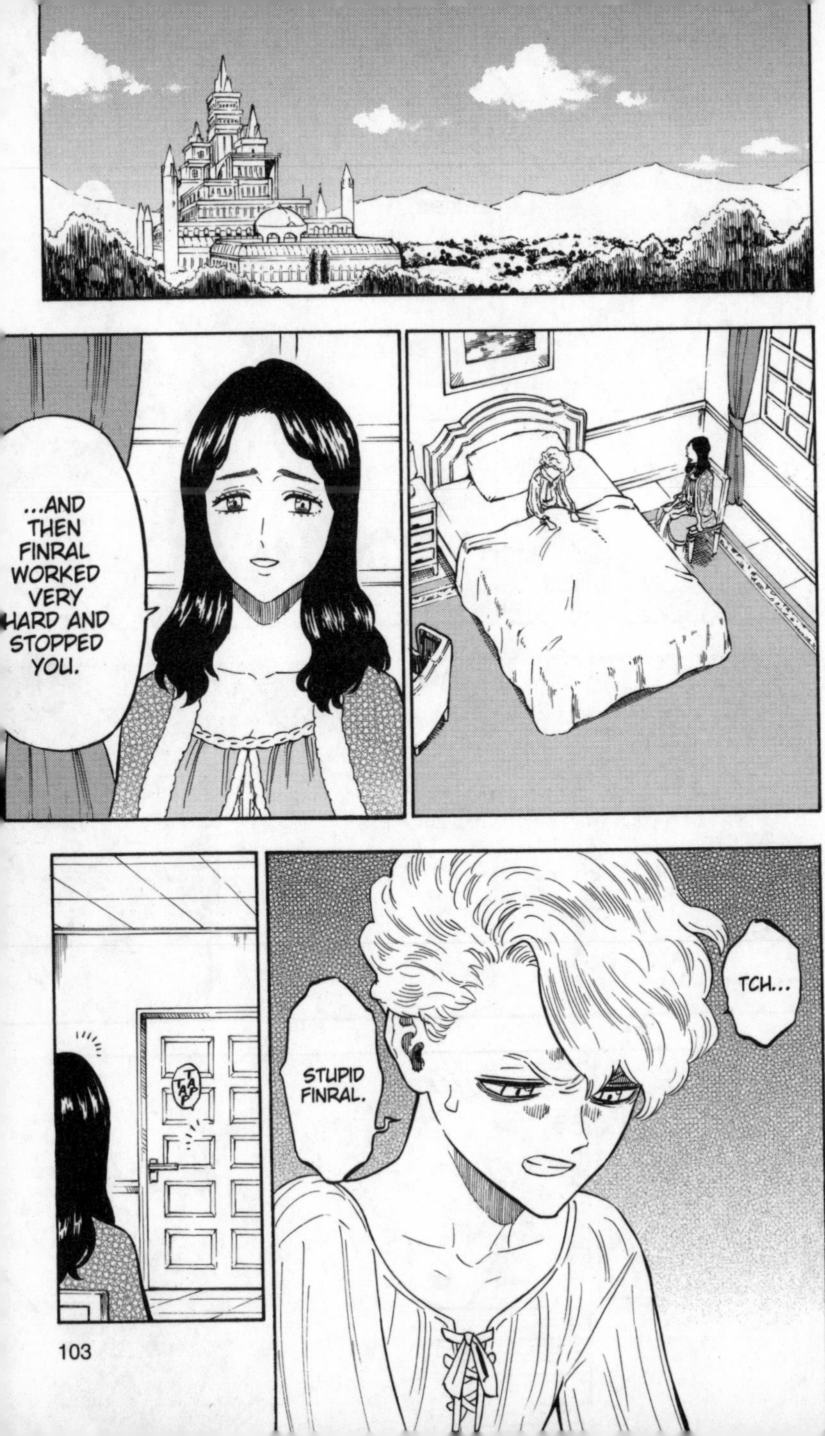

...AND THEN FINRAL WORKED VERY HARD AND STOPPED YOU.
TCH...
STUPID FINRAL.
TAP TAP

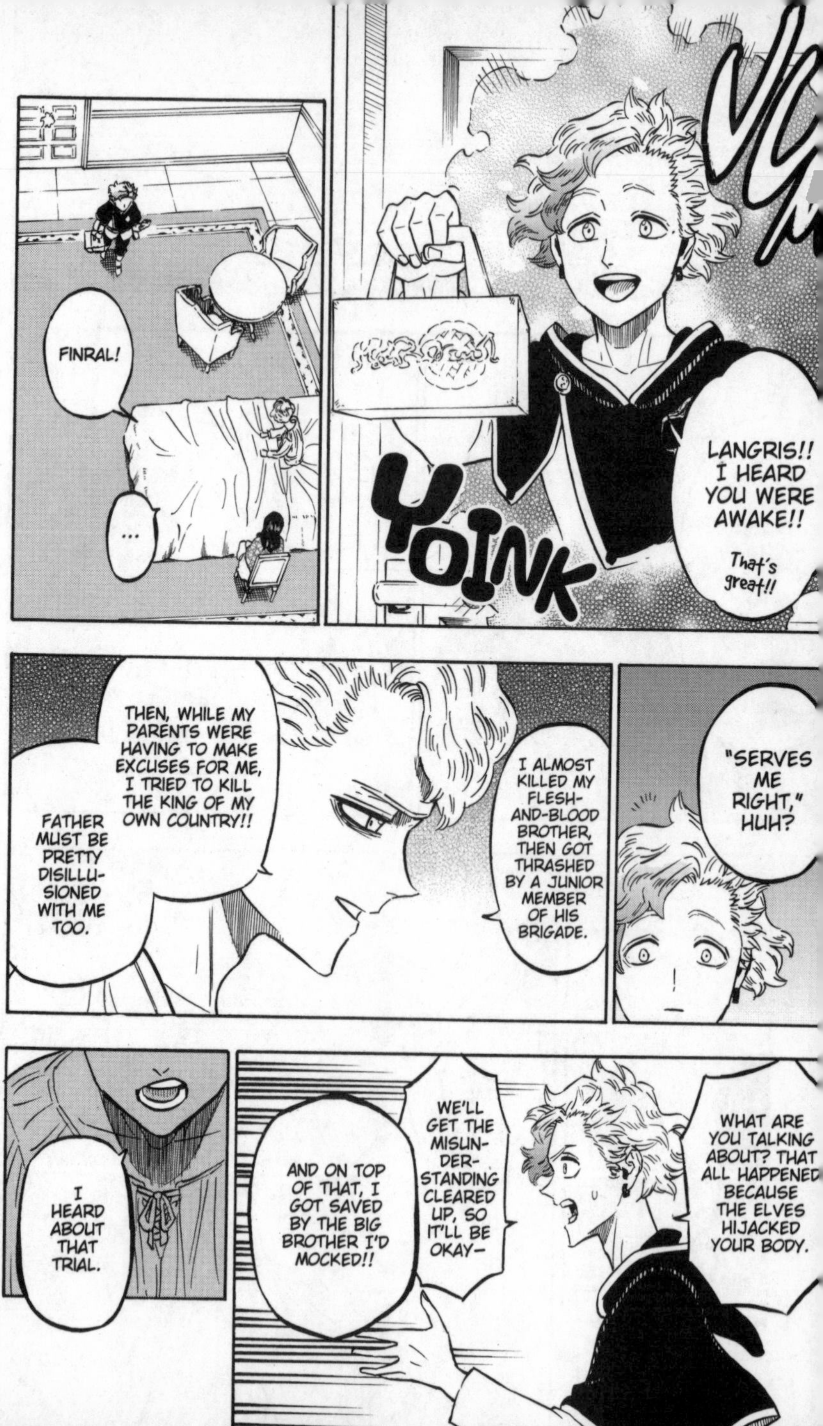
LANGRIS!! I HEARD YOU WERE AWAKE!!
That's great!!
YOINK
FINRAL!
...
"SERVES ME RIGHT," HUH?
I ALMOST KILLED MY FLESH-AND-BLOOD BROTHER, THEN GOT THRASHED BY A JUNIOR MEMBER OF HIS BRIGADE.
THEN, WHILE MY PARENTS WERE HAVING TO MAKE EXCUSES FOR ME, I TRIED TO KILL THE KING OF MY OWN COUNTRY!!
FATHER MUST BE PRETTY DISILLUSIONED WITH ME TOO.
WHAT ARE YOU TALKING ABOUT? THAT ALL HAPPENED BECAUSE THE ELVES HIJACKED YOUR BODY.
WE'LL GET THE MISUNDERSTANDING CLEARED UP, SO IT'LL BE OKAY—
AND ON TOP OF THAT, I GOT SAVED BY THE BIG BROTHER I'D MOCKED!!
I HEARD ABOUT THAT TRIAL.

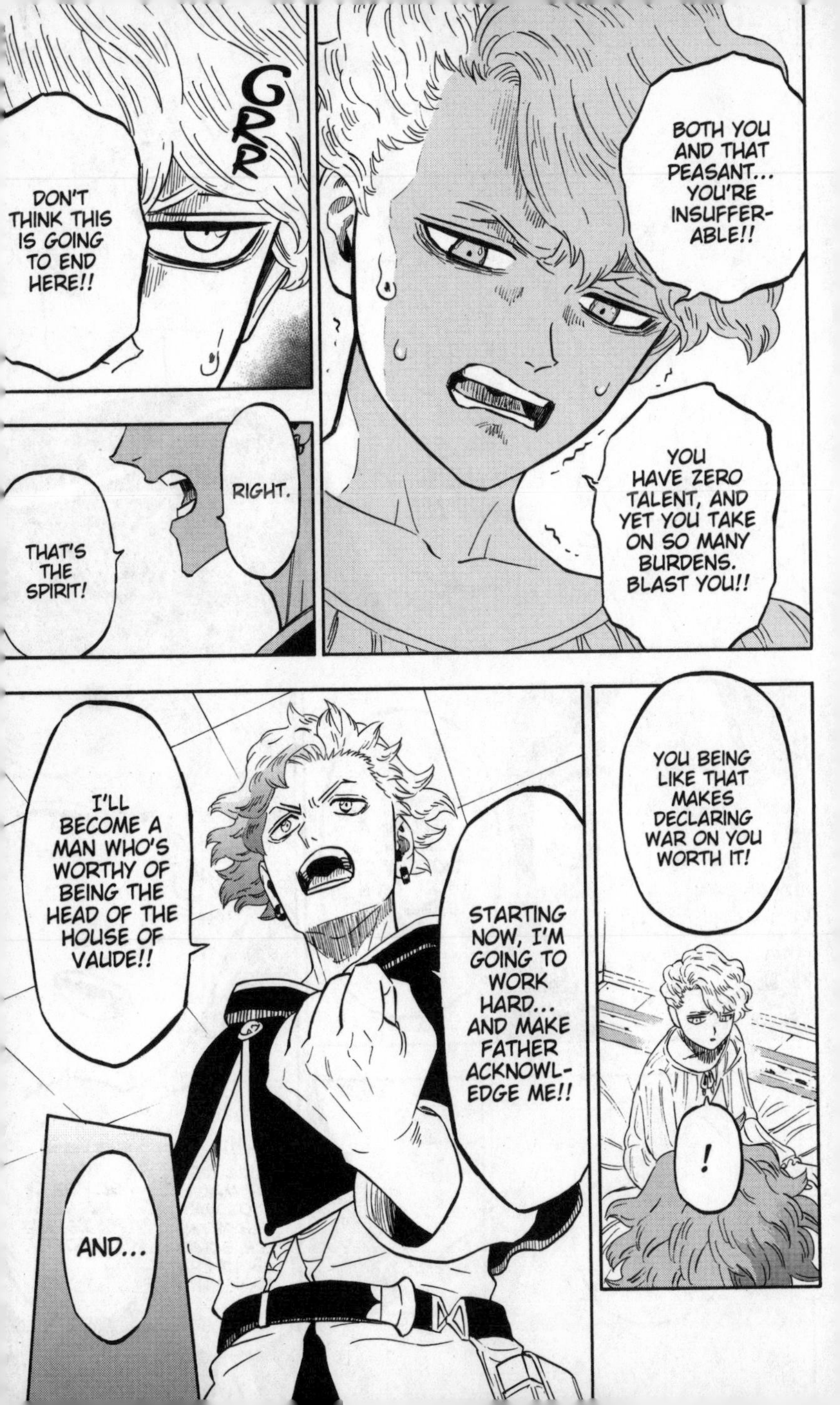
BOTH YOU AND THAT PEASANT... YOU'RE INSUFFER-ABLE!!
YOU HAVE ZERO TALENT, AND YET YOU TAKE ON SO MANY BURDENS. BLAST YOU!!
GRR
DON'T THINK THIS IS GOING TO END HERE!!
RIGHT.
THAT'S THE SPIRIT!
YOU BEING LIKE THAT MAKES DECLARING WAR ON YOU WORTH IT!
!
STARTING NOW, I'M GOING TO WORK HARD... AND MAKE FATHER ACKNOWL-EDGE ME!!
I'LL BECOME A MAN WHO'S WORTHY OF BEING THE HEAD OF THE HOUSE OF VAUDE!!
AND...

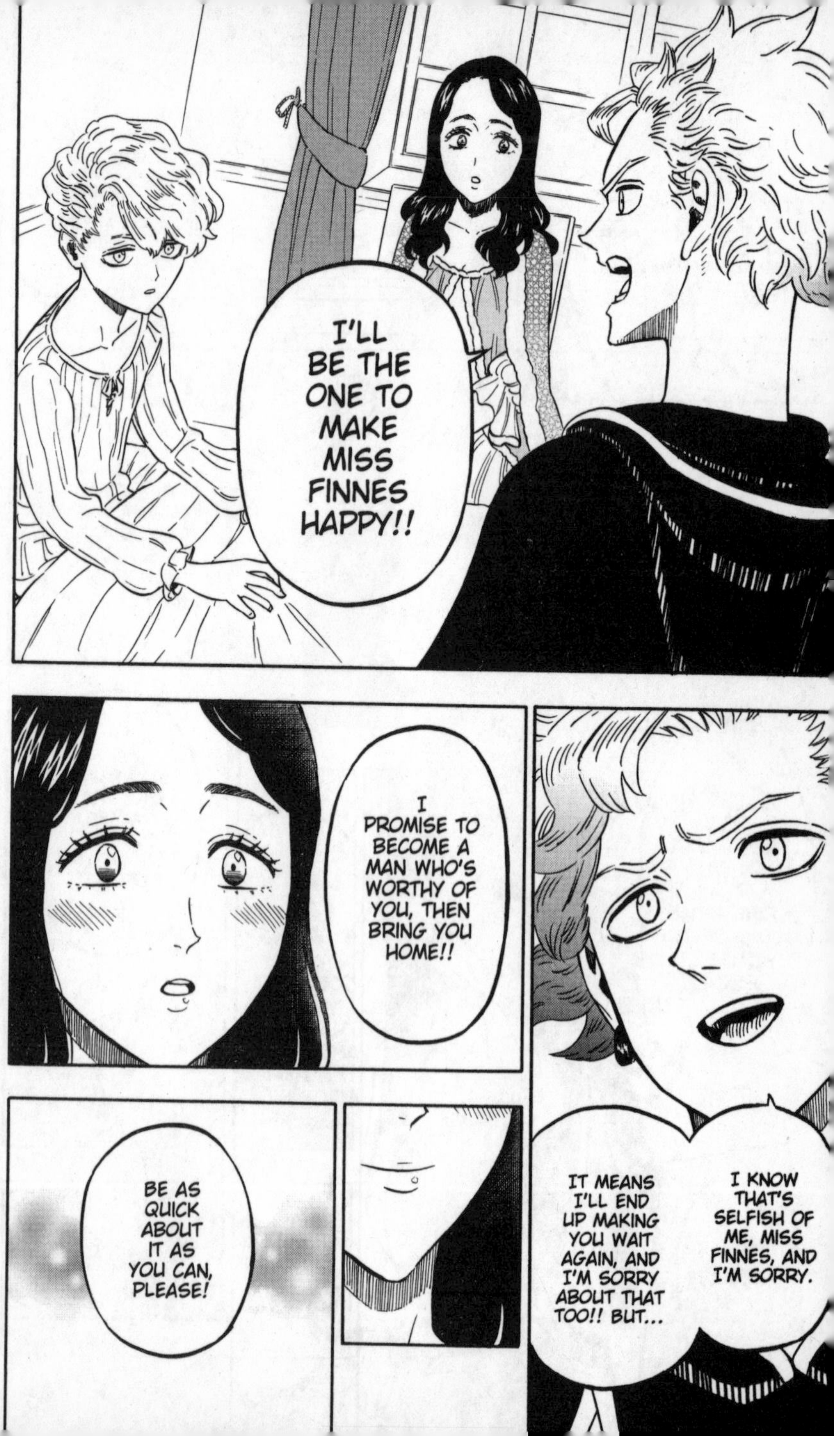
I'LL BE THE ONE TO MAKE MISS FINNES HAPPY!!
I KNOW THAT'S SELFISH OF ME, MISS FINNES, AND I'M SORRY.
IT MEANS I'LL END UP MAKING YOU WAIT AGAIN, AND I'M SORRY ABOUT THAT TOO!! BUT...
I PROMISE TO BECOME A MAN WHO'S WORTHY OF YOU, THEN BRING YOU HOME!!
BE AS QUICK ABOUT IT AS YOU CAN, PLEASE!

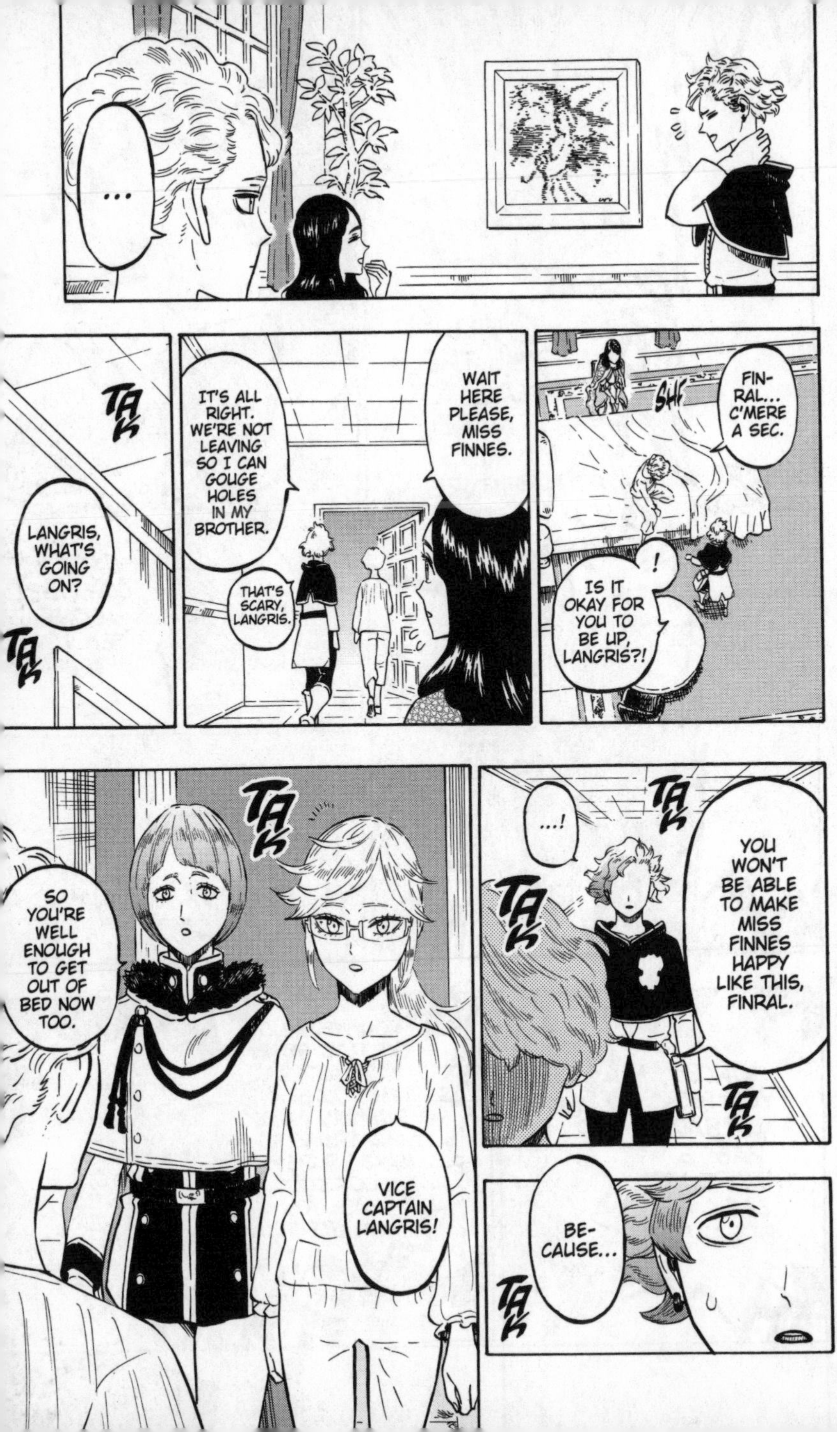
...
FIN-RAL... C'MERE A SEC.
SHF
!
IS IT OKAY FOR YOU TO BE UP, LANGRIS?!
WAIT HERE PLEASE, MISS FINNES.
IT'S ALL RIGHT. WE'RE NOT LEAVING SO I CAN GOUGE HOLES IN MY BROTHER.
THAT'S SCARY, LANGRIS.
TAK
LANGRIS, WHAT'S GOING ON?
TAK
TAK
YOU WON'T BE ABLE TO MAKE MISS FINNES HAPPY LIKE THIS, FINRAL.
...!
TAK
TAK
BE-CAUSE...
TAK
TAK
SO YOU'RE WELL ENOUGH TO GET OUT OF BED NOW TOO.
VICE CAPTAIN LANGRIS!

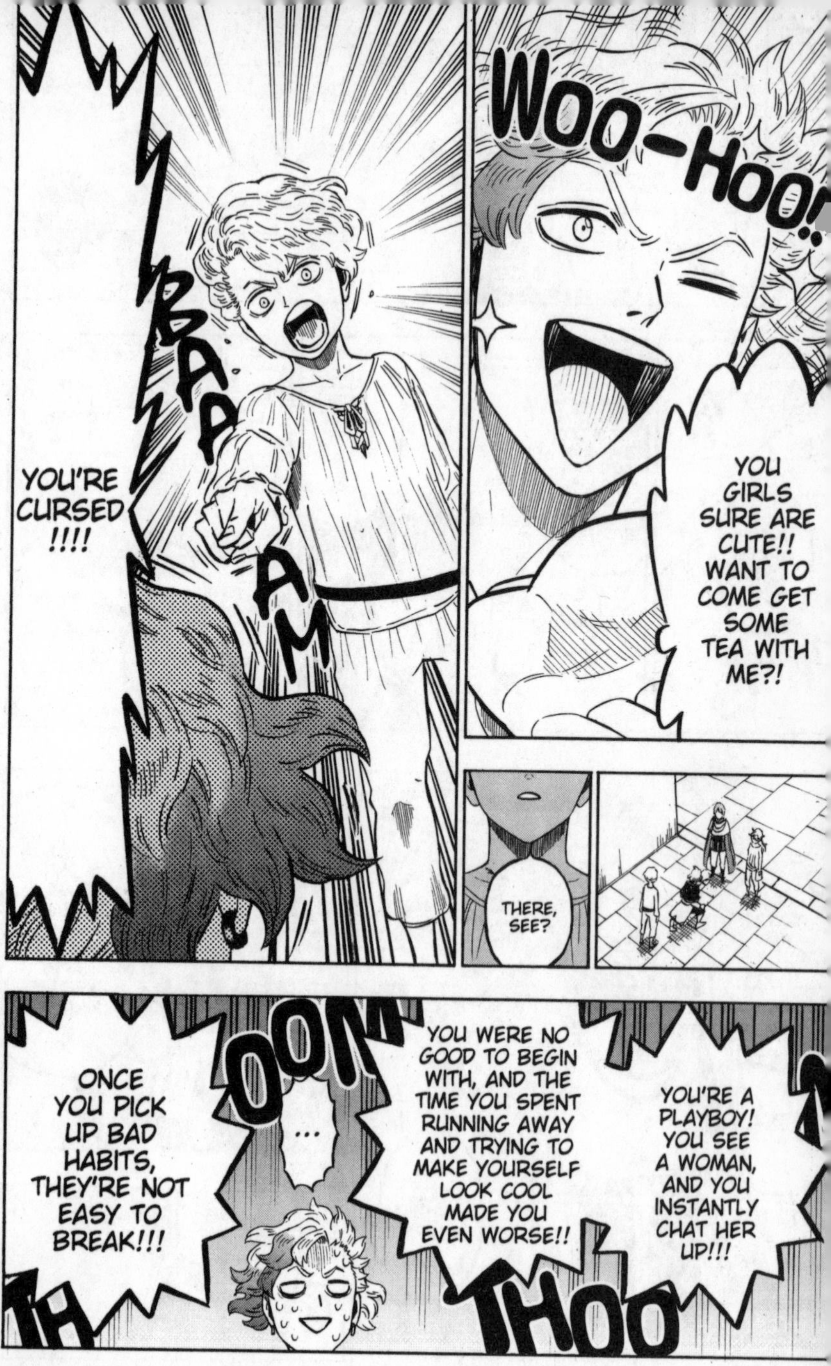
WOO-HOO!!
YOU GIRLS SURE ARE CUTE!! WANT TO COME GET SOME TEA WITH ME?!
THERE, SEE?
BAAAM
YOU'RE CURSED!!!!
YOU'RE A PLAYBOY! YOU SEE A WOMAN, AND YOU INSTANTLY CHAT HER UP!!!
YOU WERE NO GOOD TO BEGIN WITH, AND THE TIME YOU SPENT RUNNING AWAY AND TRYING TO MAKE YOURSELF LOOK COOL MADE YOU EVEN WORSE!!
...
ONCE YOU PICK UP BAD HABITS, THEY'RE NOT EASY TO BREAK!!!

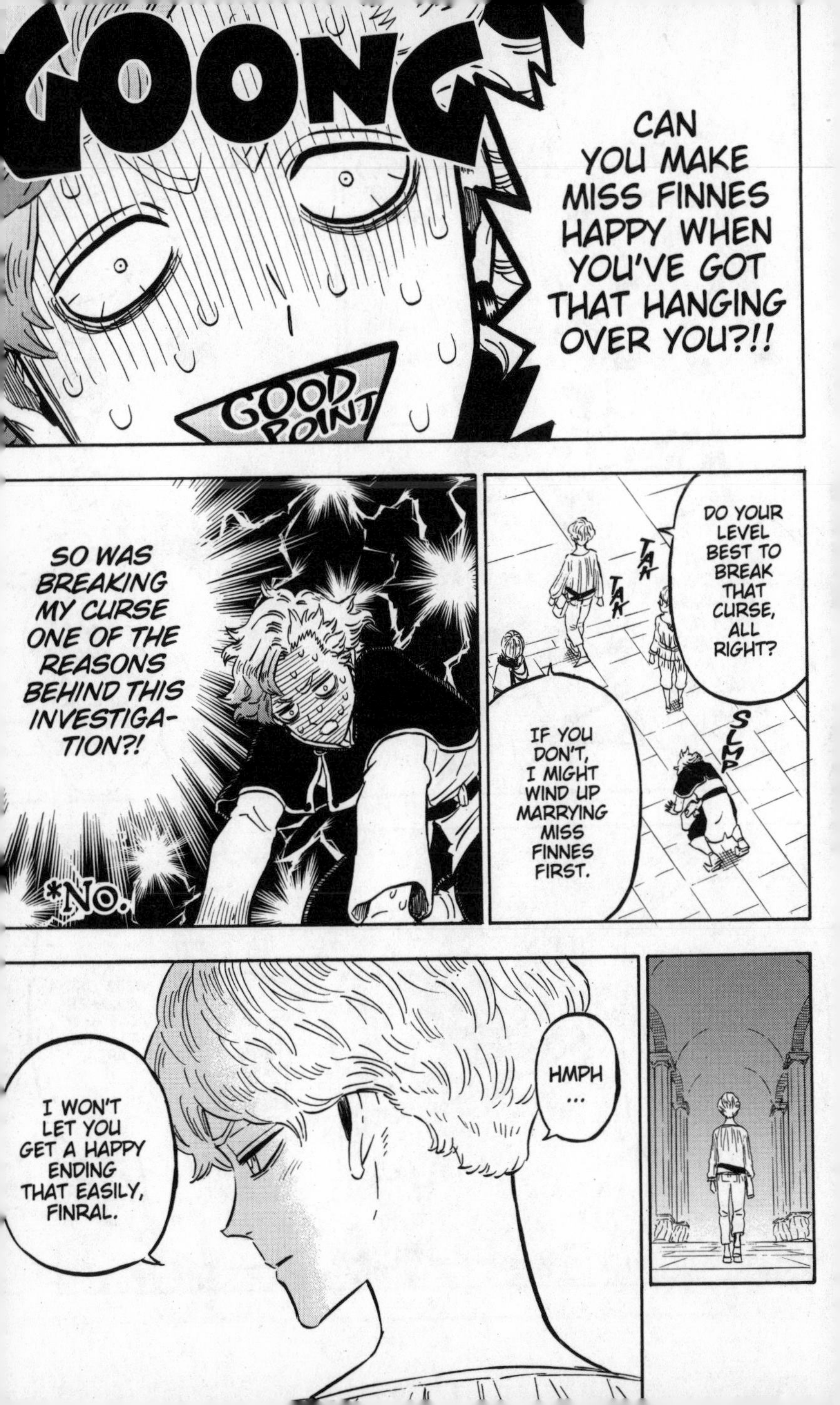
GOONG
CAN YOU MAKE MISS FINNES HAPPY WHEN YOU'VE GOT THAT HANGING OVER YOU?!!
GOOD POINT
DO YOUR LEVEL BEST TO BREAK THAT CURSE, ALL RIGHT?
TAK
TAK
IF YOU DON'T, I MIGHT WIND UP MARRYING MISS FINNES FIRST.
SLMP
SO WAS BREAKING MY CURSE ONE OF THE REASONS BEHIND THIS INVESTIGA-TION?!
*No.
HMPH...
I WON'T LET YOU GET A HAPPY ENDING THAT EASILY, FINRAL.

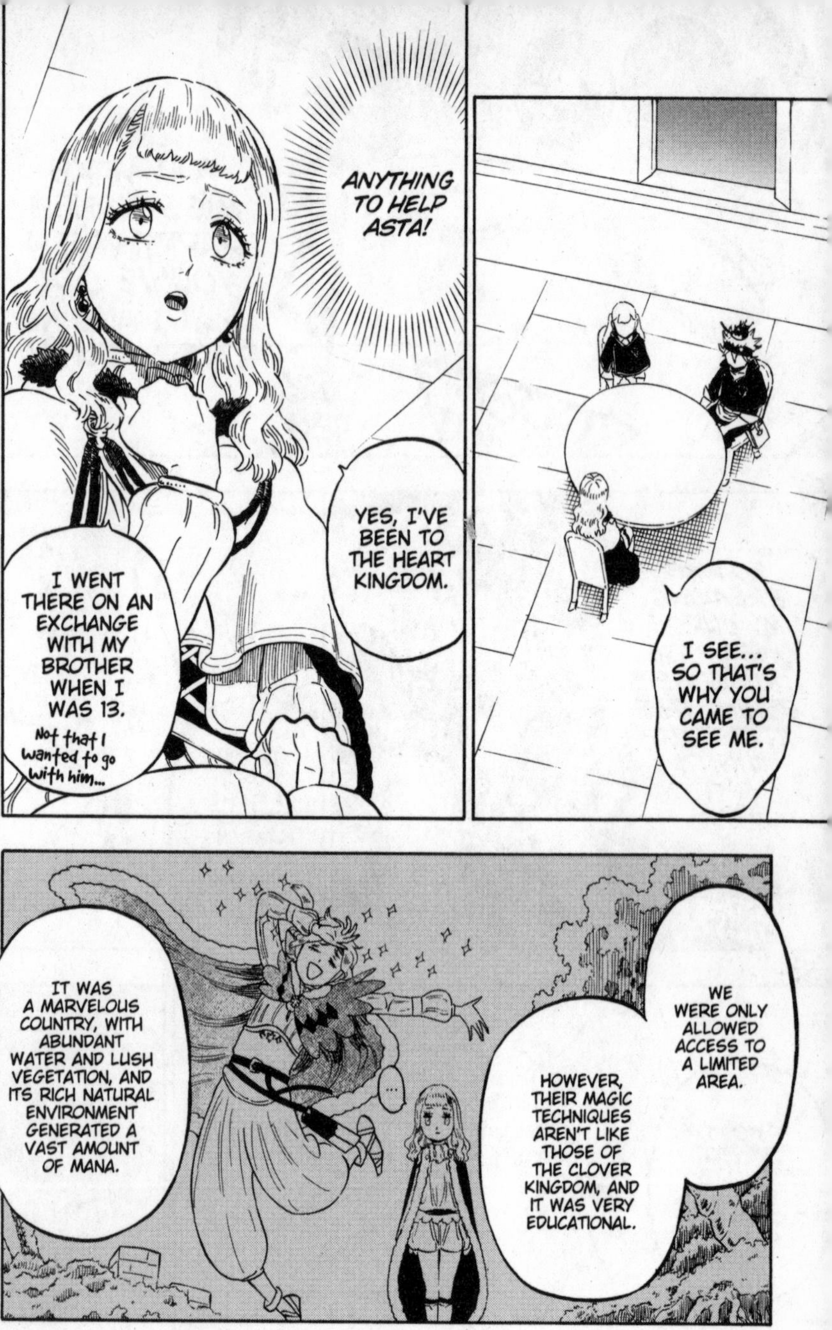
I SEE... SO THAT'S WHY YOU CAME TO SEE ME.
ANYTHING TO HELP ASTA!
YES, I'VE BEEN TO THE HEART KINGDOM.
I WENT THERE ON AN EXCHANGE WITH MY BROTHER WHEN I WAS 13.
Not that I wanted to go with him...
WE WERE ONLY ALLOWED ACCESS TO A LIMITED AREA.
HOWEVER, THEIR MAGIC TECHNIQUES AREN'T LIKE THOSE OF THE CLOVER KINGDOM, AND IT WAS VERY EDUCATIONAL.
...
IT WAS A MARVELOUS COUNTRY, WITH ABUNDANT WATER AND LUSH VEGETATION, AND ITS RICH NATURAL ENVIRONMENT GENERATED A VAST AMOUNT OF MANA.

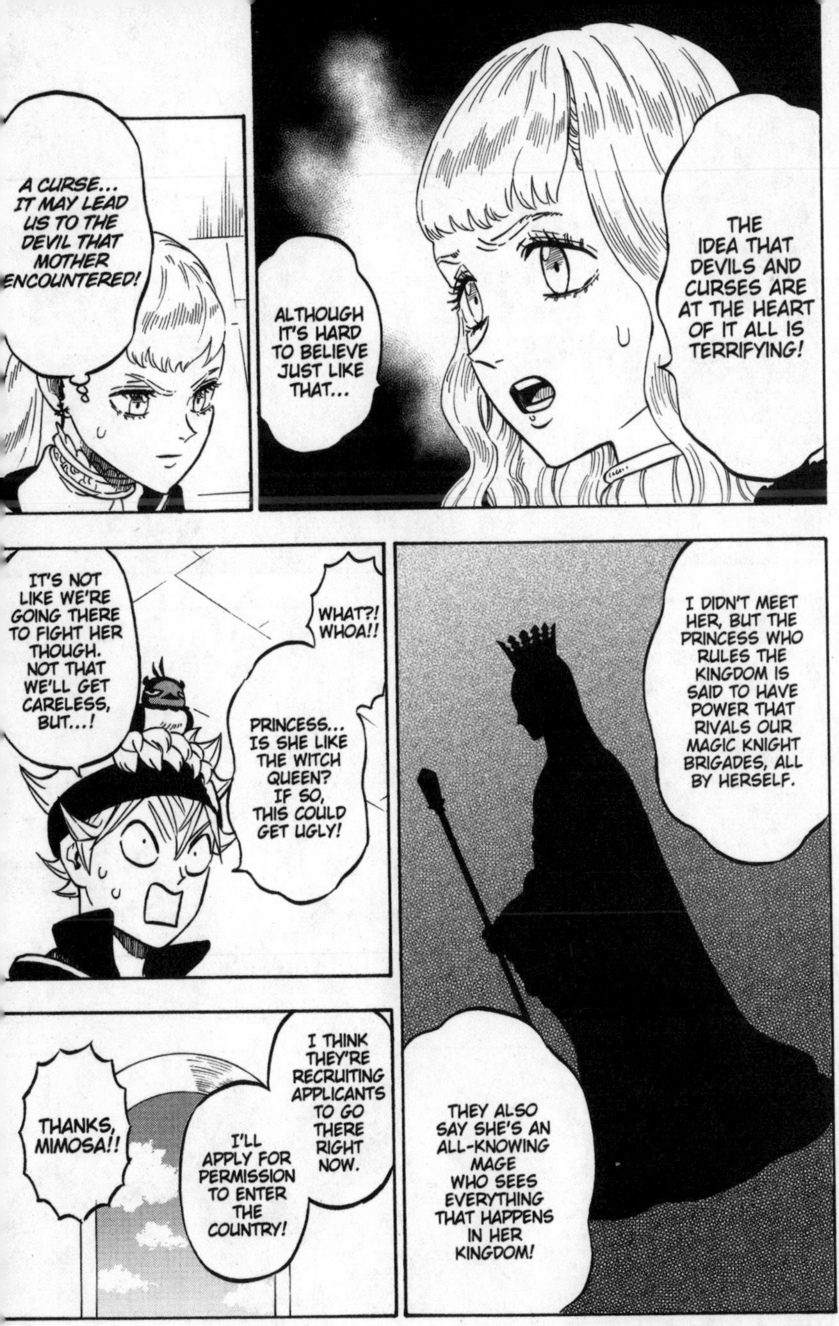
ALTHOUGH IT'S HARD TO BELIEVE JUST LIKE THAT...
THE IDEA THAT DEVILS AND CURSES ARE AT THE HEART OF IT ALL IS TERRIFYING!
A CURSE... IT MAY LEAD US TO THE DEVIL THAT MOTHER ENCOUNTERED!
I DIDN'T MEET HER, BUT THE PRINCESS WHO RULES THE KINGDOM IS SAID TO HAVE POWER THAT RIVALS OUR MAGIC KNIGHT BRIGADES, ALL BY HERSELF.
THEY ALSO SAY SHE'S AN ALL-KNOWING MAGE WHO SEES EVERYTHING THAT HAPPENS IN HER KINGDOM!
WHAT?! WHOA!!
PRINCESS... IS SHE LIKE THE WITCH QUEEN? IF SO, THIS COULD GET UGLY!
IT'S NOT LIKE WE'RE GOING THERE TO FIGHT HER THOUGH. NOT THAT WE'LL GET CARELESS, BUT...!
I THINK THEY'RE RECRUITING APPLICANTS TO GO THERE RIGHT NOW.
I'LL APPLY FOR PERMISSION TO ENTER THE COUNTRY!
THANKS, MIMOSA!!

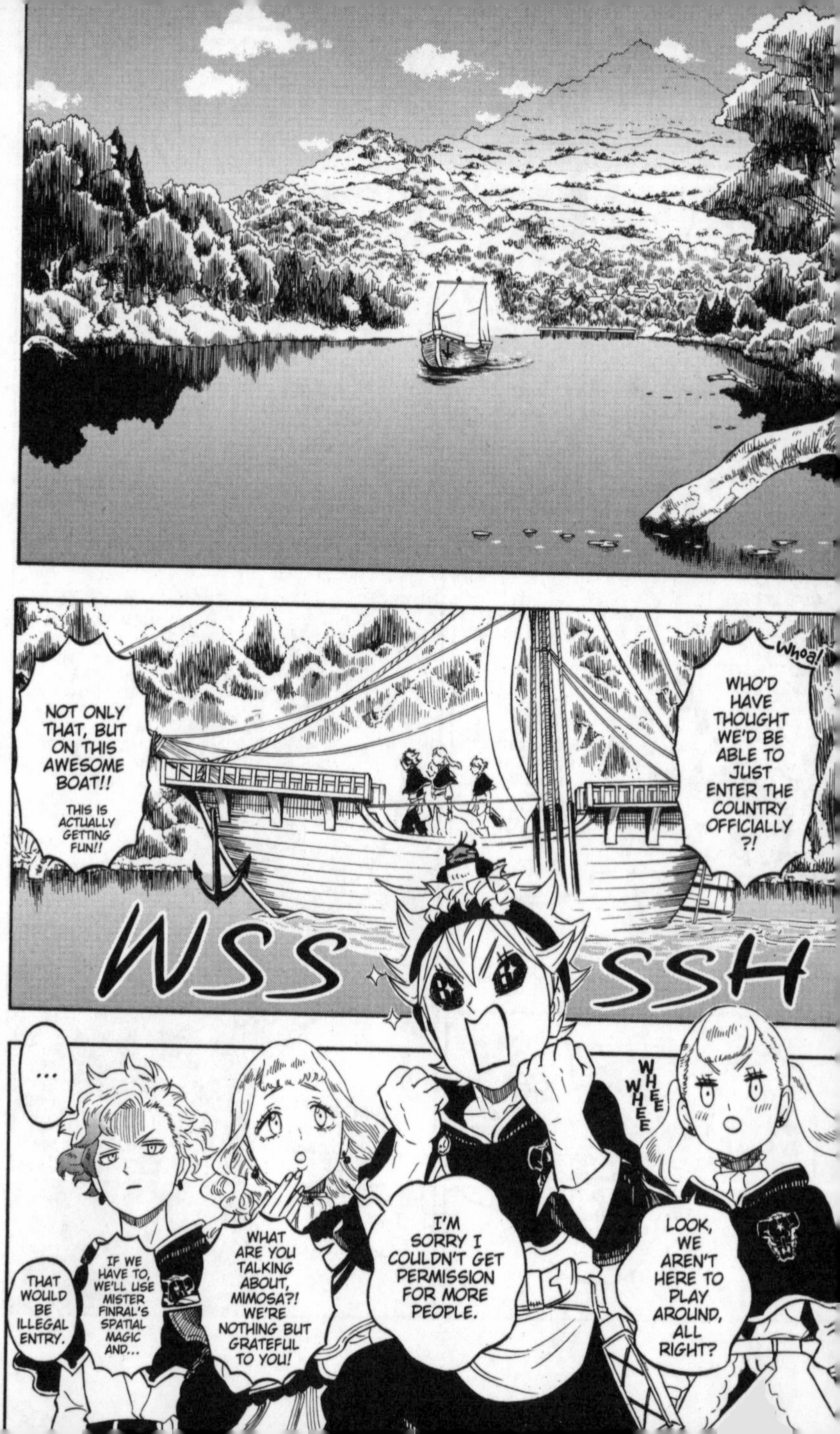
Whoa!
WHO'D HAVE THOUGHT WE'D BE ABLE TO JUST ENTER THE COUNTRY OFFICIALLY?!
NOT ONLY THAT, BUT ON THIS AWESOME BOAT!!
THIS IS ACTUALLY GETTING FUN!!
WSSSSH
WHEE WHEE
LOOK, WE AREN'T HERE TO PLAY AROUND, ALL RIGHT?
I'M SORRY I COULDN'T GET PERMISSION FOR MORE PEOPLE.
WHAT ARE YOU TALKING ABOUT, MIMOSA?! WE'RE NOTHING BUT GRATEFUL TO YOU!
IF WE HAVE TO, WE'LL USE MISTER FINRAL'S SPATIAL MAGIC AND...
THAT WOULD BE ILLEGAL ENTRY.
...

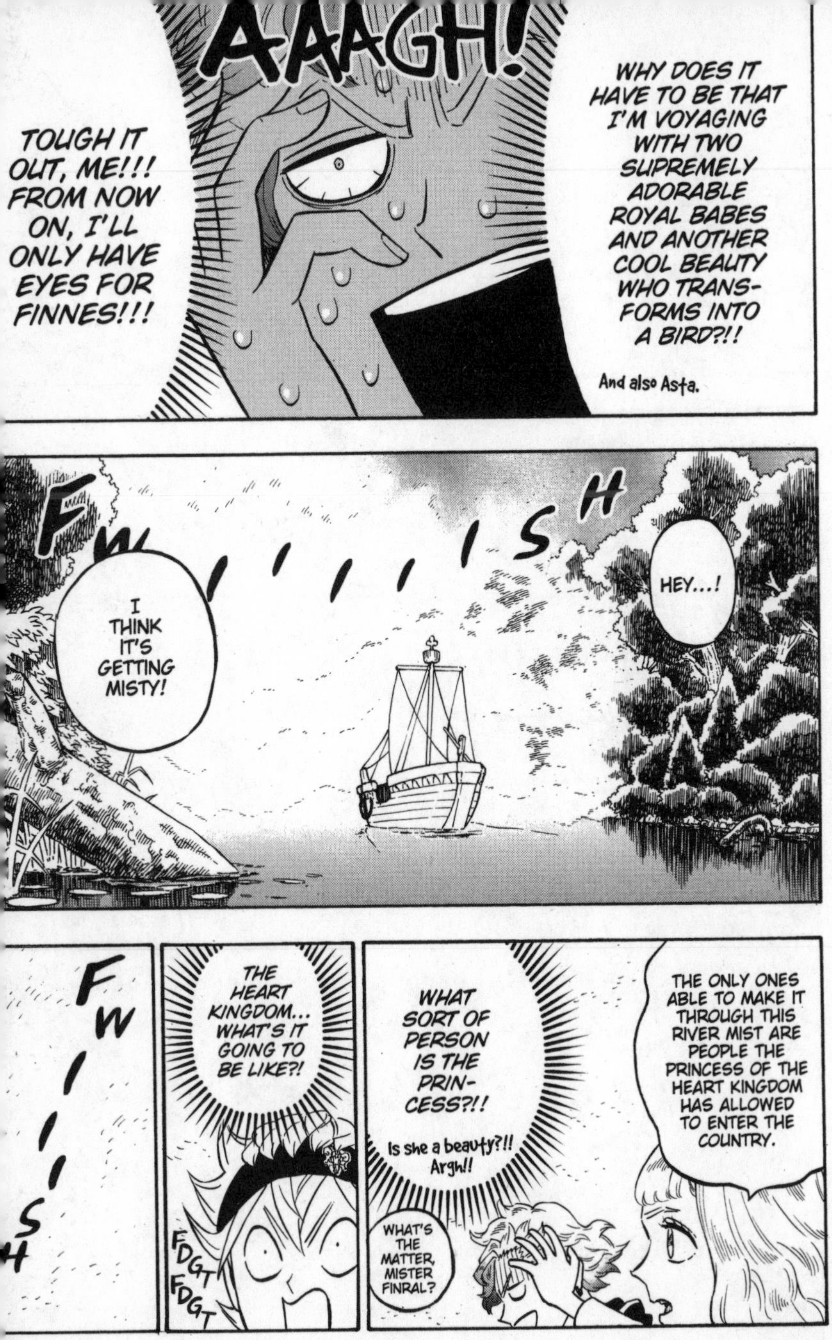
AAAGH!
WHY DOES IT HAVE TO BE THAT I'M VOYAGING WITH TWO SUPREMELY ADORABLE ROYAL BABES AND ANOTHER COOL BEAUTY WHO TRANS-FORMS INTO A BIRD?!!
And also Asta.
TOUGH IT OUT, ME!!! FROM NOW ON, I'LL ONLY HAVE EYES FOR FINNES!!!
FWIIIISH
HEY...!
I THINK IT'S GETTING MISTY!
THE ONLY ONES ABLE TO MAKE IT THROUGH THIS RIVER MIST ARE PEOPLE THE PRINCESS OF THE HEART KINGDOM HAS ALLOWED TO ENTER THE COUNTRY.
WHAT SORT OF PERSON IS THE PRIN-CESS?!!
Is she a beauty?!! Argh!!
WHAT'S THE MATTER, MISTER FINRAL?
THE HEART KINGDOM... WHAT'S IT GOING TO BE LIKE?!
FDGT FDGT
FWIIIISH

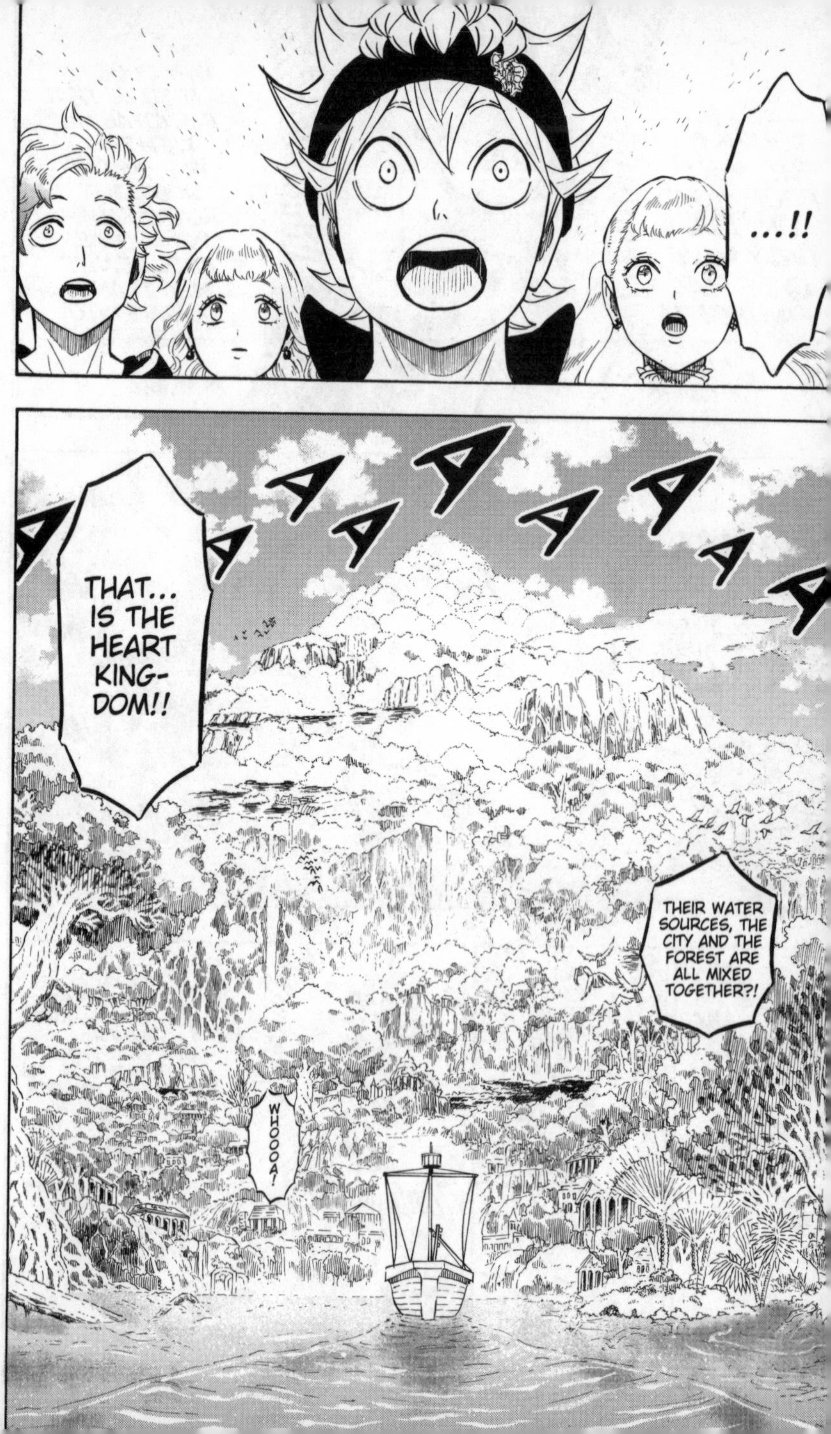
...!!
AAAAAAAAAAAA
THAT... IS THE HEART KING-DOM!!
THEIR WATER SOURCES, THE CITY AND THE FOREST ARE ALL MIXED TOGETHER?!
WHOOOA!

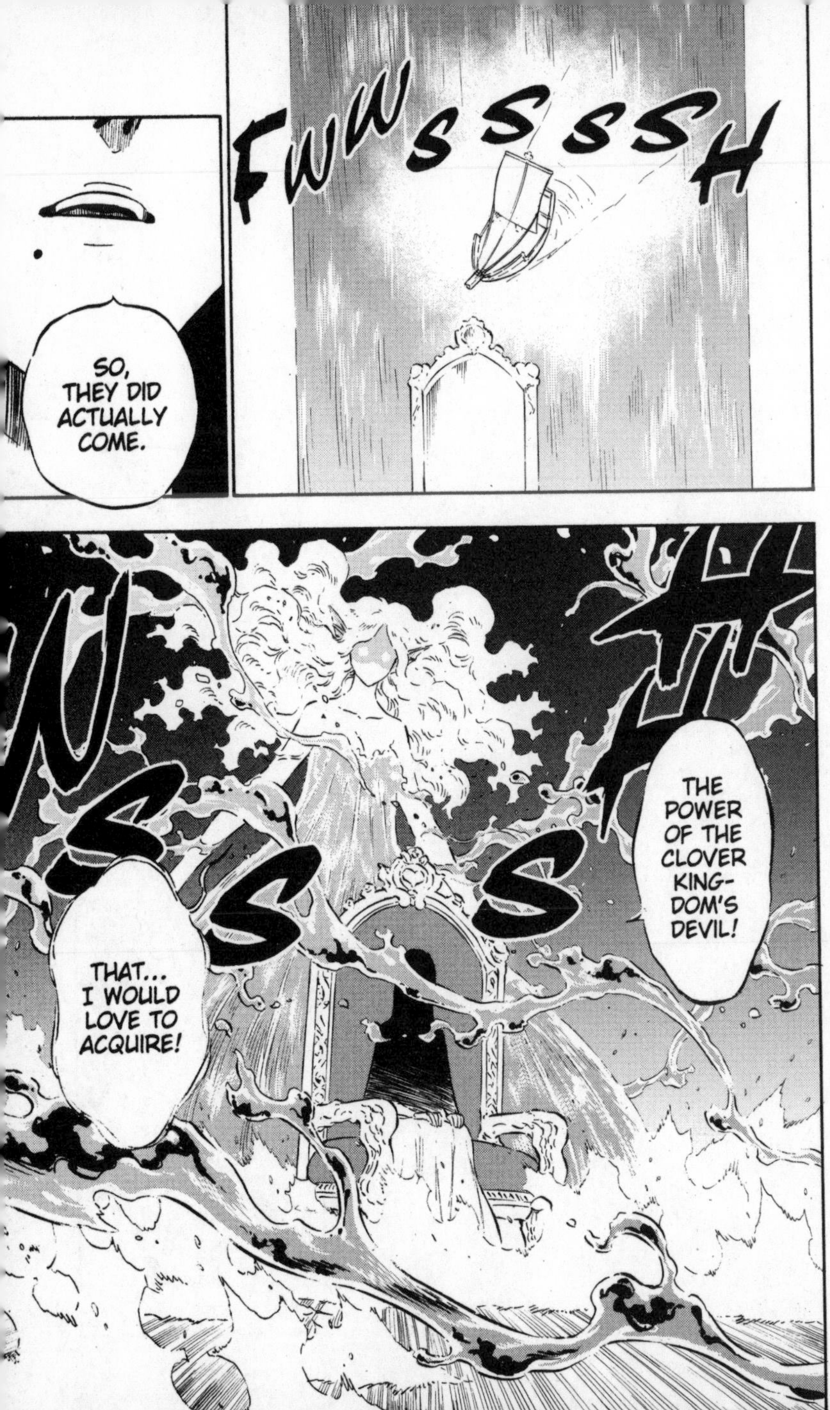
FWWSSSSH
SO, THEY DID ACTUALLY COME.
THE POWER OF THE CLOVER KING-DOM'S DEVIL!
THAT... I WOULD LOVE TO ACQUIRE!

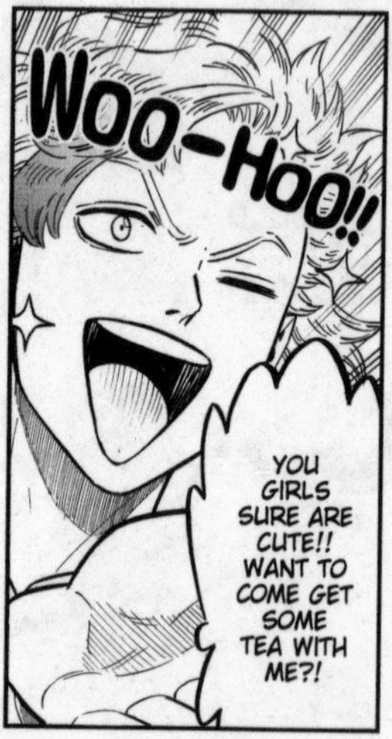
WOO-HOO!!
YOU GIRLS SURE ARE CUTE!! WANT TO COME GET SOME TEA WITH ME?!

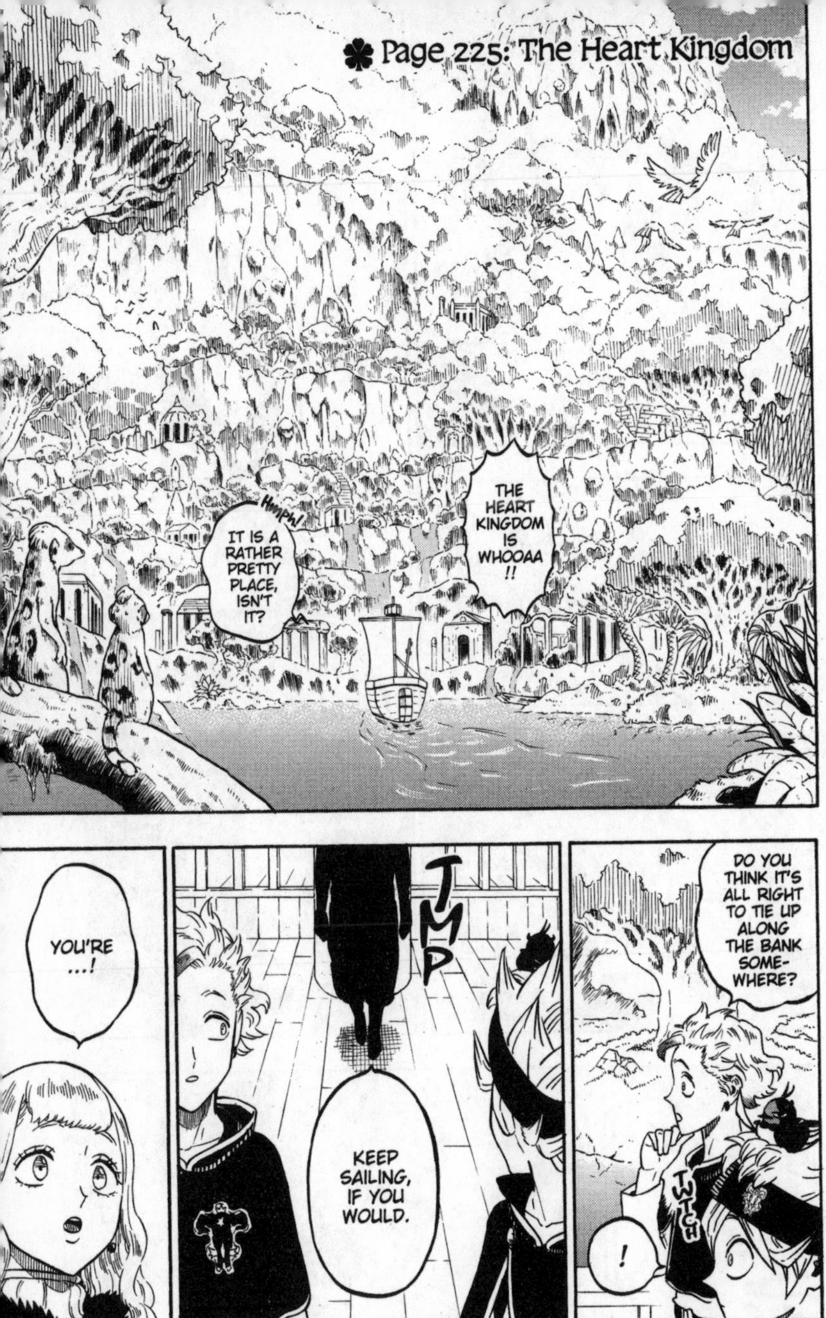
Page 225: The Heart Kingdom
THE HEART KINGDOM IS WHOOAA !!
Hmph!
IT IS A RATHER PRETTY PLACE, ISN'T IT?
DO YOU THINK IT'S ALL RIGHT TO TIE UP ALONG THE BANK SOME-WHERE?
TWITCH
!
TMP
KEEP SAILING, IF YOU WOULD.
YOU'RE ...!

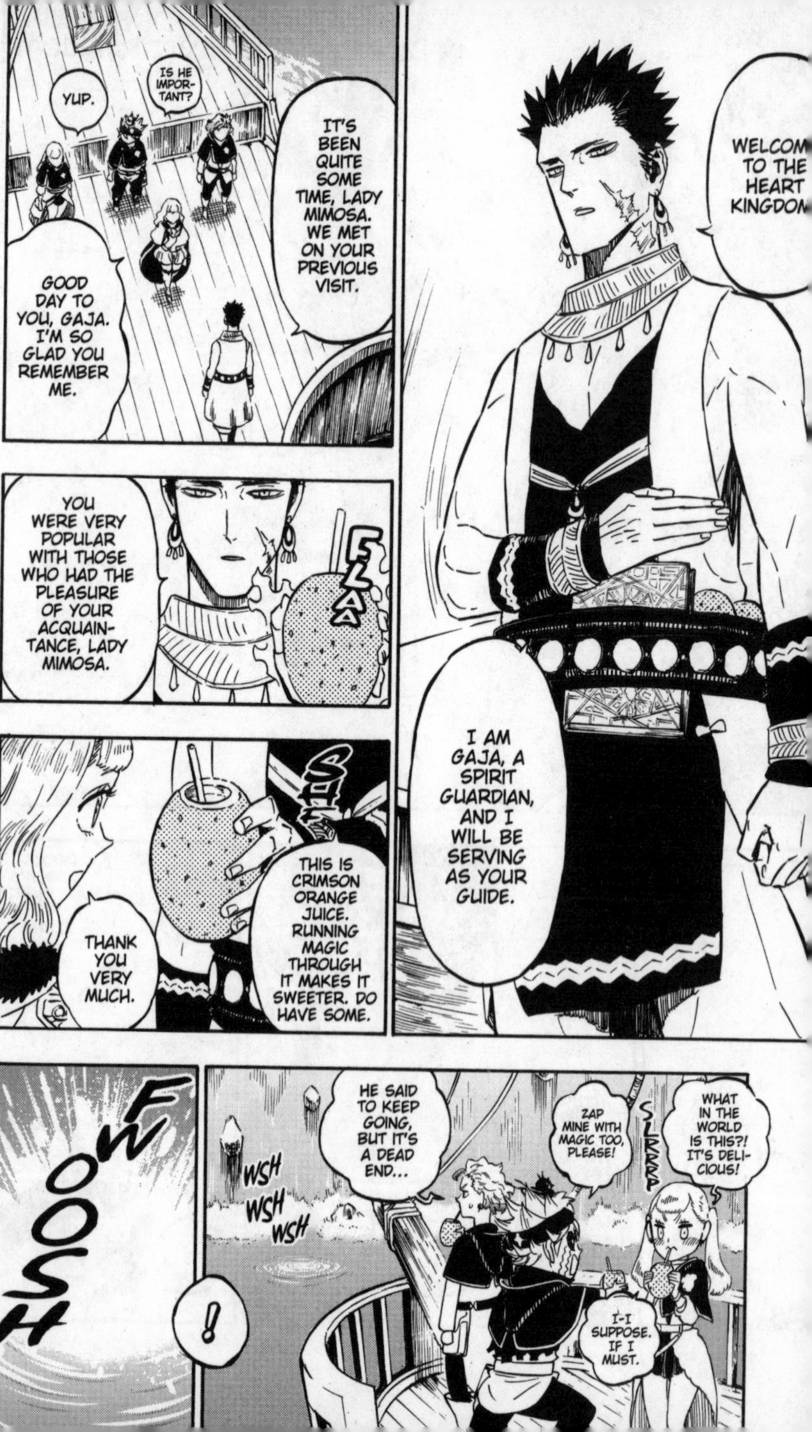
WELCOM TO THE HEART KINGDOM
I AM GAJA, A SPIRIT GUARDIAN, AND I WILL BE SERVING AS YOUR GUIDE.
IT'S BEEN QUITE SOME TIME, LADY MIMOSA. WE MET ON YOUR PREVIOUS VISIT.
IS HE IMPORTANT?
YUP.
GOOD DAY TO YOU, GAJA. I'M SO GLAD YOU REMEMBER ME.
FLAA
YOU WERE VERY POPULAR WITH THOSE WHO HAD THE PLEASURE OF YOUR ACQUAINTANCE, LADY MIMOSA.
SHF
THIS IS CRIMSON ORANGE JUICE. RUNNING MAGIC THROUGH IT MAKES IT SWEETER. DO HAVE SOME.
THANK YOU VERY MUCH.
WHAT IN THE WORLD IS THIS?! IT'S DELICIOUS!
SLRRRP
ZAP MINE WITH MAGIC TOO, PLEASE!
I-I SUPPOSE. IF I MUST.
HE SAID TO KEEP GOING, BUT IT'S A DEAD END...
WSH
WSH
WSH
!
FWOOSH

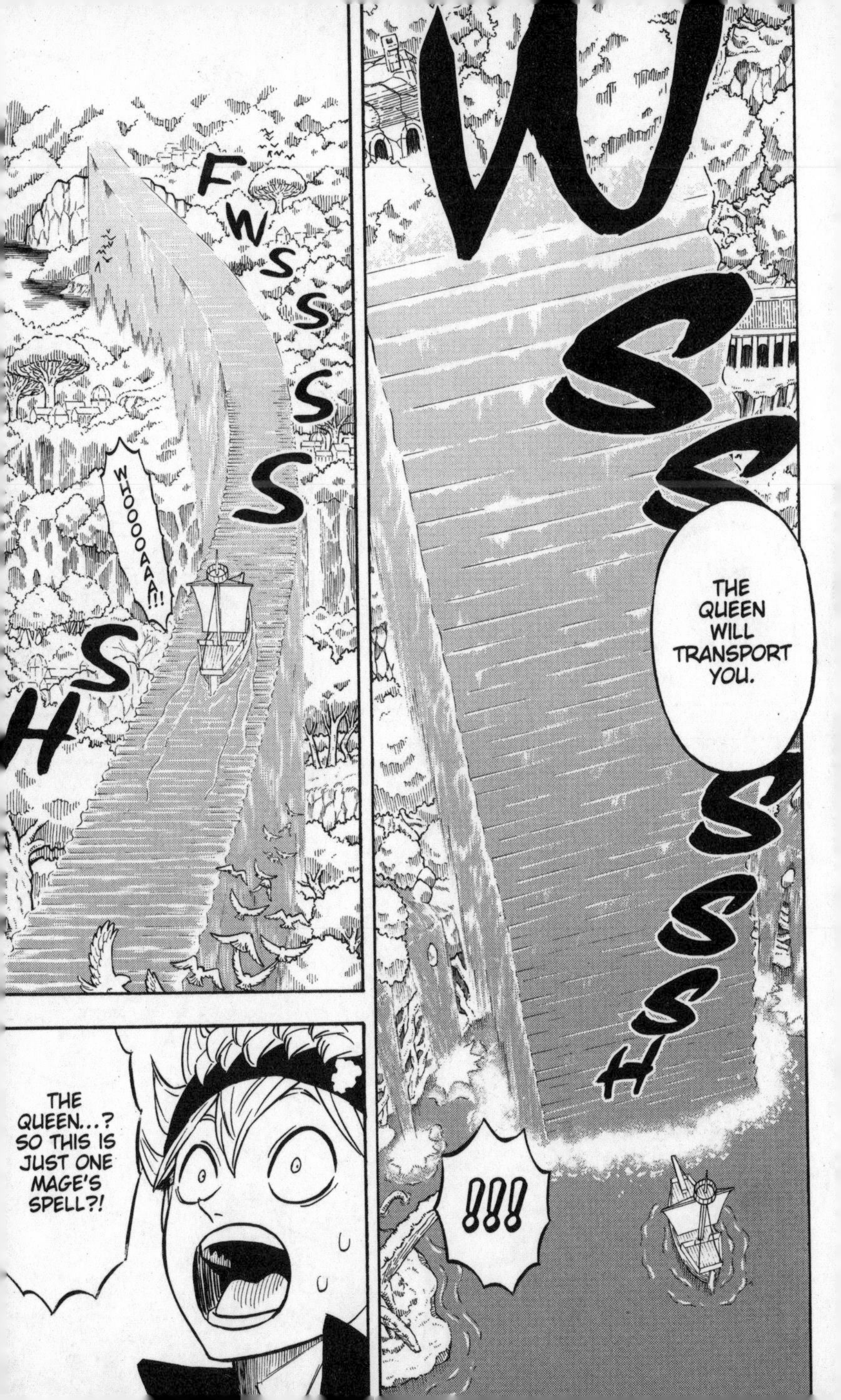
WSSSSSSSH
THE QUEEN WILL TRANSPORT YOU.
!!!
FWSSSSSH
WHOOOOAAA!!
THE QUEEN...? SO THIS IS JUST ONE MAGE'S SPELL?!

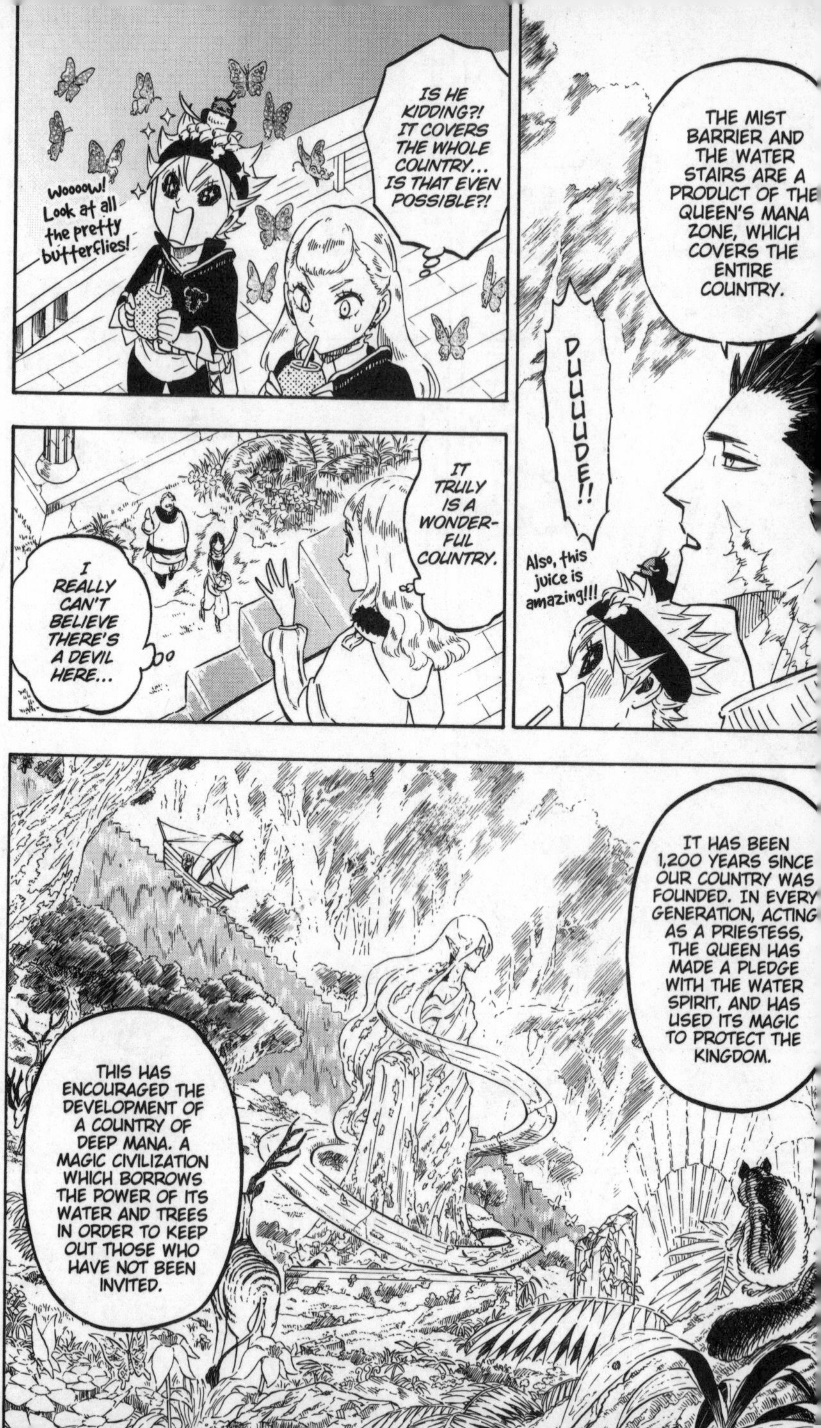
THE MIST BARRIER AND THE WATER STAIRS ARE A PRODUCT OF THE QUEEN'S MANA ZONE, WHICH COVERS THE ENTIRE COUNTRY.
DUUUUDE!!
Also, this juice is amazing!!!
IS HE KIDDING?! IT COVERS THE WHOLE COUNTRY... IS THAT EVEN POSSIBLE?!
Wooooow! Look at all the pretty butterflies!
IT TRULY IS A WONDERFUL COUNTRY.
I REALLY CAN'T BELIEVE THERE'S A DEVIL HERE...
IT HAS BEEN 1,200 YEARS SINCE OUR COUNTRY WAS FOUNDED. IN EVERY GENERATION, ACTING AS A PRIESTESS, THE QUEEN HAS MADE A PLEDGE WITH THE WATER SPIRIT, AND HAS USED ITS MAGIC TO PROTECT THE KINGDOM.
THIS HAS ENCOURAGED THE DEVELOPMENT OF A COUNTRY OF DEEP MANA. A MAGIC CIVILIZATION WHICH BORROWS THE POWER OF ITS WATER AND TREES IN ORDER TO KEEP OUT THOSE WHO HAVE NOT BEEN INVITED.

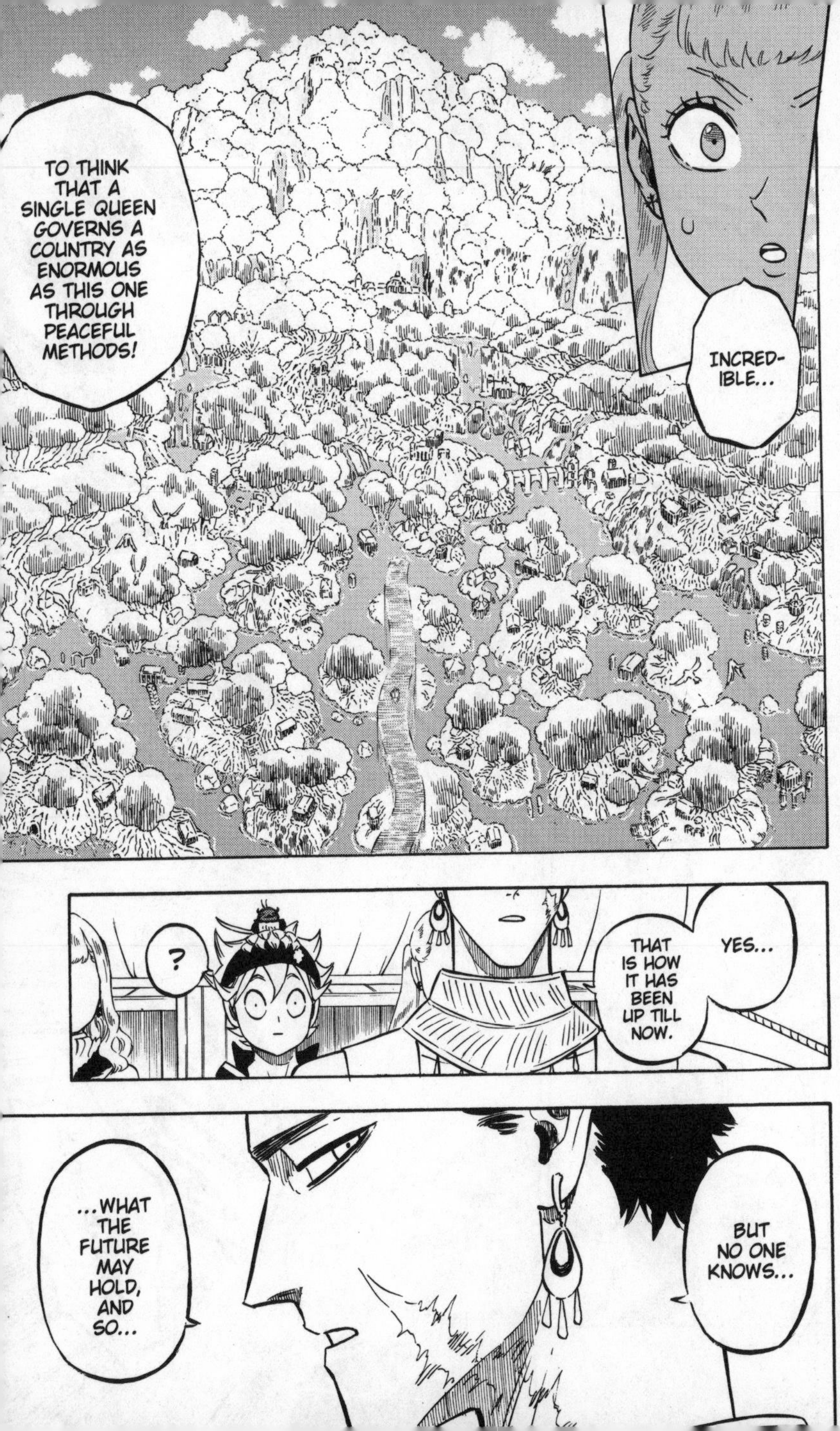
INCRED-IBLE...
TO THINK THAT A SINGLE QUEEN GOVERNS A COUNTRY AS ENORMOUS AS THIS ONE THROUGH PEACEFUL METHODS!
YES...
THAT IS HOW IT HAS BEEN UP TILL NOW.
?
BUT NO ONE KNOWS...
...WHAT THE FUTURE MAY HOLD, AND SO...

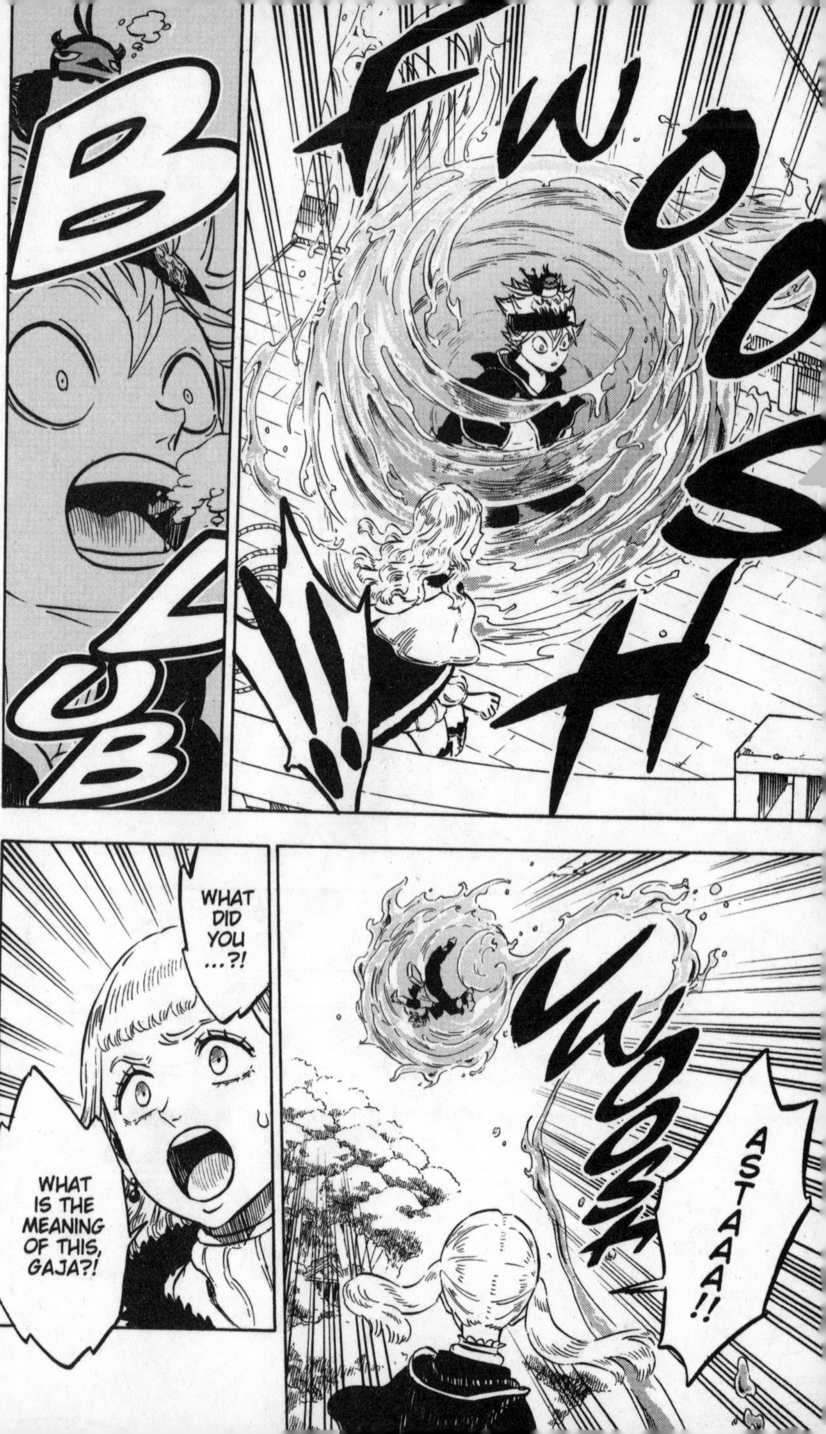
FWOOSH
!!
BLUB
ASTAAAA!!
WHAT DID YOU ...?!
WHAT IS THE MEANING OF THIS, GAJA?!

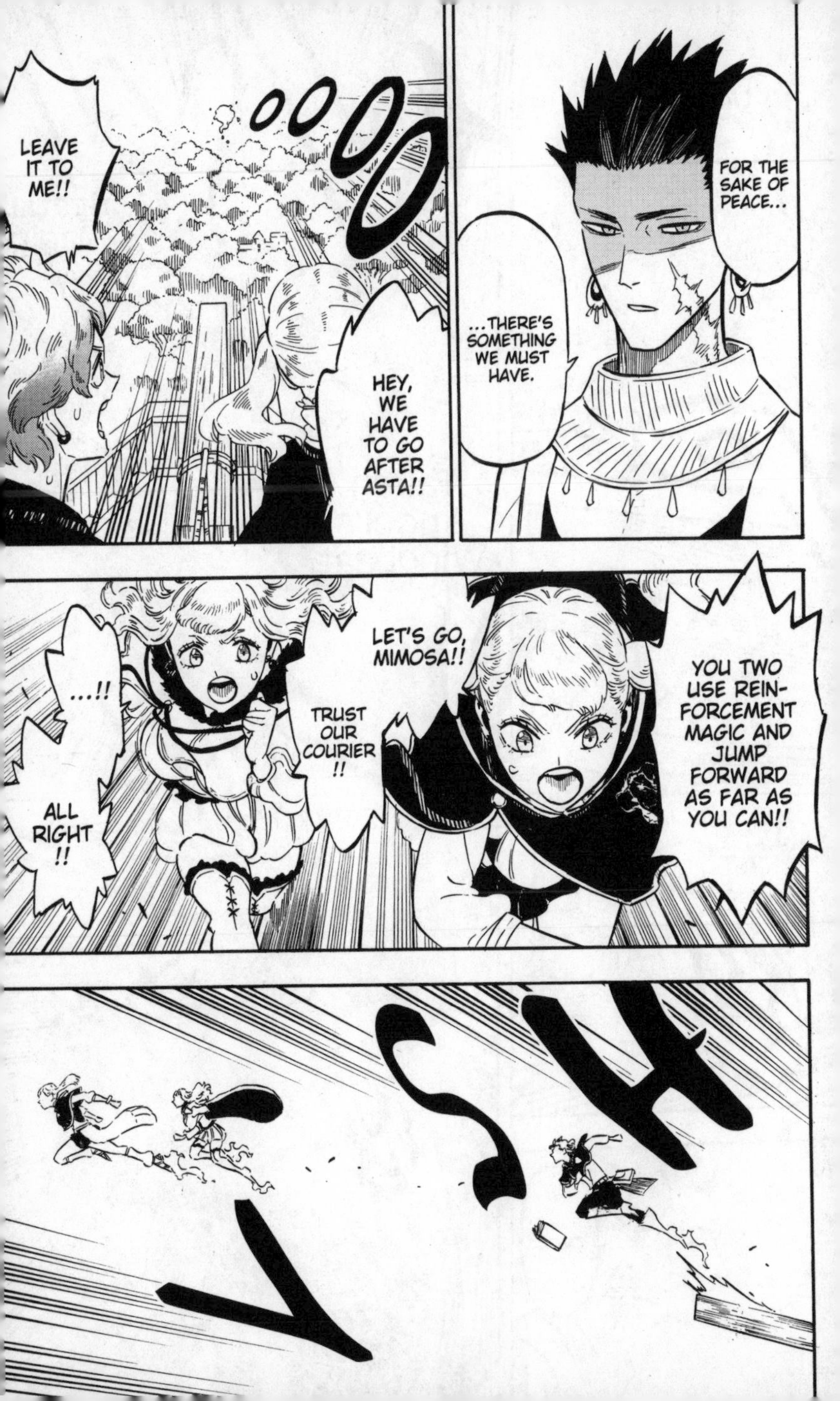
FOR THE SAKE OF PEACE...
...THERE'S SOMETHING WE MUST HAVE.
HEY, WE HAVE TO GO AFTER ASTA!!
LEAVE IT TO ME!!
YOU TWO USE REIN-FORCEMENT MAGIC AND JUMP FORWARD AS FAR AS YOU CAN!!
LET'S GO, MIMOSA!!
TRUST OUR COURIER!!
...!!
ALL RIGHT!!
VSH

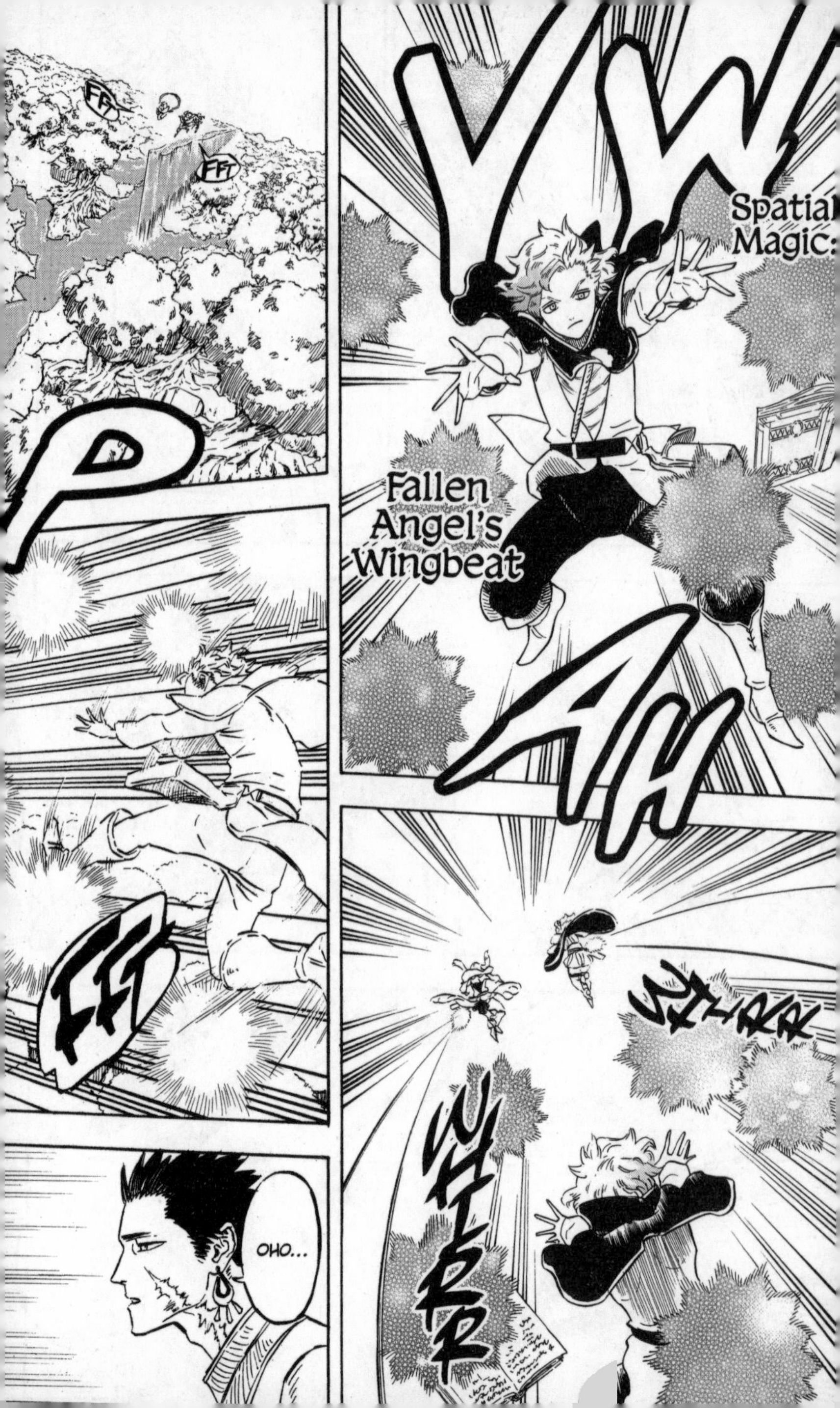
VWAH
Spatial Magic:
Fallen Angel's Wingbeat
FFT
FFT
P
FFT
OHO...

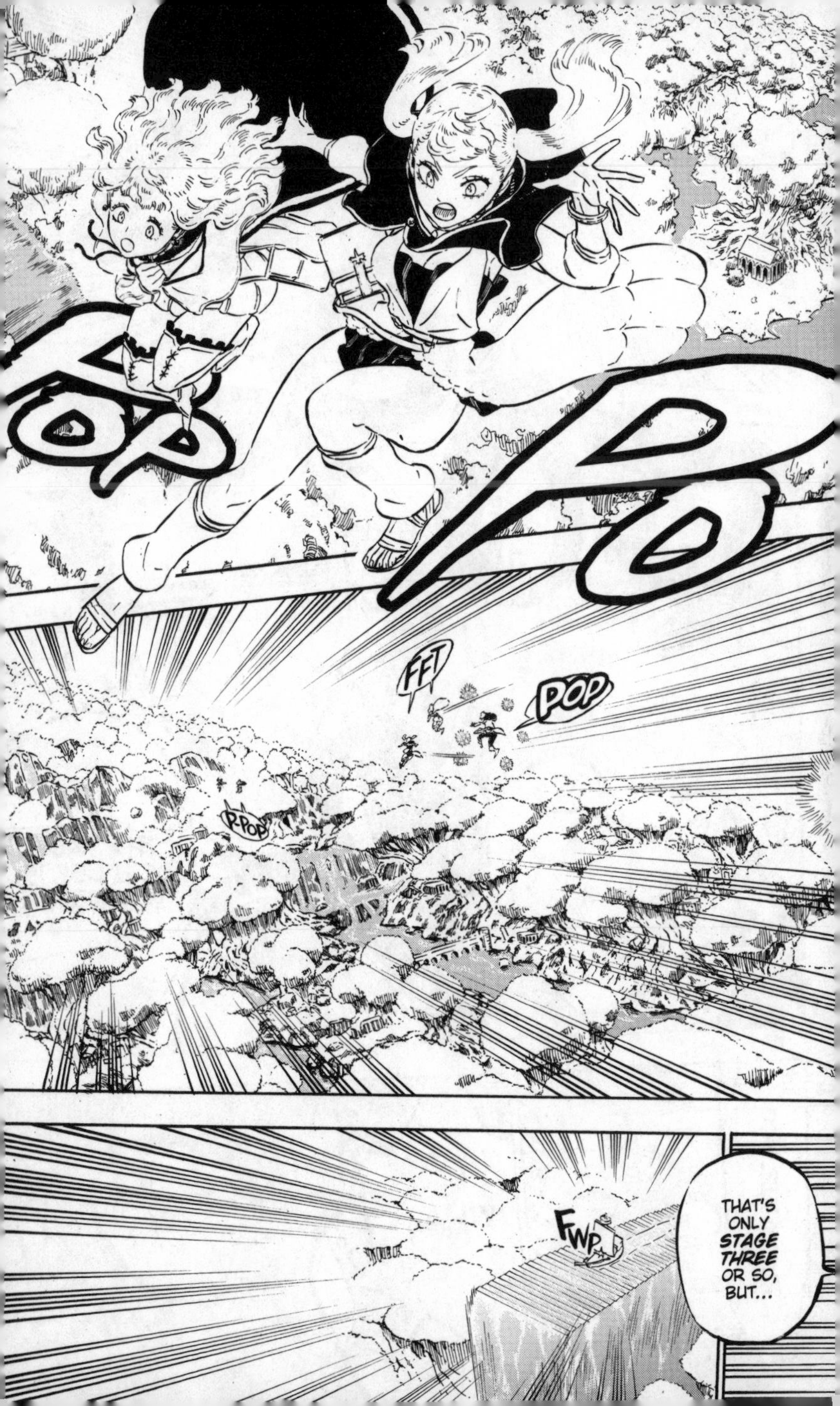
POP
FFT
POP
P-POP
THAT'S ONLY STAGE THREE OR SO, BUT...
FWP

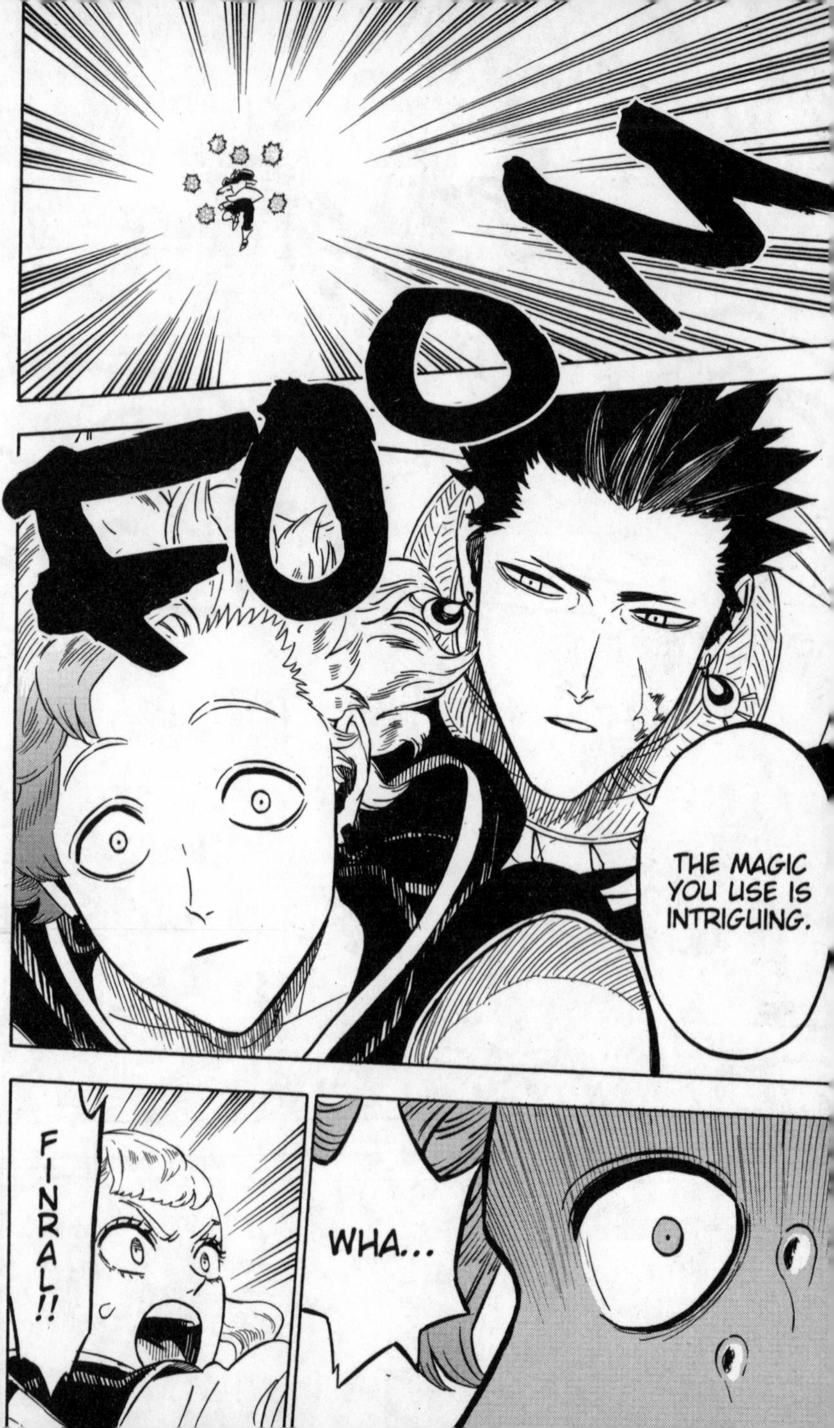
FOOM
THE MAGIC YOU USE IS INTRIGUING.
WHA...
FINRAL!!

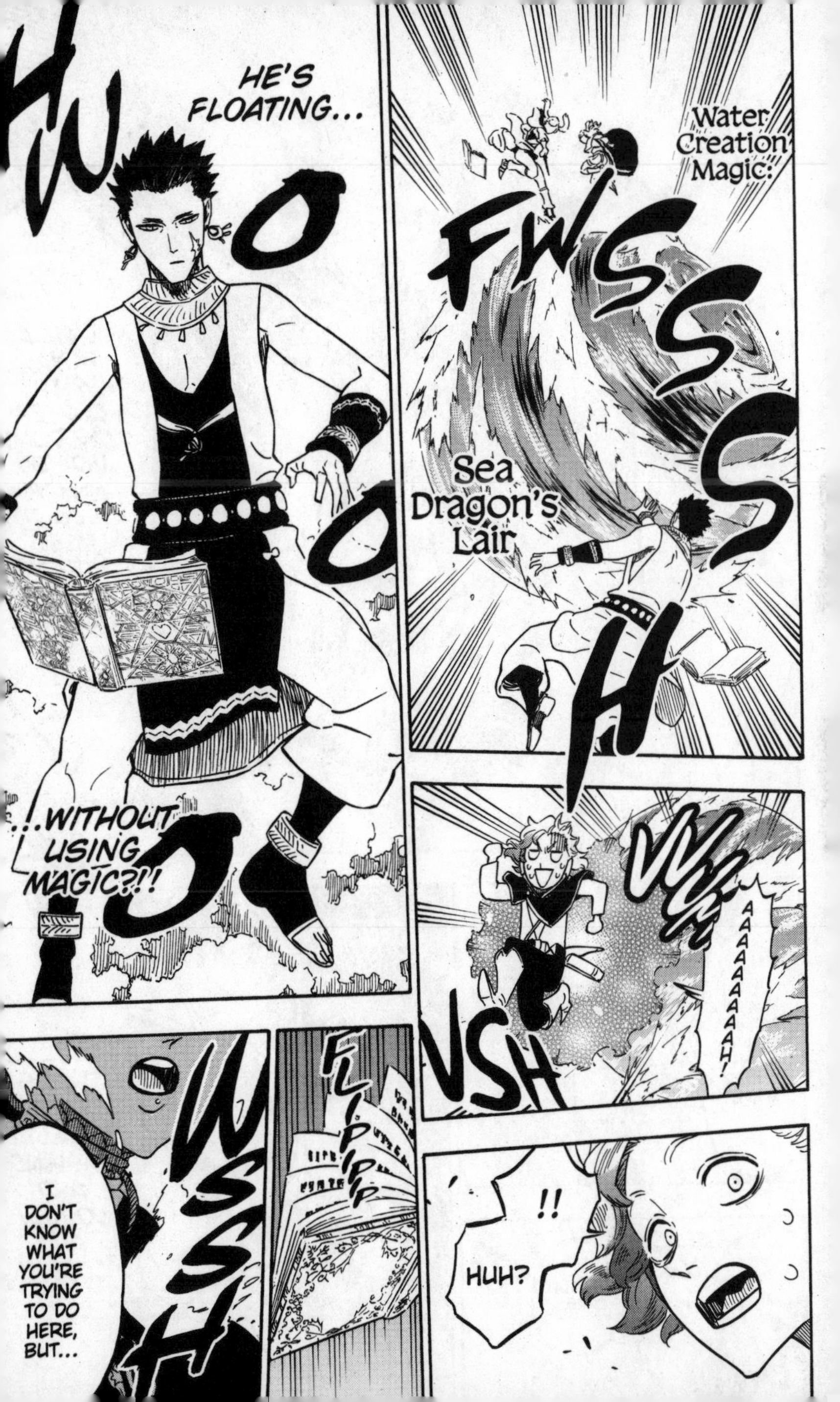

Water Creation Magic:
Sea Dragon's Lair
FWSSSH
VWSH
AAAAAAAAAH!
HWOOO
HE'S FLOATING...
...WITHOUT USING MAGIC?!!
!!
HUH?
FLIPIPIP
WSSH
I DON'T KNOW WHAT YOU'RE TRYING TO DO HERE, BUT...

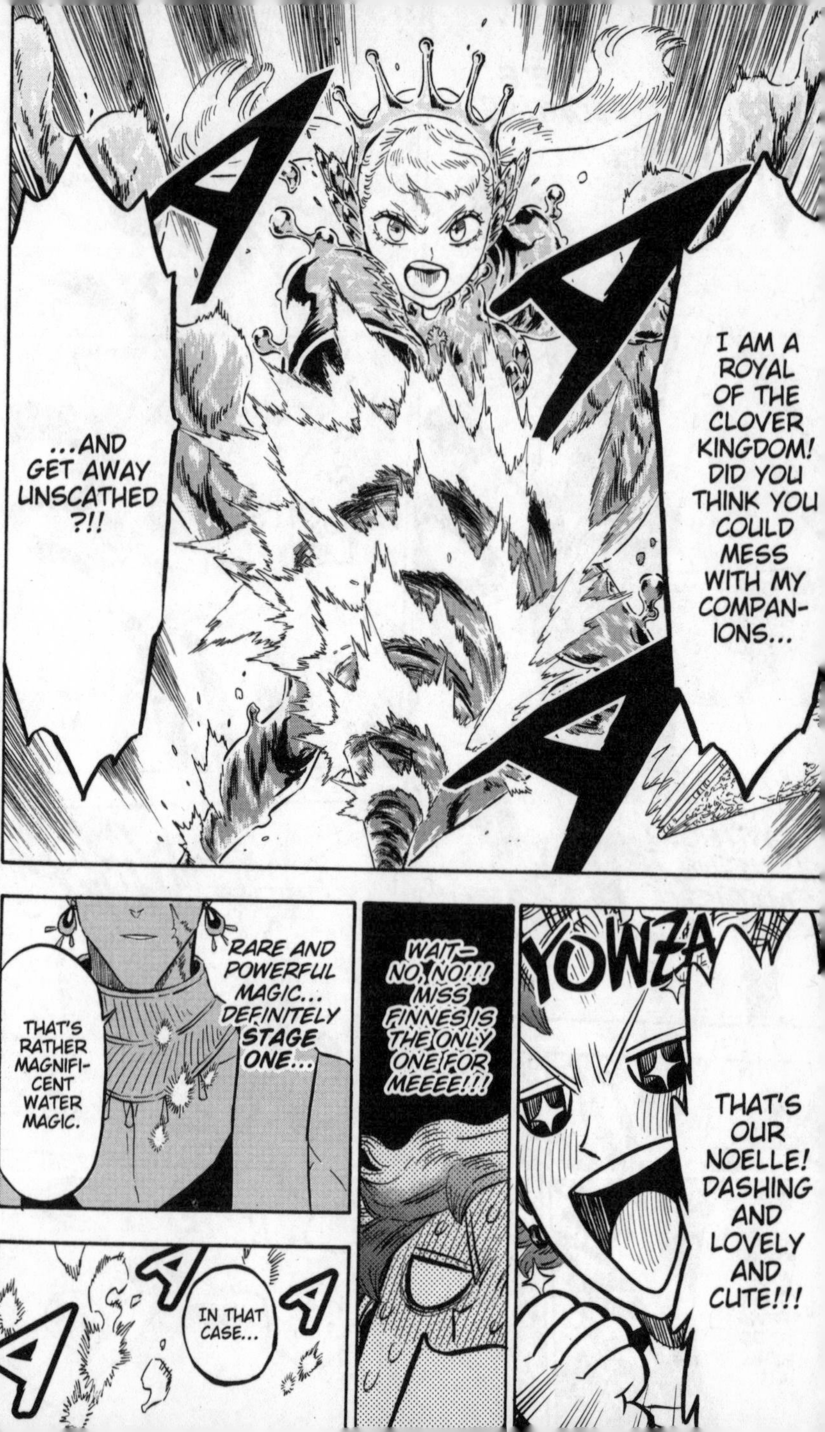
I AM A ROYAL OF THE CLOVER KINGDOM! DID YOU THINK YOU COULD MESS WITH MY COMPANIONS...
...AND GET AWAY UNSCATHED?!!
AAAA
YOWZA
THAT'S OUR NOELLE! DASHING AND LOVELY AND CUTE!!!
WAIT— NO, NO!!! MISS FINNES IS THE ONLY ONE FOR MEEEE!!!
RARE AND POWERFUL MAGIC... DEFINITELY STAGE ONE...
THAT'S RATHER MAGNIFICENT WATER MAGIC.
AAA
IN THAT CASE...

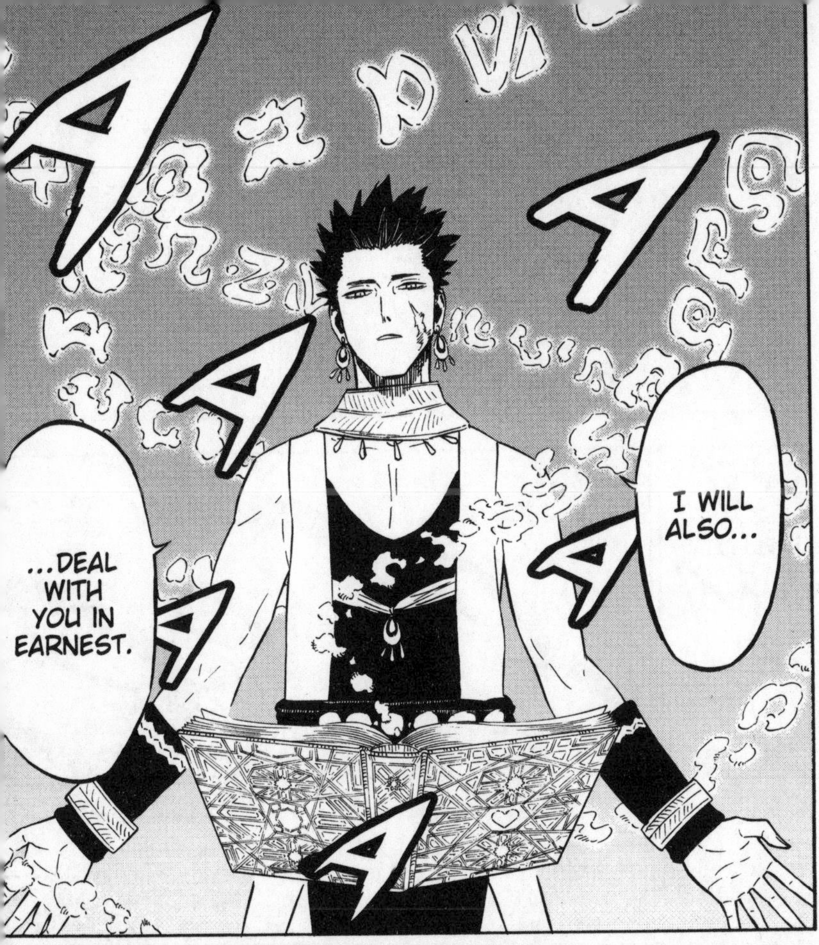
I WILL ALSO...
...DEAL WITH YOU IN EARNEST.
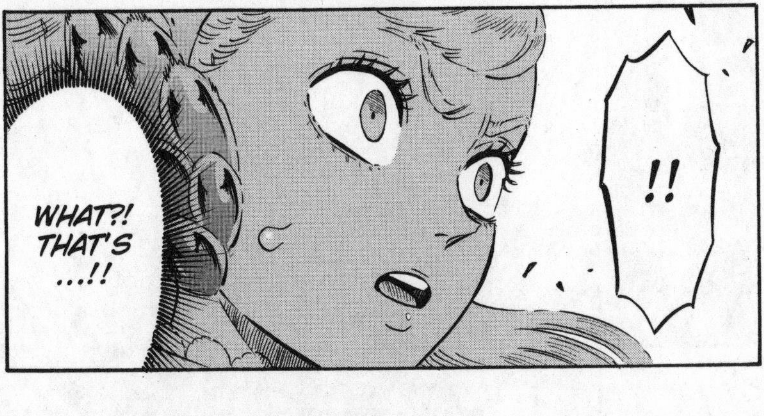
!!
WHAT?! THAT'S ...!!

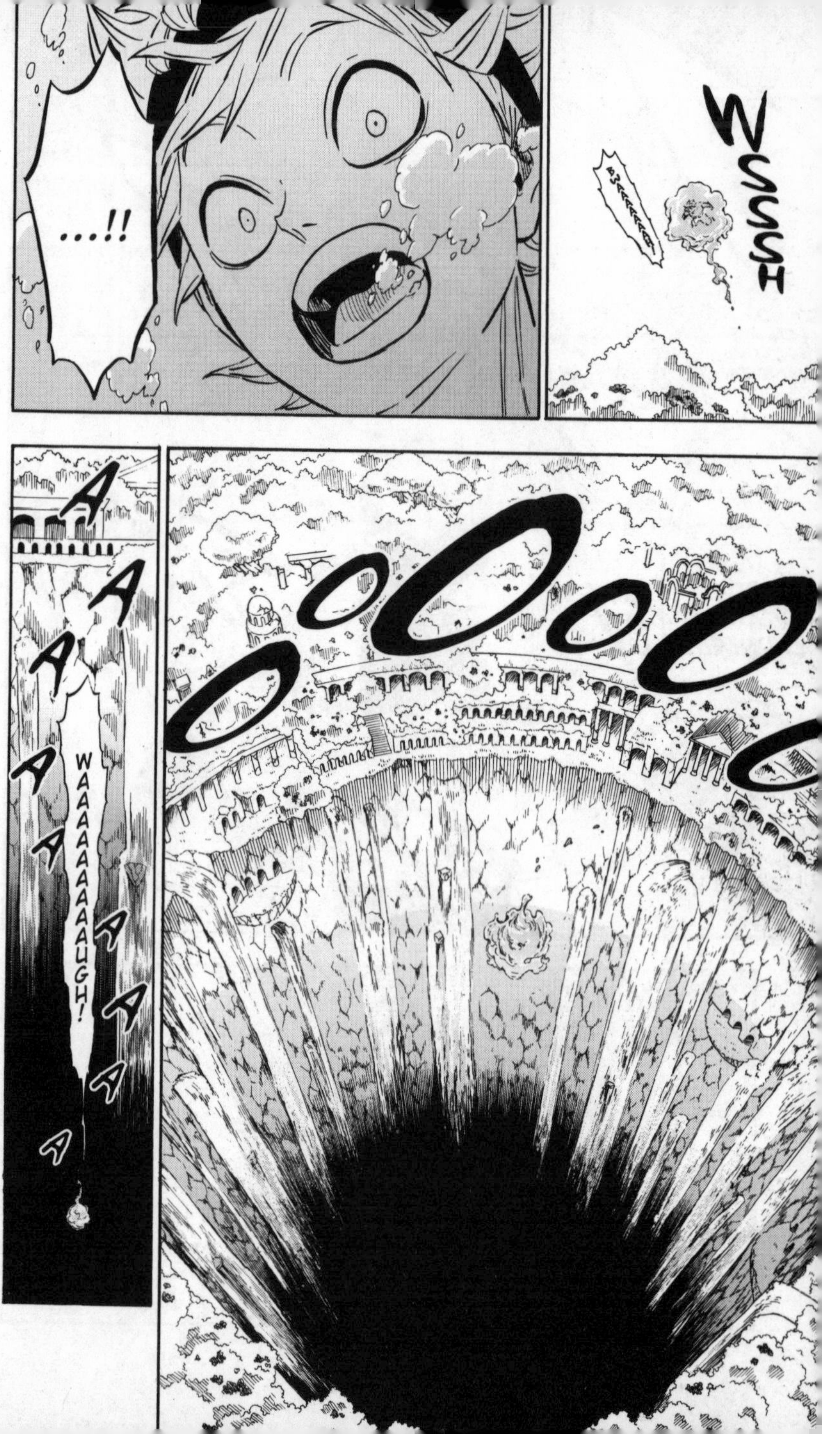
WSSSH
BJAAAAAAAH!
...!!
OOOOOOO
AAAAAAAAAA
WAAAAAAAAAAAUGH!

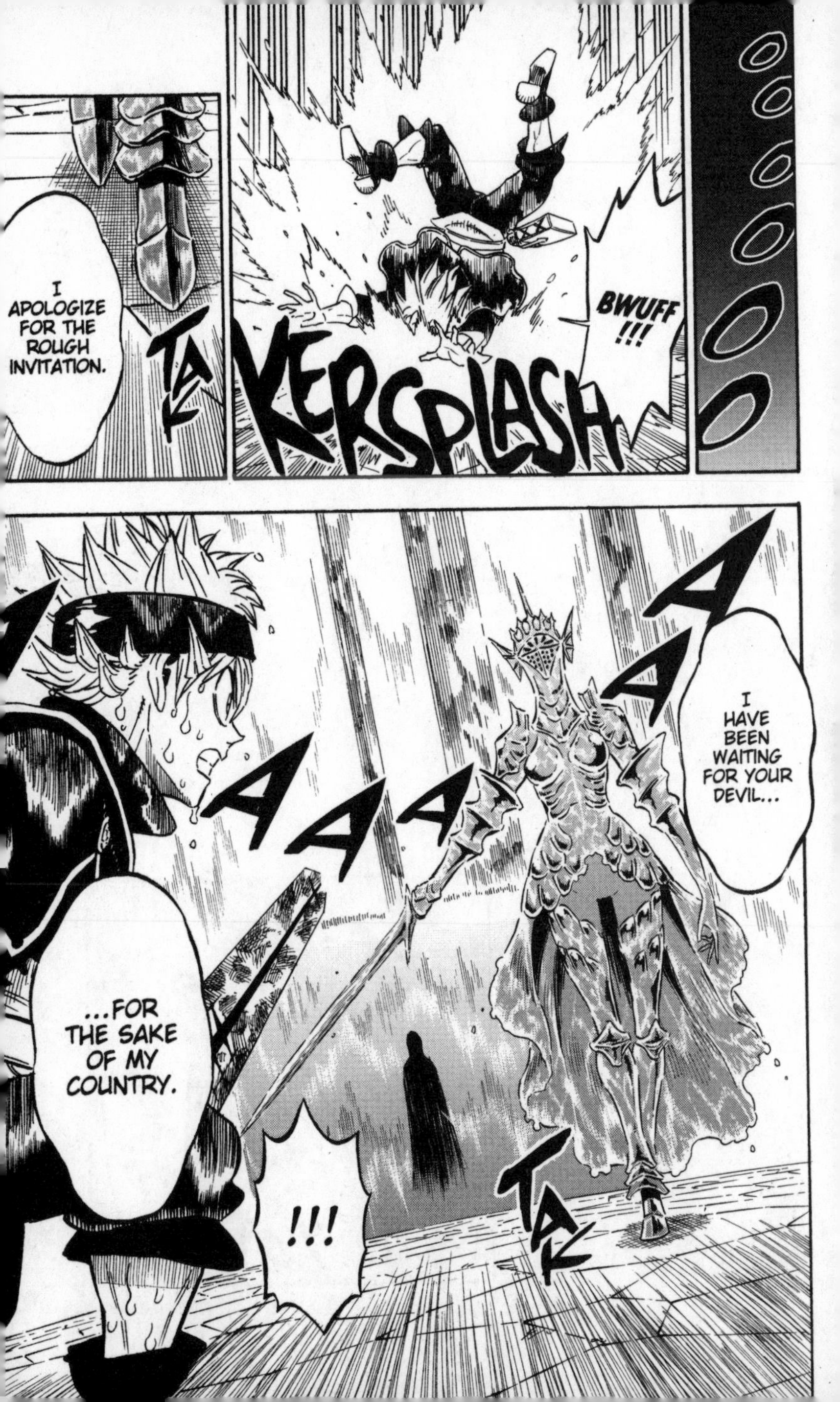

OOOOOOOO
BWUFF!!!
KERSPLASH
I APOLOGIZE FOR THE ROUGH INVITATION.
TAK
AAAAAAA
I HAVE BEEN WAITING FOR YOUR DEVIL...
...FOR THE SAKE OF MY COUNTRY.
!!!
TAK

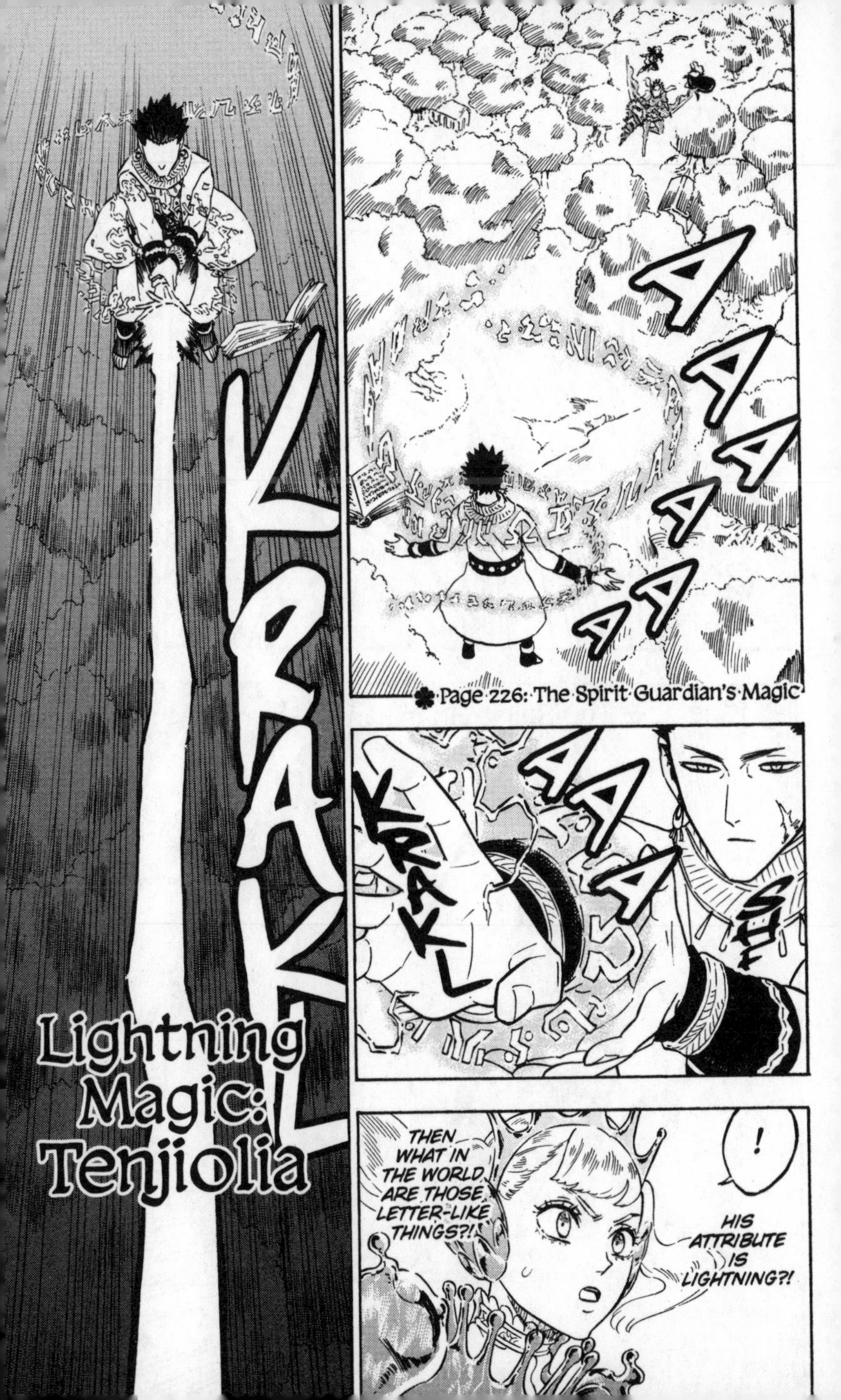

AAAAAAAA
Page 226: The Spirit Guardian's Magic
AAAA
KRAKL
!
HIS ATTRIBUTE IS LIGHTNING?!
THEN WHAT IN THE WORLD ARE THOSE LETTER-LIKE THINGS?!
KRAKL
Lightning Magic: Tenjiolia

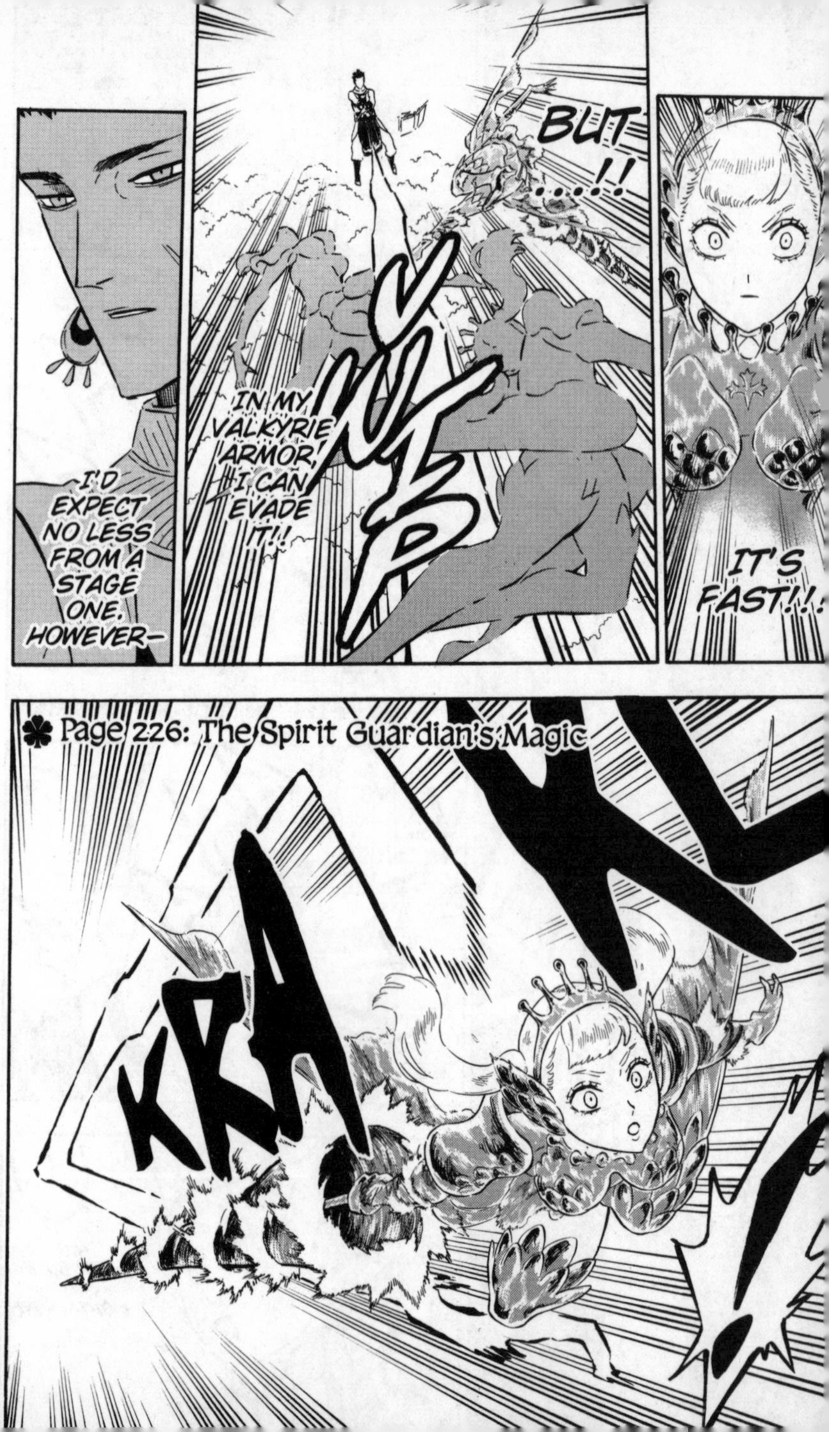
IT'S FAST!!!
BUT ...!!
IN MY VALKYRIE ARMOR, I CAN EVADE IT!!
JUMP
I'D EXPECT NO LESS FROM A STAGE ONE. HOWEVER—
Page 226: The Spirit Guardian's Magic
KRAK!

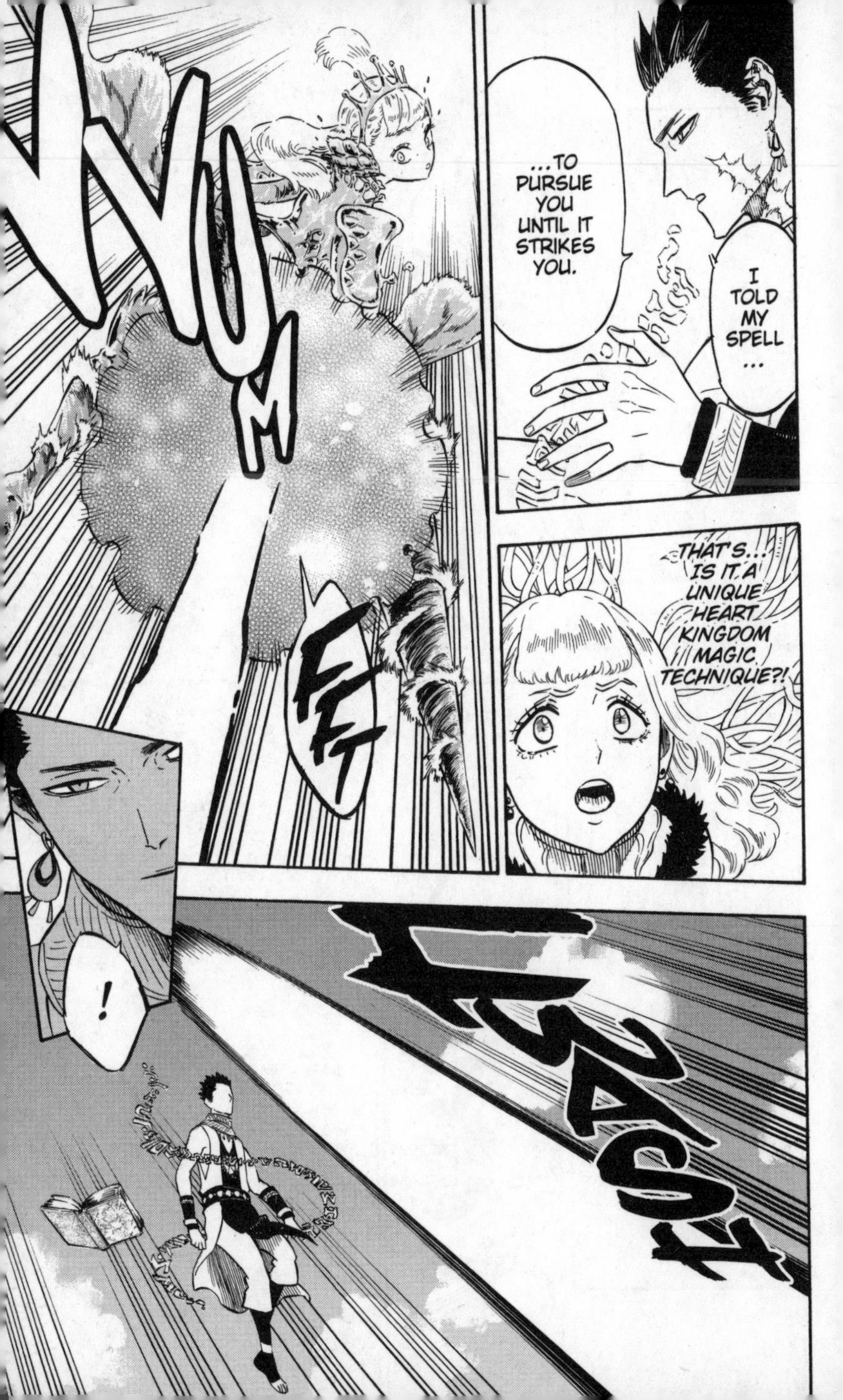
I TOLD MY SPELL...
...TO PURSUE YOU UNTIL IT STRIKES YOU.
VVOOM
FFT
THAT'S... IS IT A UNIQUE HEART KINGDOM MAGIC TECHNIQUE?!
!

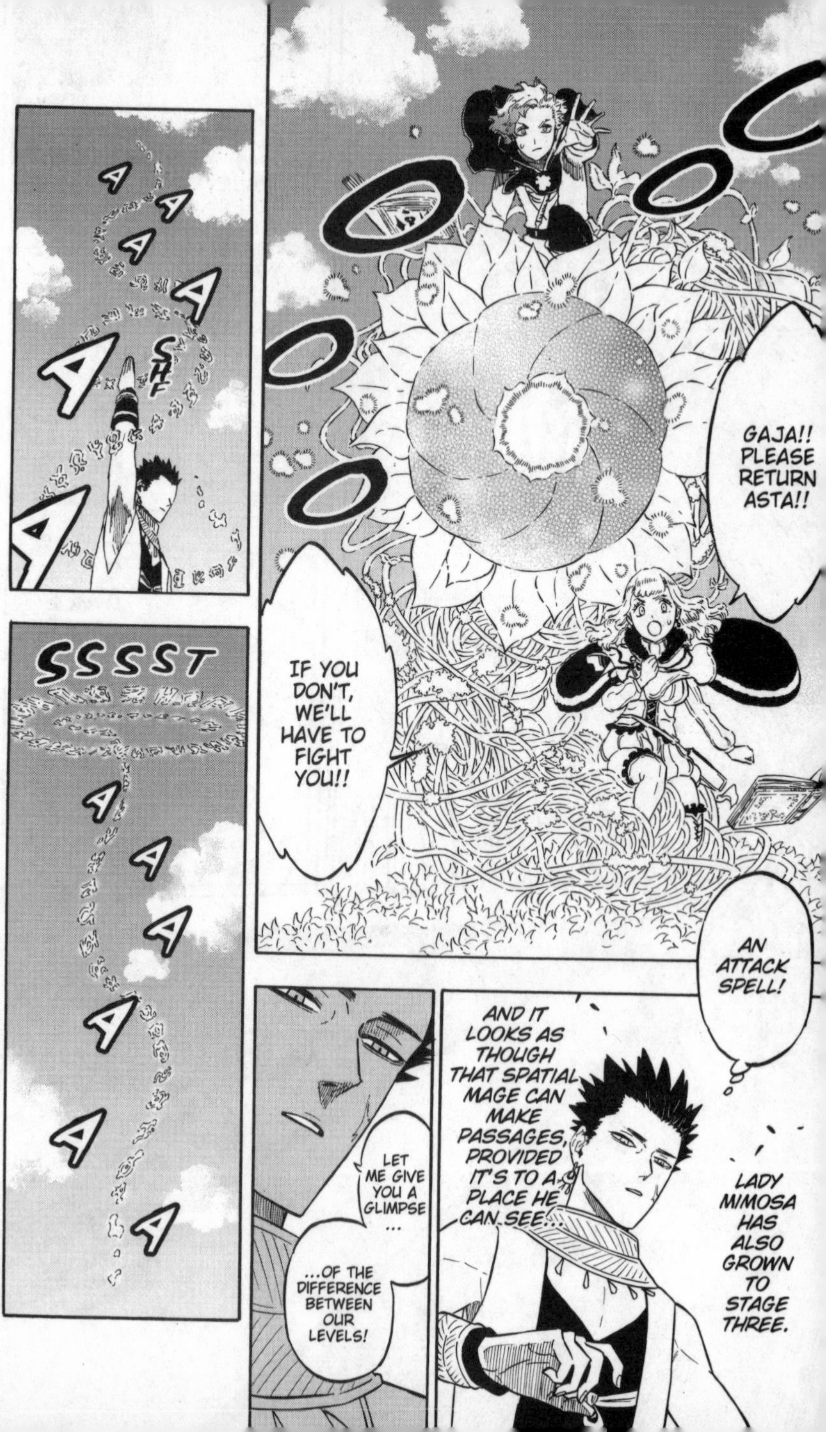

GAJA!! PLEASE RETURN ASTA!!
IF YOU DON'T, WE'LL HAVE TO FIGHT YOU!!
AN ATTACK SPELL!
LADY MIMOSA HAS ALSO GROWN TO STAGE THREE.
AND IT LOOKS AS THOUGH THAT SPATIAL MAGE CAN MAKE PASSAGES, PROVIDED IT'S TO A PLACE HE CAN SEE...
LET ME GIVE YOU A GLIMPSE...
...OF THE DIFFERENCE BETWEEN OUR LEVELS!
AAAAAA
SHF
SSSST
AAAAAA

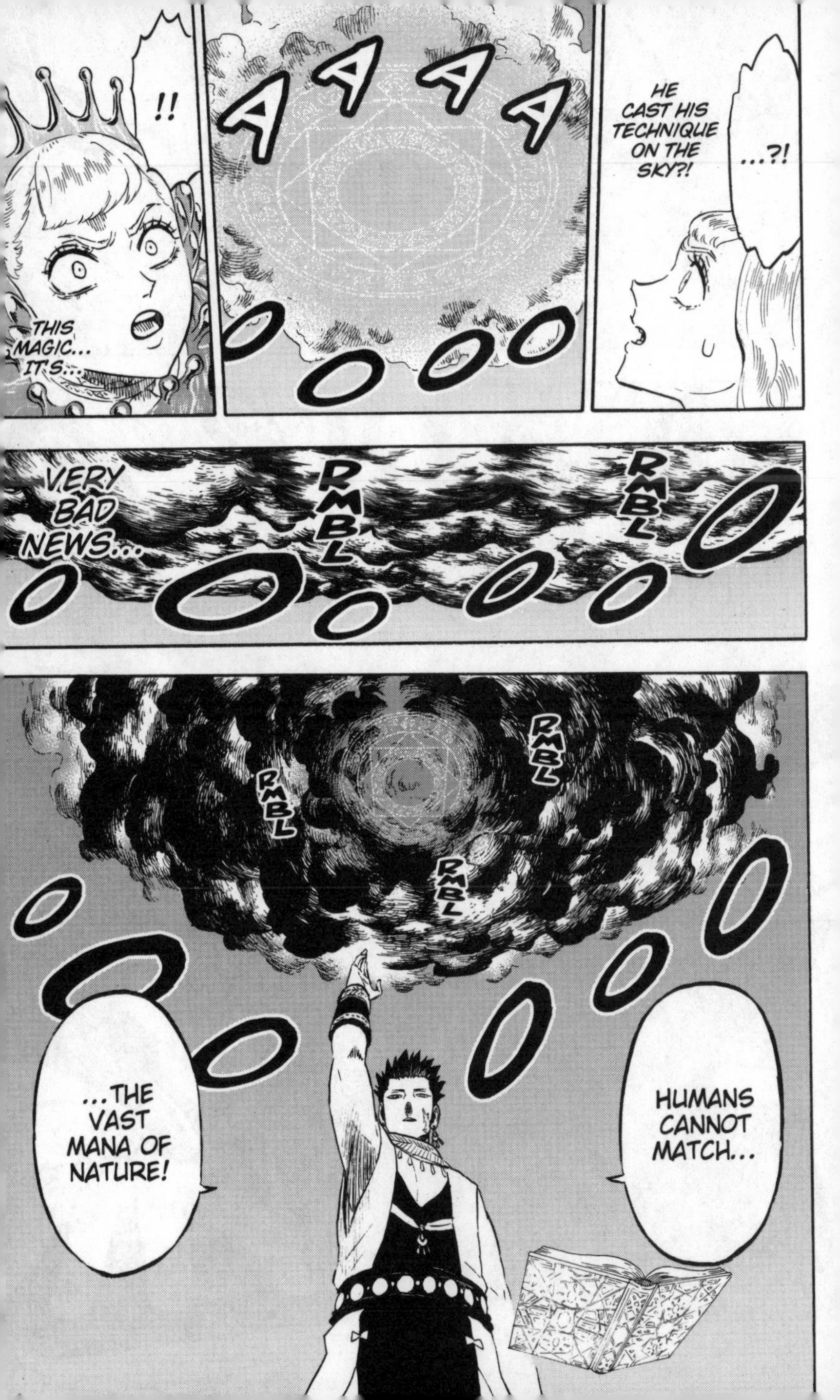

...?!
HE CAST HIS TECHNIQUE ON THE SKY?!
AAAA
OOOO
!!
THIS MAGIC... IT'S...
RMBL
RMBL
VERY BAD NEWS...
RMBL
RMBL
RMBL
HUMANS CANNOT MATCH...
...THE VAST MANA OF NATURE!

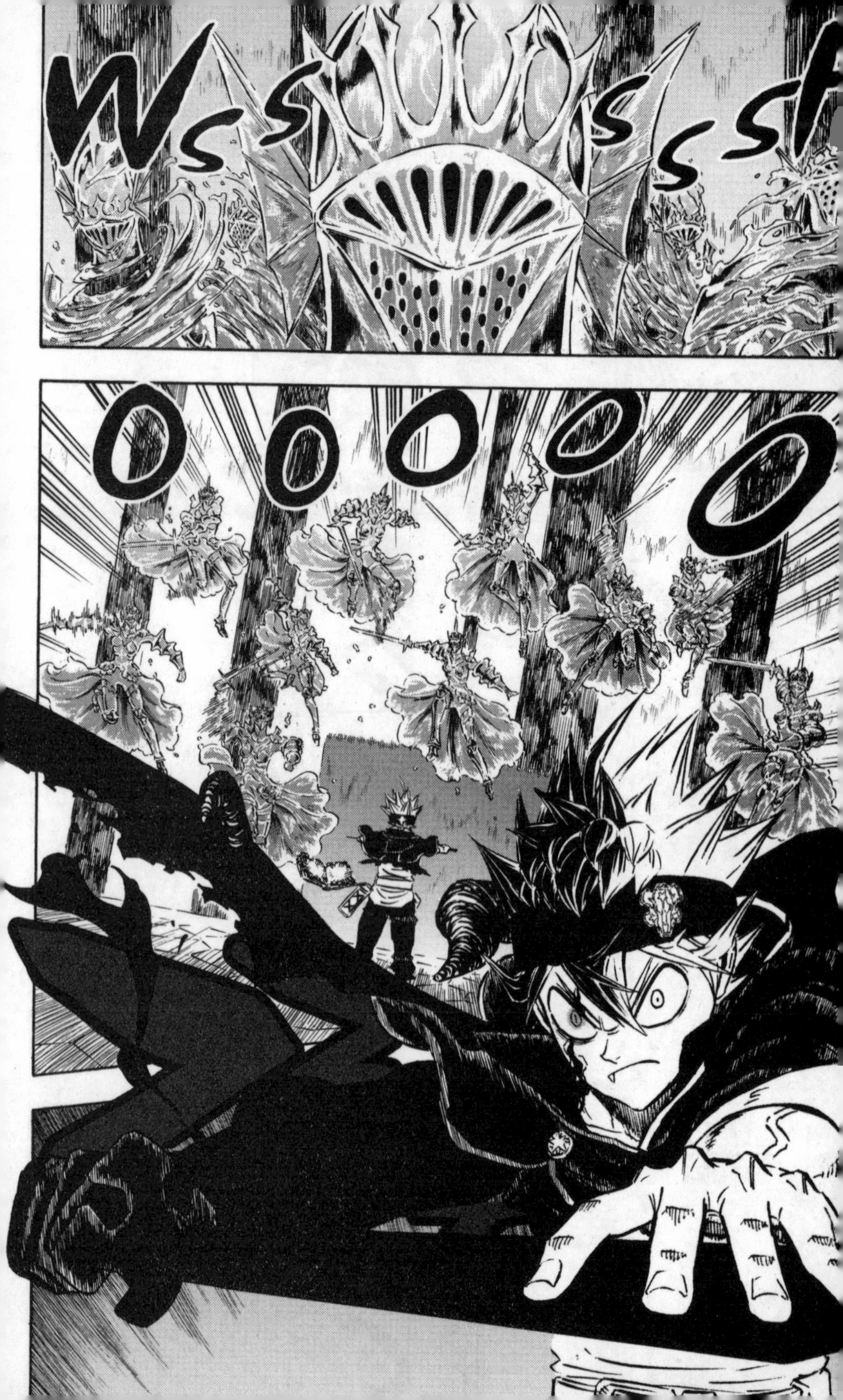
WSSSSSH
OOOOO

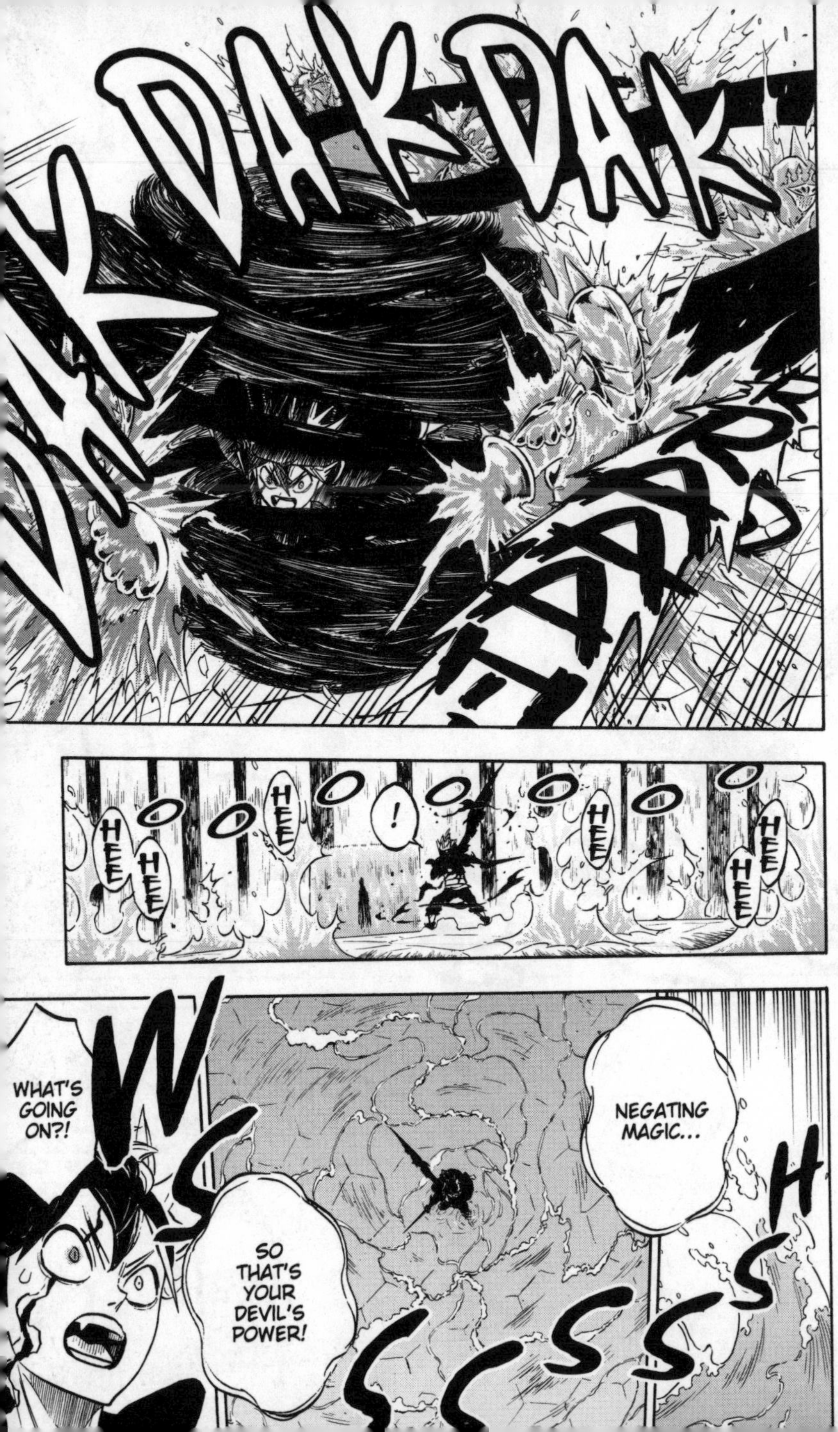
DAK-DAK-DAK
!
HEE HEE
HEE
HEE HEE
HEE
HEE
HEE
NEGATING MAGIC...
SO THAT'S YOUR DEVIL'S POWER!
WHAT'S GOING ON?!
WSSSSH

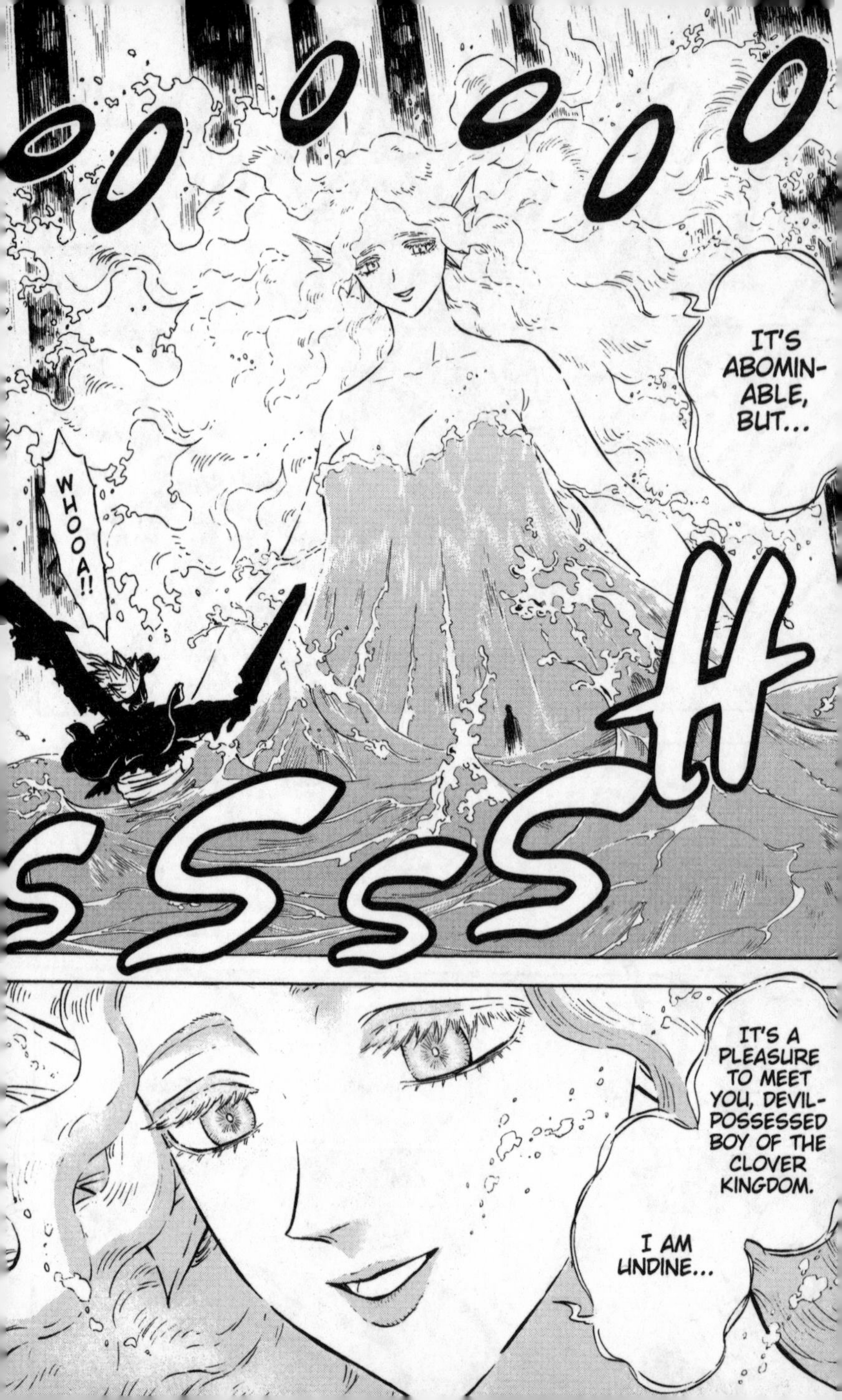
OOOOOOO
IT'S ABOMINABLE, BUT...
WHOOA!!
SSSSH
IT'S A PLEASURE TO MEET YOU, DEVIL-POSSESSED BOY OF THE CLOVER KINGDOM.
I AM UNDINE...

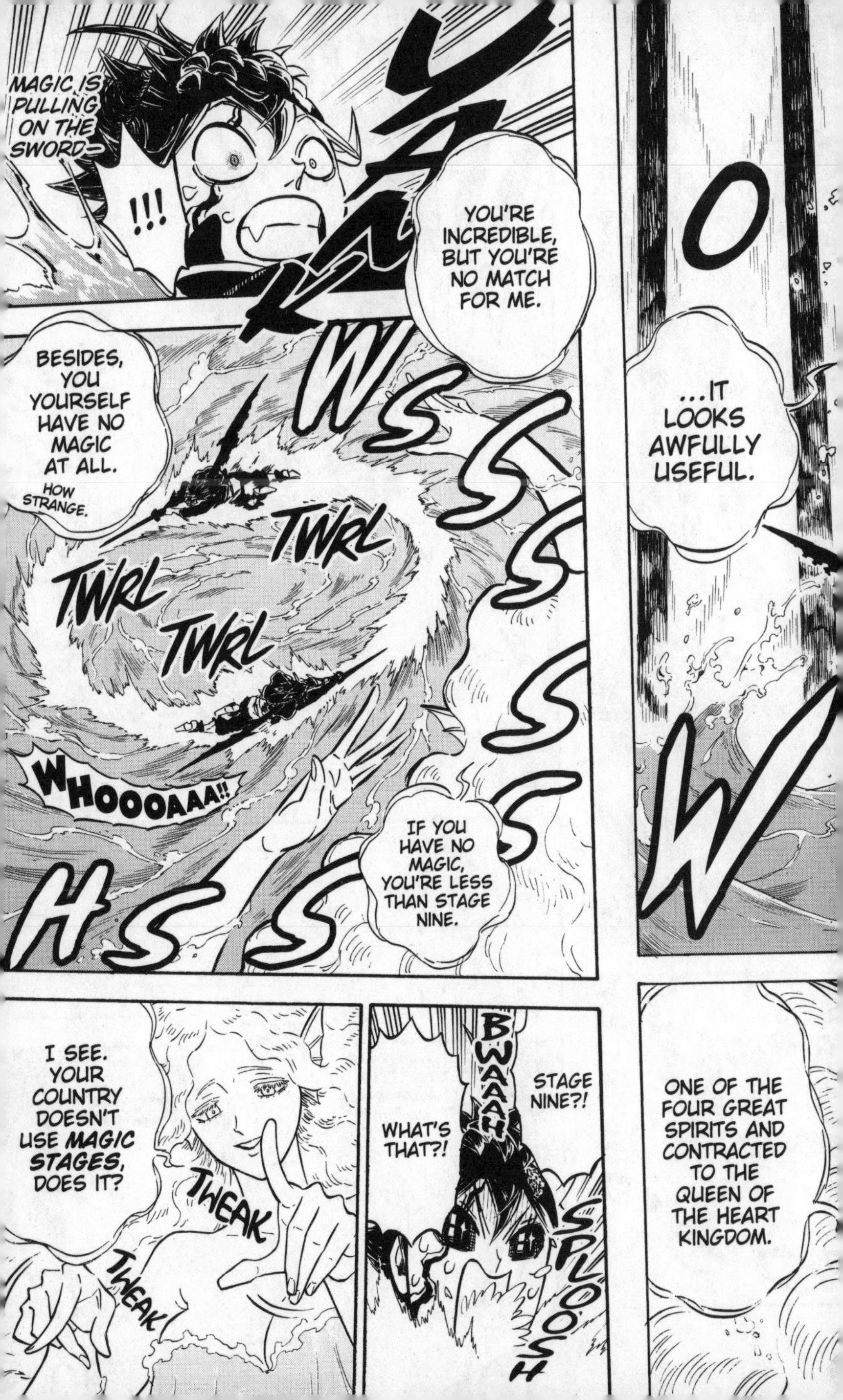
OW
...IT LOOKS AWFULLY USEFUL.
MAGIC IS PULLING ON THE SWORD—
!!!
YOU'RE INCREDIBLE, BUT YOU'RE NO MATCH FOR ME.
WSSSSSSS
BESIDES, YOU YOURSELF HAVE NO MAGIC AT ALL.
HOW STRANGE.
TWRL
TWRL
TWRL
WHOOOAAA!!
IF YOU HAVE NO MAGIC, YOU'RE LESS THAN STAGE NINE.
HS
ONE OF THE FOUR GREAT SPIRITS AND CONTRACTED TO THE QUEEN OF THE HEART KINGDOM.
STAGE NINE?!
WHAT'S THAT?!
BWAAAH
SPLOOOSH
I SEE. YOUR COUNTRY DOESN'T USE *MAGIC STAGES*, DOES IT?
TWEAK
TWEAK

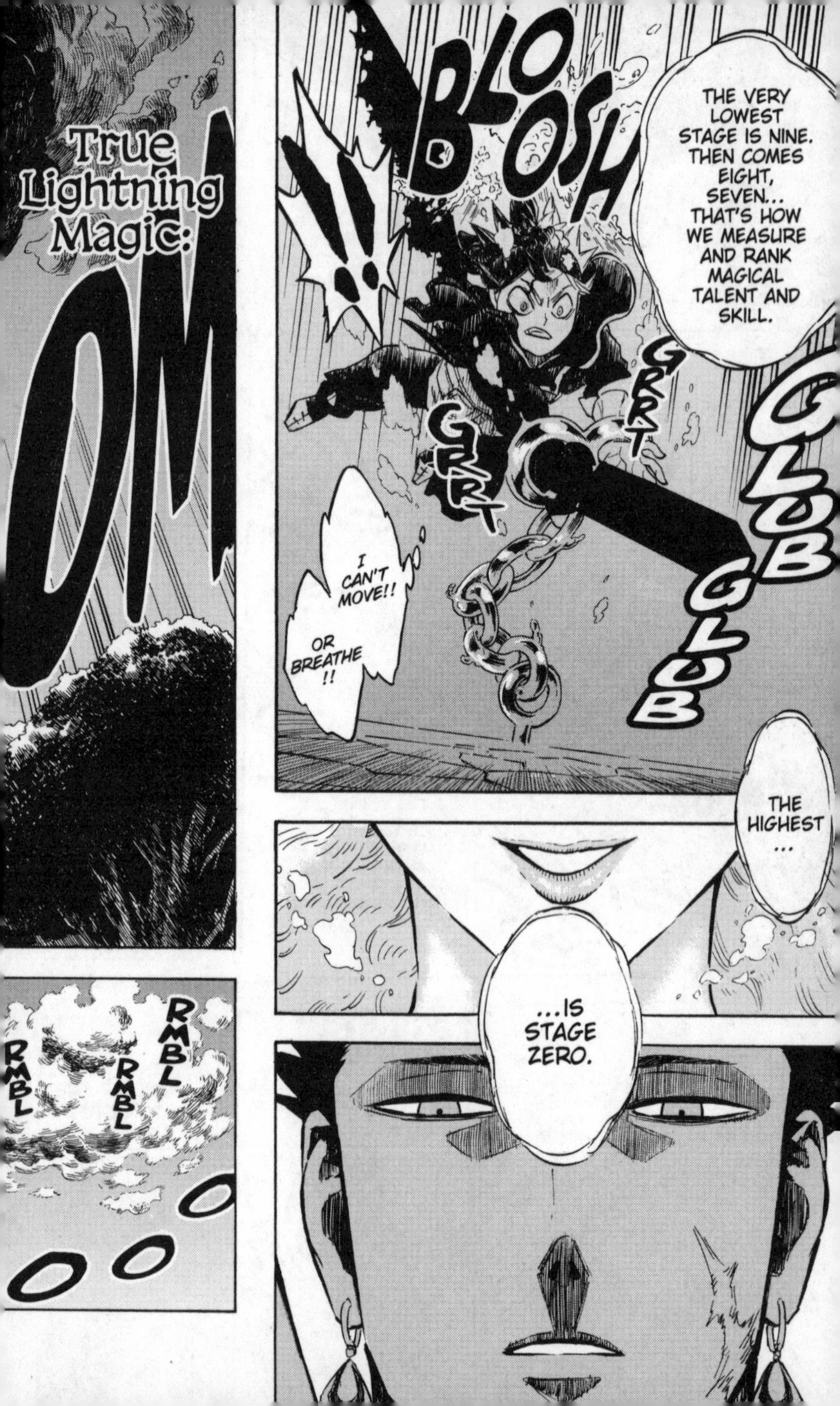
THE VERY LOWEST STAGE IS NINE. THEN COMES EIGHT, SEVEN... THAT'S HOW WE MEASURE AND RANK MAGICAL TALENT AND SKILL.
BLOSH
GRRT
GLOB GLOB
GRRT
I CAN'T MOVE!!
OR BREATHE !!
THE HIGHEST ...
...IS STAGE ZERO.
True Lightning Magic:
OM
RMBL
RMBL
RMBL
OOO

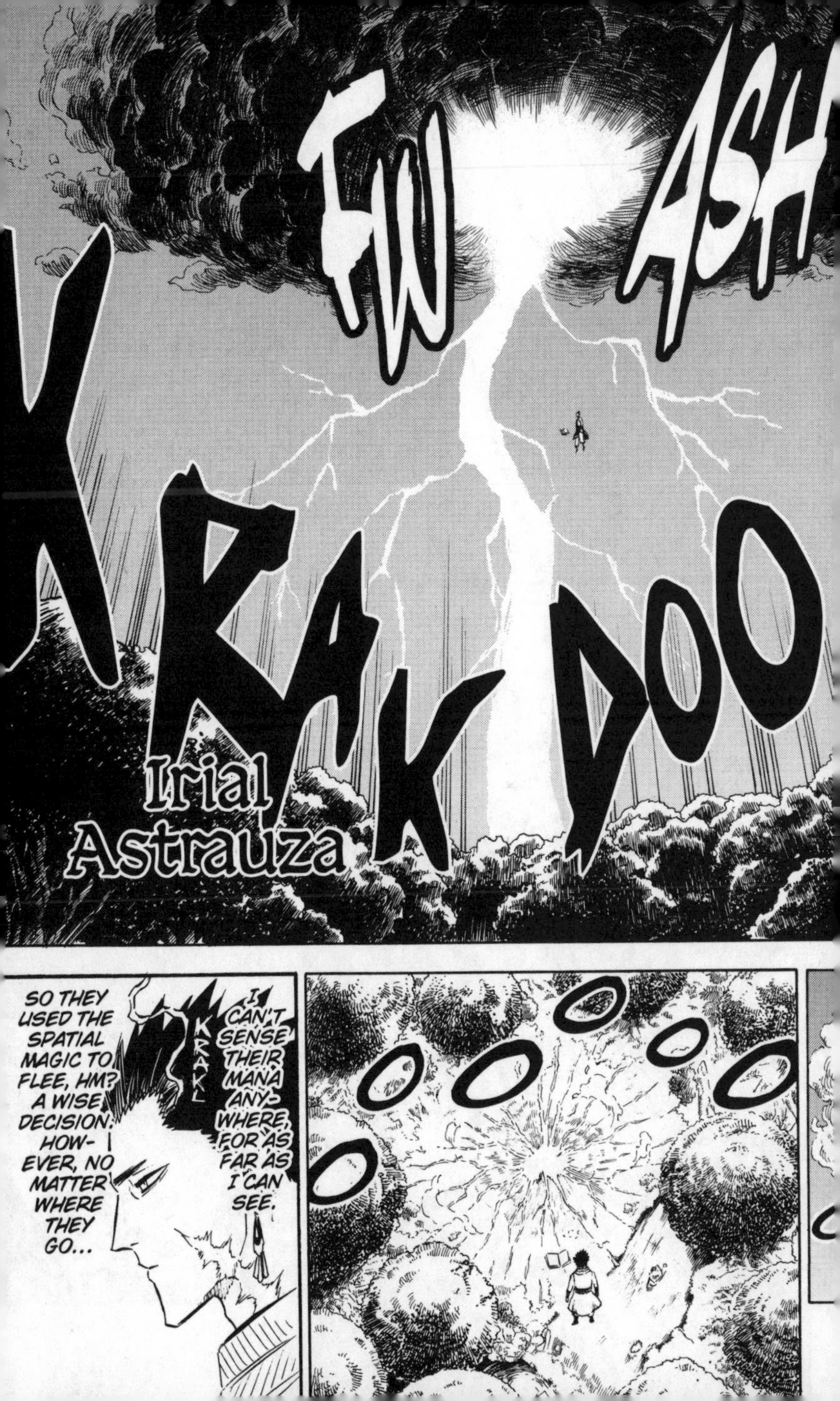
FLASH
KRAK DOOO
Irial Astrauza
OOOOOOO
I CAN'T SENSE THEIR MANA ANYWHERE, FOR AS FAR AS I CAN SEE.
KRAKL
SO THEY USED THE SPATIAL MAGIC TO FLEE, HM? A WISE DECISION. HOWEVER, NO MATTER WHERE THEY GO...

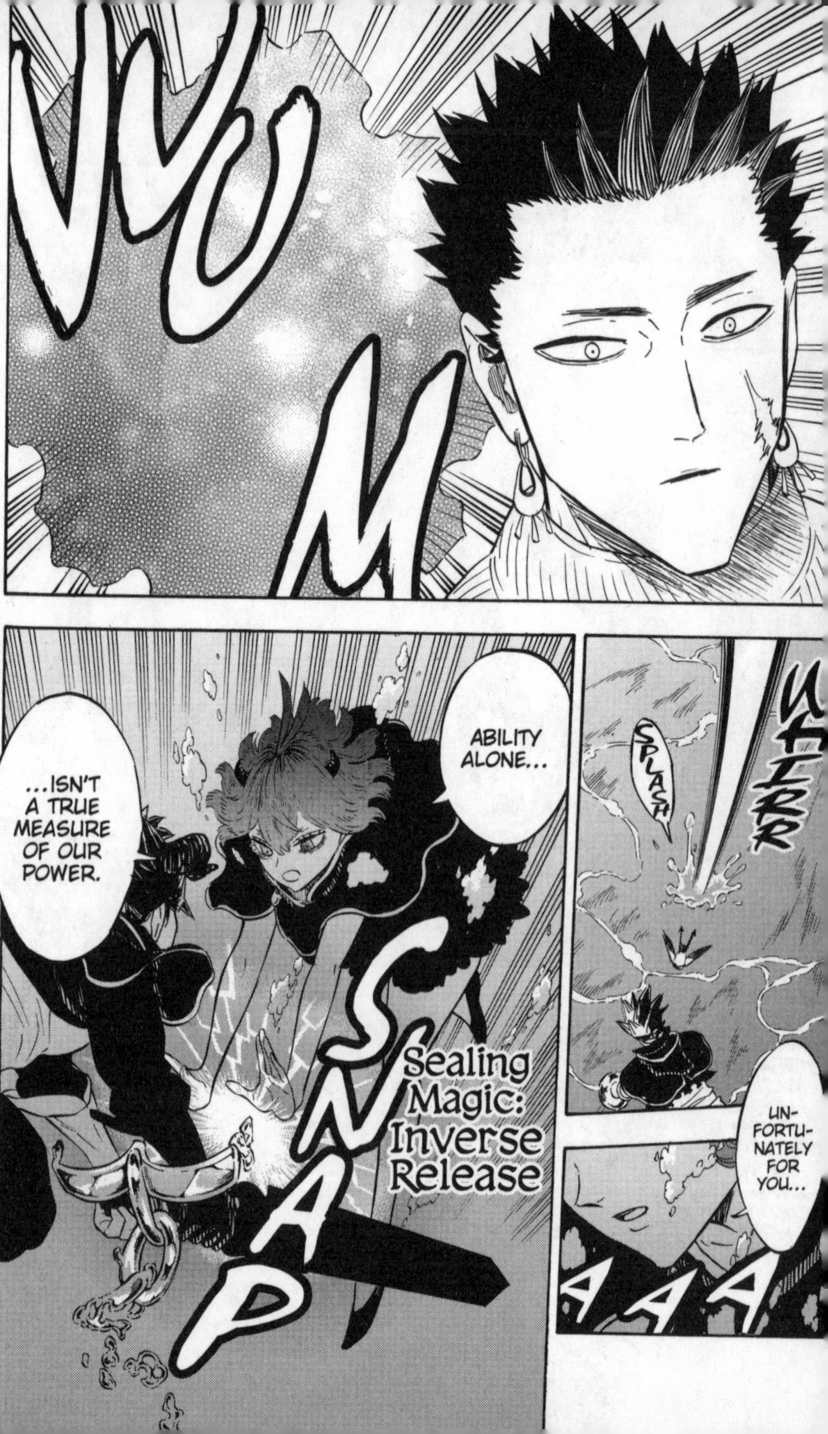
VWOM
WHIRR
SPLASH
UN-FORTU-NATELY FOR YOU...
AAA
ABILITY ALONE...
...ISN'T A TRUE MEASURE OF OUR POWER.
SNAP
Sealing Magic: Inverse Release

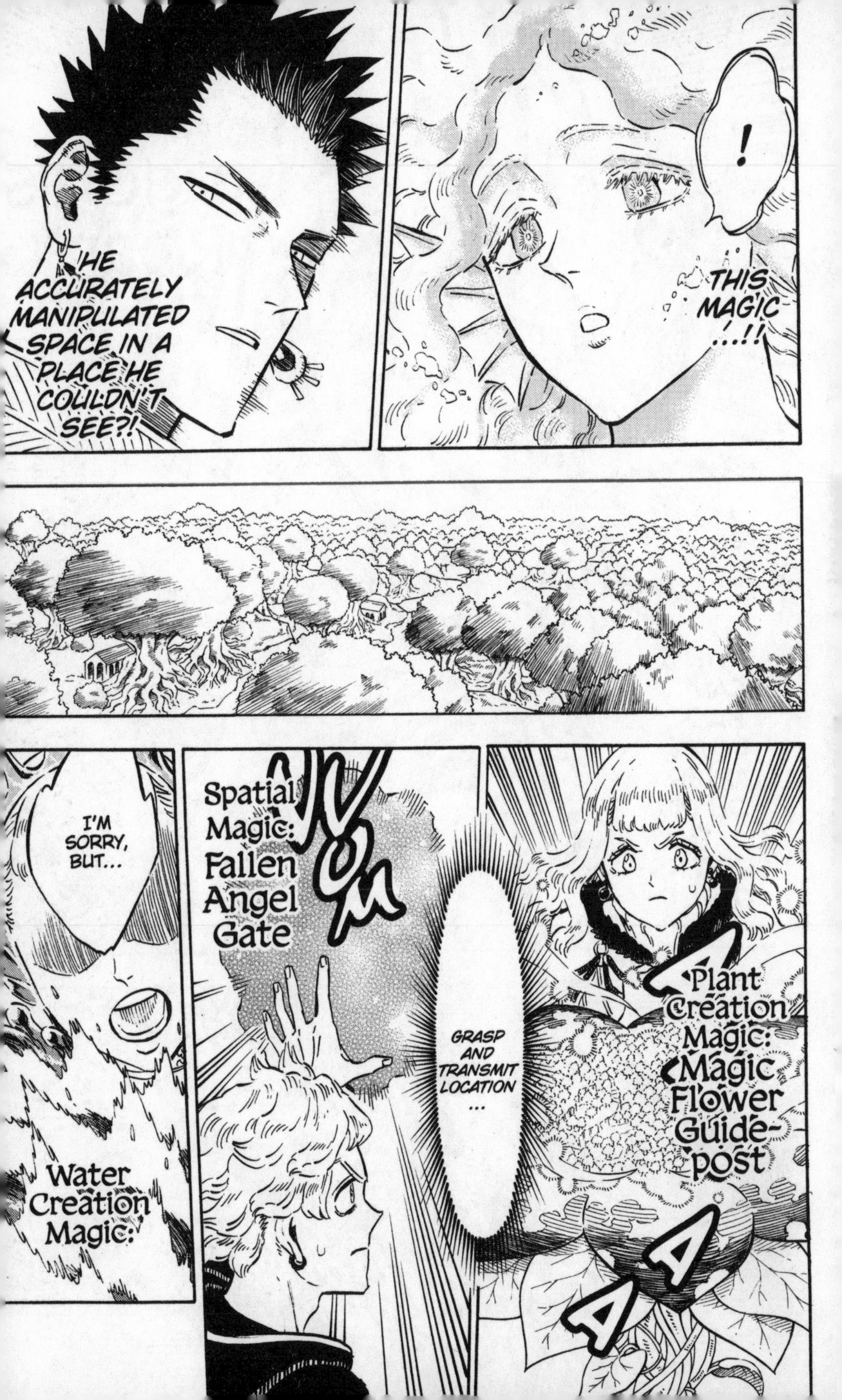
!
THIS MAGIC...!!
HE ACCURATELY MANIPULATED SPACE IN A PLACE HE COULDN'T SEE?!
Plant Creation Magic: Magic Flower Guide-post
A
A
A
GRASP AND TRANSMIT LOCATION...
Spatial Magic: Fallen Angel Gate
I'M SORRY, BUT...
Water Creation Magic:

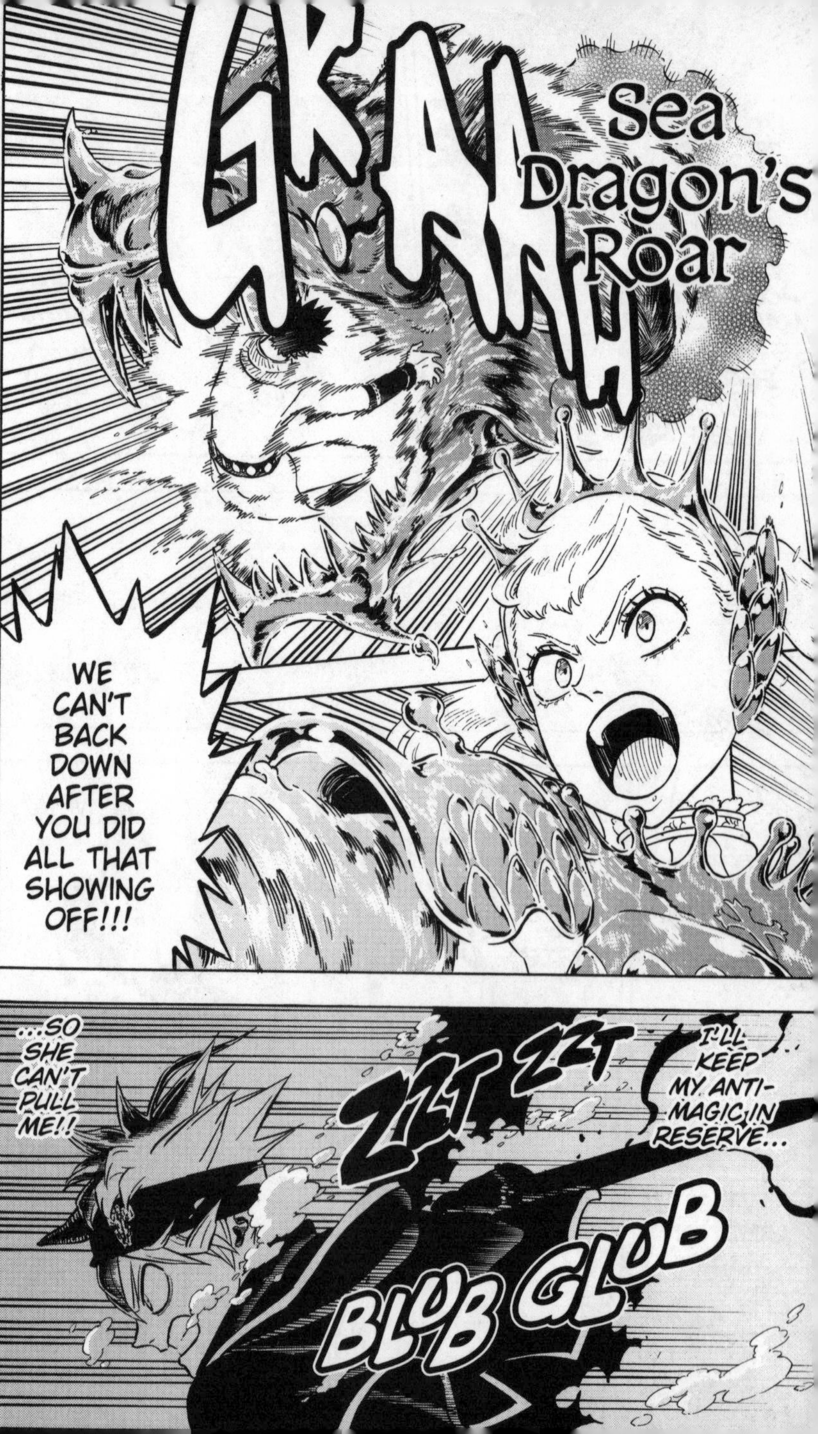
Sea Dragon's Roar
GKAAAH
WE CAN'T BACK DOWN AFTER YOU DID ALL THAT SHOWING OFF!!!
I'LL KEEP MY ANTI-MAGIC IN RESERVE...
ZZT ZZT
...SO SHE CAN'T PULL ME!!
BLUB GLUB

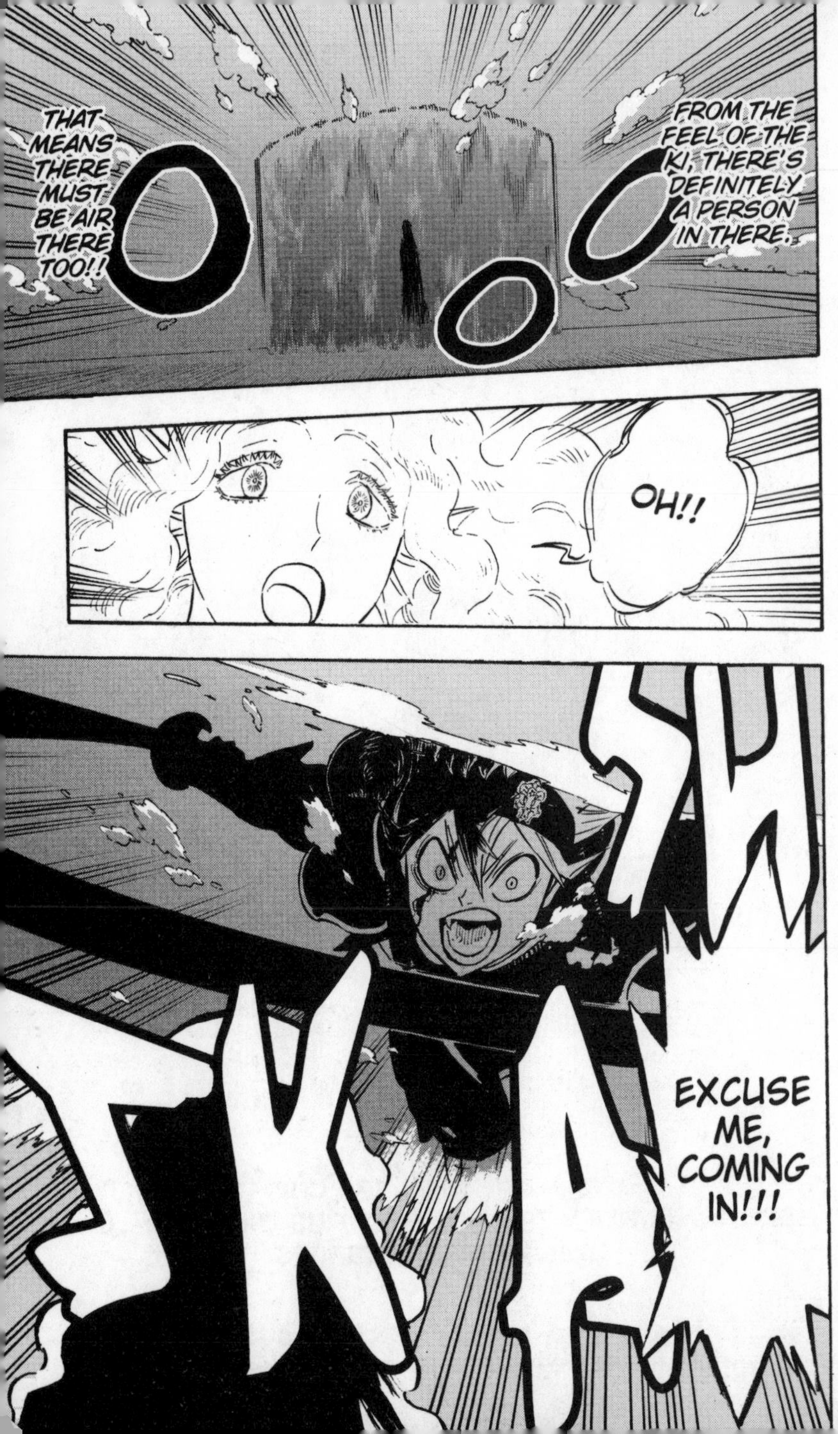
FROM THE FEEL OF THE KI, THERE'S DEFINITELY A PERSON IN THERE.
THAT MEANS THERE MUST BE AIR THERE TOO!!
OH!!
EXCUSE ME, COMING IN!!!

Gaja

Age: 27 Height: 176 cm
Birthday: January 29 Sign: Aquarius Blood Type: O
Likes: Crimson oranges

C h a r a c t e r   P r o f i l e

❧

Page 227: The All-Knowing Priestess

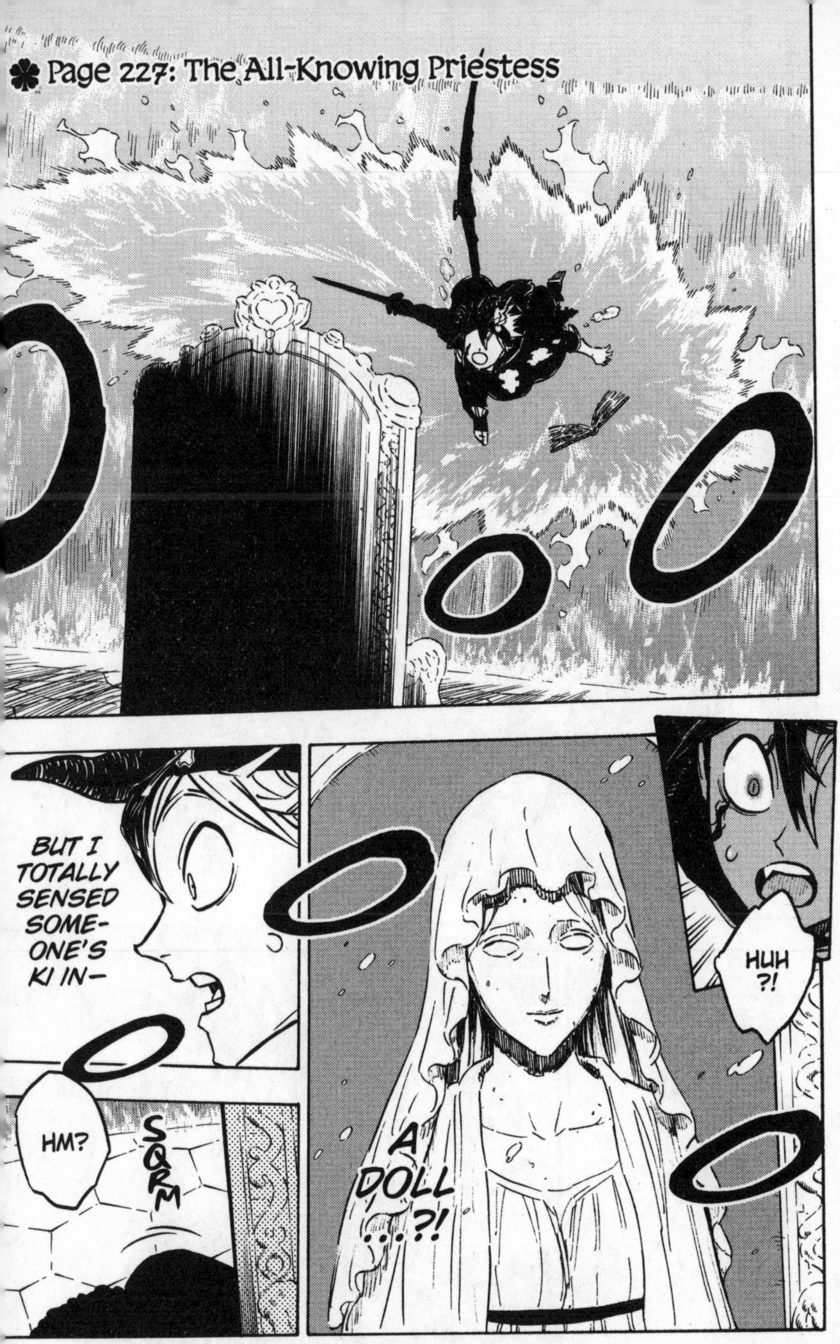
HUH ?!
A DOLL ...?!
BUT I TOTALLY SENSED SOME-ONE'S KI IN—
HM?
SQRM

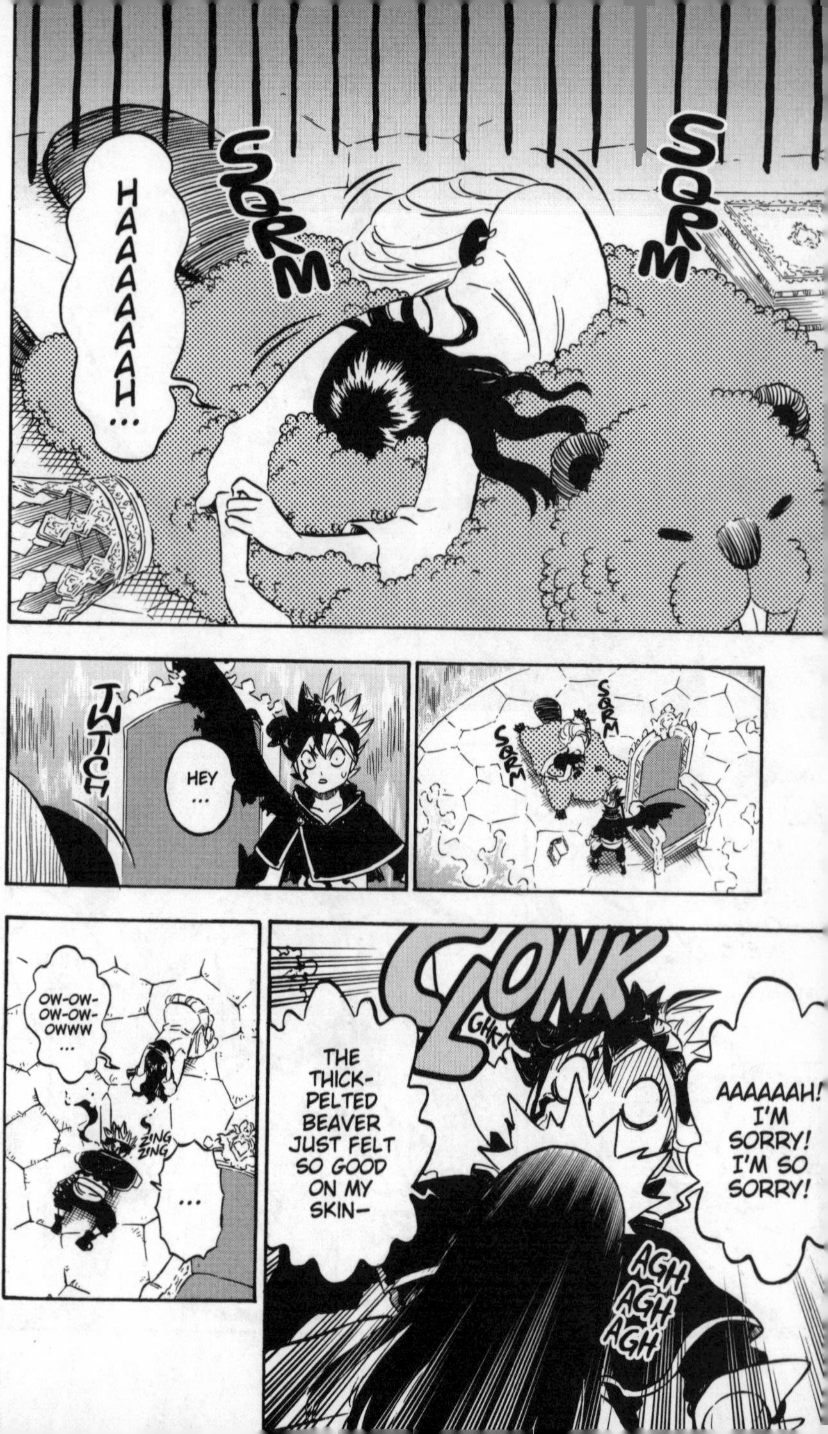
SQRM
SQRM
HAAAAAAAH...
SQRM
SQRM
TWITCH
HEY...
CLONK
GHK!
AAAAAAH! I'M SORRY! I'M SO SORRY!
THE THICK-PELTED BEAVER JUST FELT SO GOOD ON MY SKIN–
AGH AGH AGH
OW-OW-OW-OW-OWWW...
ZING ZING
...

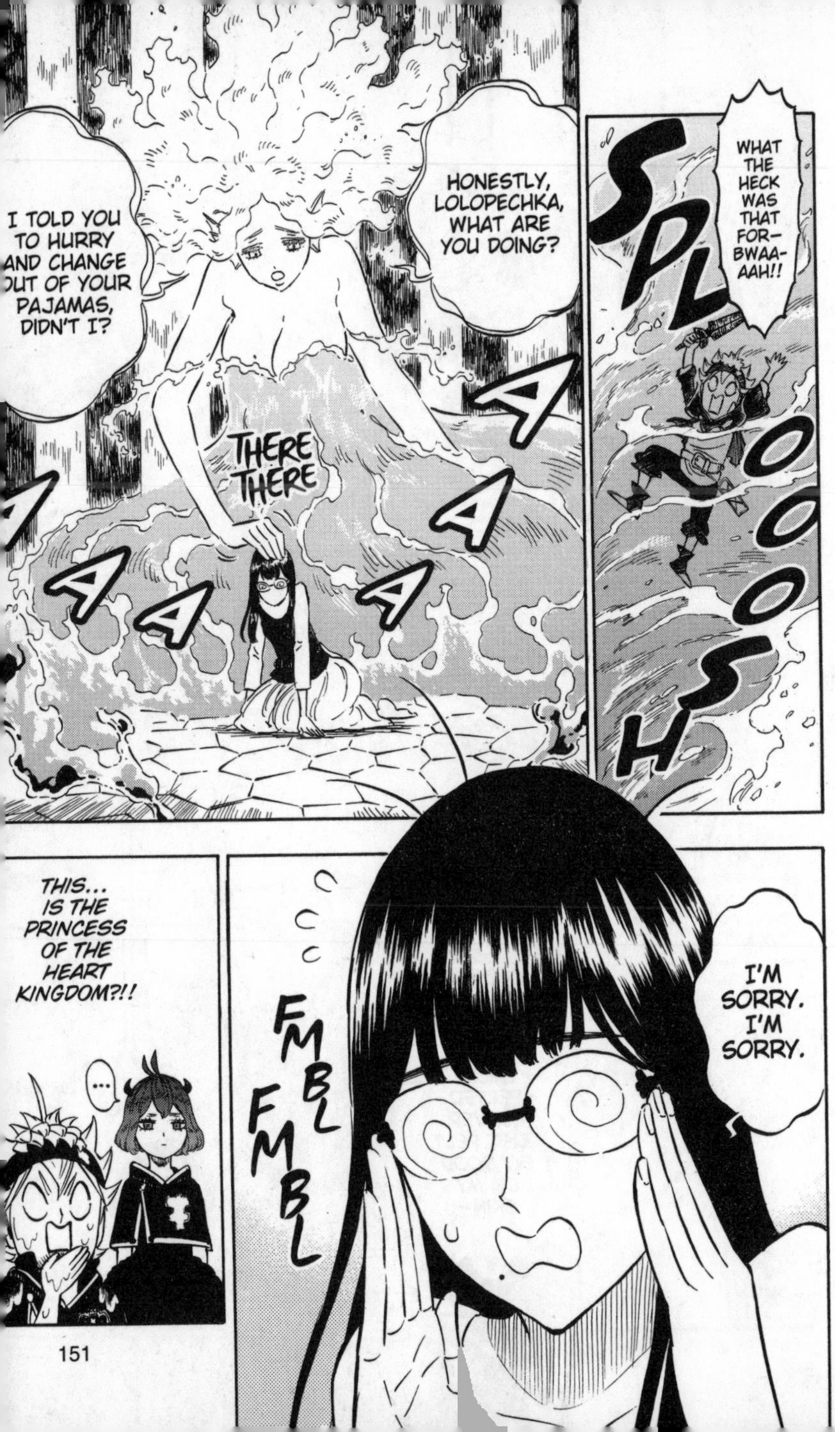

WHAT THE HECK WAS THAT FOR—BWAA-AAH!!
SPLOOOOSH
HONESTLY, LOLOPECHKA, WHAT ARE YOU DOING?
I TOLD YOU TO HURRY AND CHANGE OUT OF YOUR PAJAMAS, DIDN'T I?
AAAAA
THERE THERE
I'M SORRY. I'M SORRY.
FMBL FMBL
THIS... IS THE PRINCESS OF THE HEART KINGDOM?!!
...

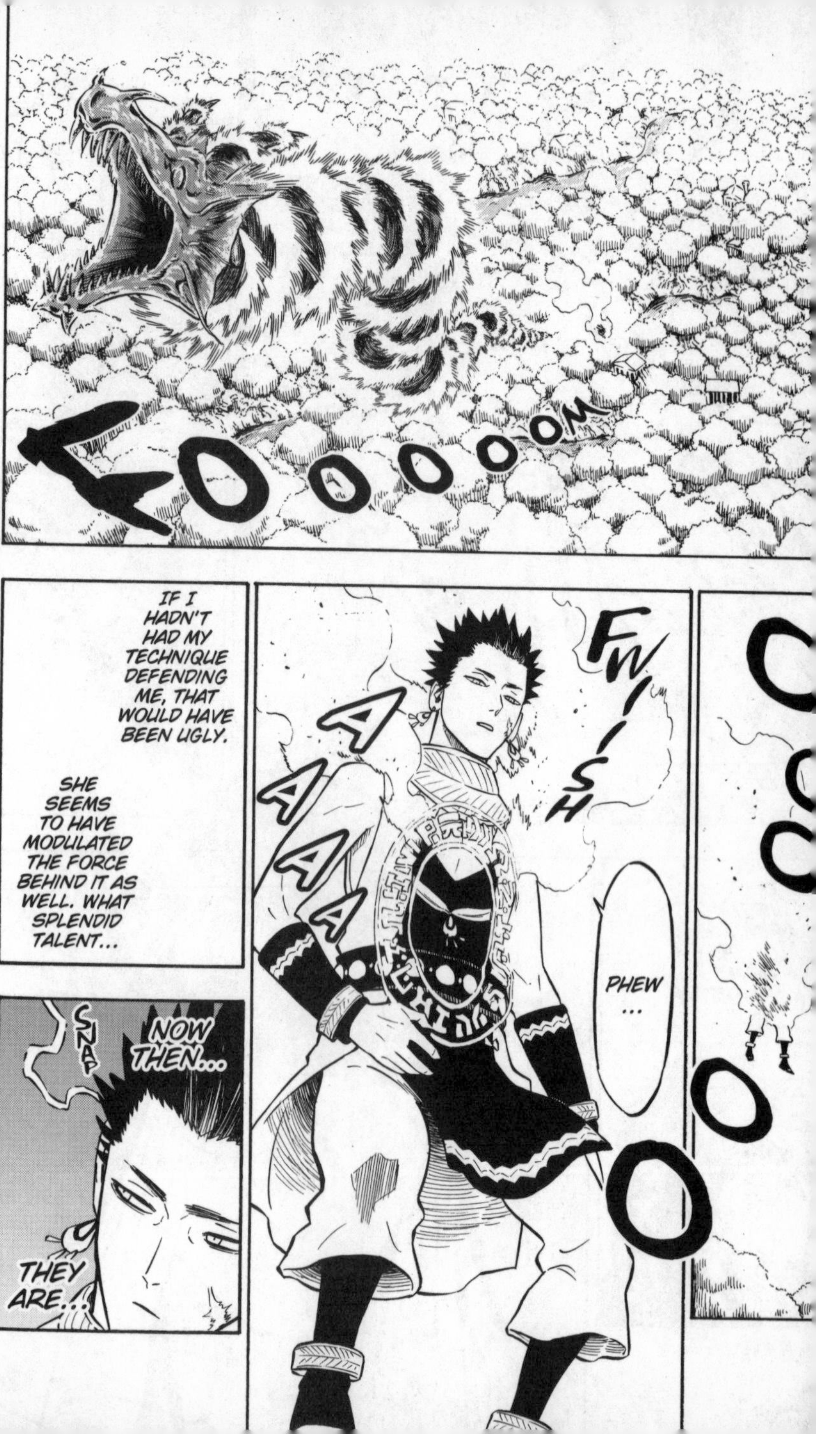
KOOOOOM
OOOOO
FWISH
PHEW ...
AAAAA
IF I HADN'T HAD MY TECHNIQUE DEFENDING ME, THAT WOULD HAVE BEEN UGLY.
SHE SEEMS TO HAVE MODULATED THE FORCE BEHIND IT AS WELL. WHAT SPLENDID TALENT...
SNAP
NOW THEN...
THEY ARE...

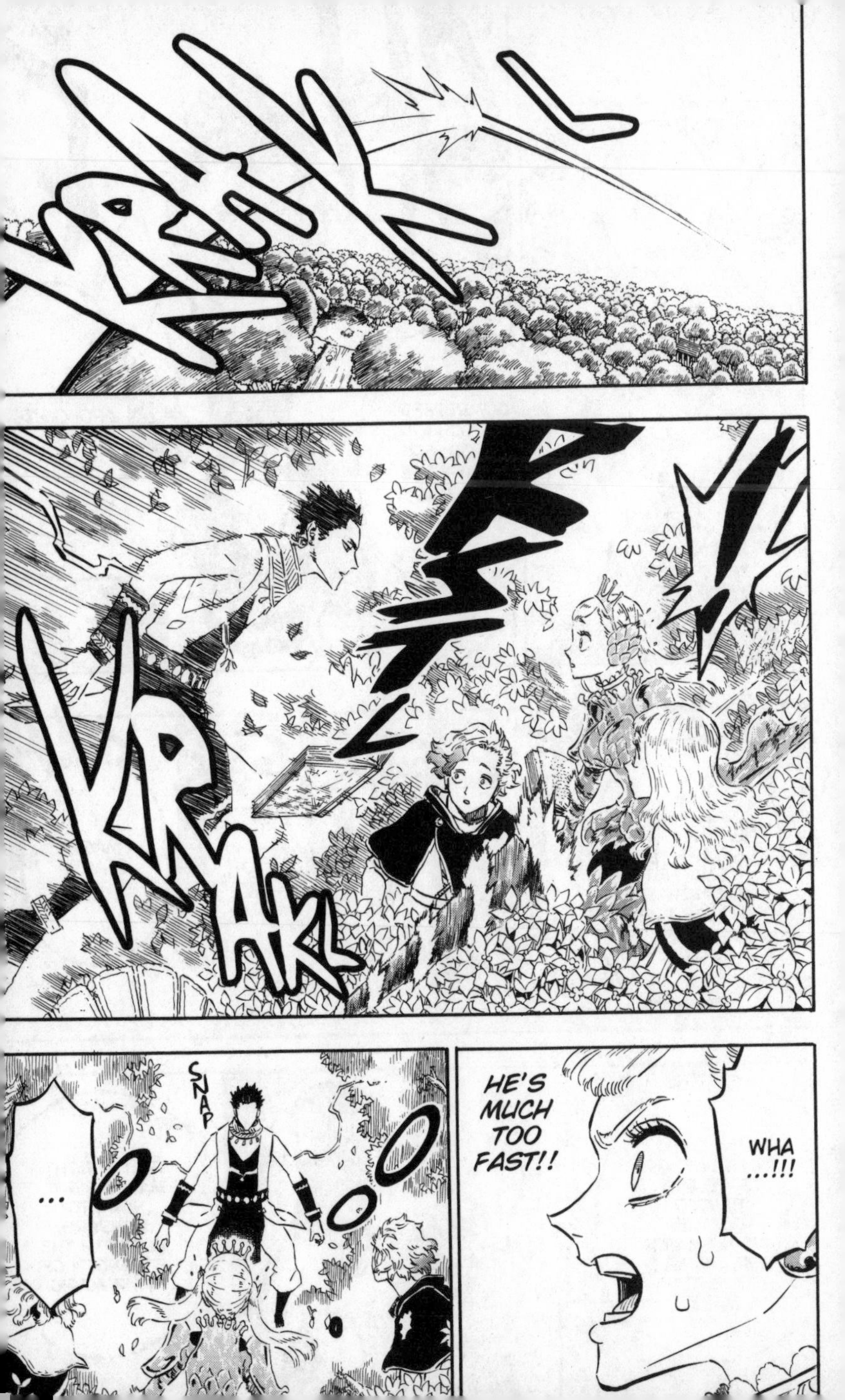

KRAK!
WHA ...!!!
HE'S MUCH TOO FAST!!
SNAP
...

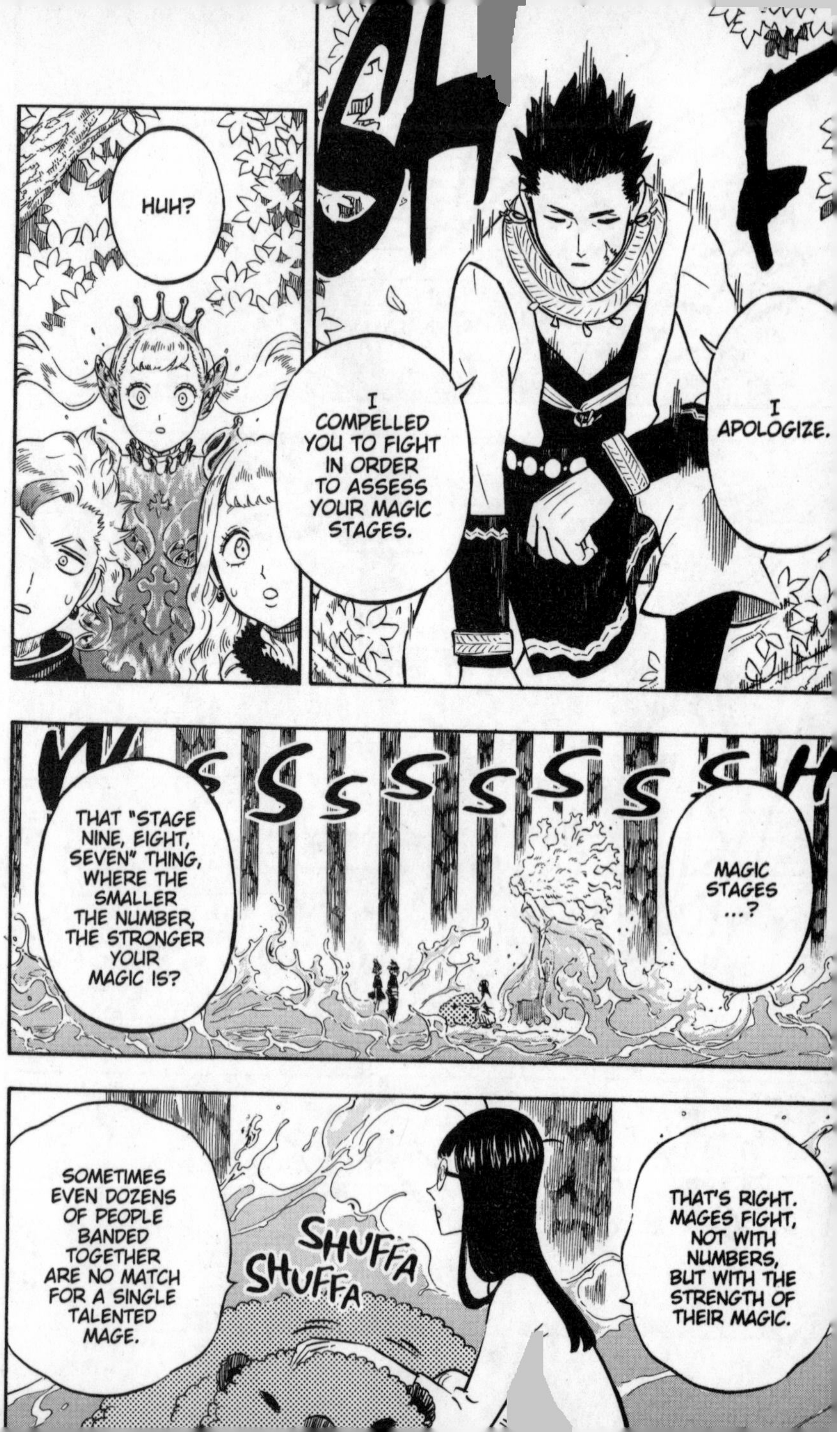
SHF
I APOLOGIZE.
I COMPELLED YOU TO FIGHT IN ORDER TO ASSESS YOUR MAGIC STAGES.
HUH?
WSSSSSSSSH
MAGIC STAGES ...?
THAT "STAGE NINE, EIGHT, SEVEN" THING, WHERE THE SMALLER THE NUMBER, THE STRONGER YOUR MAGIC IS?
THAT'S RIGHT. MAGES FIGHT, NOT WITH NUMBERS, BUT WITH THE STRENGTH OF THEIR MAGIC.
SHUFFA SHUFFA
SOMETIMES EVEN DOZENS OF PEOPLE BANDED TOGETHER ARE NO MATCH FOR A SINGLE TALENTED MAGE.

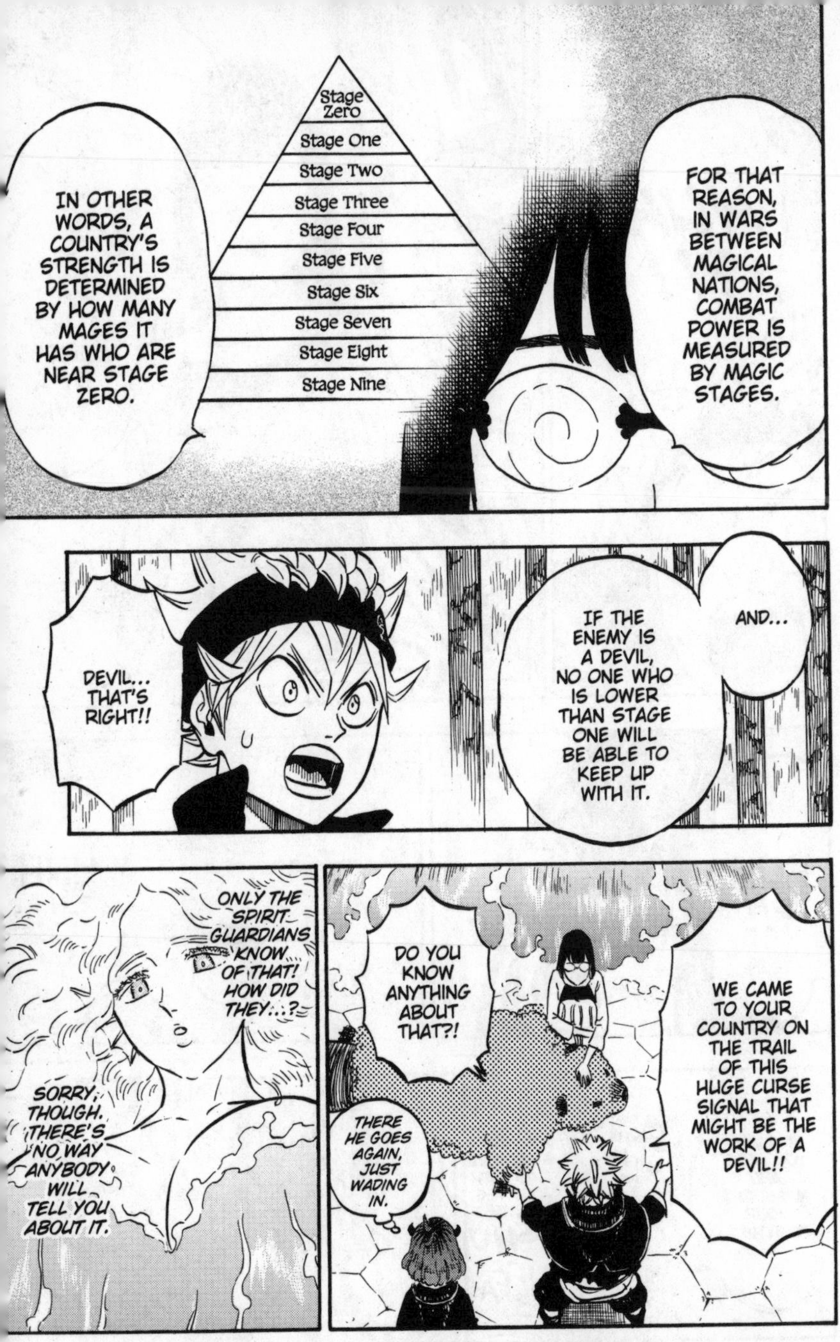
FOR THAT REASON, IN WARS BETWEEN MAGICAL NATIONS, COMBAT POWER IS MEASURED BY MAGIC STAGES.
Stage Zero
Stage One
Stage Two
Stage Three
Stage Four
Stage Five
Stage Six
Stage Seven
Stage Eight
Stage Nine
IN OTHER WORDS, A COUNTRY'S STRENGTH IS DETERMINED BY HOW MANY MAGES IT HAS WHO ARE NEAR STAGE ZERO.
AND...
IF THE ENEMY IS A DEVIL, NO ONE WHO IS LOWER THAN STAGE ONE WILL BE ABLE TO KEEP UP WITH IT.
DEVIL... THAT'S RIGHT!!
WE CAME TO YOUR COUNTRY ON THE TRAIL OF THIS HUGE CURSE SIGNAL THAT MIGHT BE THE WORK OF A DEVIL!!
DO YOU KNOW ANYTHING ABOUT THAT?!
THERE HE GOES AGAIN, JUST WADING IN.
ONLY THE SPIRIT GUARDIANS KNOW OF THAT! HOW DID THEY...?
SORRY, THOUGH. THERE'S NO WAY ANYBODY WILL TELL YOU ABOUT IT.

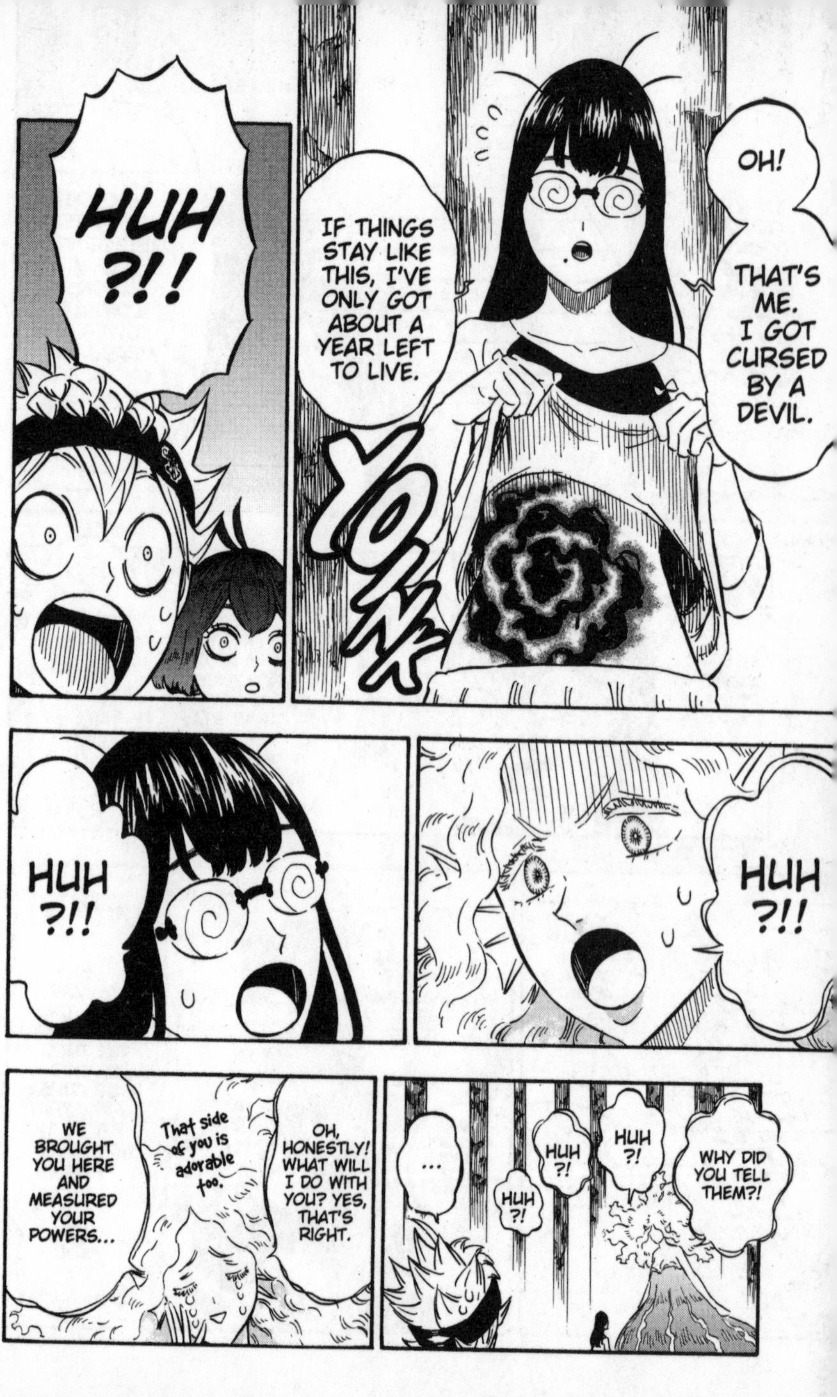
OH!
THAT'S ME. I GOT CURSED BY A DEVIL.
IF THINGS STAY LIKE THIS, I'VE ONLY GOT ABOUT A YEAR LEFT TO LIVE.
YOINK
HUH ?!!
HUH ?!!
HUH ?!!
WHY DID YOU TELL THEM?!
HUH ?!
HUH ?!
HUH ?!
...
OH, HONESTLY! WHAT WILL I DO WITH YOU? YES, THAT'S RIGHT.
That side of you is adorable too.
WE BROUGHT YOU HERE AND MEASURED YOUR POWERS...

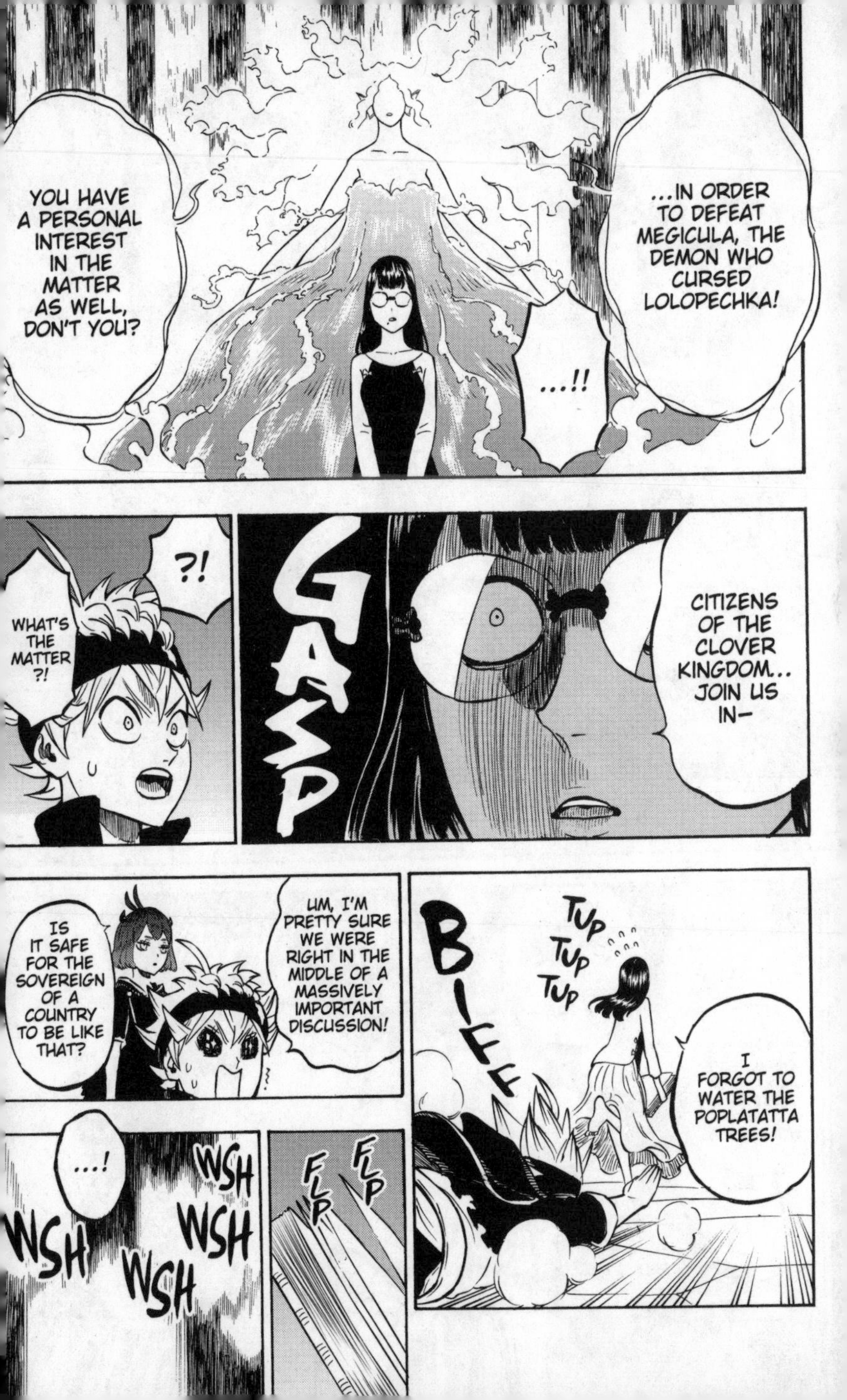

...IN ORDER TO DEFEAT MEGICULA, THE DEMON WHO CURSED LOLOPECHKA!
...!!
YOU HAVE A PERSONAL INTEREST IN THE MATTER AS WELL, DON'T YOU?
CITIZENS OF THE CLOVER KINGDOM... JOIN US IN—
GASP
?!
WHAT'S THE MATTER ?!
TUP TUP TUP
BIFF
I FORGOT TO WATER THE POPLATATTA TREES!
UM, I'M PRETTY SURE WE WERE RIGHT IN THE MIDDLE OF A MASSIVELY IMPORTANT DISCUSSION!
IS IT SAFE FOR THE SOVEREIGN OF A COUNTRY TO BE LIKE THAT?
FLP FLP
...!
WSH WSH WSH WSH

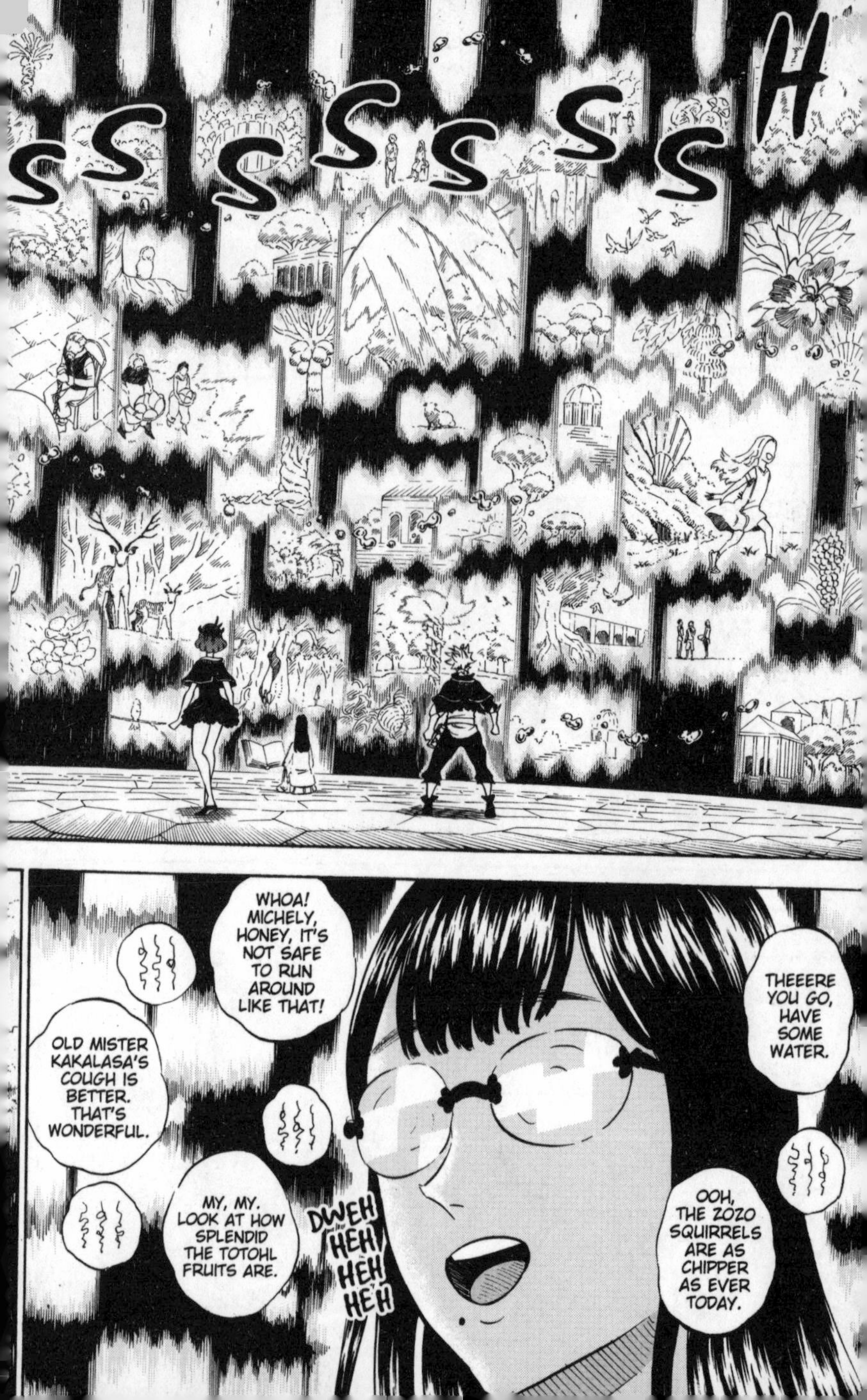
SSSSSSSH
THEEERE YOU GO, HAVE SOME WATER.
WHOA! MICHELY, HONEY, IT'S NOT SAFE TO RUN AROUND LIKE THAT!
OLD MISTER KAKALASA'S COUGH IS BETTER. THAT'S WONDERFUL.
OOH, THE ZOZO SQUIRRELS ARE AS CHIPPER AS EVER TODAY.
DWEH HEH HEH HEH HEH
MY, MY. LOOK AT HOW SPLENDID THE TOTOHL FRUITS ARE.

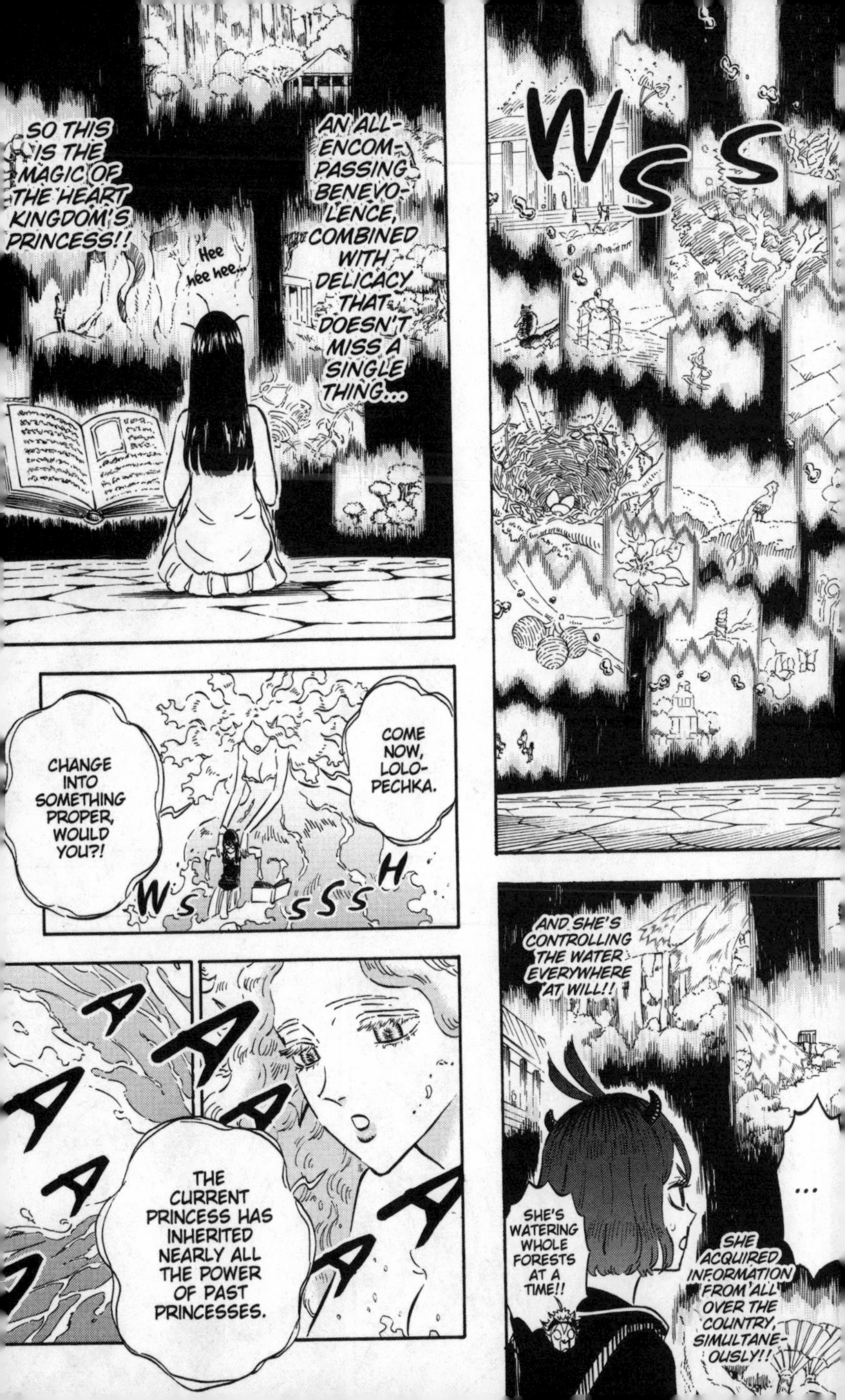
WSS
AN ALL-ENCOMPASSING BENEVOLENCE, COMBINED WITH DELICACY THAT DOESN'T MISS A SINGLE THING...
SO THIS IS THE MAGIC OF THE HEART KINGDOM'S PRINCESS!!
Hee hee hee...
COME NOW, LOLOPECHKA.
CHANGE INTO SOMETHING PROPER, WOULD YOU?!
WSSSSH
AND SHE'S CONTROLLING THE WATER EVERYWHERE AT WILL!!
...
SHE ACQUIRED INFORMATION FROM ALL OVER THE COUNTRY, SIMULTANEOUSLY!!
SHE'S WATERING WHOLE FORESTS AT A TIME!!
AAAAAAAA
THE CURRENT PRINCESS HAS INHERITED NEARLY ALL THE POWER OF PAST PRINCESSES.

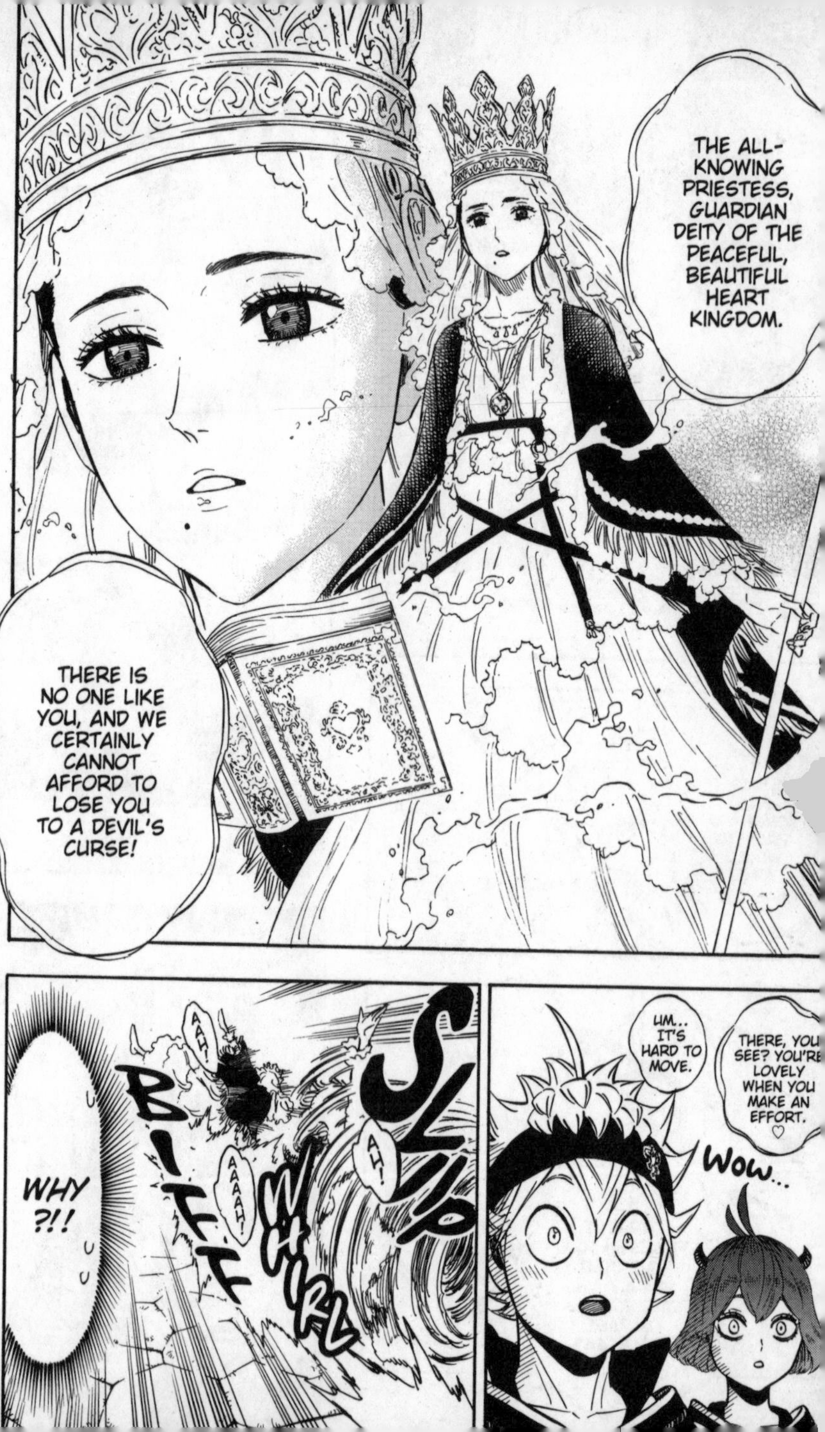
THE ALL-KNOWING PRIESTESS, GUARDIAN DEITY OF THE PEACEFUL, BEAUTIFUL HEART KINGDOM.
THERE IS NO ONE LIKE YOU, AND WE CERTAINLY CANNOT AFFORD TO LOSE YOU TO A DEVIL'S CURSE!
THERE, YOU SEE? YOU'RE LOVELY WHEN YOU MAKE AN EFFORT. ♡
UM... IT'S HARD TO MOVE.
WOW...
SLIP
AH!
WHIRL
AAAAH!
BIFFF
AAH!
WHY?!!

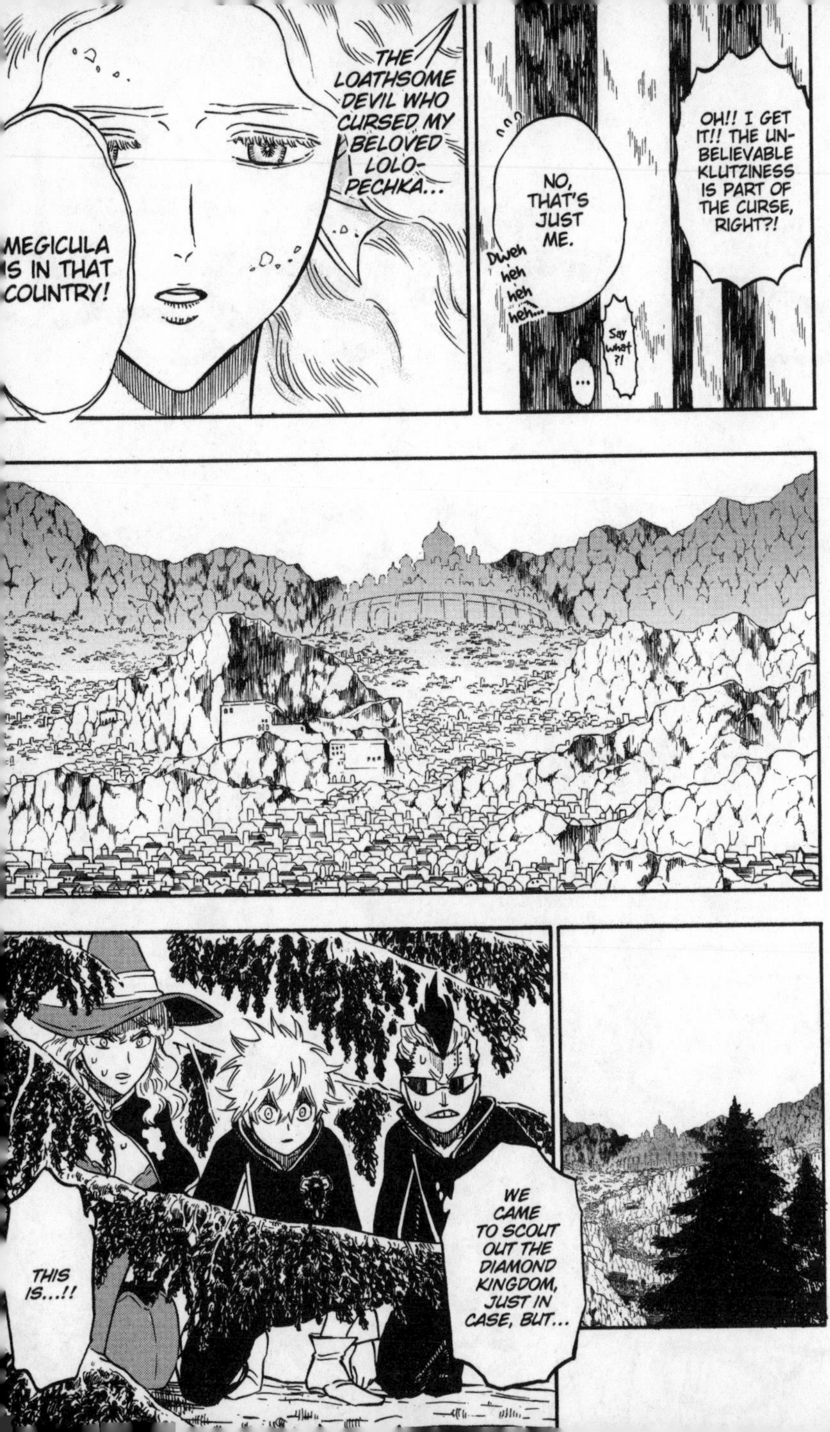

OH!! I GET IT!! THE UN-BELIEVABLE KLUTZINESS IS PART OF THE CURSE, RIGHT?!
NO, THAT'S JUST ME.
Dweh heh heh heh...
Say what?!
...
THE LOATHSOME DEVIL WHO CURSED MY BELOVED LOLO-PECHKA...
MEGICULA IS IN THAT COUNTRY!
WE CAME TO SCOUT OUT THE DIAMOND KINGDOM, JUST IN CASE, BUT...
THIS IS...!!

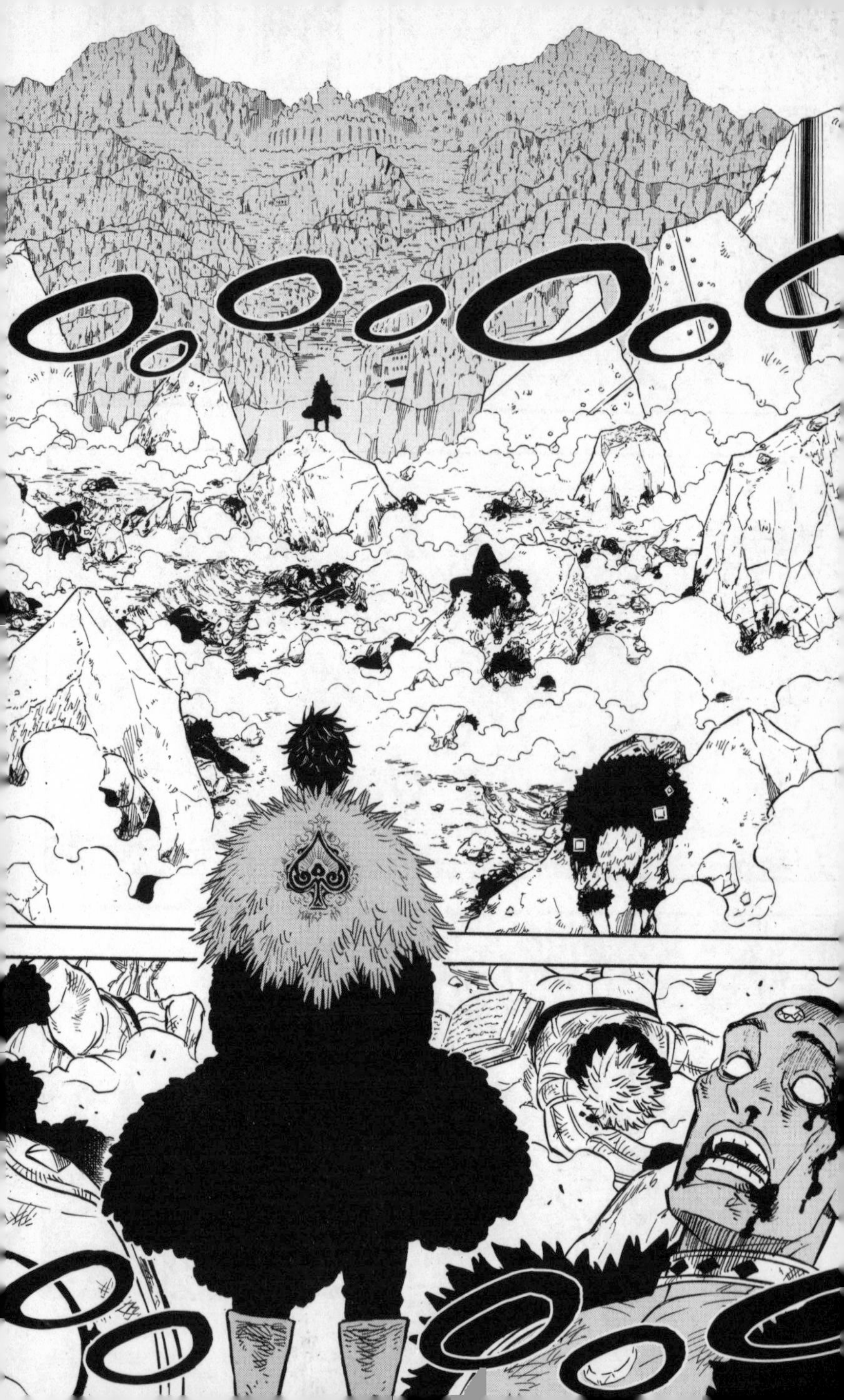

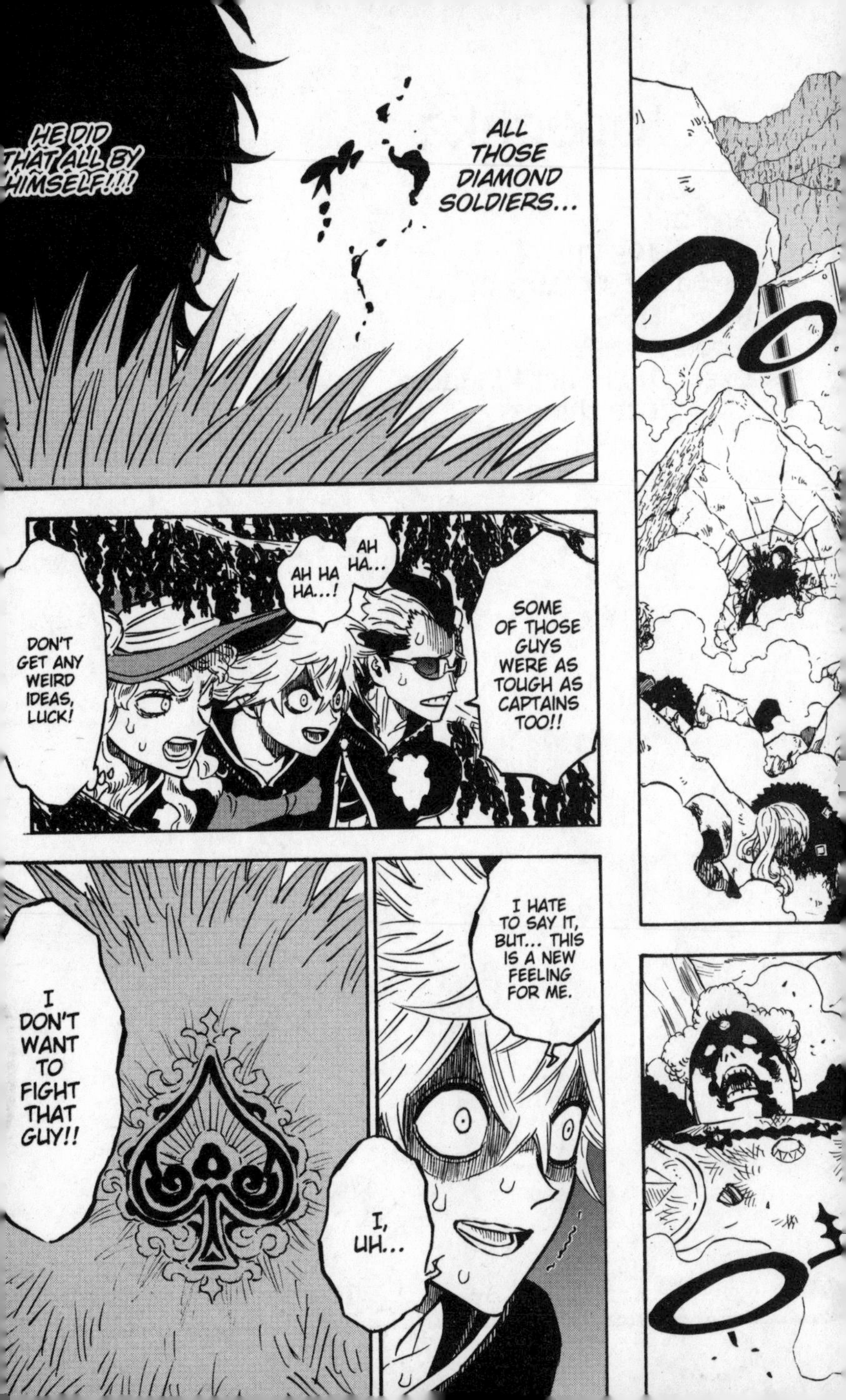
ALL THOSE DIAMOND SOLDIERS...
HE DID THAT ALL BY HIMSELF!!!
SOME OF THOSE GUYS WERE AS TOUGH AS CAPTAINS TOO!!
AH HA...
AH HA HA...!
DON'T GET ANY WEIRD IDEAS, LUCK!
I HATE TO SAY IT, BUT... THIS IS A NEW FEELING FOR ME.
I, UH...
I DON'T WANT TO FIGHT THAT GUY!!

Lolopechka

Age: 21
Height: 165 cm
Birthday: February 21
Sign: Pisces
Blood Type: A
Likes: The Heart Kingdom
Cute things

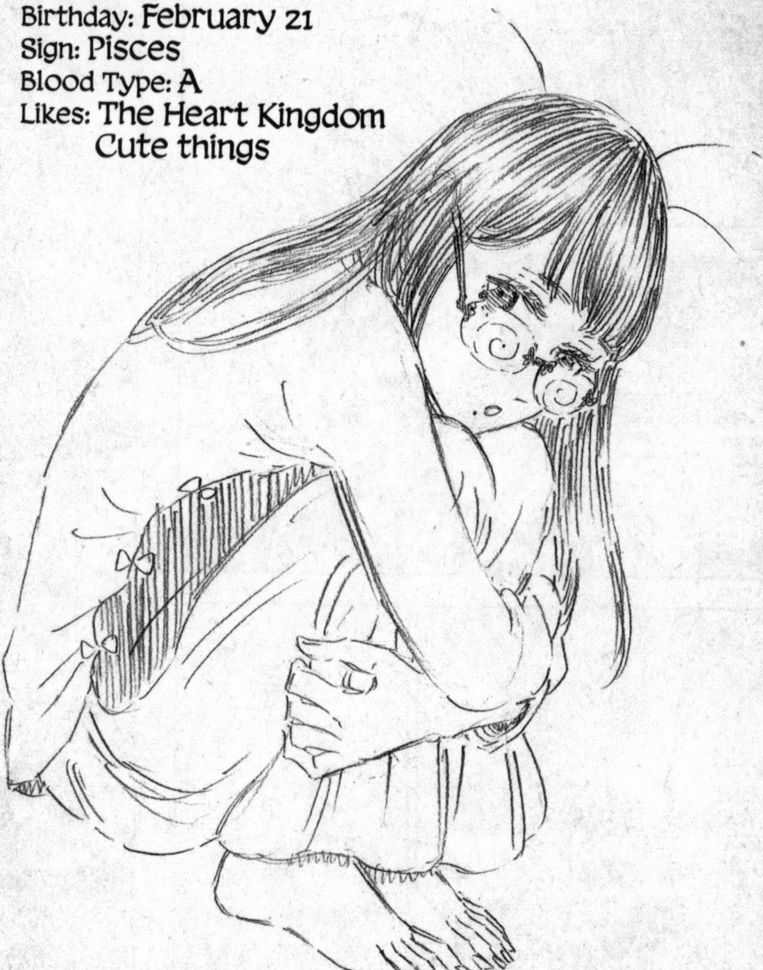

Character Profile

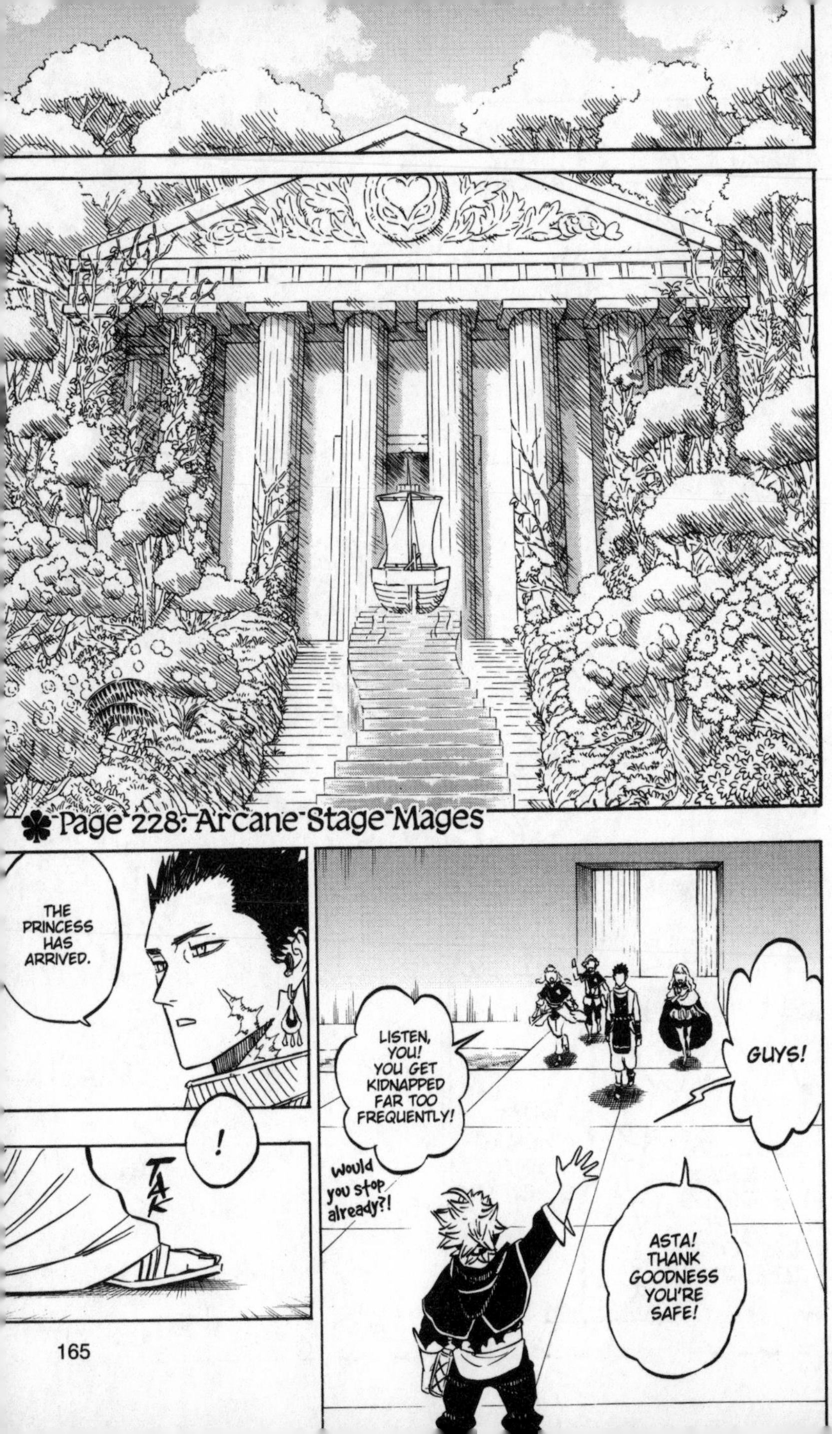
Page 228: Arcane Stage Mages
GUYS!
ASTA! THANK GOODNESS YOU'RE SAFE!
LISTEN, YOU! YOU GET KIDNAPPED FAR TOO FREQUENTLY!
Would you stop already?!
THE PRINCESS HAS ARRIVED.
!
TAK

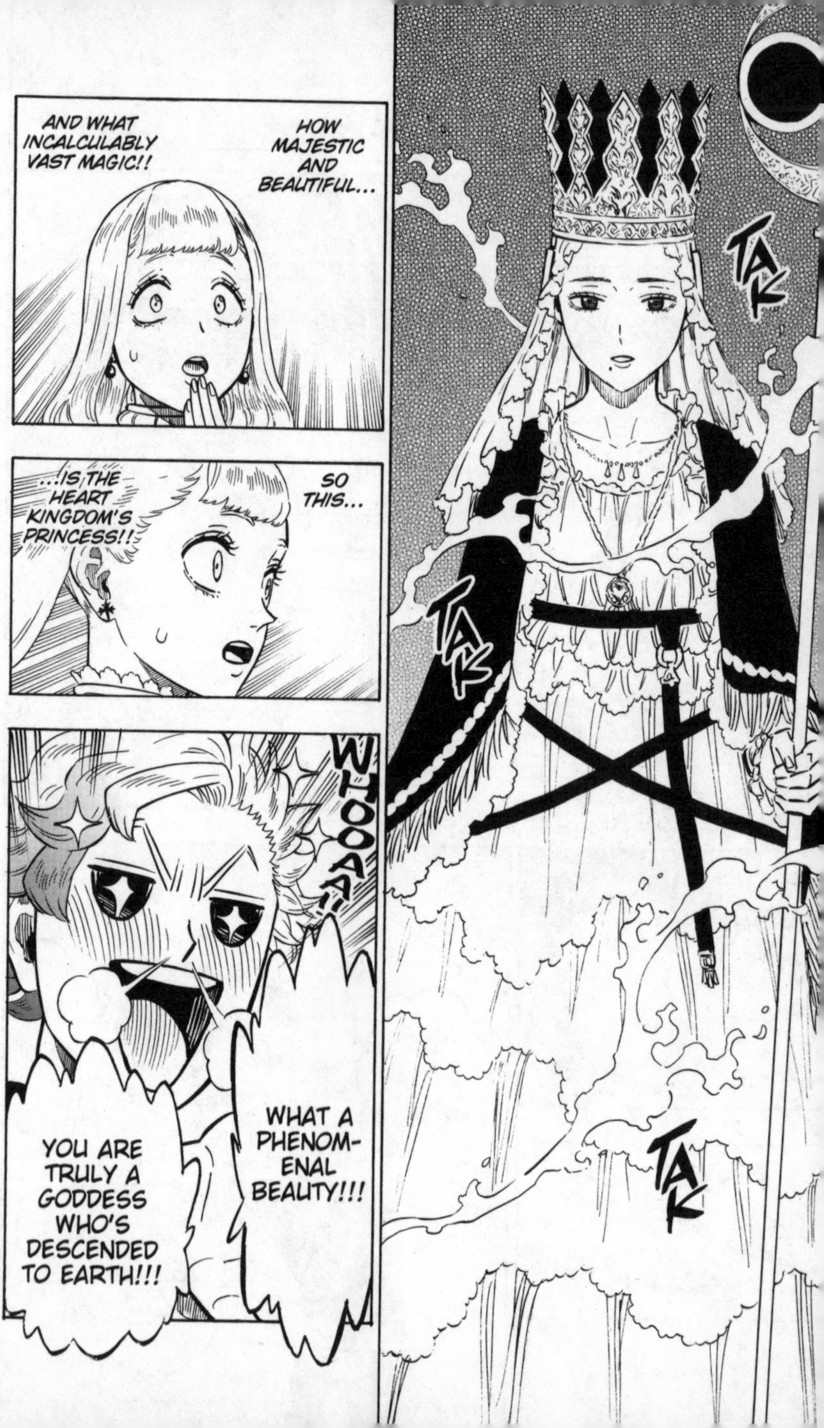
TAK
TAK
TAK
HOW MAJESTIC AND BEAUTIFUL...
AND WHAT INCALCULABLY VAST MAGIC!!
SO THIS...
...IS THE HEART KINGDOM'S PRINCESS!!
WHOOOAA!!
WHAT A PHENOM-ENAL BEAUTY!!!
YOU ARE TRULY A GODDESS WHO'S DESCENDED TO EARTH!!!

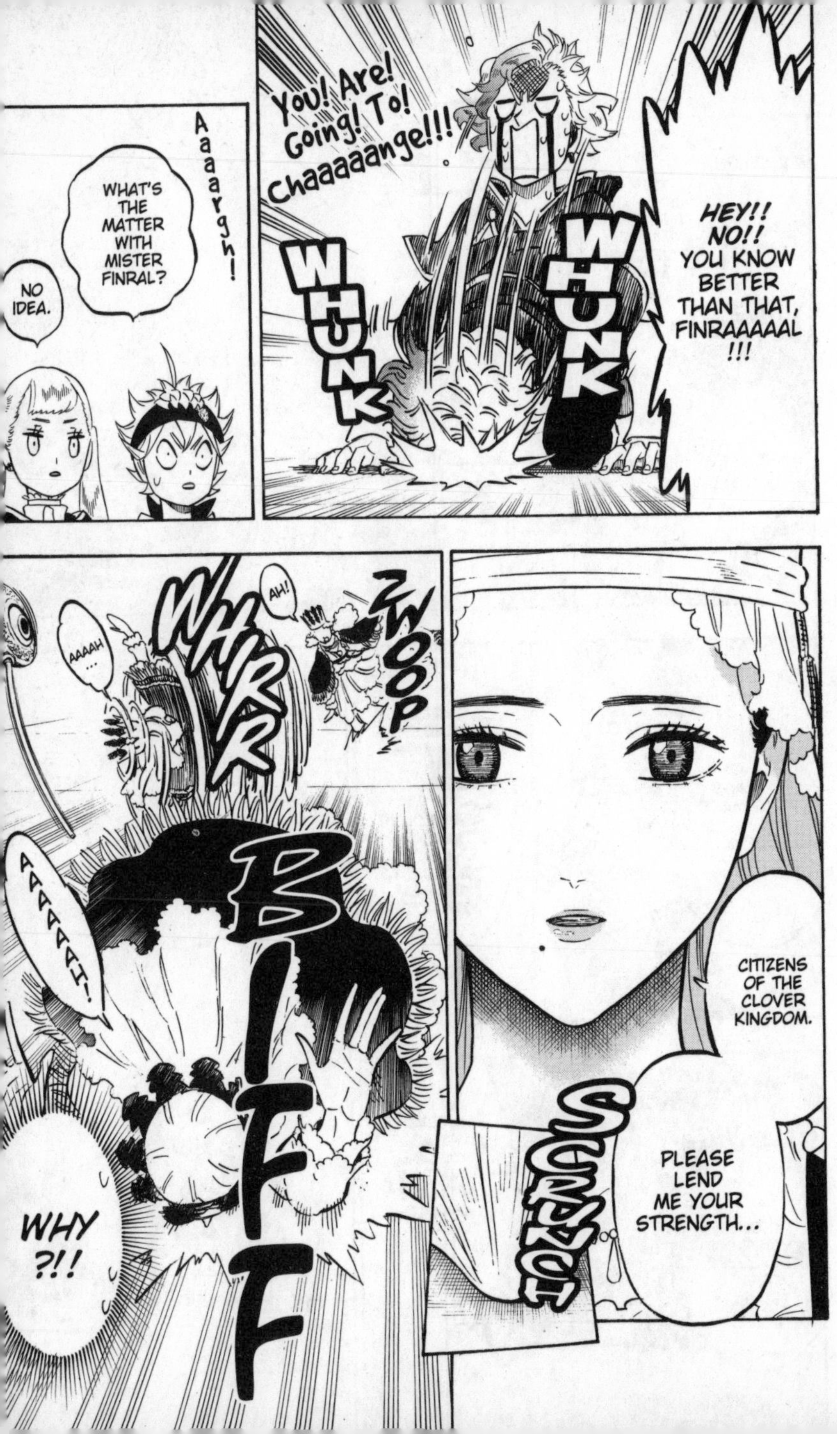
HEY!! NO!! YOU KNOW BETTER THAN THAT, FINRAAAAAL!!!
You! Are! Going! To! Chaaaaange!!!
WHUNK
WHUNK
Aaaaargh!
WHAT'S THE MATTER WITH MISTER FINRAL?
NO IDEA.
CITIZENS OF THE CLOVER KINGDOM.
PLEASE LEND ME YOUR STRENGTH...
SCRUNCH
ZWOOP
AH!
WHIRR
AAAAH...
BIFF
AAAAAAH!
WHY?!!

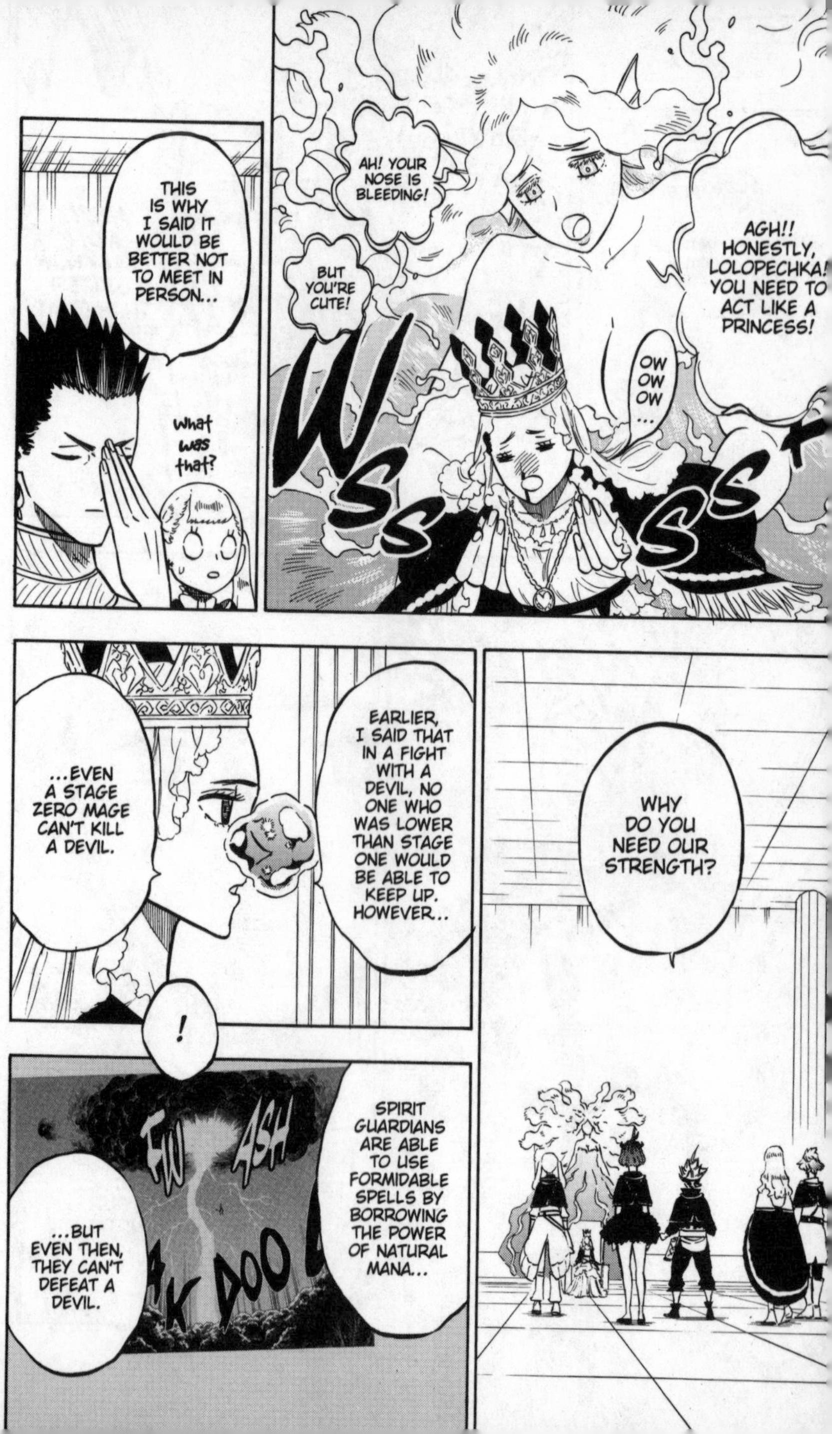
AGH!! HONESTLY, LOLOPECHKA! YOU NEED TO ACT LIKE A PRINCESS!
AH! YOUR NOSE IS BLEEDING!
BUT YOU'RE CUTE!
OW OW OW...
WSS SSS
THIS IS WHY I SAID IT WOULD BE BETTER NOT TO MEET IN PERSON...
what was that?
WHY DO YOU NEED OUR STRENGTH?
EARLIER, I SAID THAT IN A FIGHT WITH A DEVIL, NO ONE WHO WAS LOWER THAN STAGE ONE WOULD BE ABLE TO KEEP UP. HOWEVER...
...EVEN A STAGE ZERO MAGE CAN'T KILL A DEVIL.
!
SPIRIT GUARDIANS ARE ABLE TO USE FORMIDABLE SPELLS BY BORROWING THE POWER OF NATURAL MANA...
FWASH
KADOO
...BUT EVEN THEN, THEY CAN'T DEFEAT A DEVIL.

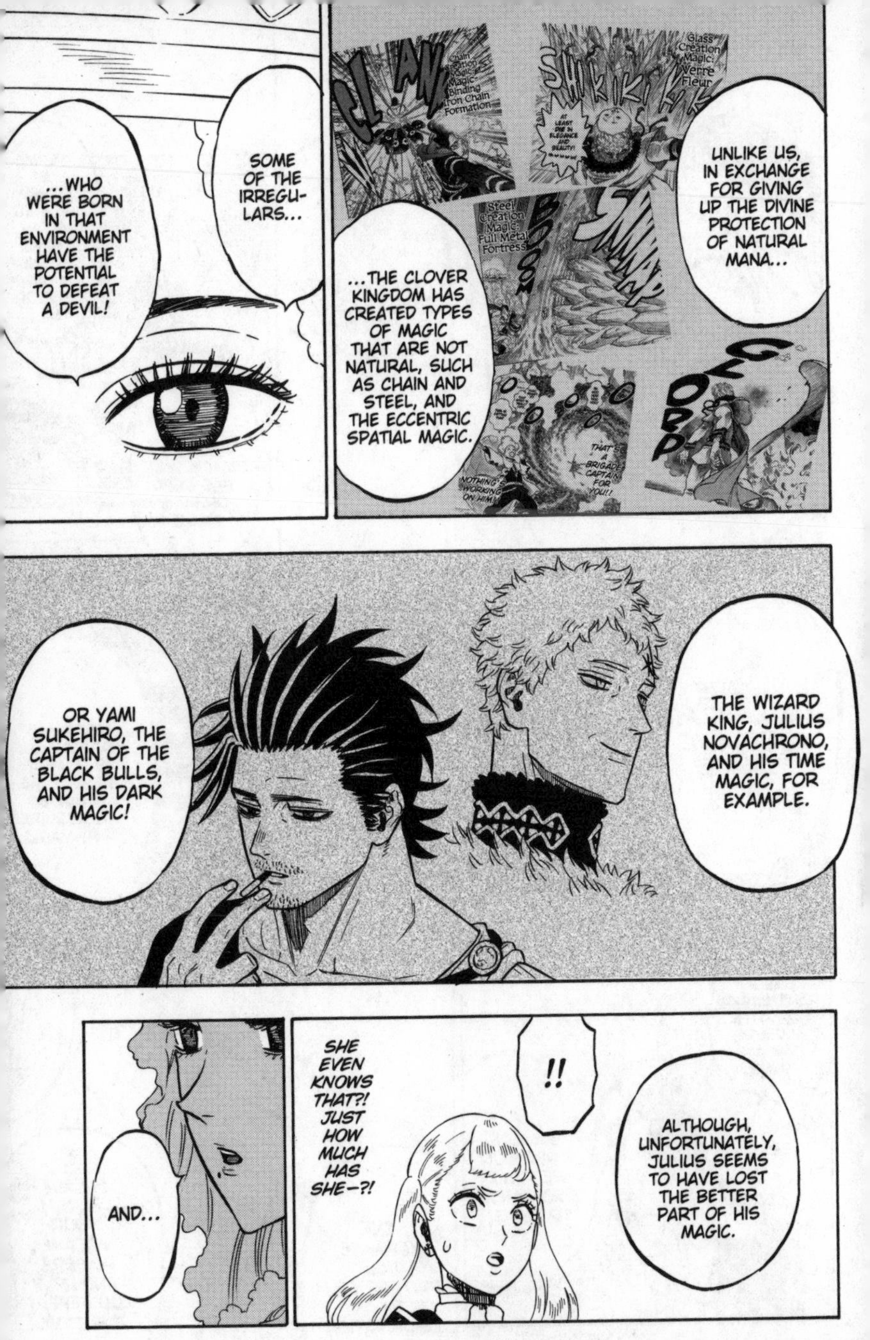
UNLIKE US, IN EXCHANGE FOR GIVING UP THE DIVINE PROTECTION OF NATURAL MANA...
Glass Creation Magic: Verre Fleur
Chain Creation Magic: Magic-Binding Iron Chain Formation
Steel Creation Magic: Full Metal Fortress
THAT'S A BRIGADE CAPTAIN FOR YOU!!
NOTHING'S WORKING ON HIM!
...THE CLOVER KINGDOM HAS CREATED TYPES OF MAGIC THAT ARE NOT NATURAL, SUCH AS CHAIN AND STEEL, AND THE ECCENTRIC SPATIAL MAGIC.
SOME OF THE IRREGULARS...
...WHO WERE BORN IN THAT ENVIRONMENT HAVE THE POTENTIAL TO DEFEAT A DEVIL!
THE WIZARD KING, JULIUS NOVACHRONO, AND HIS TIME MAGIC, FOR EXAMPLE.
OR YAMI SUKEHIRO, THE CAPTAIN OF THE BLACK BULLS, AND HIS DARK MAGIC!
!!
ALTHOUGH, UNFORTUNATELY, JULIUS SEEMS TO HAVE LOST THE BETTER PART OF HIS MAGIC.
SHE EVEN KNOWS THAT?! JUST HOW MUCH HAS SHE—?!
AND...

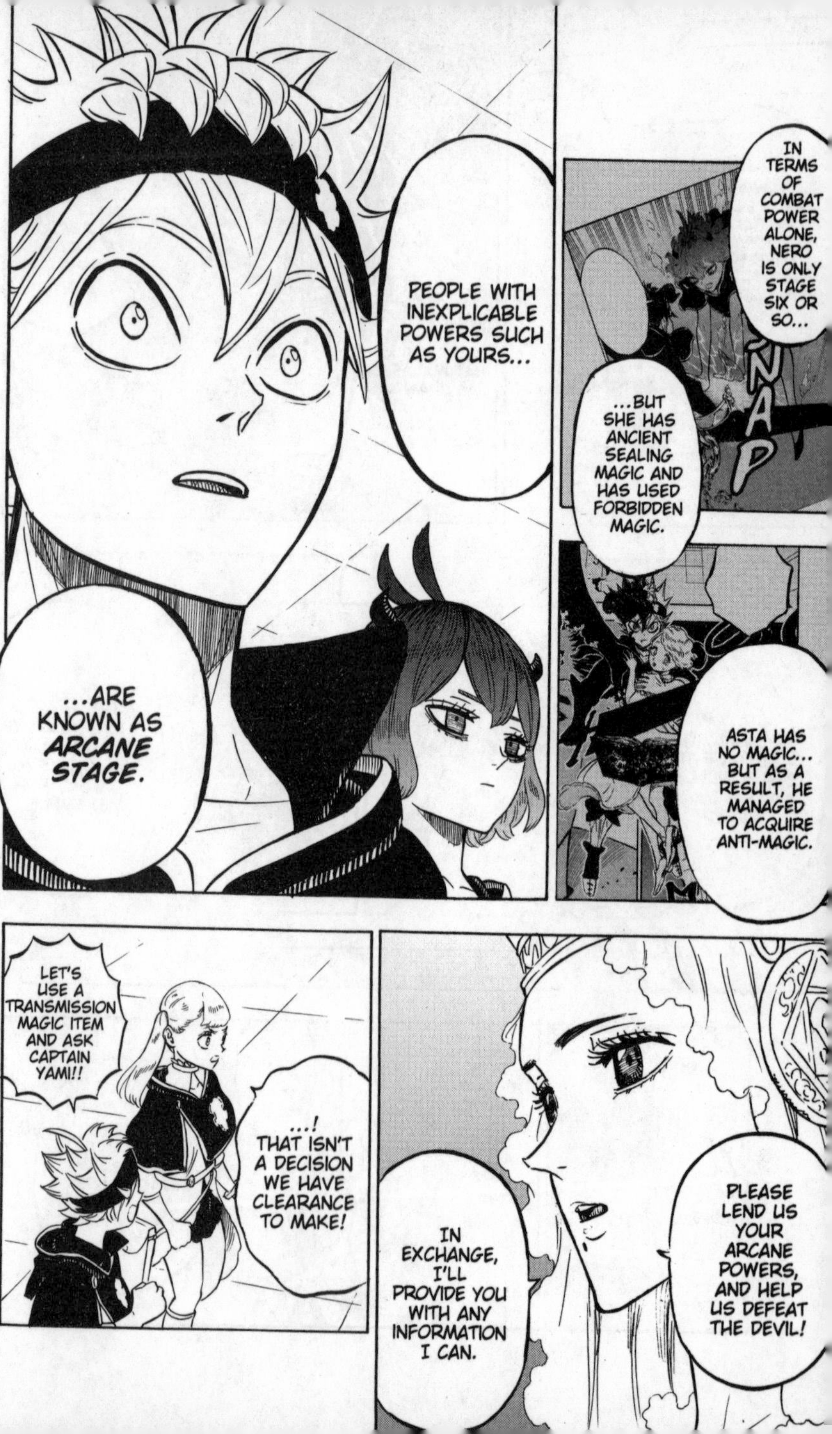
IN TERMS OF COMBAT POWER ALONE, NERO IS ONLY STAGE SIX OR SO...
...BUT SHE HAS ANCIENT SEALING MAGIC AND HAS USED FORBIDDEN MAGIC.
ASTA HAS NO MAGIC... BUT AS A RESULT, HE MANAGED TO ACQUIRE ANTI-MAGIC.
PEOPLE WITH INEXPLICABLE POWERS SUCH AS YOURS...
...ARE KNOWN AS ARCANE STAGE.
PLEASE LEND US YOUR ARCANE POWERS, AND HELP US DEFEAT THE DEVIL!
IN EXCHANGE, I'LL PROVIDE YOU WITH ANY INFORMATION I CAN.
...! THAT ISN'T A DECISION WE HAVE CLEARANCE TO MAKE!
LET'S USE A TRANSMISSION MAGIC ITEM AND ASK CAPTAIN YAMI!!

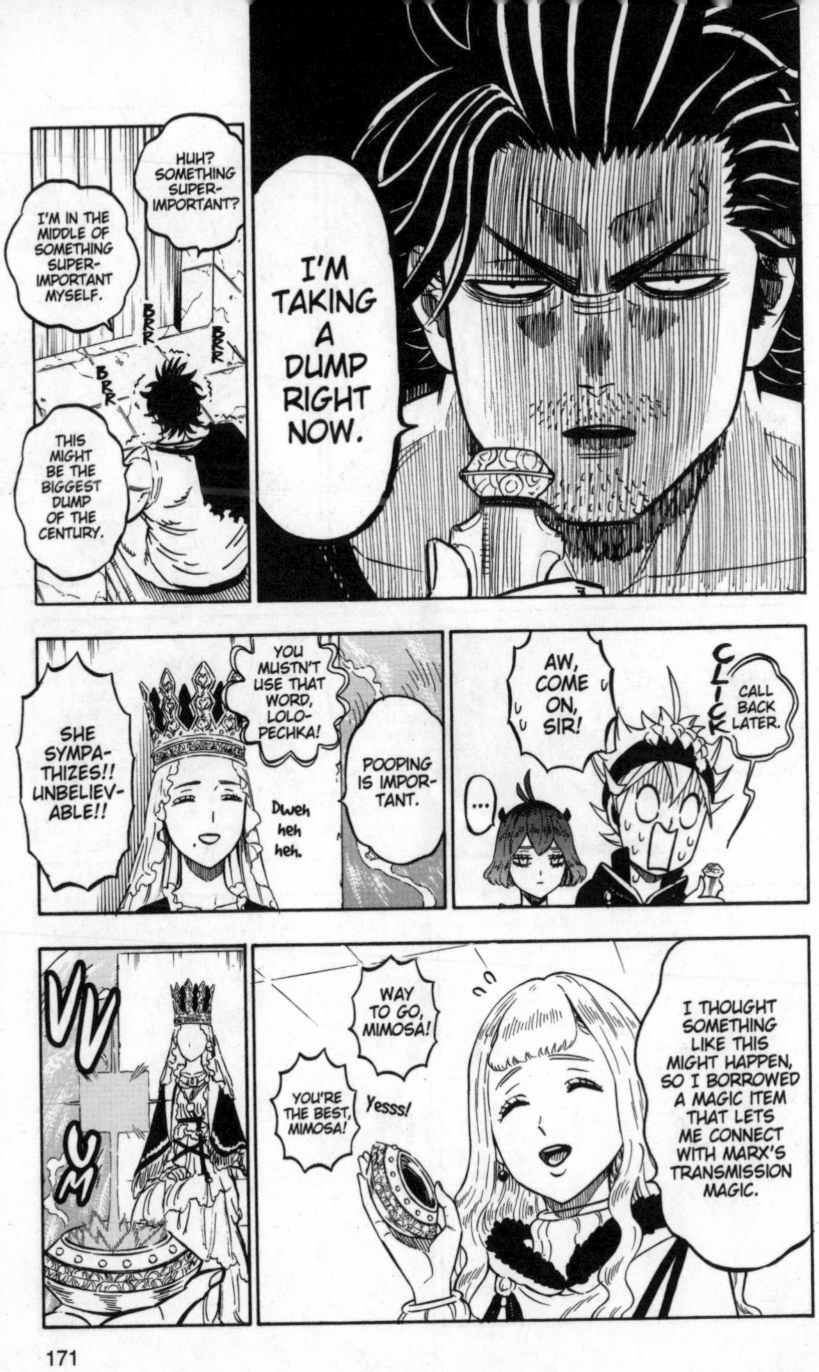
I'M TAKING A DUMP RIGHT NOW.
HUH? SOMETHING SUPER-IMPORTANT?
I'M IN THE MIDDLE OF SOMETHING SUPER-IMPORTANT MYSELF.
BRR BRR BRR
THIS MIGHT BE THE BIGGEST DUMP OF THE CENTURY.
CALL BACK LATER.
CLICK
AW, COME ON, SIR!
...
YOU MUSTN'T USE THAT WORD, LOLOPECHKA!
POOPING IS IMPORTANT.
Dweh heh heh.
SHE SYMPATHIZES!! UNBELIEVABLE!!
I THOUGHT SOMETHING LIKE THIS MIGHT HAPPEN, SO I BORROWED A MAGIC ITEM THAT LETS ME CONNECT WITH MARX'S TRANSMISSION MAGIC.
WAY TO GO, MIMOSA!
Yesss!
YOU'RE THE BEST, MIMOSA!
VVVUM

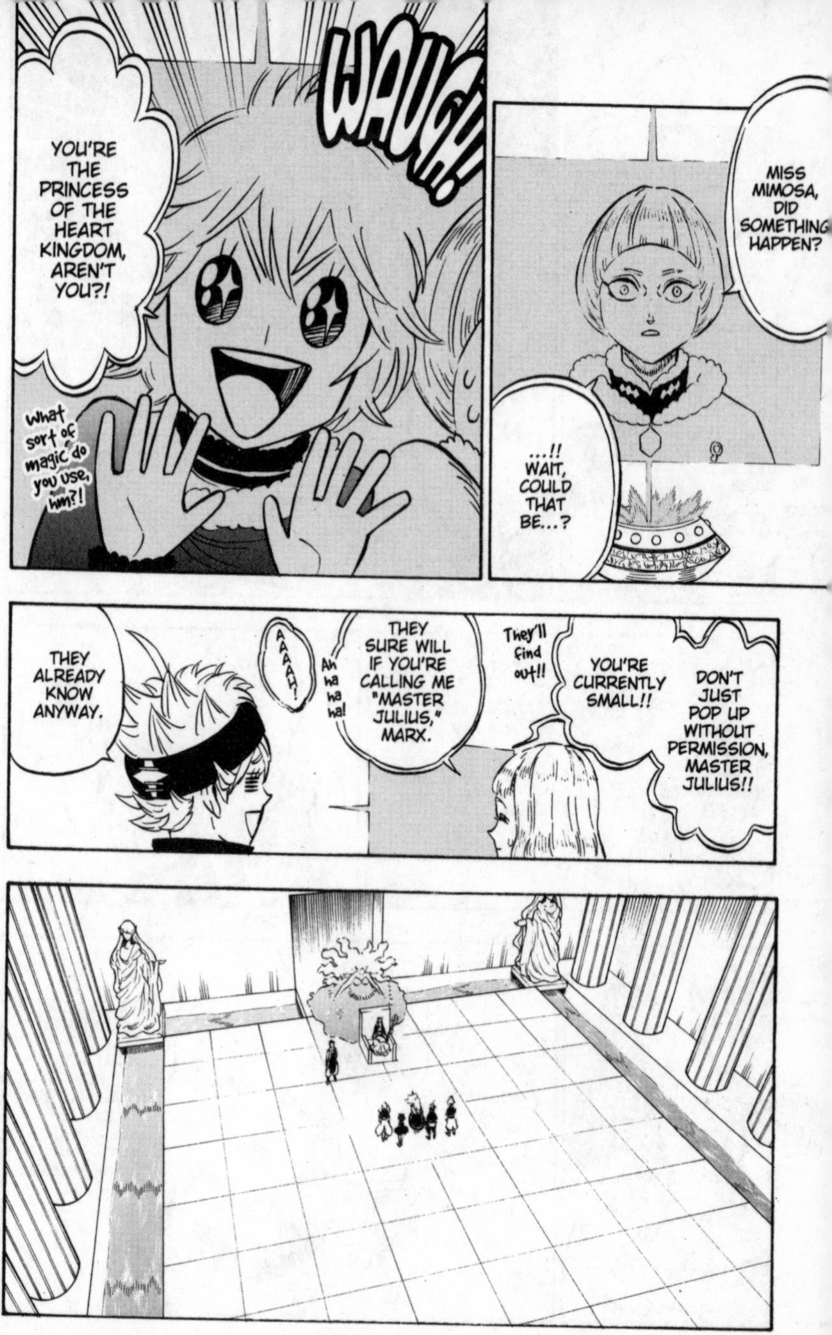
MISS MIMOSA, DID SOMETHING HAPPEN?
...!! WAIT, COULD THAT BE...?
WAUGH!!
YOU'RE THE PRINCESS OF THE HEART KINGDOM, AREN'T YOU?!
What sort of magic do you use, hm?!
DON'T JUST POP UP WITHOUT PERMISSION, MASTER JULIUS!!
YOU'RE CURRENTLY SMALL!!
They'll find out!!
THEY SURE WILL IF YOU'RE CALLING ME "MASTER JULIUS," MARX.
AAAAH!
Ah ha ha ha!
THEY ALREADY KNOW ANYWAY.

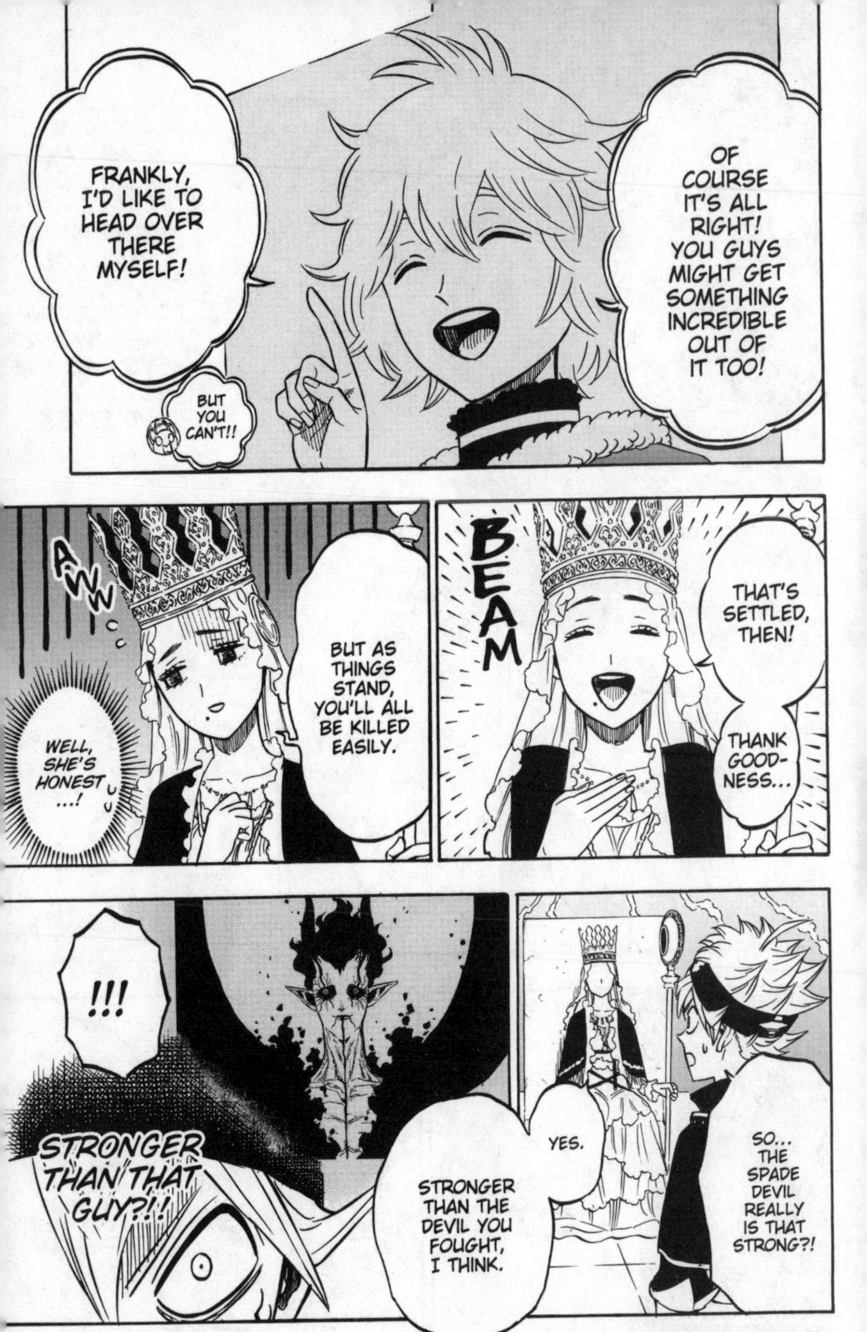
OF COURSE IT'S ALL RIGHT! YOU GUYS MIGHT GET SOMETHING INCREDIBLE OUT OF IT TOO!
FRANKLY, I'D LIKE TO HEAD OVER THERE MYSELF!
BUT YOU CAN'T!!
BEAM
THAT'S SETTLED, THEN!
THANK GOODNESS...
AWW
BUT AS THINGS STAND, YOU'LL ALL BE KILLED EASILY.
WELL, SHE'S HONEST...!
SO... THE SPADE DEVIL REALLY IS THAT STRONG?!
YES.
STRONGER THAN THE DEVIL YOU FOUGHT, I THINK.
!!!
STRONGER THAN THAT GUY?!!

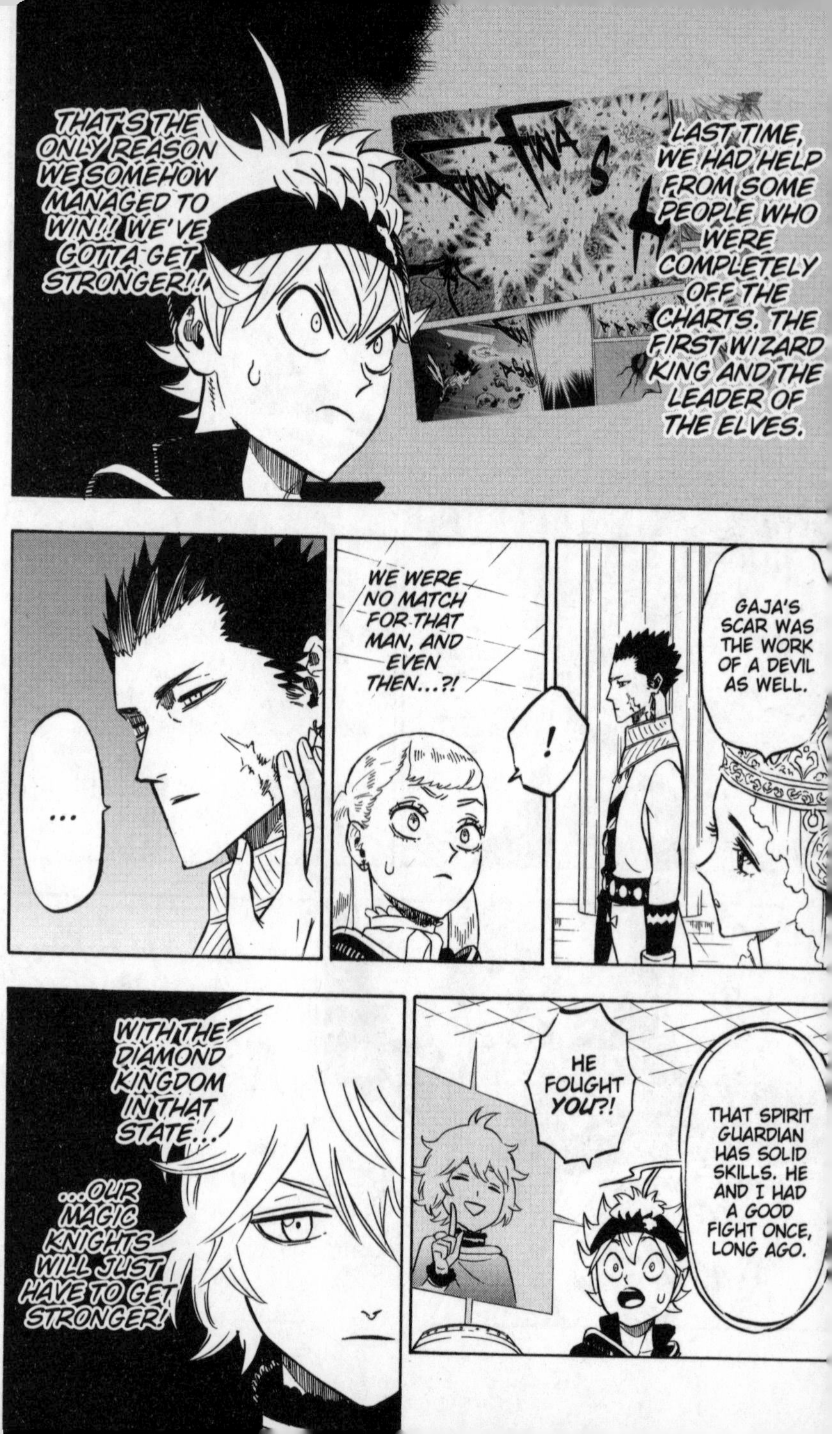
LAST TIME, WE HAD HELP FROM SOME PEOPLE WHO WERE COMPLETELY OFF THE CHARTS. THE FIRST WIZARD KING AND THE LEADER OF THE ELVES.
THAT'S THE ONLY REASON WE SOMEHOW MANAGED TO WIN!! WE'VE GOTTA GET STRONGER!!
GAJA'S SCAR WAS THE WORK OF A DEVIL AS WELL.
!
WE WERE NO MATCH FOR THAT MAN, AND EVEN THEN...?!
...
THAT SPIRIT GUARDIAN HAS SOLID SKILLS. HE AND I HAD A GOOD FIGHT ONCE, LONG AGO.
HE FOUGHT *YOU*?!
WITH THE DIAMOND KINGDOM IN THAT STATE...
...OUR MAGIC KNIGHTS WILL JUST HAVE TO GET STRONGER!

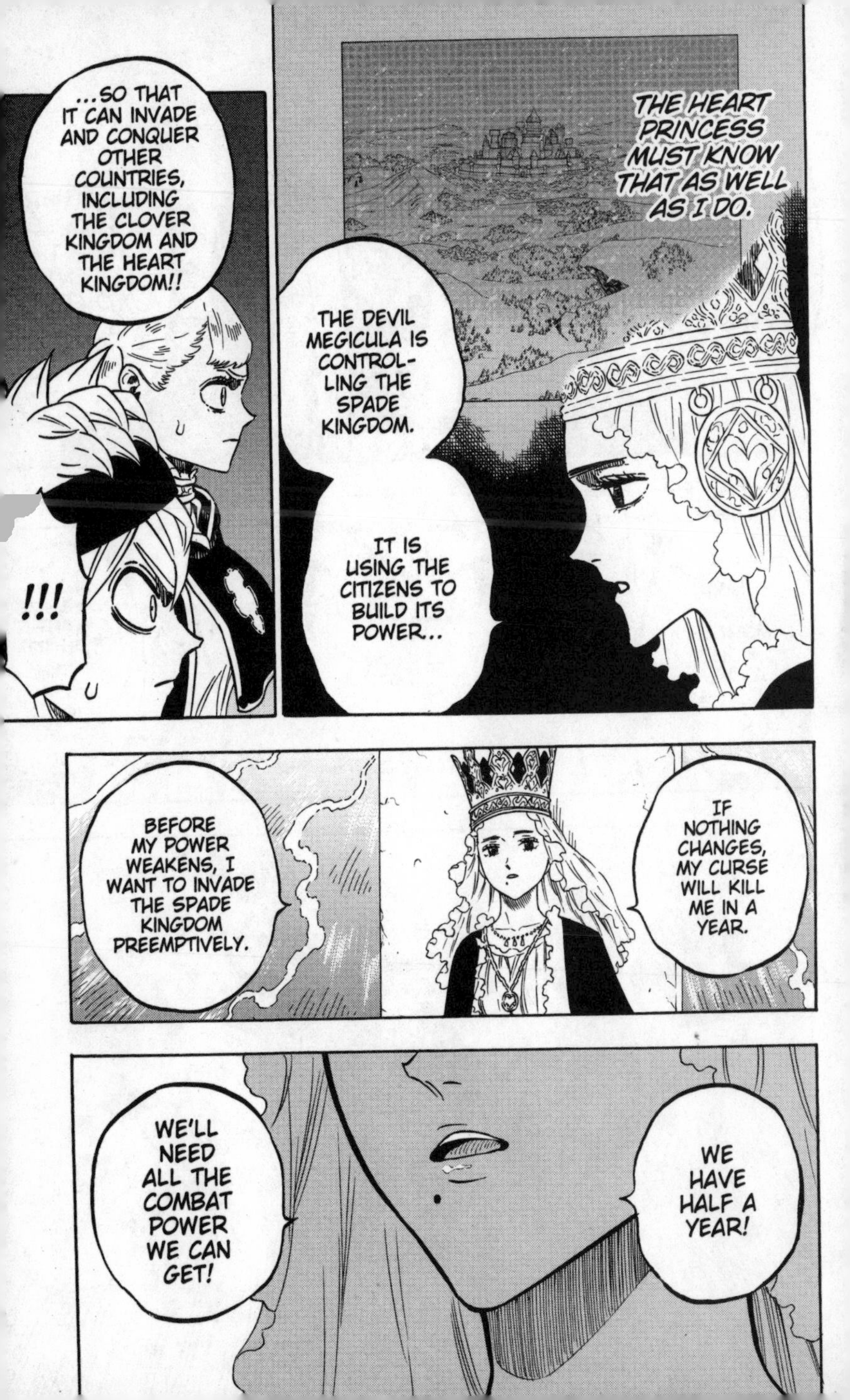
THE HEART PRINCESS MUST KNOW THAT AS WELL AS I DO.
THE DEVIL MEGICULA IS CONTROL-LING THE SPADE KINGDOM.
IT IS USING THE CITIZENS TO BUILD ITS POWER...
...SO THAT IT CAN INVADE AND CONQUER OTHER COUNTRIES, INCLUDING THE CLOVER KINGDOM AND THE HEART KINGDOM!!
!!!
IF NOTHING CHANGES, MY CURSE WILL KILL ME IN A YEAR.
BEFORE MY POWER WEAKENS, I WANT TO INVADE THE SPADE KINGDOM PREEMPTIVELY.
WE HAVE HALF A YEAR!
WE'LL NEED ALL THE COMBAT POWER WE CAN GET!

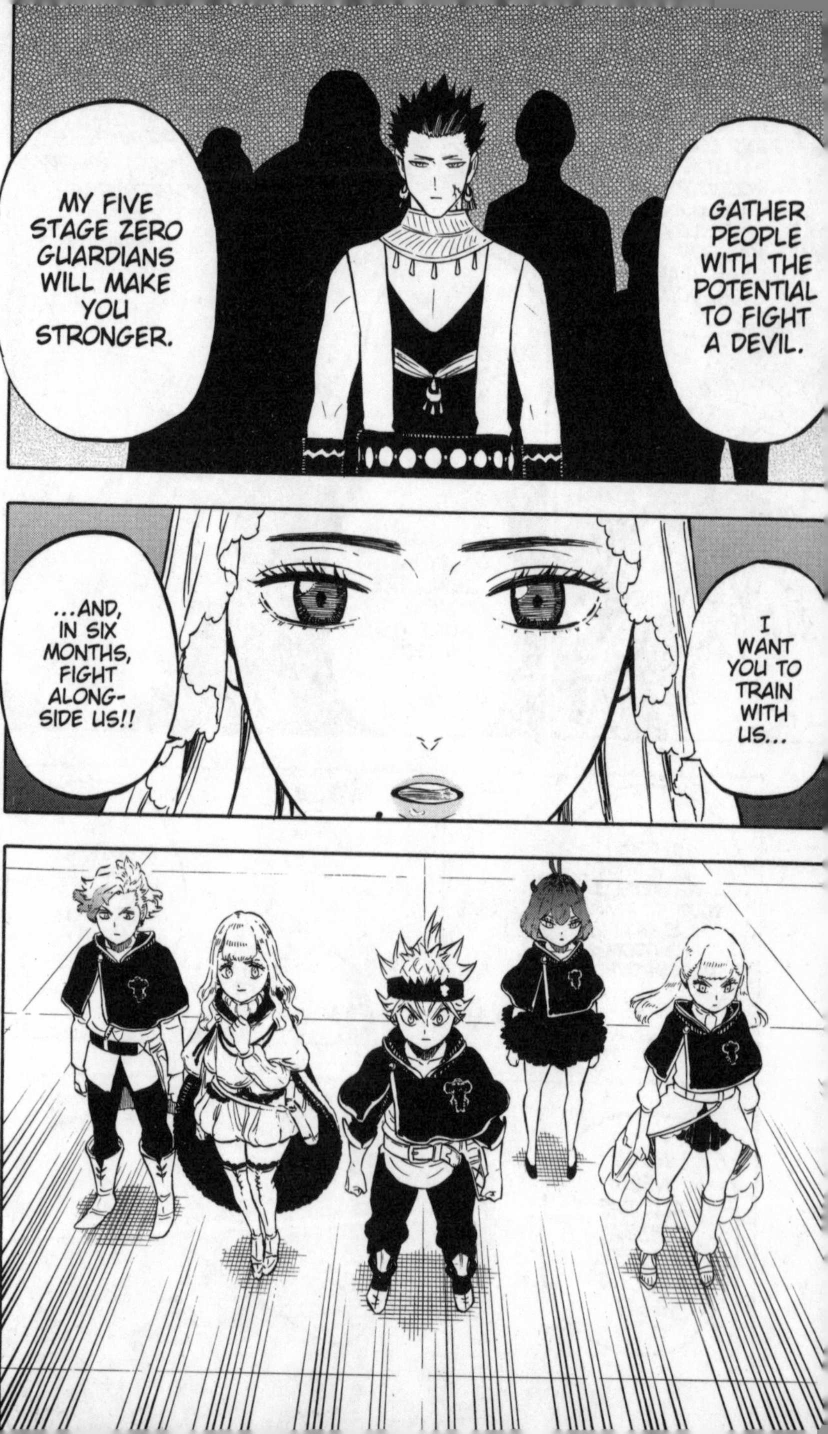
GATHER PEOPLE WITH THE POTENTIAL TO FIGHT A DEVIL.
MY FIVE STAGE ZERO GUARDIANS WILL MAKE YOU STRONGER.
I WANT YOU TO TRAIN WITH US...
...AND, IN SIX MONTHS, FIGHT ALONG-SIDE US!!

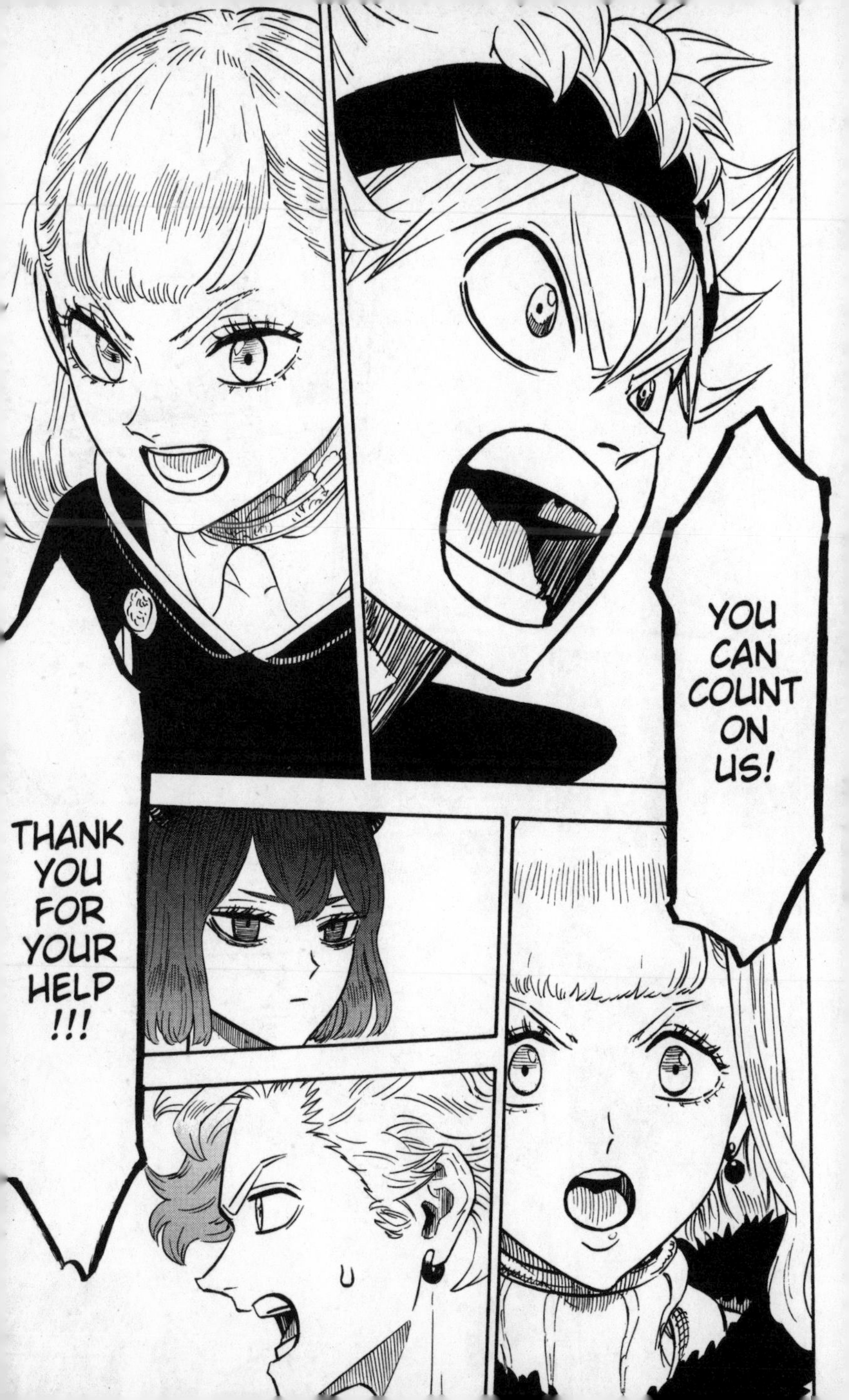
YOU CAN COUNT ON US!
THANK YOU FOR YOUR HELP!!!

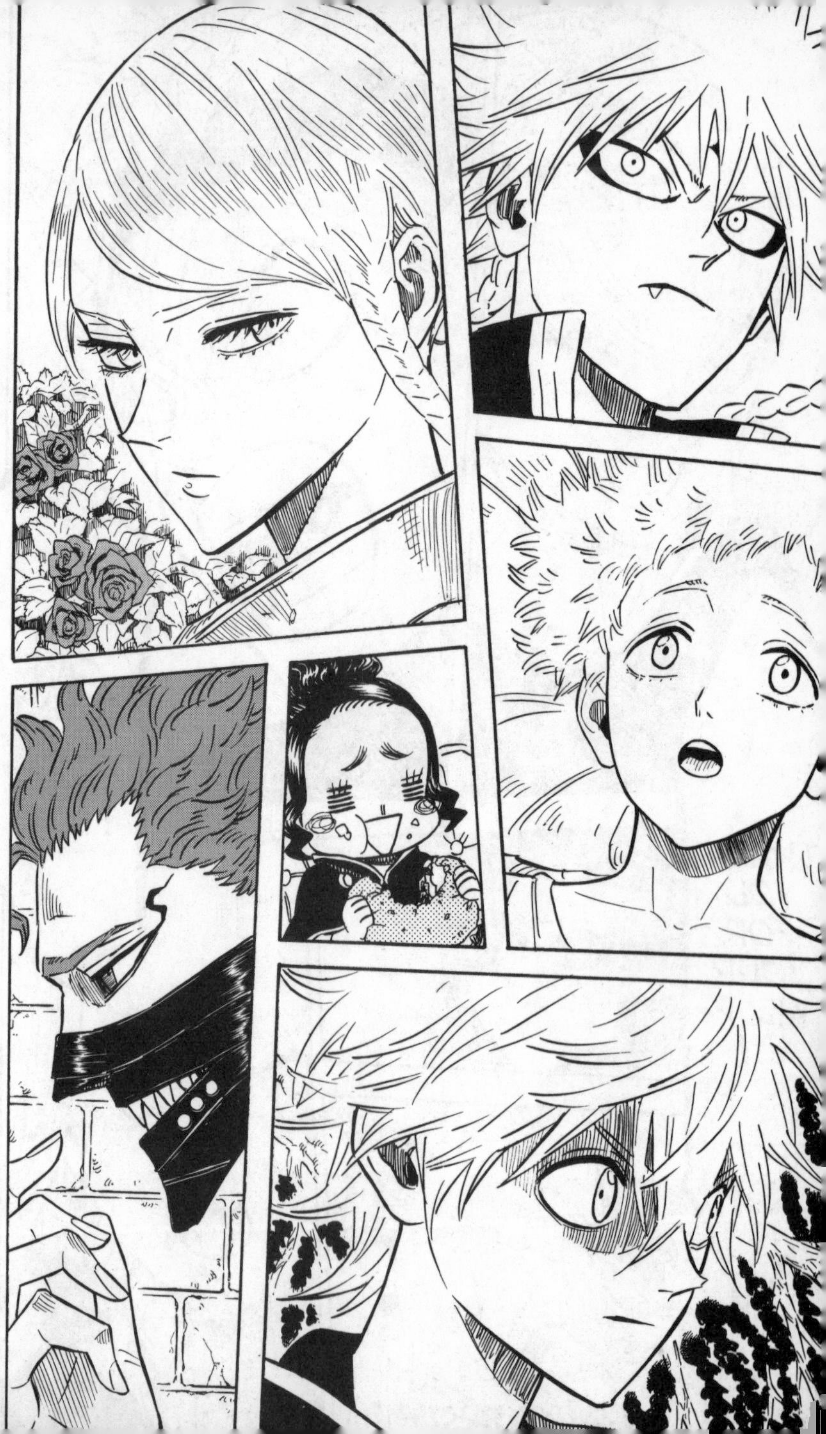

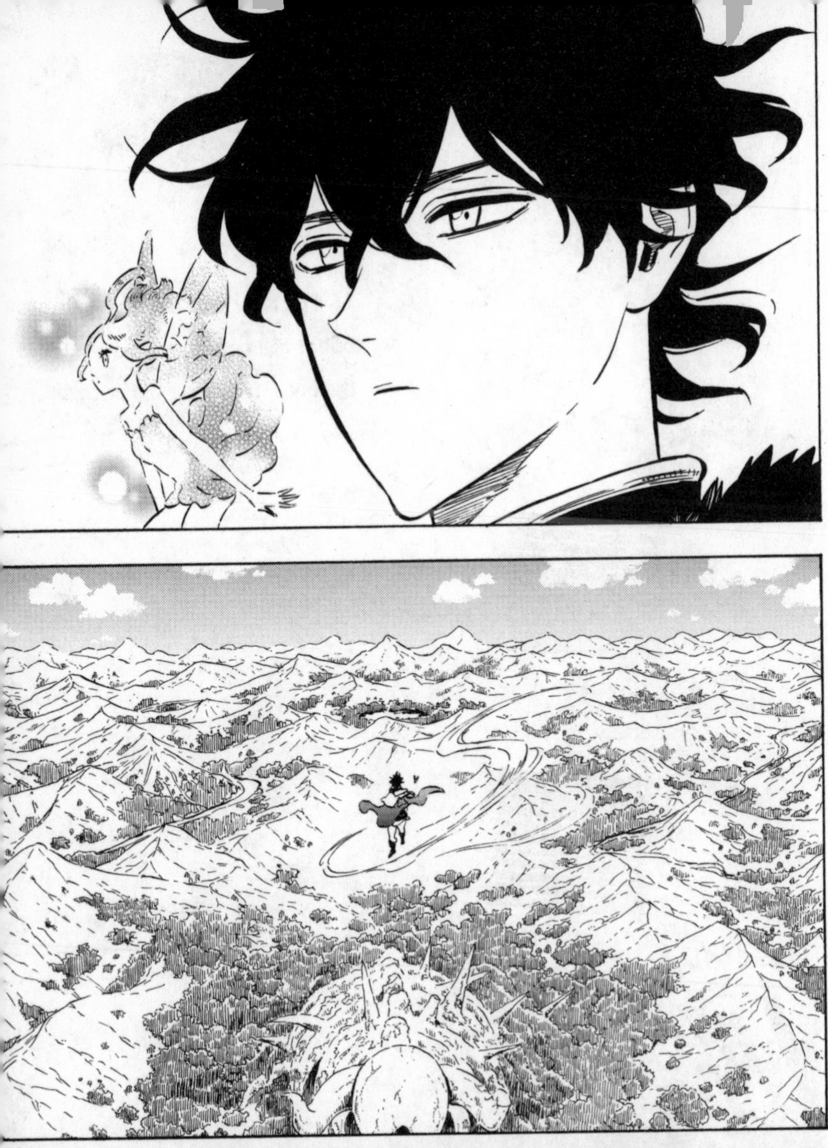

The Blank Page Brigade

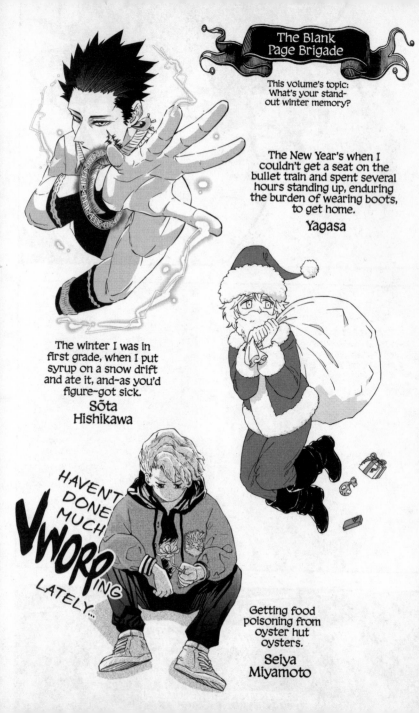

This volume's topic: What's your stand-out winter memory?

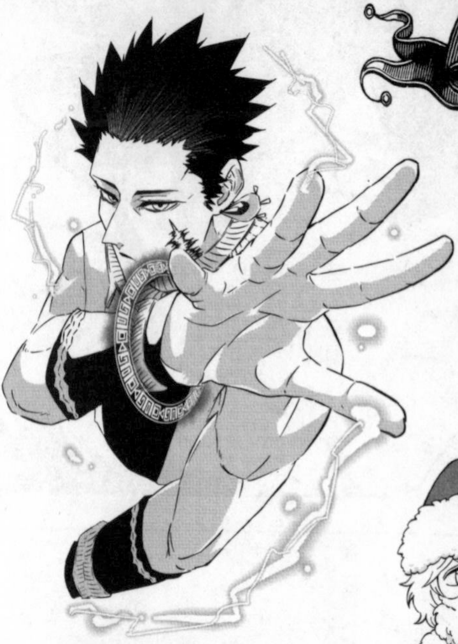

The New Year's when I couldn't get a seat on the bullet train and spent several hours standing up, enduring the burden of wearing boots, to get home.

Yagasa

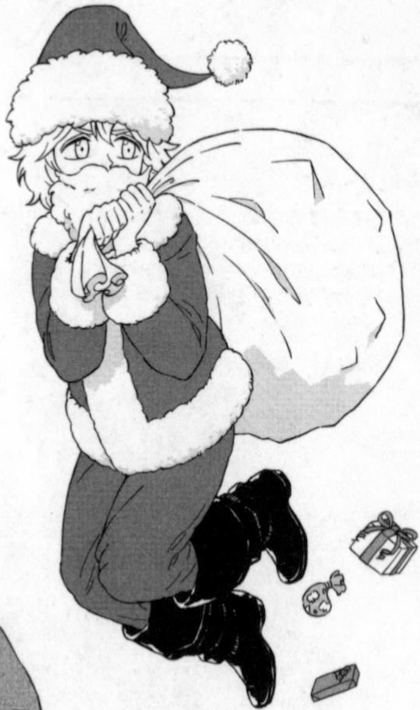

The winter I was in first grade, when I put syrup on a snow drift and ate it, and–as you'd figure–got sick.

Sōta Hishikawa

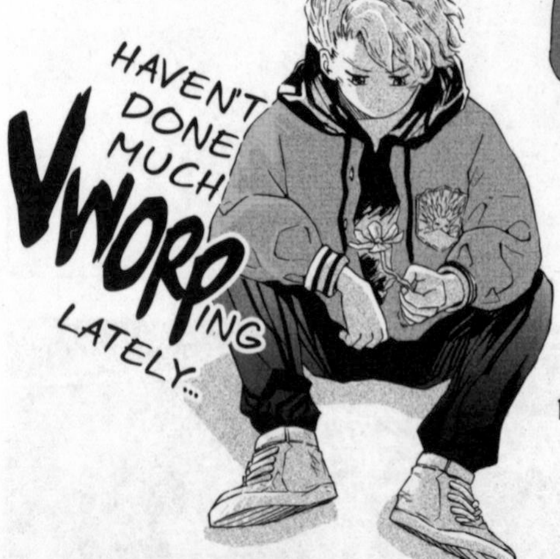
HAVEN'T DONE MUCH VWORPING LATELY...

Getting food poisoning from oyster hut oysters.

Seiya Miyamoto

New Year's, when I stayed up all night playing board games with people from work.

Hayato Gotō

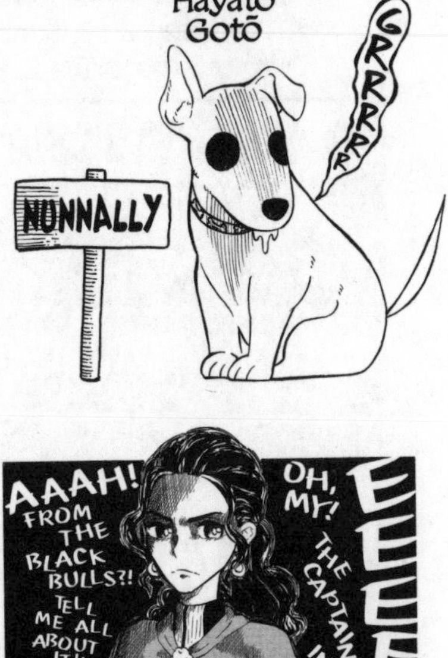
GRRRRR
NUNNALLY

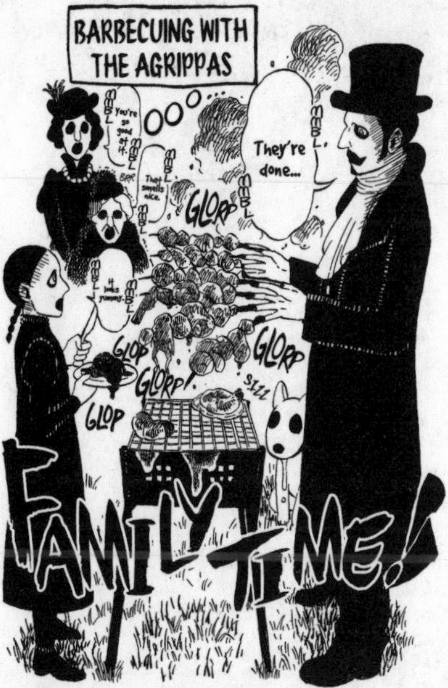
BARBECUING WITH THE AGRIPPAS
MMBL
They're done...
OOO...
MMBL
You're so good at it.
MMBL
That smells nice.
BRR
GLORP
MMBL
It was yummy.
GLORP
GLOP
GLORP!
SIZZ
GLOP
FAMILY TIME!

The winter of my third year in middle school, when I put too much effort into a snowball fight and farted but kept insisting that it wasn't me.

Kazuhiro Wakao

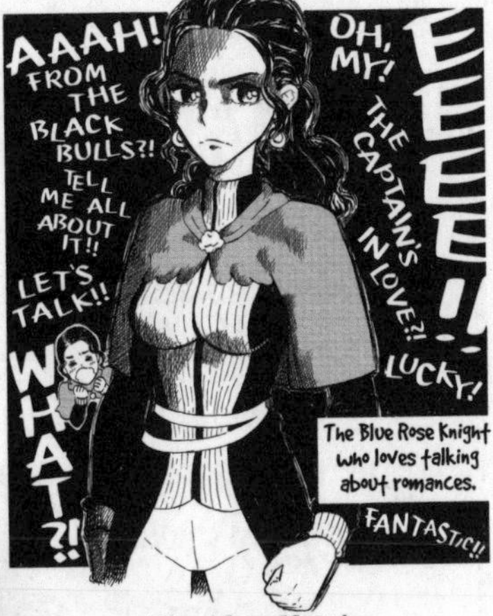
EEEE!!
OH, MY!
THE CAPTAIN'S IN LOVE?!
LUCKY!
The Blue Rose Knight who loves talking about romances.
FANTASTIC!!
AAAH! FROM THE BLACK BULLS?!
TELL ME ALL ABOUT IT!!
LET'S TALK!!
WHAT?!

The New Year's all-night board game tournament when I stood up the whole time so I wouldn't fall asleep.

Yōtarō Hayakawa

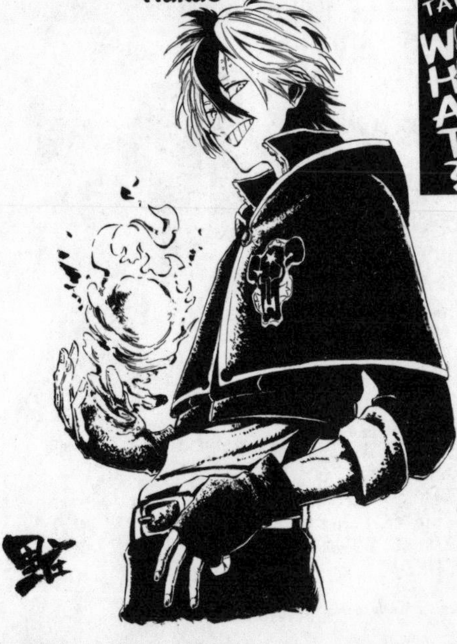

The winter of my third year of middle school, when the stress of the entrance exams wrecked my health, and I couldn't move properly unless I had an I.V. administered daily.

Masayoshi Satoshō

Toide's graduation article brigade

GOODBYE...

So we're doing a feature on former editor Toide!!

❀ WHO IS TOIDE, ANYWAY?! ❀

BLACK CLOVER'S SECOND EDITOR. IN TERMS OF THE BOOKS, HE'S BEEN IN CHARGE SINCE VOLUME 16. DUE TO AN EDITORIAL SHUFFLE, HE'S NOW LEAVING *BLACK CLOVER*. HIS HOBBIES ARE READING AND EXPLORING THE FINE FOODS AREAS IN DEPARTMENT STORE BASEMENTS. SINGLE.

TOIDE IS THIS GUY IN THE BACK-OF-THE-VOLUME COMMENTS!!

A COMMENT FROM TOIDE

I'M SORRY FOR ABRUPTLY SHOWING UP LIKE THIS!! THIS IS TOIDE, FROM THE *JUMP* EDITORIAL DEPARTMENT! TABATA SENSEI, YOU'D MAKE YOUR EDITOR COME UP WITH TWO BONUS PAGES WHEN HE'S GETTING SWITCHED OUT? SERIOUSLY, WHAT IS WITH YOU?!

THE SERIES HAS SOLD OVER A MILLION COPIES NOW, AND ALL SORTS OF PEOPLE READ IT. PUTTING PAGES FOR SOME UNKNOWN OLD GUY LIKE ME IN THE BACK OF A BOOK IS JUST NUTS!

IF I WROTE DOWN ALL THE VAST FEELINGS OF GRATITUDE I HAVE FOR TABATA SENSEI AND *BLACK CLOVER*, AND ALL THE SNAPPY COMEBACKS, IT WOULD NEVER FIT IN A SINGLE VOLUME. SINCE THAT'S THE CASE, I'LL WRITE DOWN JUST A FEW ANECDOTES ABOUT *BLACK CLOVER* AND TABATA SENSEI FROM AN EDITOR'S PERSPECTIVE, SO THAT YOU CAN ENJOY THIS UNREASONABLE REQUEST FROM TABATA SENSEI—WHO'S STILL A KID AT HEART—AS MUCH AS POSSIBLE. IF YOU'RE NOT INTERESTED, CUT THESE PAGES OUT AND USE THEM AS SCRATCH PAPER OR TISSUES!

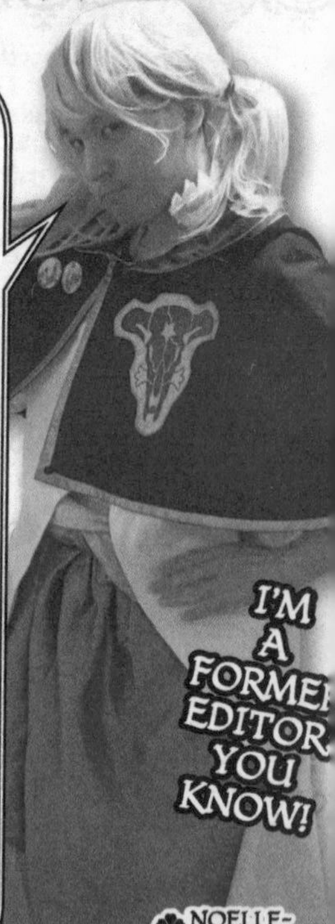

I'M A FORMER EDITOR YOU KNOW!

❀ NOELLE-TOIDE... SHE LOOKS TOUGH.

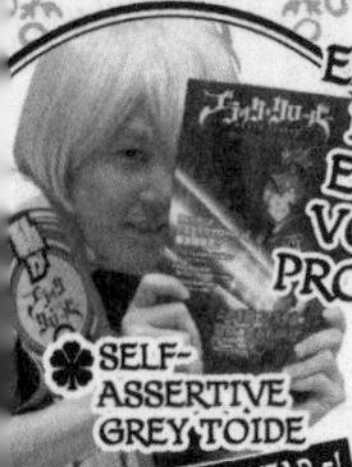

EEEEEEEP! IT'S AN END-OF-VOLUME PROJEEECT!

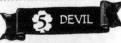

A tearful farewell! Editor

SELF-ASSERTIVE GREY TOIDE

RIGHT BEFORE YEAR 5!

Black Clover's getting a new editor!

FIVE HARD-LUCK STOR-UM, GREAT MEMORIES, ONE FOR EACH CLOVER LEAF!!

1 GOOD FAITH

WHAT MADE ME HAPPY ABOUT *BLACK CLOVER*!

THE FACT THAT WHEN I DRESSED AS GREY FOR A *JUMP* EVENT, TABATA SENSEI LAUGHED. AFTER THAT, I MADE A NEW OUTFIT FOR EACH EVENT AND TOOK A SHOT AT BEING EVERY MEMBER OF THE BLACK BULLS, BUT DIDN'T MAKE IT. I'LL LEAVE THE REST OF THAT ENDEAVOR TO THE NEW EDITOR... TABATA SENSEI WAS A GOOD, CHEERFUL PERSON, SO FOR THE WHOLE OF MY TWO YEARS AS SERIES EDITOR, I WAS ABLE TO KEEP WANTING TO GIVE MY BEST FOR EVERYTHING, NOT ONLY DURING THE CREATION OF THE WEEKLY MANGA, BUT ALSO FOR EVENTS AND EVEN WHEN BRINGING IN SNACKS.

2 HOPE

WHAT WAS FUN ABOUT *BLACK CLOVER*!

MEETINGS WITH TABATA SENSEI! I TOOK OVER AROUND THE TIME THE ELVES REINCARNATED, SO ASKING HIM "WHAT'S GOING TO HAPPEN NEXT?!" WAS FUN FOR ME. AFTER THAT, THE LEGEND FROM 500 YEARS AGO, NERO AND REVEALING ALL THE EARLIER FORESHADOWING WAS REALLY EXCITING! I ALSO REALLY LOVED MULLING OVER HOW TO DEFEAT SUPER-TOUGH OPPONENTS, LIKE THE ONE DURING THE DREAM MAGIC BATTLE IN VOL. 20, WITH HIM.

3 LOVE

WHAT SURPRISED ME ABOUT *BLACK CLOVER*!

WHEN I WAS WAITING FOR COLOR PAGES FOR THE FRONT OF THE MAGAZINE, I GOT A SUDDEN PHONE CALL FROM TABATA SENSEI. THINKING, "WHAT AM I GONNA DO IF HE SAYS HE WON'T MAKE IT IN TIME?", I ANSWERED THE PHONE, AND TABATA SENSEI SAID, "I'M SORRY... I DREW MORE THAN I WAS SUPPOSED TO." WHAT HE SENT IN WERE SUPER-EXPLOSIVELY-GORGEOUS OPENING COLOR PAGES WITH A FULL BACKGROUND AND A TON OF CHARACTERS, ALL OF THEM IN SCHOOL UNIFORMS. I WAS BOWLED OVER! ALL THE PAGES WERE FILLED WITH LOVE, AND IT REALLY LOOKED AS IF THEY WERE SHINING...

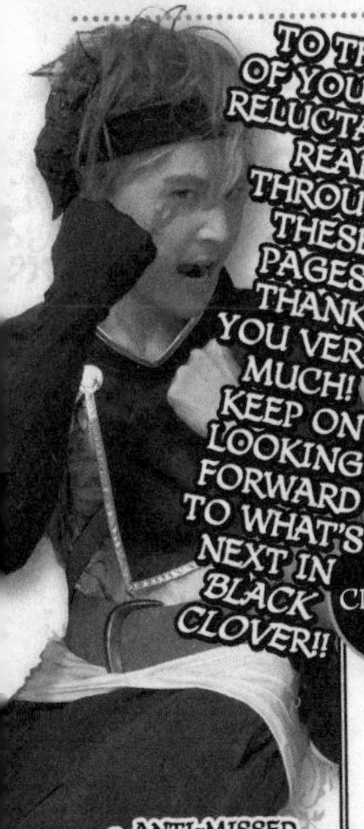

TO THOSE OF YOU WHO RELUCTANTLY READ THROUGH THESE PAGES, THANK YOU VERY MUCH! KEEP ON LOOKING FORWARD TO WHAT'S NEXT IN *BLACK CLOVER*!!

4 LUCK

WHAT MADE ME GRATEFUL ABOUT *BLACK CLOVER*!

BEING THE EDITOR FOR *BLACK CLOVER* GAVE ME THE CHANCE TO EXPERIENCE A VARIETY OF JOBS, AND I WAS BLESSED WITH THE OPPORTUNITY TO MEET LOTS OF INCREDIBLY TALENTED PEOPLE. AND THEN THERE WERE THE DINNERS TABATA SENSEI'S WIFE SERVED ME WHEN WE HAD PLANNING SESSIONS! AND LITTLE AMELIE, WHO'D COME RUNNING UP TO ME! I WAS INSPIRED BY AMAZING PEOPLE, AND SUPPORTED BY WARM PEOPLE, AND IT GAVE ME THE FUEL I NEEDED TO WORK HARD ON *BLACK CLOVER*!

5 DEVIL

WHAT WAS ROUGH ABOUT *BLACK CLOVER*!

WAITING FOR THE CHAPTERS EVERY SINGLE WEEK... THOSE TIMES WHEN I'D LOOK AT TABATA SENSEI'S BACK, AND THE PAGES THAT STILL HAD WHITE SPACE ON THEM. I'D LOOK AT THE CLOCK AND SLOWLY CLOSE MY EYES AND PRAY "HELP ME..." WHEN HE TURNED IN AN AWESOME CHAPTER THOUGH, IT FELT AS IF ALL OF THAT PATIENCE HAD BEEN REWARDED. WAITING FOR FINAL PAGES IS ROUGH, BUT IF THE CHAPTER ENDS UP BEING AMAZING, IT'S FINE. IF IT'S AMAZING AND THE PAGES GET TURNED IN EARLY, THAT'S EVEN BETTER. HELP ME OUT, TABATA SENSEI!

IN CLOSING

BLACK CLOVER IS ABOUT TO PLUNGE INTO ITS OVERSEAS ARC! THE MAGIC BATTLES WILL GET FIERCER, AND TOUGHER ENEMIES WILL SHOW UP! WHAT'S GOING TO HAPPEN TO ASTA, YUNO AND THE OTHER MAGIC KNIGHTS?! IT'S A SHAME I WON'T GET TO BE THE EDITOR FOR THESE THRILLING NEW DEVELOPMENTS AND THE SERIES' MOMENTOUS FIFTH ANNIVERSARY. NOT FAIR, NEW EDITOR! I'M SURE HE'LL MAKE THE SERIES WAY MORE FASCINATING AND SURPRISING THAN IT WAS WHEN I WAS ITS EDITOR THOUGH!! IT'S UP TO YOU NOW, TABATA SENSEI AND NEW EDITOR IWASAKI!

ANTI-MISSED DEADLINES BLACK ASTA TOIDE

Special Bonus Material!

Illustration for the 2019 Reader Gift Campaign

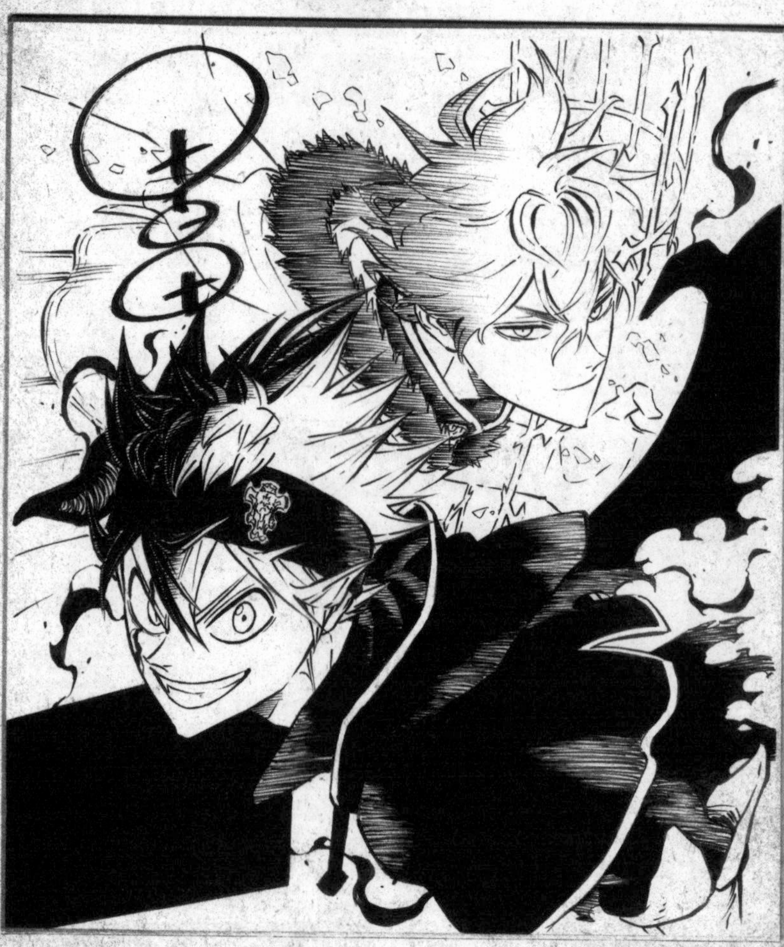

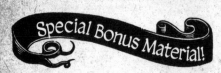

The Blank Page Brigade

This volume's topic: What's your standout winter memory?

My honeymoon, when we rode the sleeper express Hokutosei to Hokkaido. There was all sorts of delicious food!

©

On the way back from my fun honeymoon, I got a phone call at New Chitose Airport notifying me that *Black Clover* was going to be a series in *Jump*. Whoa!!

Captain Tabata

The winter I was 20, when I went snowboarding for the first time with an experienced friend, and almost died on a dangerous course.

Comics editor Fujiwara

When I got *Beast Wars* from Santa, and I was so happy about it I thought "This is no time to take a bathroom break!", then wet my pants while I was playing.

Editor Toide

AFTERWORD

With this volume, it feels as though we've reached the end of an era in the story, so I brought the way the back of the graphic novel cover shows the grimoire of the character who'll be on the next cover full circle, ending it on this volume. As if to say "So what?" *Black Clover* is going to keep right on going, so please keep an eye out for the next volume as well!!!

DEMON SLAYER

KIMETSU NO YAIBA

Story and Art by

KOYOHARU GOTOUGE

In Taisho-era Japan, kindhearted Tanjiro Kamado makes a living selling charcoal. But his peaceful life is shattered when a demon slaughters his entire family. His little sister Nezuko is the only survivor, but she has been transformed into a demon herself! Tanjiro sets out on a dangerous journey to find a way to return his sister to normal and destroy the demon who ruined his life.

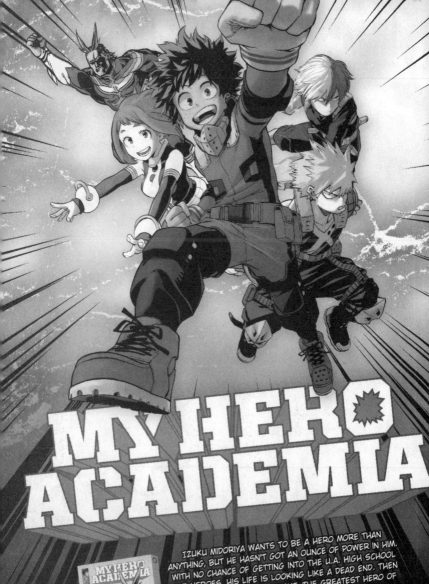

MY HERO ACADEMIA

IZUKU MIDORIYA WANTS TO BE A HERO MORE THAN ANYTHING, BUT HE HASN'T GOT AN OUNCE OF POWER IN HIM. WITH NO CHANCE OF GETTING INTO THE U.A. HIGH SCHOOL FOR HEROES, HIS LIFE IS LOOKING LIKE A DEAD END. THEN AN ENCOUNTER WITH ALL MIGHT, THE GREATEST HERO OF ALL, GIVES HIM A CHANCE TO CHANGE HIS DESTINY...

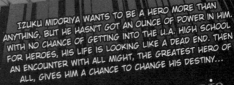

www.viz.com

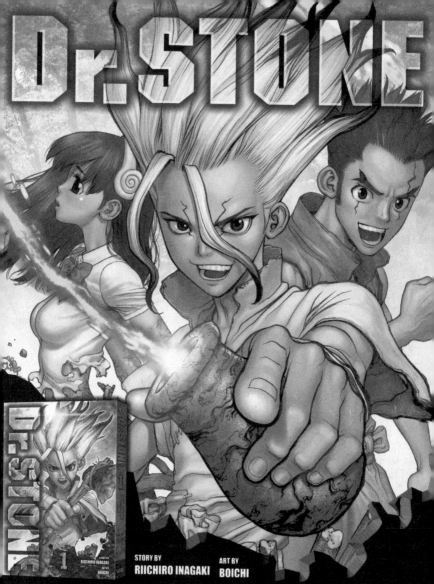

Dr.STONE

STORY BY
RIICHIRO INAGAKI

ART BY
BOICHI

One fateful day, all of humanity turned to stone. Many millennia later, Taiju frees himself from petrification and finds himself surrounded by statues. The situation looks grim—until he runs into his science-loving friend Senku! Together they plan to restart civilization with the power of science!

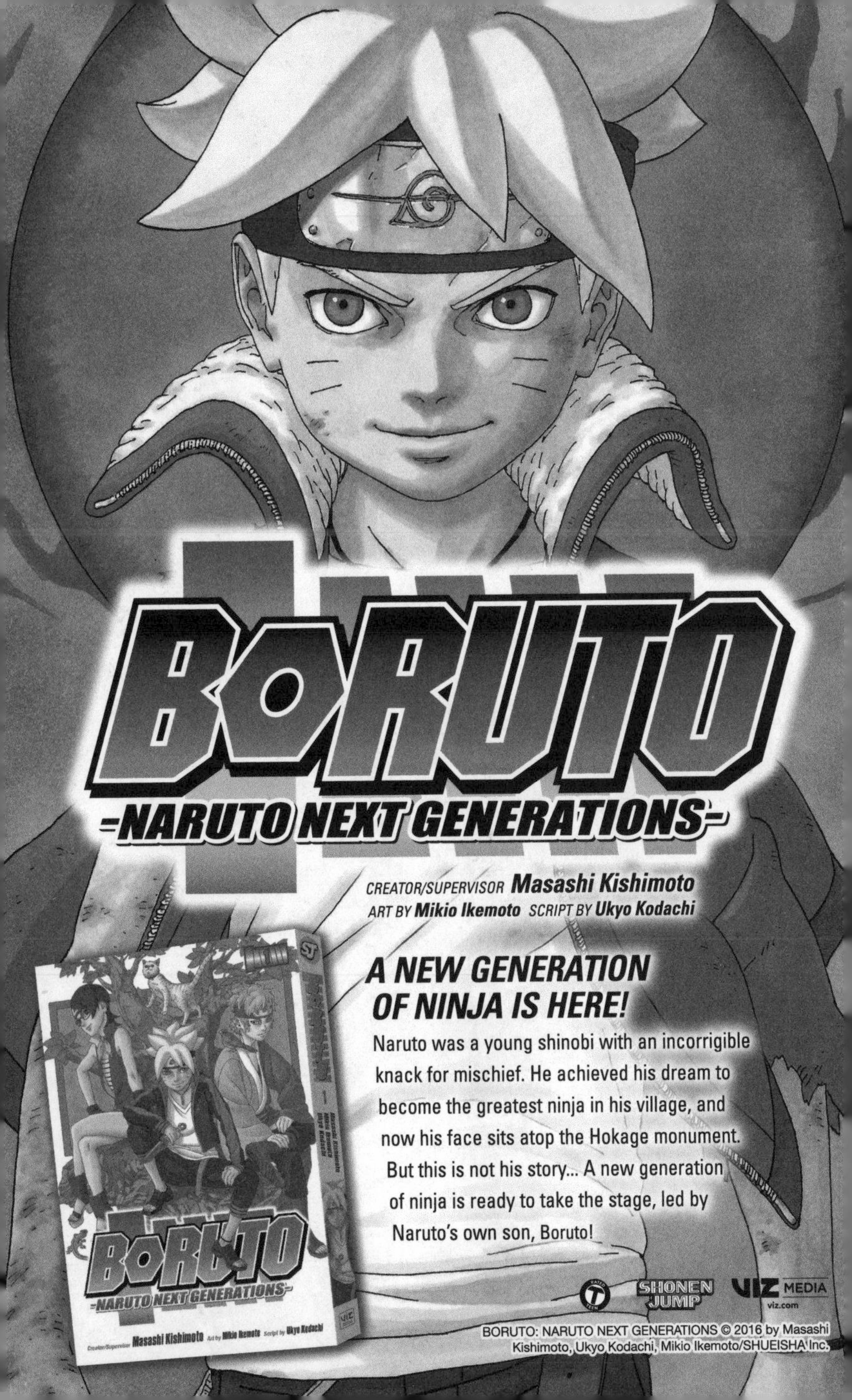
BORUTO
-NARUTO NEXT GENERATIONS-
CREATOR/SUPERVISOR Masashi Kishimoto
ART BY Mikio Ikemoto SCRIPT BY Ukyo Kodachi
A NEW GENERATION OF NINJA IS HERE!
Naruto was a young shinobi with an incorrigible knack for mischief. He achieved his dream to become the greatest ninja in his village, and now his face sits atop the Hokage monument. But this is not his story... A new generation of ninja is ready to take the stage, led by Naruto's own son, Boruto!
BORUTO
-NARUTO NEXT GENERATIONS-
Creator/Supervisor Masashi Kishimoto Art by Mikio Ikemoto Script by Ukyo Kodachi
SHONEN JUMP
VIZ MEDIA
viz.com
BORUTO: NARUTO NEXT GENERATIONS © 2016 by Masashi Kishimoto, Ukyo Kodachi, Mikio Ikemoto/SHUEISHA Inc.